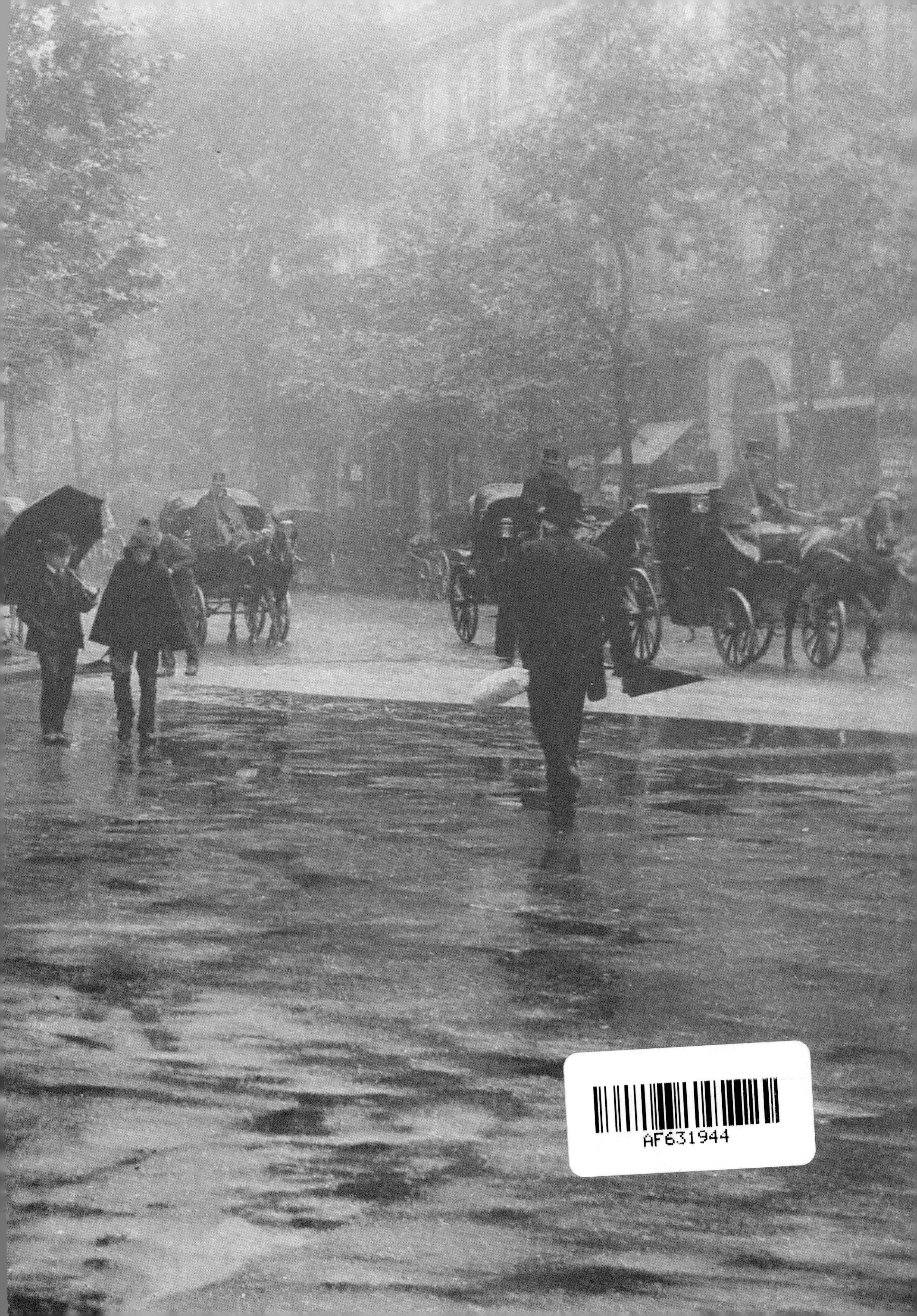

The Places of the Impressionists

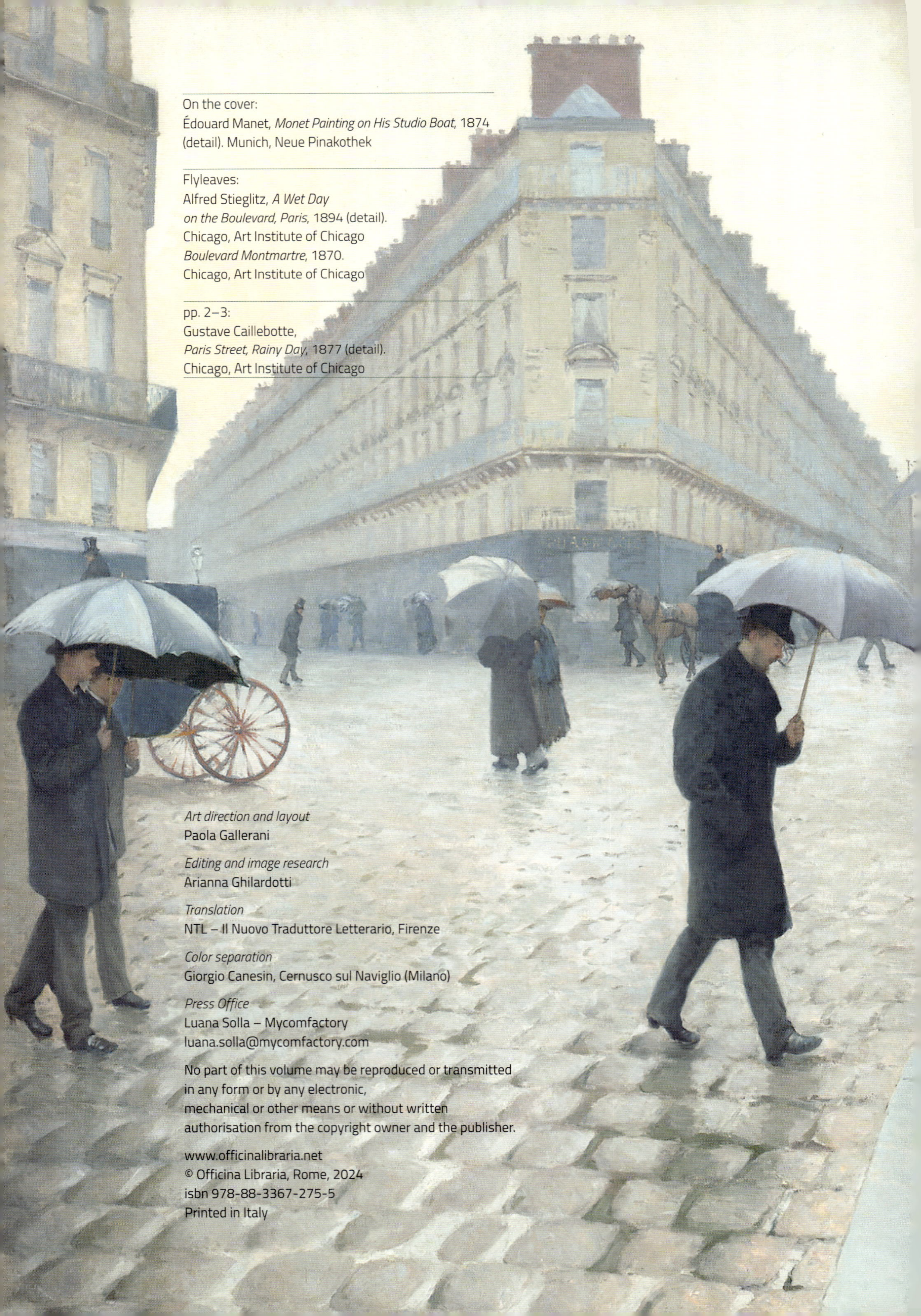

On the cover:
Édouard Manet, *Monet Painting on His Studio Boat*, 1874 (detail). Munich, Neue Pinakothek

Flyleaves:
Alfred Stieglitz, *A Wet Day on the Boulevard, Paris*, 1894 (detail).
Chicago, Art Institute of Chicago
Boulevard Montmartre, 1870.
Chicago, Art Institute of Chicago

pp. 2–3:
Gustave Caillebotte,
Paris Street, Rainy Day, 1877 (detail).
Chicago, Art Institute of Chicago

Art direction and layout
Paola Gallerani

Editing and image research
Arianna Ghilardotti

Translation
NTL – Il Nuovo Traduttore Letterario, Firenze

Color separation
Giorgio Canesin, Cernusco sul Naviglio (Milano)

Press Office
Luana Solla – Mycomfactory
luana.solla@mycomfactory.com

www.officinalibraria.net

isbn 978-88-3367-275-5
Printed in Italy

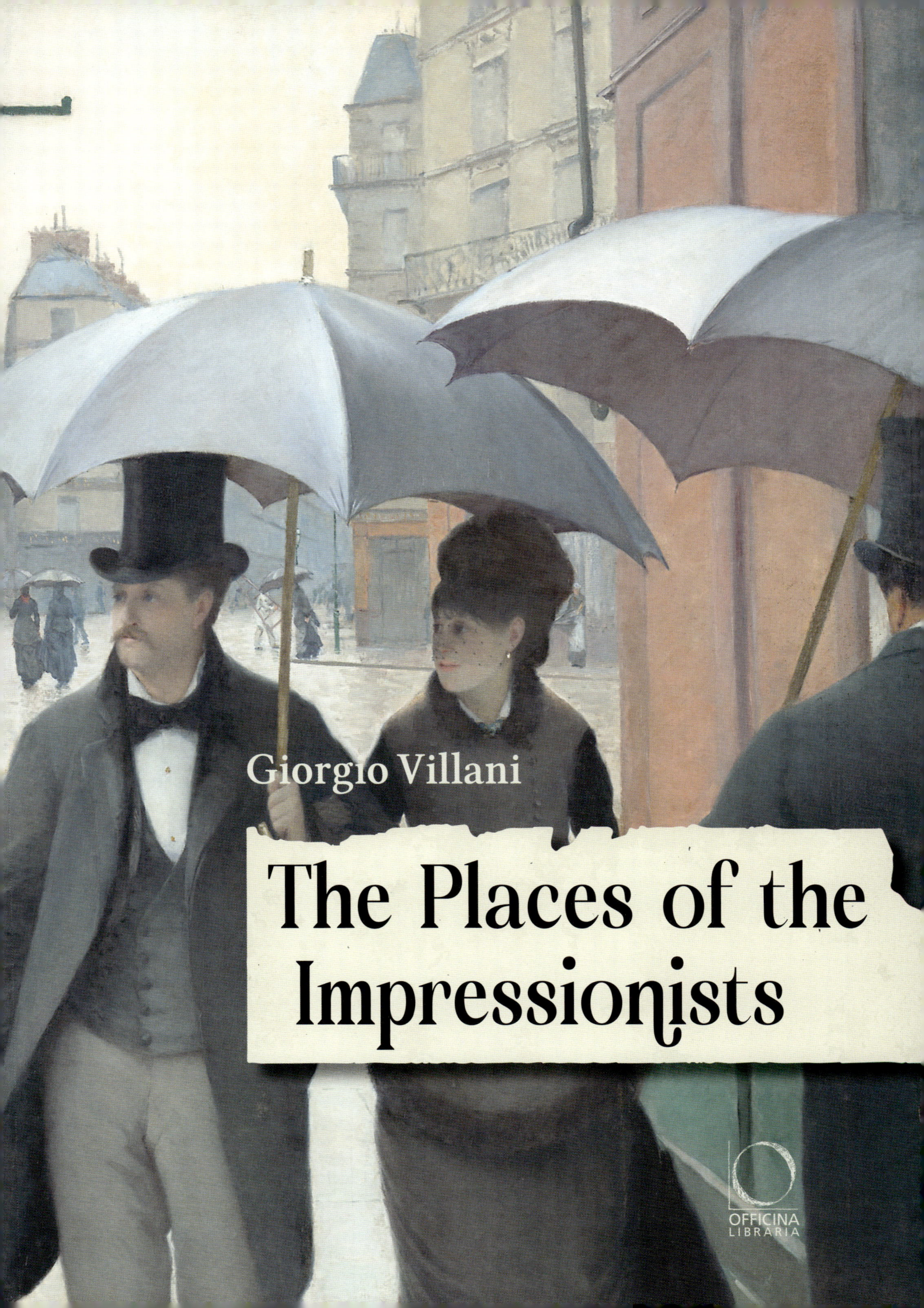

Giorgio Villani

The Places of the Impressionists

OFFICINA LIBRARIA

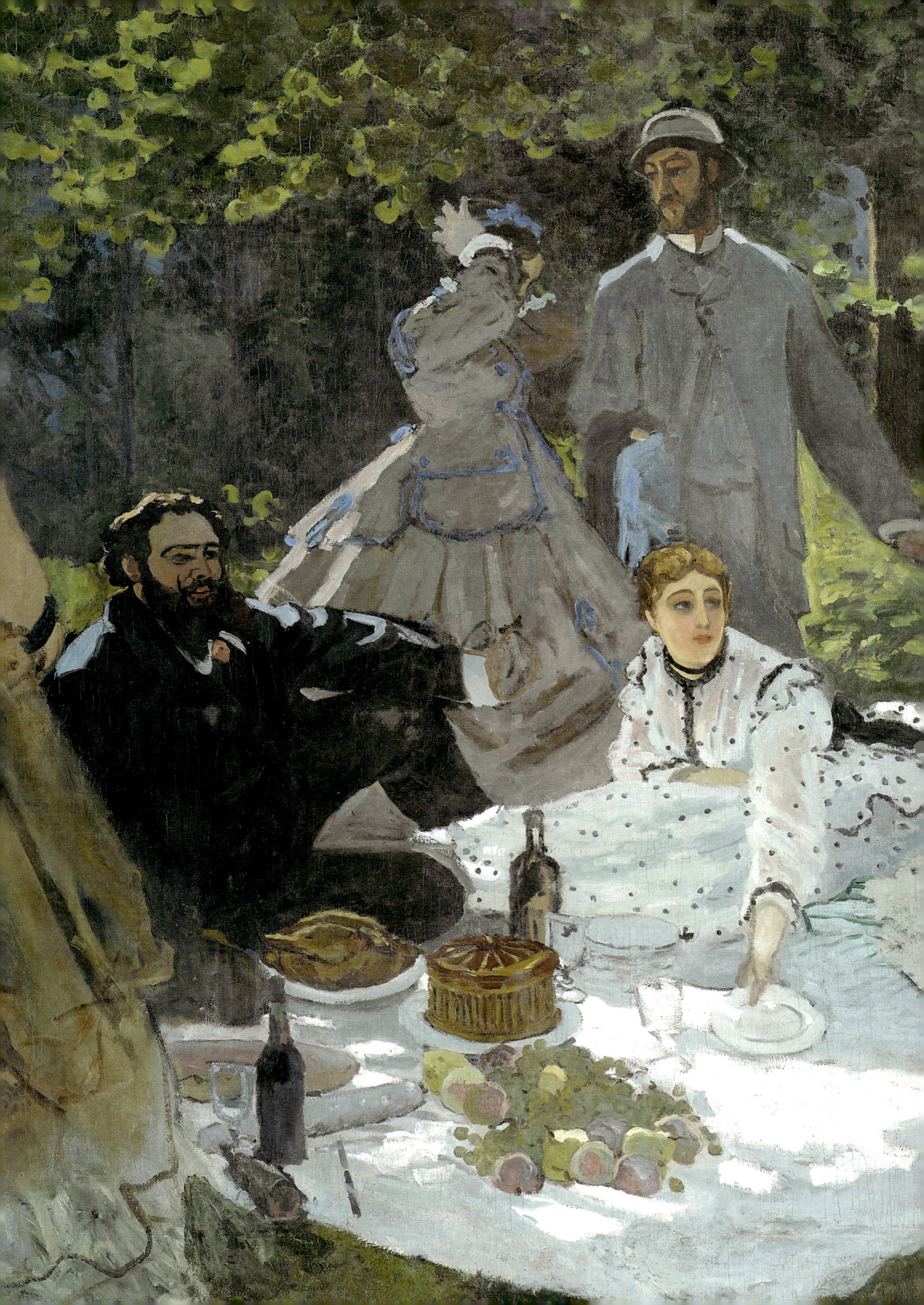

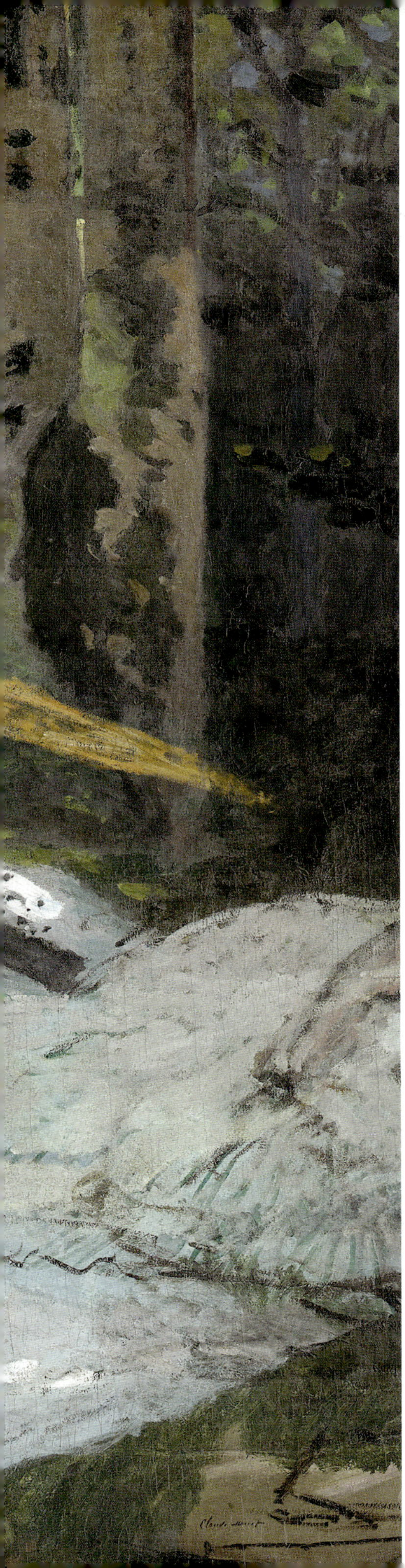

Contents

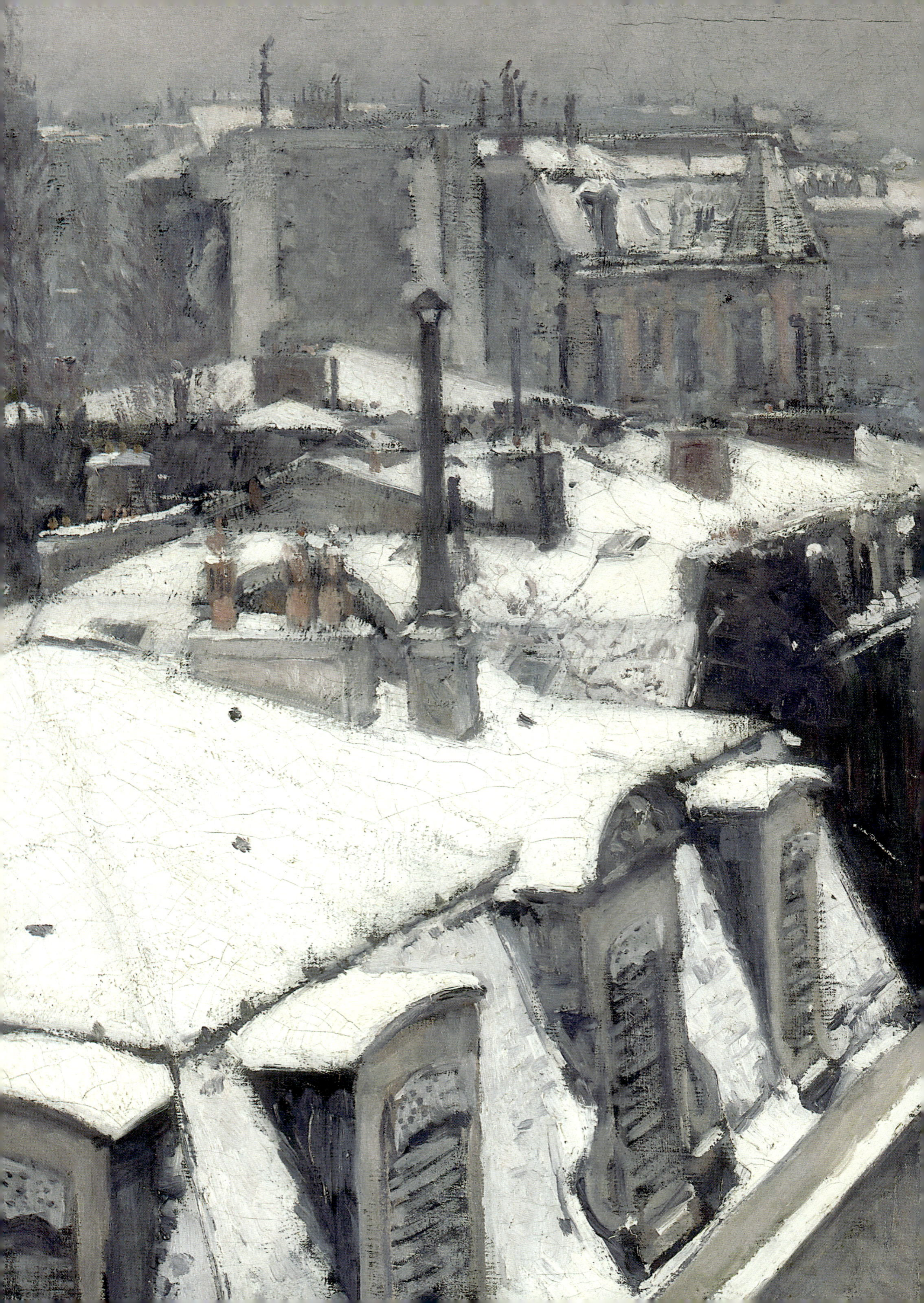

Introduction

A book about the places of Impressionism, as would be the case for any other group or current, risks falling into simple anecdote or, even worse, historical fetish, the kind that fuels the mania for putting up a plaque on a street where something happened or on a lane where something once was but is no more. What is the importance, you might ask, of the fleeting reality of inns, roads, villages and cafés that are now gone, if we still have the immortal image of them made by the artist? Would it not perhaps be degrading to reduce a painting to its subject or incidental motif? For many of the old masters, this would certainly be the case. But information about the real world, almost insignificant for other painters, is instead of fundamental importance in the case of the Impressionists, who developed their technique *en plein air* and their ideas inside cafés.

p. 4
Claude Monet, *Luncheon on the Grass*, 1865–1866 (detail). Paris, Musée d'Orsay

The art historian Rudolf Wittkower, who wrote a famous book with his wife about artists and melancholy,[1] would never have been able to include Monet, Renoir, Manet or their companions in it, not because they all had an excellent character (that of Cézanne was often, on the contrary, anything but easy-going), but because their art was inseparable from their social lives and their wanderings in search of sites where they could paint together, later comparing the results and discussing them in the evening in a tavern or art supply shop. It is this shared existence that makes an everyday life seem carefree and merry that must have instead been—at least for some of them—tormented by poverty and saddened by the public's derision. The artist no longer created closed up in the studio, like an absorbed Renaissance alchemist. Now, he was roaming the streets, in the city and elsewhere. He was following the crowds to concerts and dances, and meeting friends, who were just as flushed as he was with the fever for the new and with whom he got worked up talking about his latest painting.

From the above, it will be clear that the streets of Montmartre, the trees of Fontainebleau, the banks of the Seine with their lively gathering places, the circuses and the galleries were always more than simple painting motifs or incidental liminal places.

The aim of this volume is to render them in all their freshness, sometimes drawing on literature, sometimes music, other times the memories of the artists themselves or their dealers or patrons, since, starting in the middle of the nineteenth century, painters were no longer just painters, writers were no longer just writers, and not even musicians were just musicians: they were all brethren in art, as portrayed by Puccini in the garret in *La Bohème*.

Gustave Caillebotte, *View of rooftops (Effect of snow)*, 1878. Paris, Musée d'Orsay

The centre of Paris

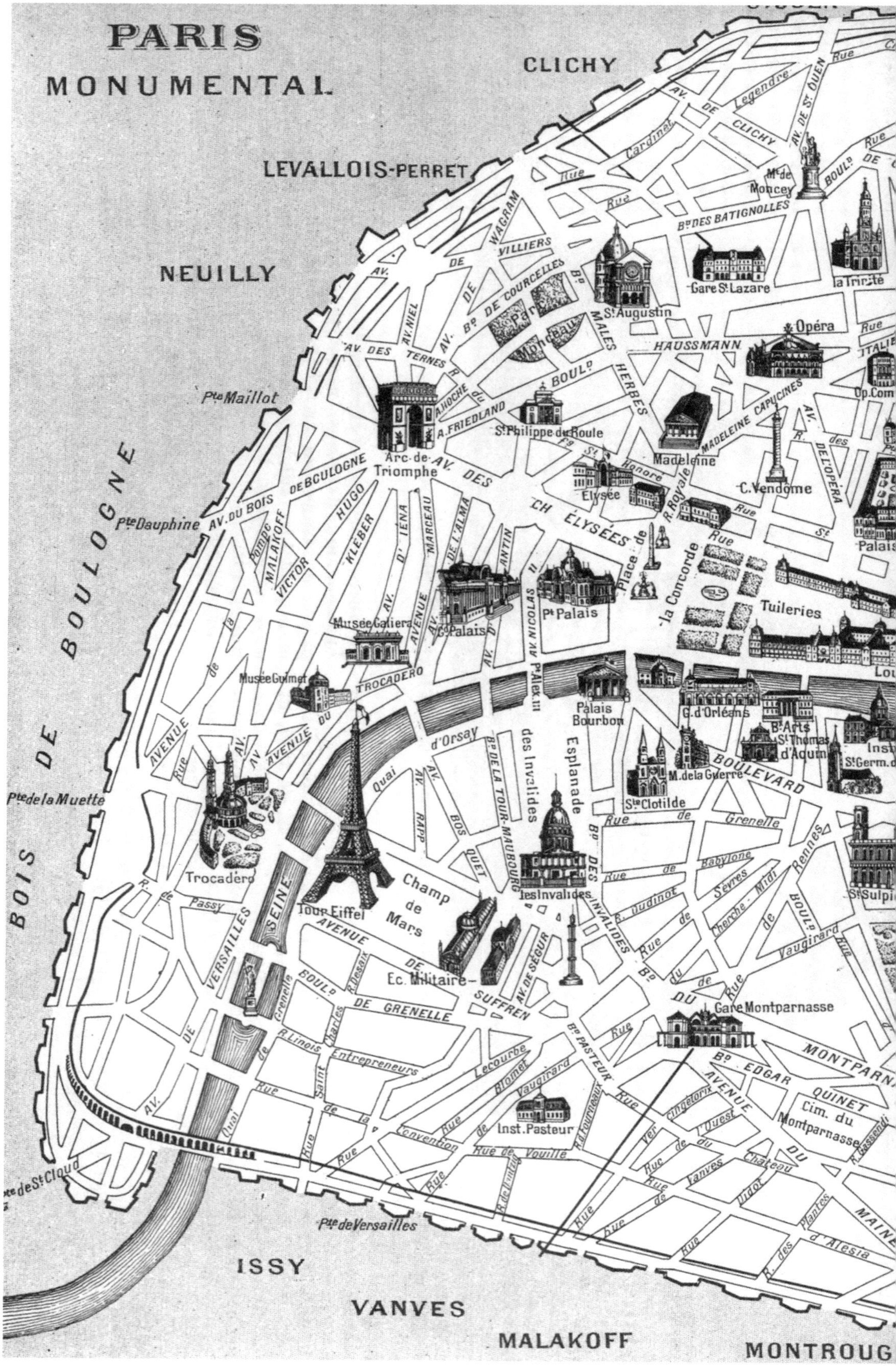

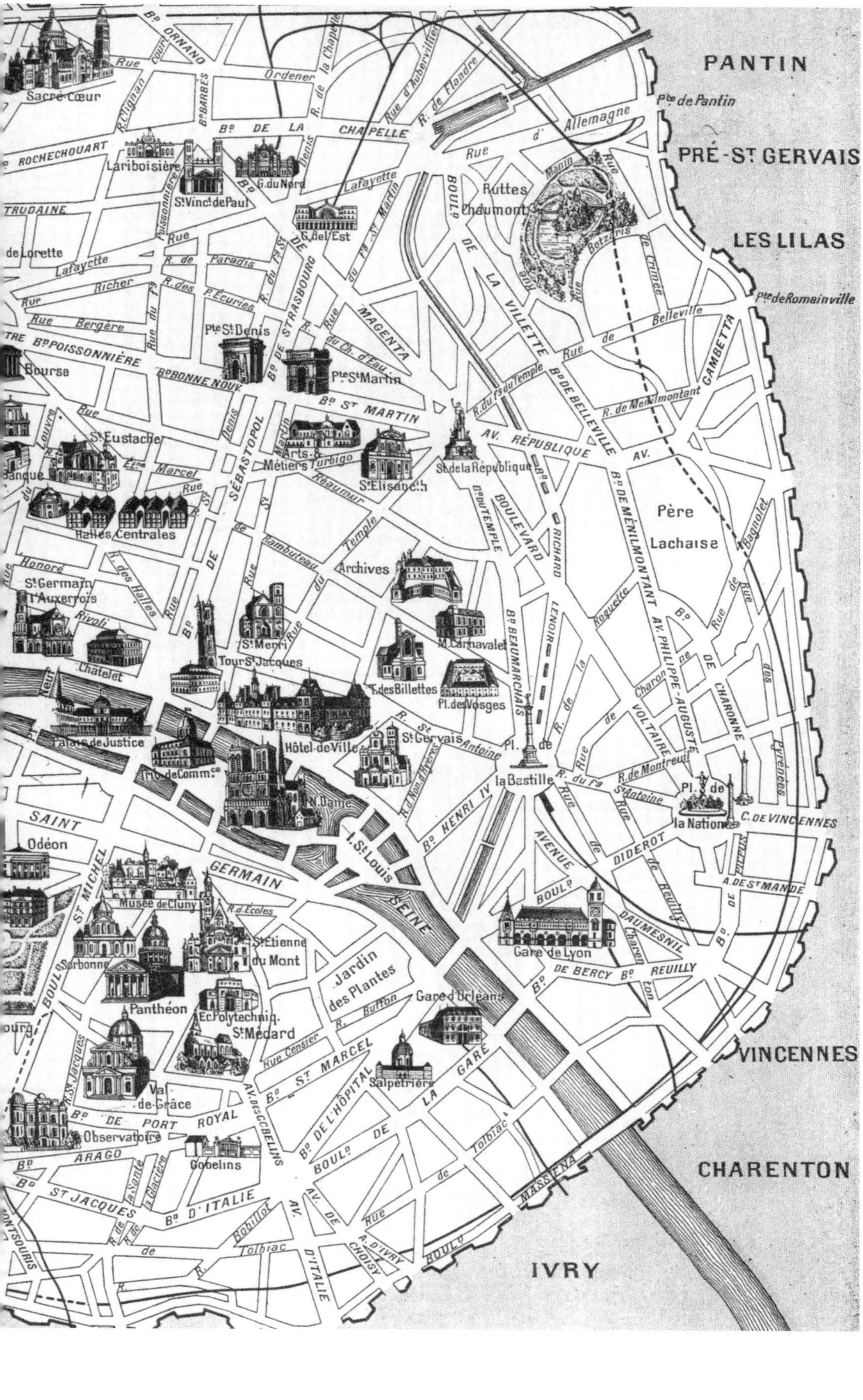

pp. 10–11
Maurice Denis, *Homage to Cézanne*, 1900. Paris, Musée d'Orsay

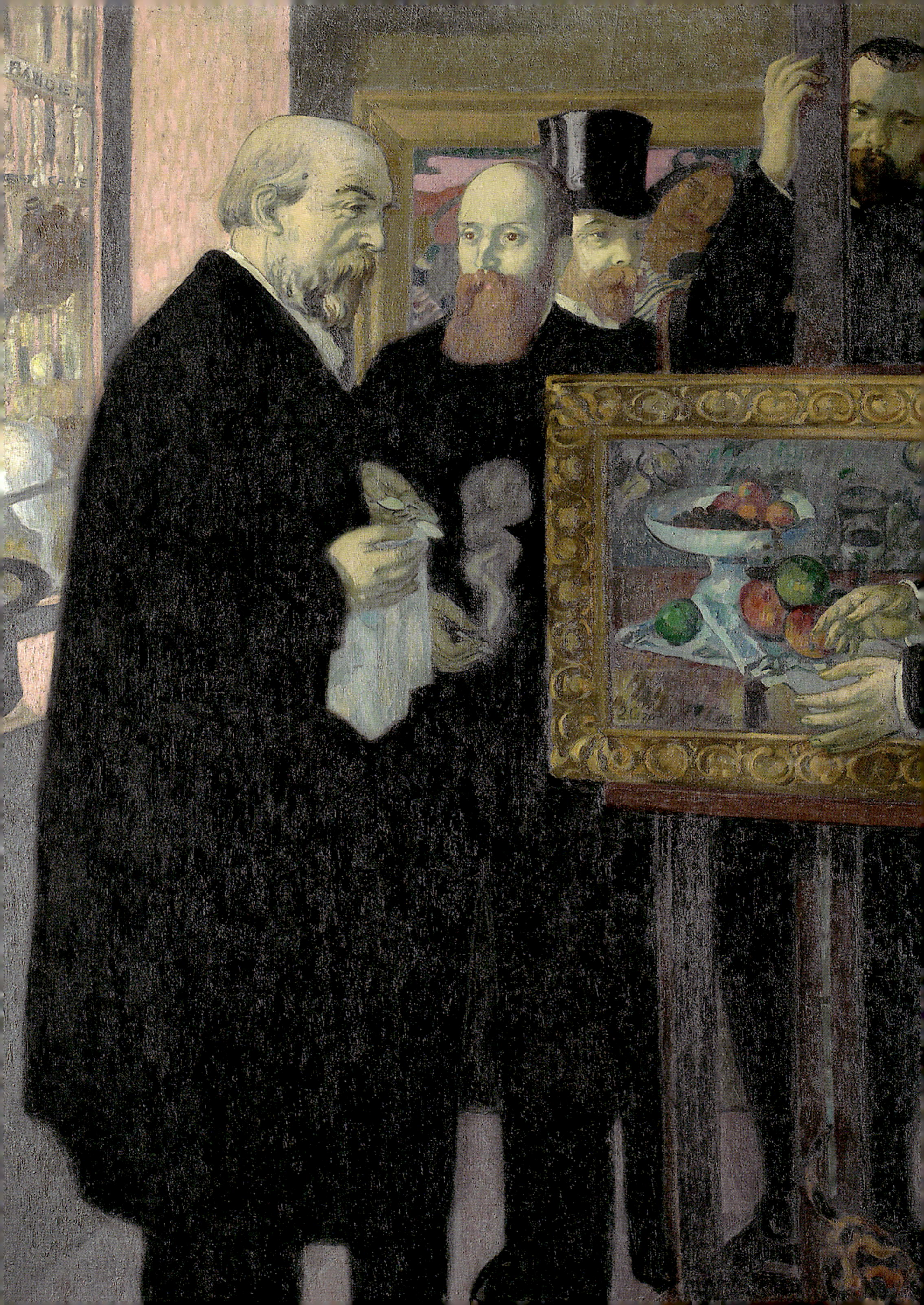

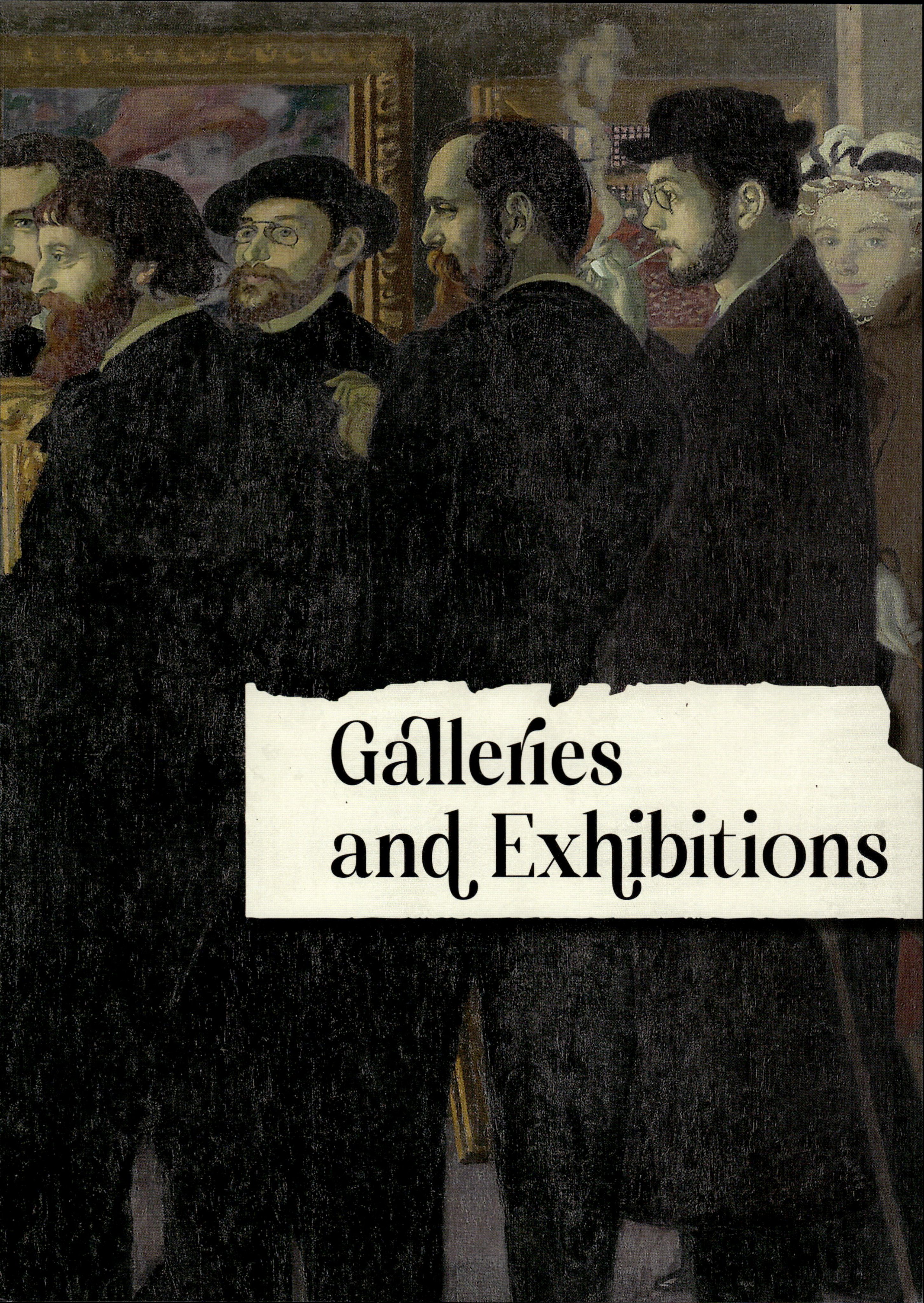

Galleries and Exhibitions

1. Père Tanguy's Shop

14 rue Clauzel

The work of the Impressionists was not displayed in the windows of the grand galleries decorated with damasked walls and ornamental plants on the broad boulevards in the city centre. Those who wanted to see it had to climb up Montmartre, which was dotted with little vegetable gardens and shacks at the time. Way up at the top, there were a few small junk shops, where artists could buy canvases and paint. The owners were often paid with a few paintings, or simply agreed to display them. One of the most popular of these little shops was the one owned by Père Tanguy, a small, lean man with a thick frizzy beard. We do not have any photographs of his humble shop, but we can imagine that it was like that of Portier and many others, where the paintings were stacked up or hung haphazardly among junk of every kind. Julien Tanguy loved the young painters who were fighting against middle-class idiocy, enthusiasm that might have been partly fed by nostalgia for his years as a Communard. He had a great many Van Goghs, a good number of Gauguins, a few things by Seurat and Signac and, most importantly, works by Cézanne. There was a time when the paintings of Monet, Renoir, Pissarro and other Impressionists passed through his shop as well, but then those artists became famous and their works went to the more qualified dealers, like Georges Petit. The good-hearted old man was not bothered by this, however.

Tanguy only wanted his friends to be successful, nothing more. Whenever a visitor to the shop showed interest, the shopkeeper would disappear into the back room and return a few minutes later with five or six paintings under his arm and two in his hands, which he would then carefully arrange on chairs or against the walls, moving them around until he found the right light. An American art critic who visited the humble little shop in rue Clauzel, remembers Tanguy's 'curious way of first looking

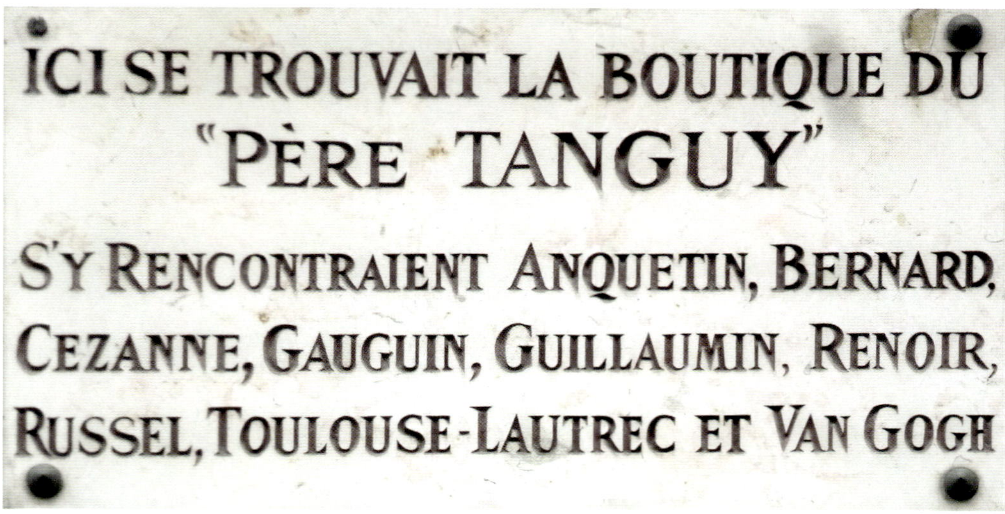

Commemorative plaque in rue Clauzel

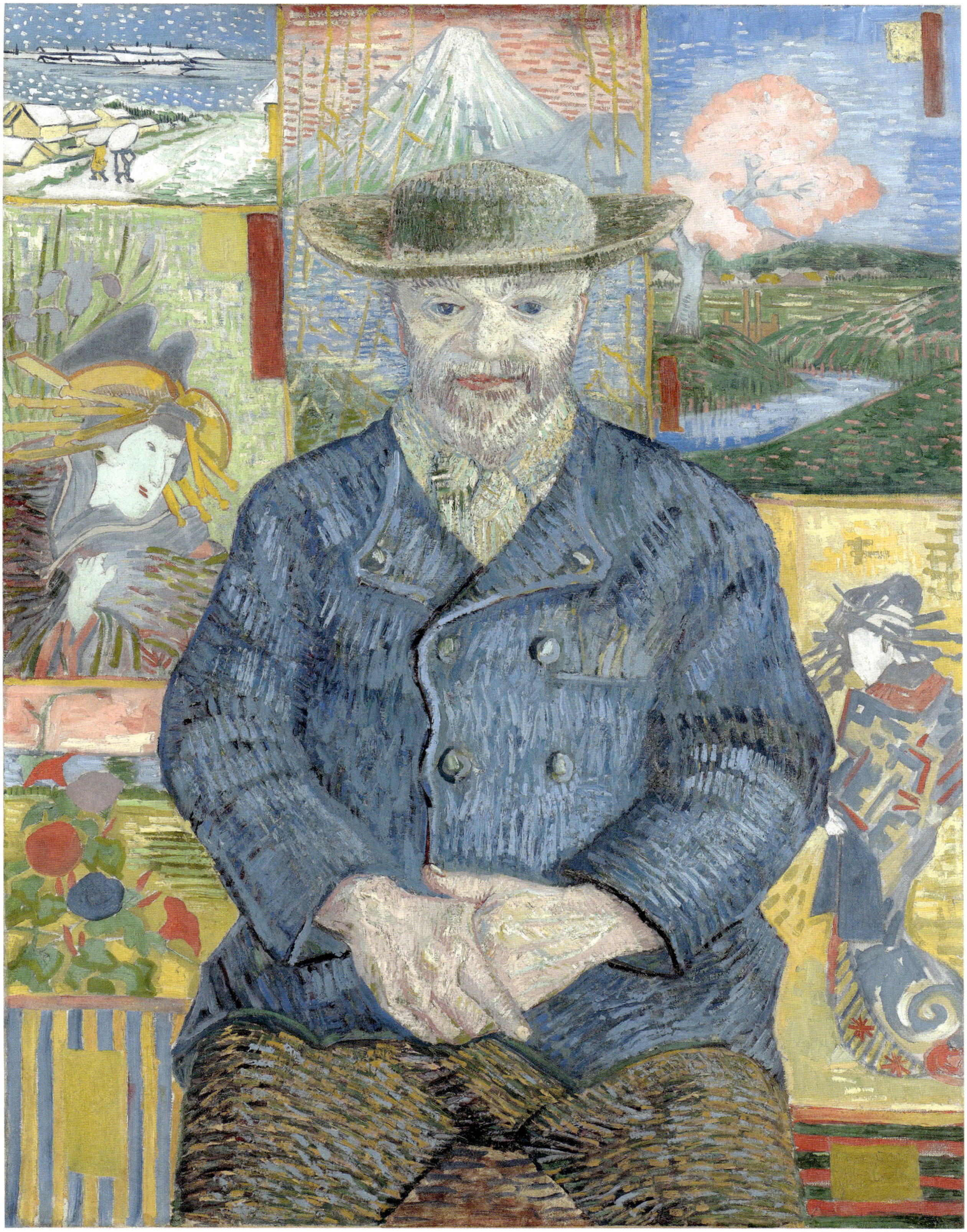

Vincent van Gogh, *Portrait of Père Tanguy*, 1887. Paris, Musée Rodin

Émile Bernard, *Portrait of Père Tanguy*, 1887. Basel, Kunstmuseum Basel

down at his picture with all the fond love of a mother, and then looking up at you over his glasses, as if begging you to admire his beloved children'.[2] He had no thirst for profit. On the contrary, he often helped the painters to the detriment of his small business, accepting paintings in lieu of payment that were worth less than the price of the canvas. But not only that, his support sometimes extended so far as providing the necessities of life. Before being an art dealer of the Impressionists, like Durand-Ruel or Vollard, he was first and foremost their friend. And, if Montmartre ever had a poetic, wretched romantic period, it is represented by this old paint seller and his little shop. These aspects of his character might have been what endeared him so much to the surly Cézanne, whose paintings, after the 1877 group show, could not be seen anywhere else in Paris. This lent further allure to the cramped shop, which was slowly becoming the scruffy Bayreuth of new art, as we read in these lines by Émile Bernard, writing about Cézanne:

> Members of the Institute, influential and avant-garde critics, visited the modest shop in the Rue Clauzel, which thus became the fable of Paris and the conversation of the studios. Nothing seemed more disconcerting than these canvases, where the most outstanding gifts were coupled with a childlike naiveté. The young felt the genius, the old the folly of the paradox; the jealous saw only impotence.[3]

It is said that when Cardinal Mazzarino was at the point of death he sighed for his paintings, which he would be soon forced to abandon: Tanguy, who had been a Communard and perhaps did not put much stock in the promise of consolation in the afterlife, must have had even more reason than the old cardinal to regret that irremediable loss. Dying of stomach cancer, he wanted to be brought home from the hospital so that he could spend his final days among his paintings. When he was near the end, he had them all brought into his room in order to draw up an inventory. Then, this task complete, he died as he had lived, surrounded by the art he had always loved.

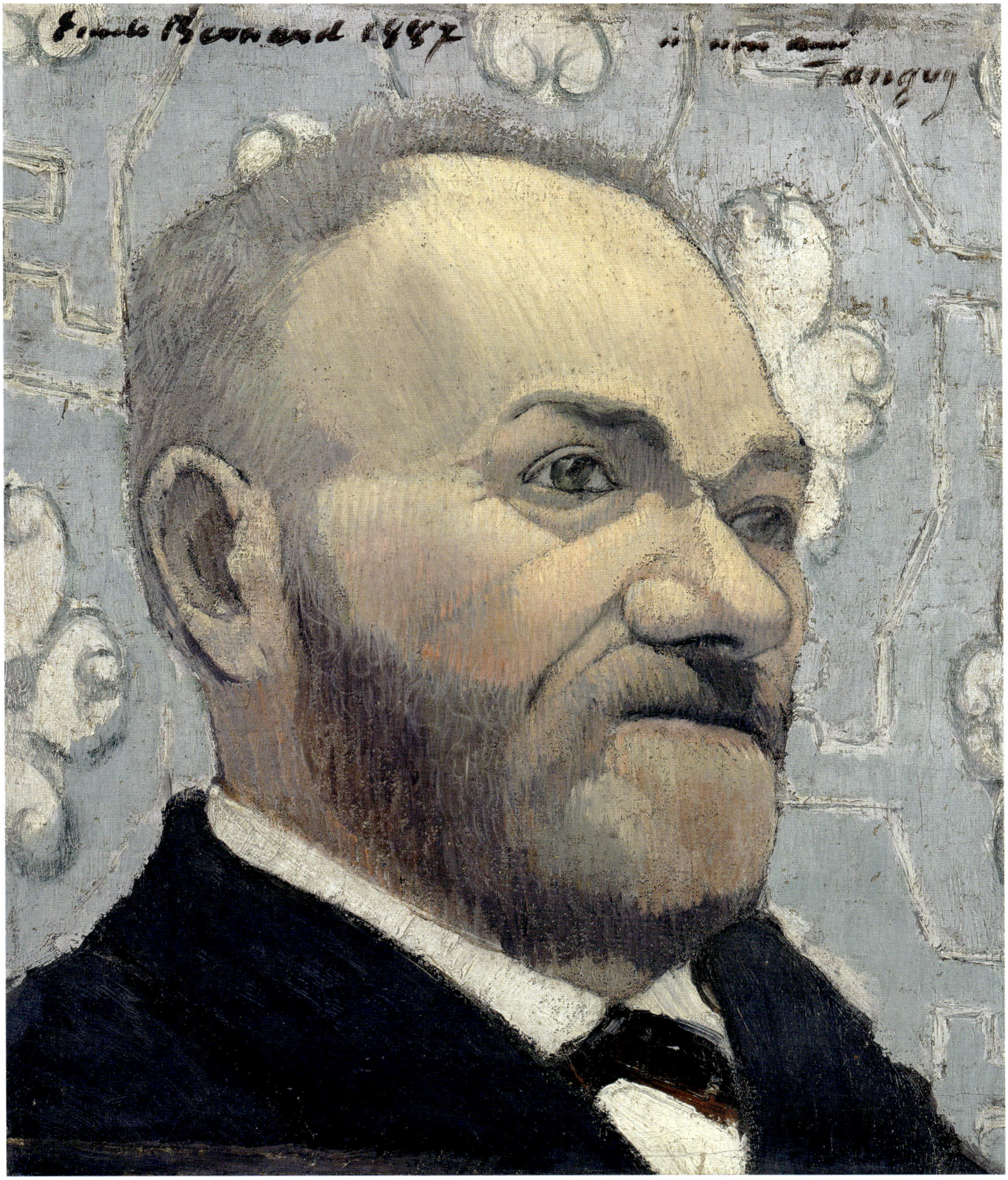
Emile Bernard 1887
Tanguy

2. The Gallery of Durand-Ruel

16 rue Laffitte
11 rue Le Peletier

For many years, the Durand-Ruel family conducted its business in rue de la Paix, near Place Vendôme. This magnificent square, at once both intimate and majestic, with rounded corners and softly modelled symmetries, was where Paris's high society gathered, even then. In his memoires, Paul Durand-Ruel wrote of his regret at having left that space (which was modest, but well located, and his family had made its fortune there, first selling paper and paints and then paintings) in 1869 in order to rent a larger one in a street that received less traffic and was far less elegant: the eighteenth-century rue Le Paul, from which one could get to the foot of Montmartre. Which is not to say that this street lacked its own allure. It was home to the old Opera House, which had provided so much material to Degas before it was destroyed by a fire in 1873, and the renowned Divan Le Peletier restaurant, the bohemian clientele of which was the subject of a popular poem by Théodore de Banville. The space, however, was awkward and needed to be renovated. Moreover, wealthy people and foreigners preferred to walk along the grand boulevards rather than turn onto rue Le Peletier or rue Laffitte, where one found the gallery's other entrance.

Paul's father, Jean, was not wealthy, but it did not take large sums to be a patron of the new painters: in 1850, you could get a painting by Théodore Rousseau for just 300 or 400 francs, whereas those of Corot, although prices had gone up after Napoleon III purchased one of them in 1861, rarely cost more than 1,200. When his father died, Paul inherited his business as well as his taste, and it was he who handled the sale of one of the masterpieces of the past generation: Millet's *The Angelus*.

The Durand-Ruel Gallery at 16 rue Laffitte, 1920

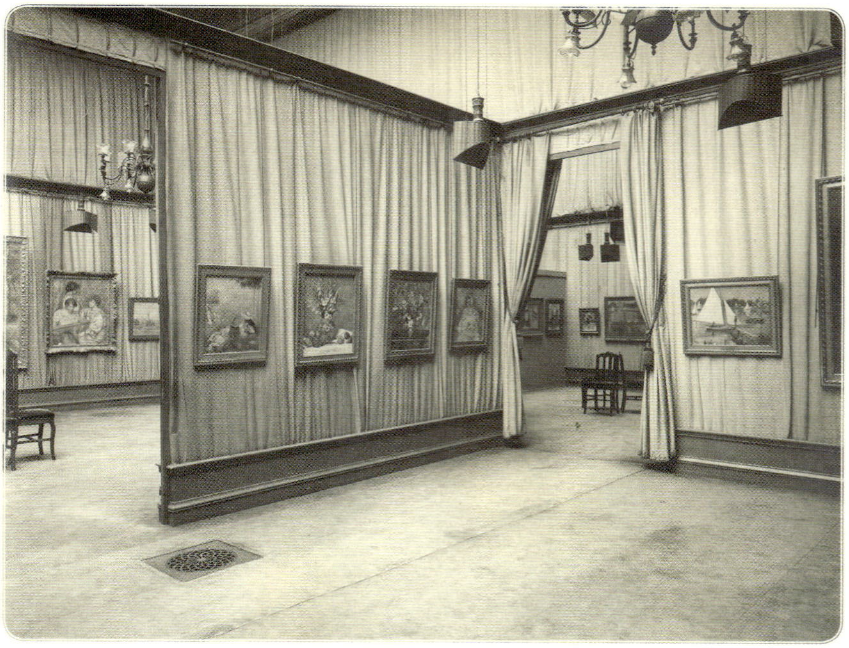

When Paul met Monet, it was 1871; not long after, he met Pissarro as well. He bought a few paintings from each: the former offered them at 300 francs apiece, the latter, even less—just 200 francs. Although risible, these amounts were in any case larger than what Impressionists in general were getting for selling their work at the time. Furthermore, the dealer offered them a small income because they painted regularly for him. And so, when Monet said, many

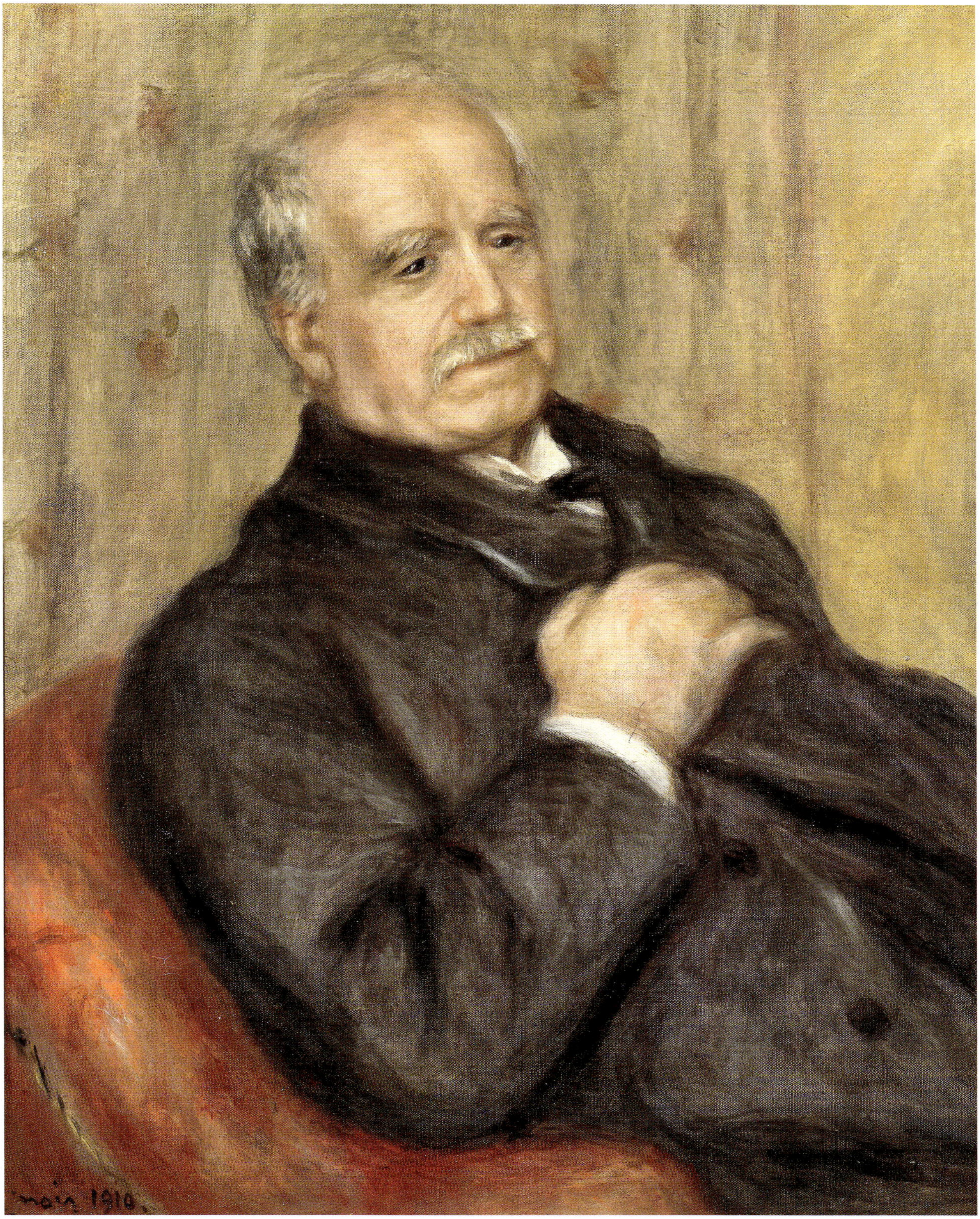

Pierre-Auguste Renoir, *Paul Durand-Ruel*, 1910. Private Collection

years later, that if it had not been for Durand-Ruel, he and his friends would have starved to death, it was not mere rhetoric. Manet also benefited from the generosity of the gallerist, who had discovered his work in Alfred Stevens's studio. The next day, Durand-Ruel went to Manet's studio and bought all twenty-three paintings he found there, including the dead bullfighter, the guitarist and the absinthe drinker. He paid a generous sum: 35,000 francs.

From then on, Durand-Ruel determinedly devoted himself to the Impressionist cause, organising numerous exhibitions, the most famous of which was the one in his gallery in 1876, with a total of 252 works. This was the Impressionists' second group show, the first having been the one in the photographer Nadar's studio in 1874. Degas showed twenty-four paintings, Monet eighteen, Morisot seventeen, Pissarro twelve and Renoir fifteen, while Sisley limited himself to eight. Manet, as on other occasions, did not participate, but he did open his own studio to the public. This time, it was decided to keep the works by each artist separate rather than display them together, but the result was the same and the reactions consisted of the usual mix of criticism and sneers: In *Le Figaro*, Albert Wolff's pen was in a state of malevolent grace:

> The Rue Peletier is unfortunate. Following upon the burning of the Opera-House, a new disaster has fallen upon the quarter. There has just been opened at M. Durand-Ruel's an exhibition of what is said to be painting. The innocent passer-by enters, and a cruel spectacle meets his terrified gaze. Here five or six lunatics, of whom one is a woman, have chosen to exhibit their works. There are people who burst out into laughter in front of these objects. Personally I am saddened by them. These so-called artists style themselves Intransigeants, Impressionists. They take paint, brushes, and canvases; they throw a few colours on to the canvas at random, and then they sign the lot. In the same way the inmates of a madhouse pick up the stones on the road and believe they have found diamonds. It is an appalling spectacle of human vanity gone astray to the point of complete dementia. Try to make M Pissarro understand that trees are not violet, that sky is not the color of fresh butter, that in no country do we see the things he paints and that no intelligence can accept such aberrations! You might as well waste your time trying to explain to an inmate of Dr Blanche, who thinks he's the Pope, that he lives in the Batignolles and not in the Vatican. Try indeed to make M. Degas see reason; tell him that in art there are certain qualities called drawing, color, execution, control, and he will laugh in your face and treat you as a reactionary. Or try to explain to M. Renoir that a woman's torso is not a mass of flesh in the process of decomposition with green and violet spots which denote the state of complete putrefaction of a corpse! There's also a woman in the group. She is called Berthe Morisot and she is interesting to observe. In her case, a feminine grace is maintained amid the outpourings of a delirious mind.[4]

The mocked paintings included Monet's *Autumn Effect at Argenteuil*, Degas's *A Cotton Office in New Orleans*, Sisley's *The Watering Place at Marly-le-Roi* and a *Self-Portrait* by Renoir. Durand-Ruel did not, however, lose heart. In 1882, he organised another group show in rue Saint-Honoré and, the following year, a series of solo exhibitions in his new space in boulevard de la Madeleine. His galleries were

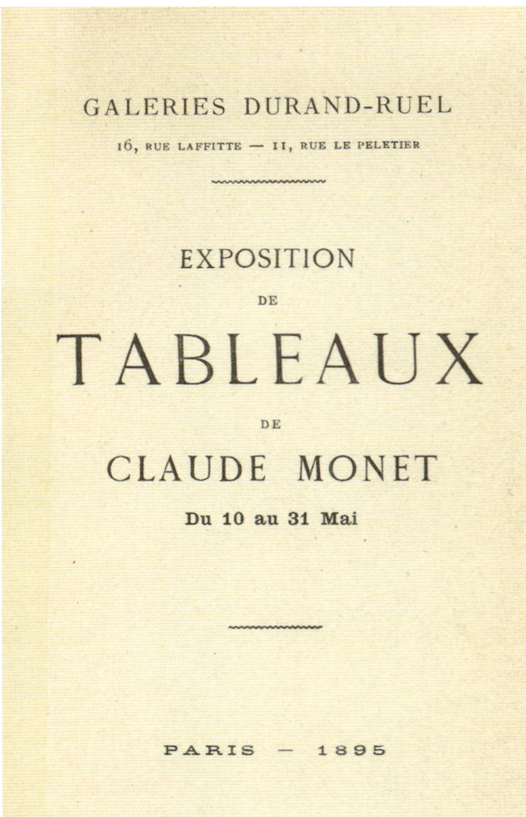
GALERIES DURAND-RUEL
16, RUE LAFFITTE — 11, RUE LE PELETIER
EXPOSITION
DE
TABLEAUX
DE
CLAUDE MONET
Du 10 au 31 Mai
PARIS — 1895

Cover of the catalogue of a solo exhibition by Monet. Paris, Galeries Durand-Ruel, 10–31 May 1895

p. 19
Exhibition of Paul Durand-Ruel's Collection of Impressionists. London, Grafton Galleries, 1905

known for their attention to light: first gas, then electric and finally, natural, making use of large windows. Despite his efforts, however, in 1884 the dealer was on the brink of ruin, to the point that some of his painters, no longer getting the support from him they needed, signed a contract with his rival, Georges Petit. Durand-Ruel was also the first to bring the Impressionists to the United States, when he was invited by the American Art Association to organise an exhibition in New York. The exhibition was held in 1886, and marked the first time that the new painting received a positive reaction. The Impressionists could at least console themselves with the adage 'no man is a prophet in his own land', but they were too occupied with their indigence to fantasise about future affluence. And indeed, when they returned from America all their usual financial problems returned. The dealer resumed his struggle. As Renoir recalled: 'At the Exposition Universelle in 1855, Durand-Ruel, not yet twenty-five, sprang to the defence of Delacroix against the Emperor, who liked only Winterhalter.'[5] Politically, he was a legitimist, and often went to the Netherlands to pay homage to the count of Chambord,[6] but in art he was a progressive. He lived just long enough to see the reassessment of his friends' art, who he survived by just a bit, dying in 1922.

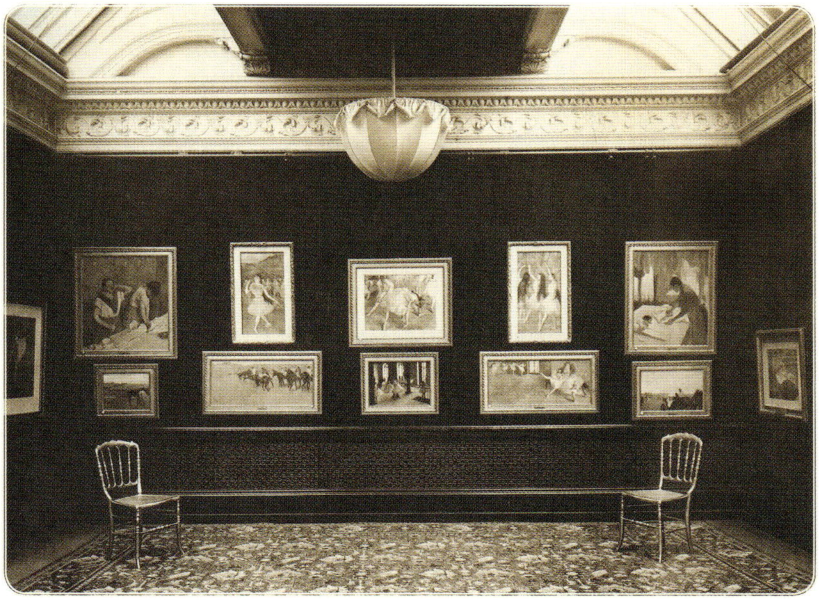

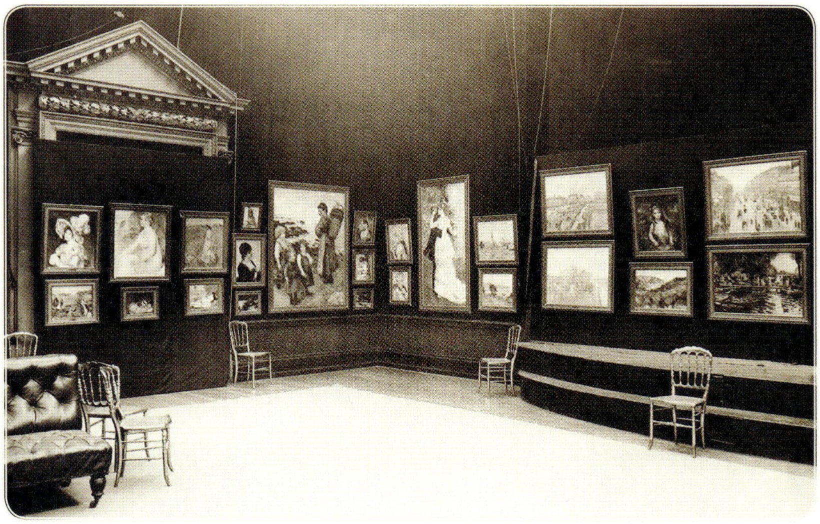

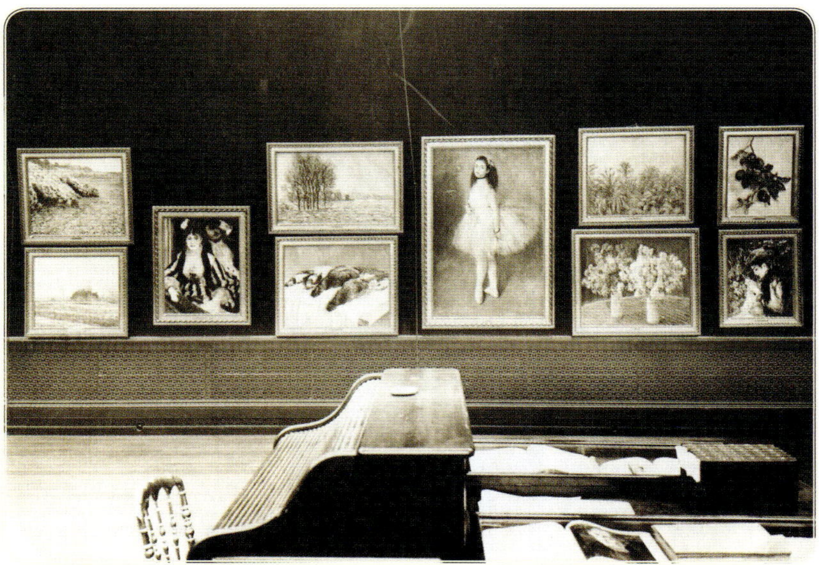

3. Ambroise Vollard's Gallery

39 rue Laffitte
then 41, later 6

Ambroise Vollard was not Parisian: his grandfather had emigrated to Réunion Island, which was a French colony at the time, and married a girl whose family was from Provence. Many years later, in his *Recollections of a Picture Dealer*, Vollard told of how his early taste for colour harmonies originated in a chance encounter between a parrot and a bed of sunflowers. Discovering the unexpected harmonies between the plumage and the hues of the flowers, little Ambroise then moved the perch to the carnation beds, then the balsam and the roses. As for his taste for collecting, he started with pebbles and then moved on to broken bits of porcelain, ending up with his parents severely forbidding him to collect anything of any kind. In the meantime, separation had filled his soul with 'distant love' for Paris, the irresistible allure of which was also coming to be felt in geographically closer countries, like England and Italy. And so Vollard moved to Paris, where his first job was under Alphonse Dumas, the wealthy owner of a picture gallery. Their tastes, however, did not coincide. Vollard found Impressionist painting interesting, Dumas found it unseemly, so they went their separate ways. Vollard opened his first little shop in rue des Apennines in Montmartre, and then moved to rue Laffitte, where, although changing street number multiple times, he remained for years. Rue Laffitte is a small street that briefly runs parallel to rue Le Peletier, where, at no. 11, the second Impressionists show had been held, not far from the famous boulevard des Capucines, which had hosted the first. As Vollard recalled:

Ambroise Vollard in his gallery, in front of Picasso's *Evocation: The Burial of Casagemas* (1901), before 1910

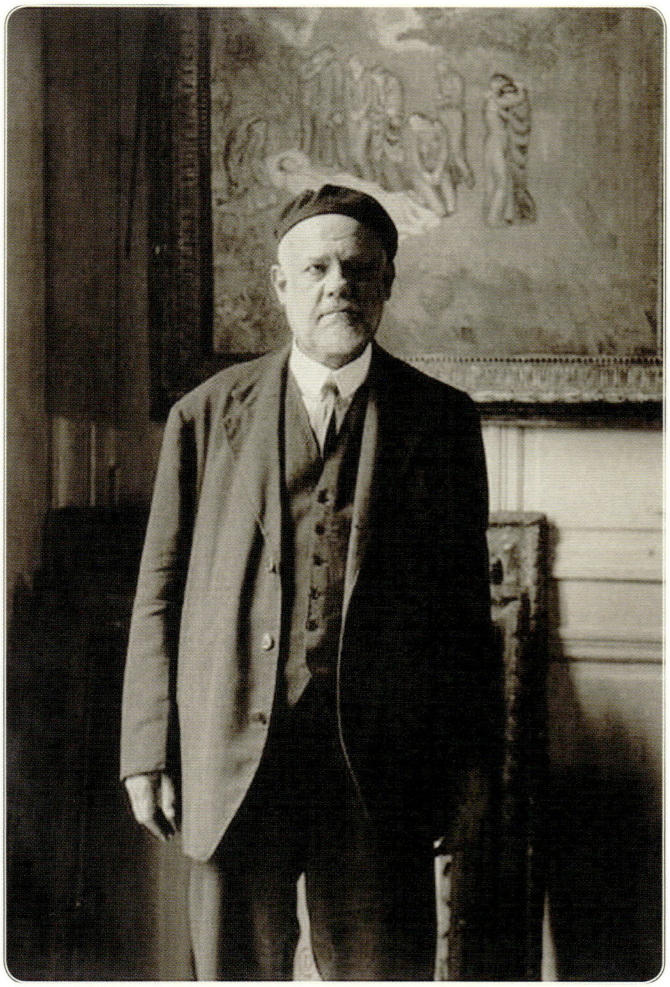

> In those days the rue Laffitte was the rue des tableaux. If you heard a man say, 'I'm going to take a turn in the rue Laffitte,' you might be sure he was a collector of pictures. On the other hand, when Manet said, 'It's a good thing to go to the rue Laffitte,' or Claude Monet asked, 'Why go to the rue Laffitte?' they meant respectively that it was a good thing, or that it was useless, for a painter to keep in touch with hisfellow-artists.[7]

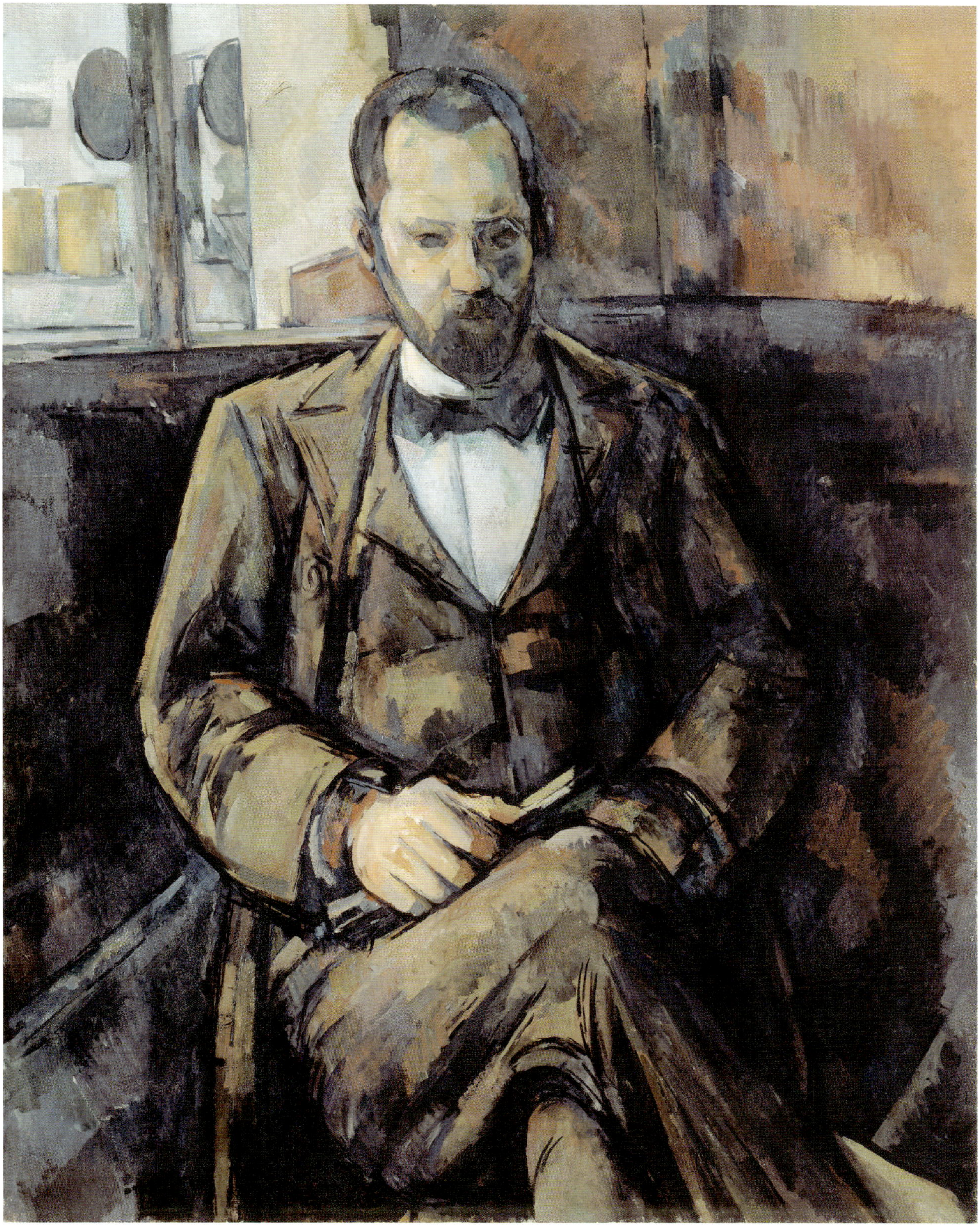

Paul Cézanne,
Ambroise Vollard, 1899.
Paris, Petit Palais,
Musée des Beaux-Arts
de la Ville

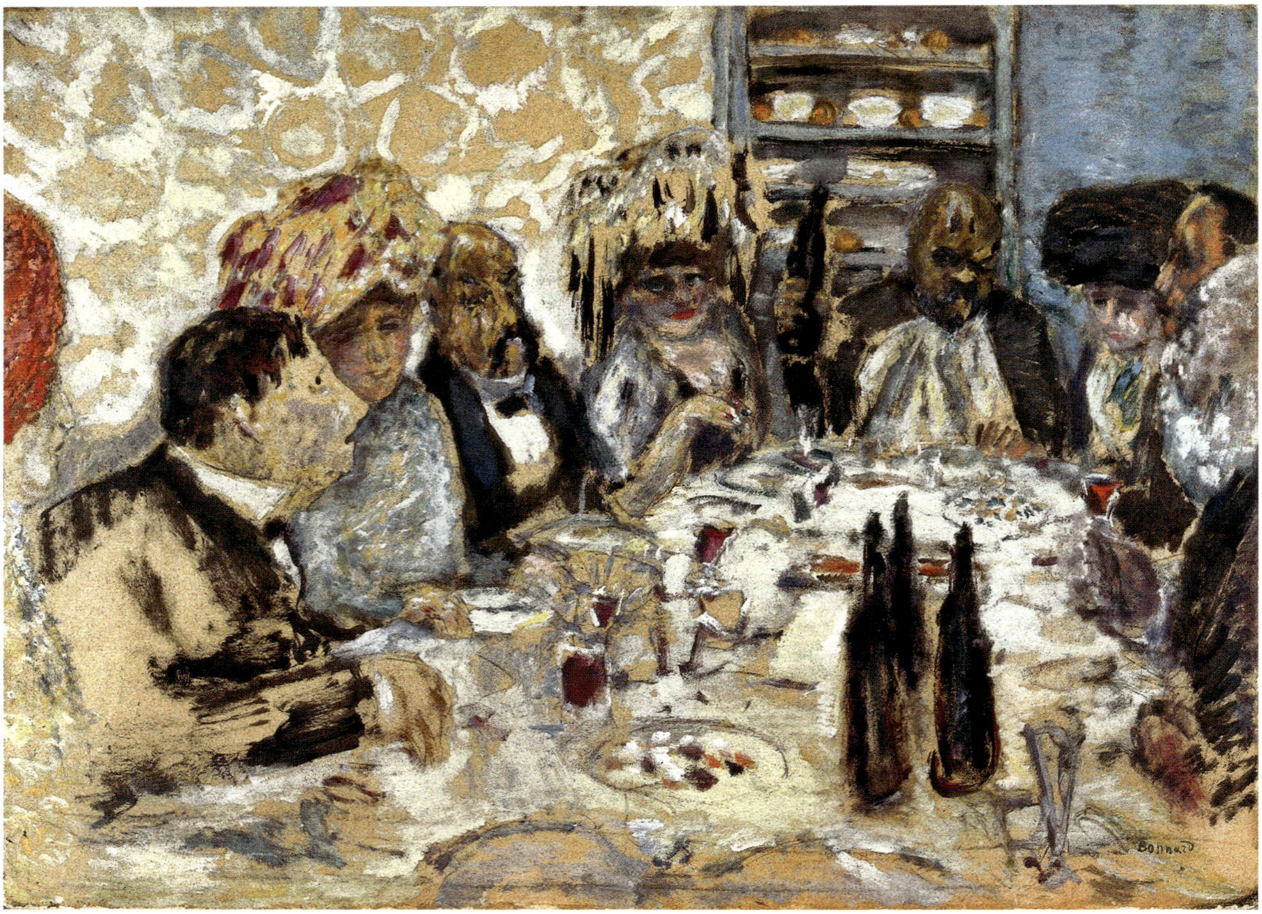

Pierre Bonnard,
Dinner at Vollard's, 1907.
Private Collection

Of his gallery's various locations, the most famous was the one at no. 6, a large shop with a mezzanine floor, below which Vollard hosted friends, artists and writers, especially in the evening. Dinners in Vollard's cellar, as the spartan space where he hosted his guests came to be called, became famous all over Paris and was passed down to posterity in numerous accounts and at least one famous painting: Pierre Bonnard's *Dinner at Vollard's*. We have a description of it penned by the dealer himself:

> My cellar in the rue Laffitte was divided in two by a partition. One part, which had a ventilator, served as a kitchen, the other, which had no opening, did duty as my dining-room. Here, where there was no communication with the outer air, the heat from the kitchen condensed in heavy moisture. Renoir, dining with me one night, said, as he picked up his walking-stick that he had stood against the wall 'There must be a water-pipe leaking somewhere about here.' 'Water-pipe leaking? Where?' 'Look at my stick! It's all wet!'[8]

Vollard had a method of selling that was all his own. When a prospective buyer entered the gallery, he would pretend to be dozing, almost as if he were absent or distracted. Some said that he would even hide himself in the closet to secretly observe the client. He was certainly a capable dealer, far more so than Père Tanguy, who had been, until his death in 1894, the sole keeper of the works of Cezanne. The year after Tanguy's death, Vollard organised the first major solo exhibition of the work of the painter from Aix, although more on the advice of Pissarro and Degas than

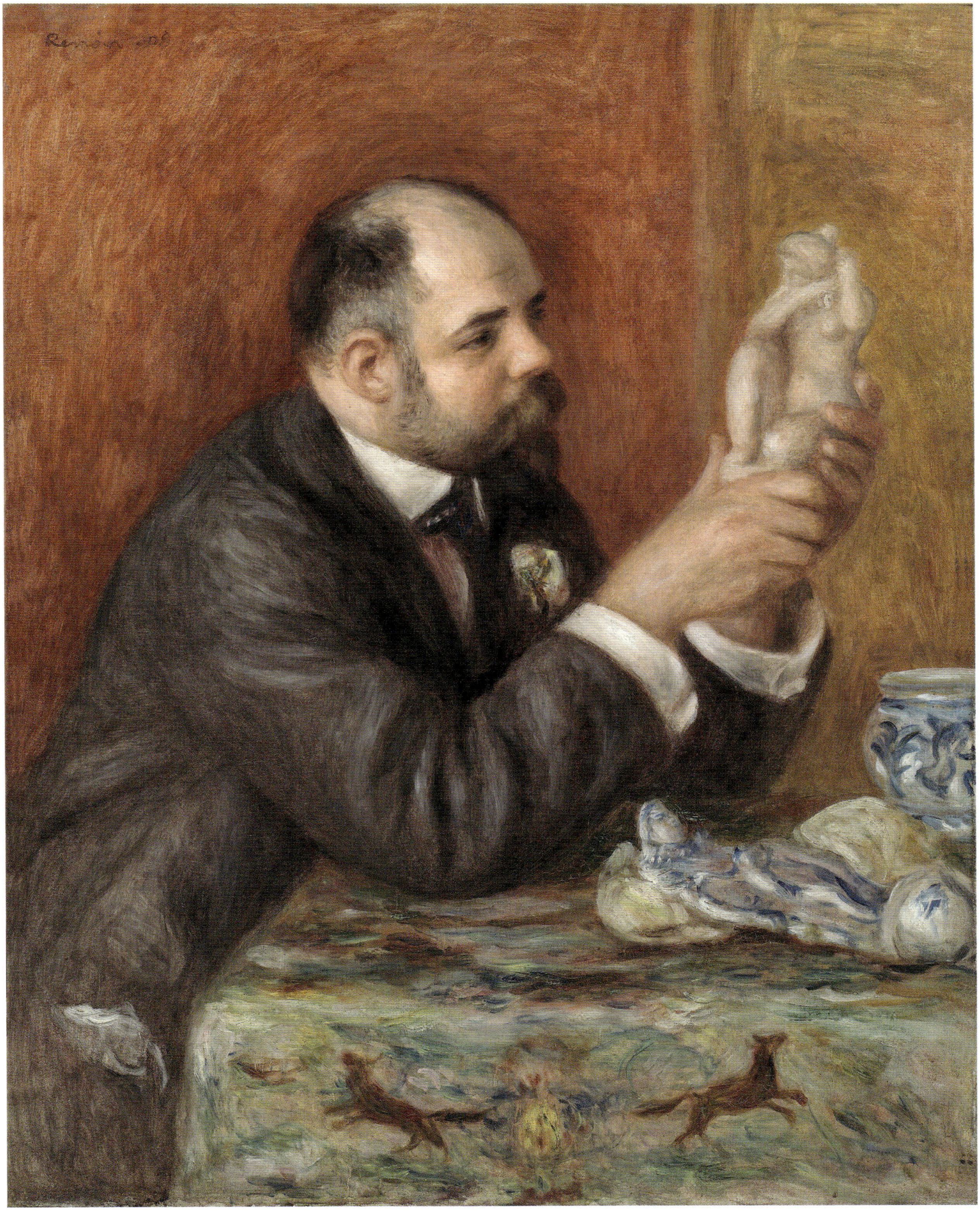

Pierre-Auguste Renoir, *Ambroise Vollard,* 1908. London, Courtauld Gallery

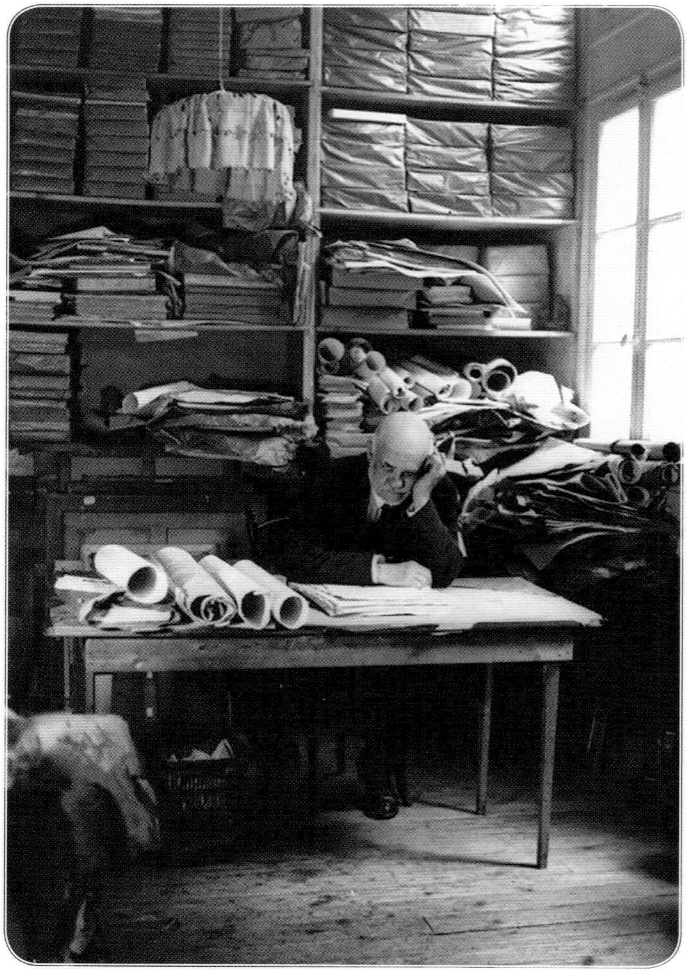

Ambroise Vollard in his home in rue Martignac, *c.* 1933 (photo by Thérèse Bonney)

his own inclinations. In any case, the dealer's role in the establishment of Cézanne's fame, at a time when the artist was living an existence of disdainful isolation in his hometown, was decisive, as attested by the portrait that the artist made of him, full of gratitude, a few years later. In Maurice Denis's *Homage to Cézanne* (pp. 10–11), Vollard is shown in profile on the left, in the place reserved for the patron on old altarpieces. In 1896, he wrote to Gauguin, who was in Tahiti, and drew up a contract with him ensuring him all the artist's production. In 1900, it was Van Gogh's turn, with a vast exhibition of hundreds of paintings to mark the tenth anniversary of his death. Of course, Vollard was also a friend of talented young artists like Picasso, who painted his portrait as well.

When the gallery in rue Laffitte became a success, the romantic period of Impressionism, when the artists were sometimes so poor that they had to scrape their canvases in order to reuse them, was coming to a close. And its definitive end came with the deaths of Alfred Jarry and Toulouse-Lautrec. Vollard supported and financed the painters, but, although he had temporarily lifted Gauguin out of poverty in 1896, he did not share their straitened circumstances with the naive camaraderie of Père Tanguy, nor did he have to show the faith and tenacity of Durand-Ruel, who was almost on the brink of bankruptcy: he stepped on the scene when Impressionism had already begun to be highly regarded. Even Montmartre had changed and lost its simple, rustic air, along with its mills and little vegetable gardens.

Vollard died in 1939, three years after publishing *Recollections of a Picture Dealer.*

4. The Palais de l'Industrie

between the Champs Élysées and the Seine

The Palais de l'Industrie. Above, the entrance portico; below, the interior.

Inaugurated in 1855, in time for the Exposition Universelle, the Palais de l'Industrie was a bombastic building, for which Jean-Marie-Victor Viel and Alexis Barrault were at least in part inspired by the Crystal Palace in London; 'in part' because the slender iron and glass members were in this case caged within a powerful carapace in a distinctive eclectic style. It had impressive dimensions: 234 metres long, 108 wide and 35 metres high, more or less the same as Notre-Dame. This massive structure was, however, still not big enough to house all the events that were slated to be held in it, and in some cases a building in avenue Montaigne had to be added: that was where the Salon de peinture et de sculpture, which took place every two years, was held.

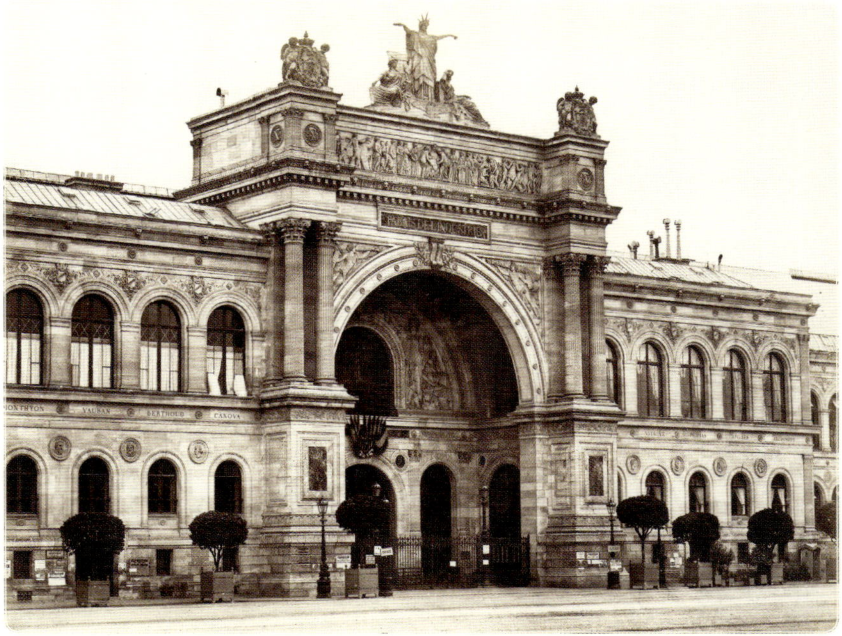

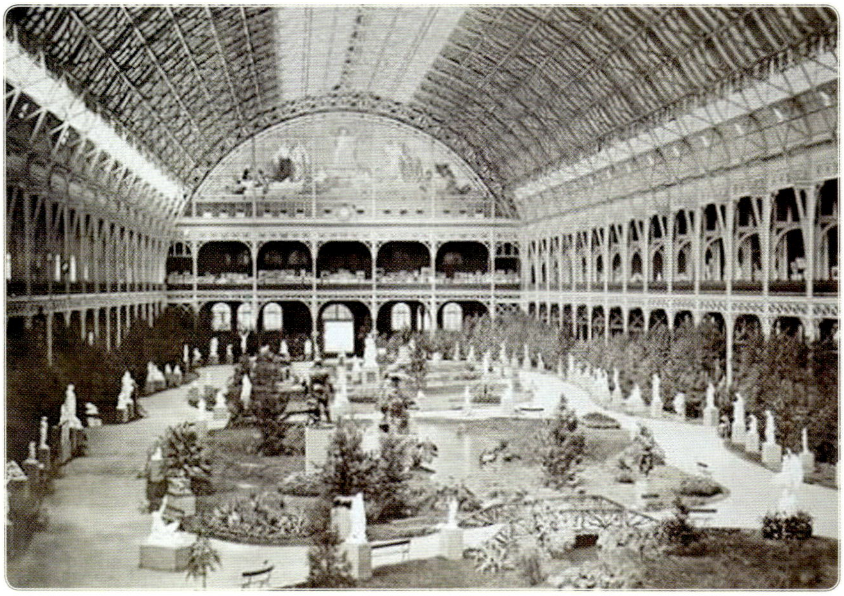

The importance placed by nineteenth-century artists on the chance to participate in the major official exhibition surprises us today. However, we need to keep in mind that the jury's rejection did not only influence the good opinion one generally had of a painter, but also determined the economic value of his work and the probability of receiving public commissions, one example being that of Johan Barthold Jongkind, who, when one of his landscapes was rejected, had to refund the buyer the entire sum that had already been paid. And so, there is some truth in Honoré Daumier's caricature *Marche funebre!!*, which shows an artist dressed in black, wet handkerchief dangling from his hand, and following behind his own paintings, which

The Exposition Universelle of 1855 at the Palais de l'Industrie

Honoré Daumier, *Marche funèbre!!*, from the series 'L'Exposition Universelle', *Le Charivari*, April 1855

p. 27
Édouard Manet, *Olympia*, 1863. Paris, Musée d'Orsay

Honoré Daumier, *Still more Venuses this Year*, from the series 'Sketches from the Salon', *Le Charivari*, 10 May 1864

Honoré Daumier, *In front of Mr. Manet's Painting*, from the series 'Sketches from the Salon', *Le Charivari*, 19 June 1865

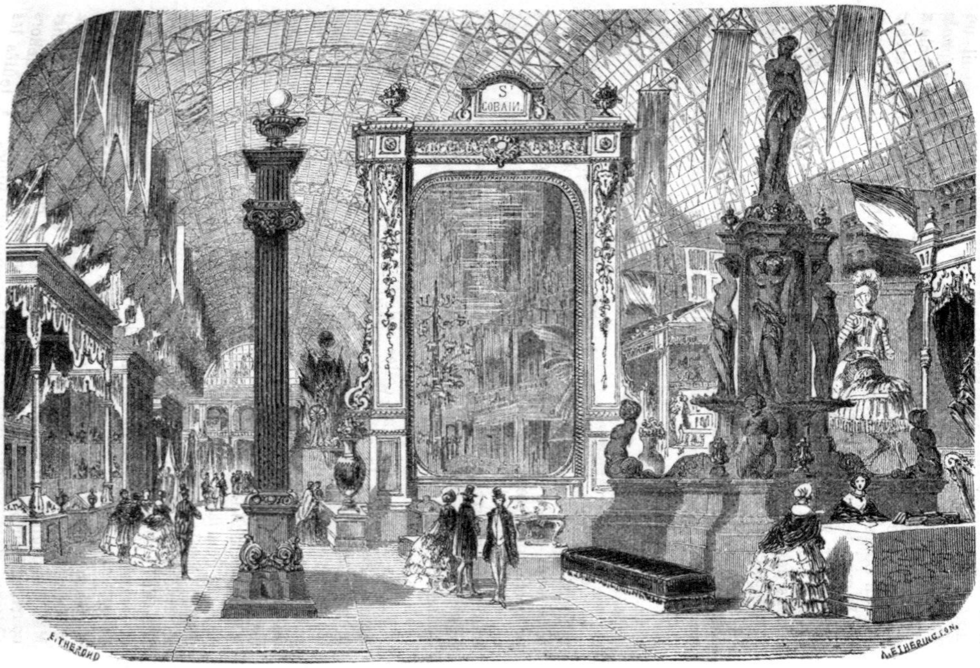

Palais de l'Industrie. (Exposition universelle de 1855.)

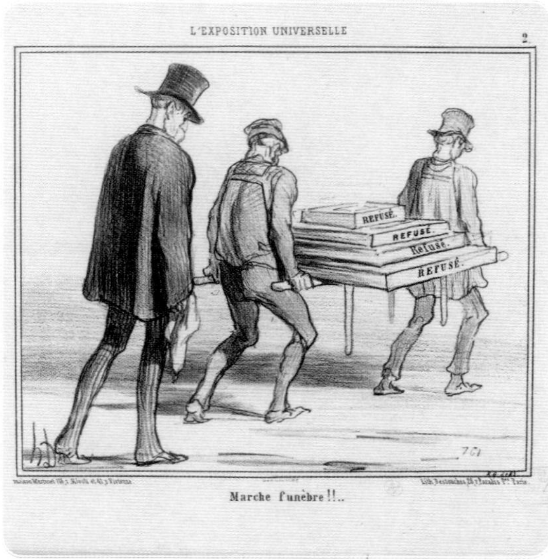

have been ignominiously labelled *refusé* and are being carried away on a stretcher by two workers in shirtsleeves. Cheerless Minoses, the members of the committee separated the professionals from the mere dilettantes, who, having lost their professional legitimacy, ended up swelling the ranks of prostitutes, pimps, wastrels, drinkers and other *rejetés*, censured by society, who flooded the narrow streets of Montmartre like a muddy river.

At the time when the Impressionists began to venture onto the Paris scene, Academic taste was particularly fossilised. Landscapes and still lifes were still looked upon with scornful condescension and it was believed that a great painting had to have a historical or at least classical subject. In 1855, Courbet set up his own pavilion near the Salon, in protest against his rejection by the committee. As for Corot and his school, they were just barely tolerated. In any case, in the view of Comte Émilien de Nieuwerkerke, director of the imperial museums, realism was painting made by 'people who don't change their underwear'. The monotony that emerged from the rigidity of these precepts was discouraging. In his novel *The Masterpiece*, Zola describes the kind of spectacle that was offered to visitors at these feeble exhibitions:

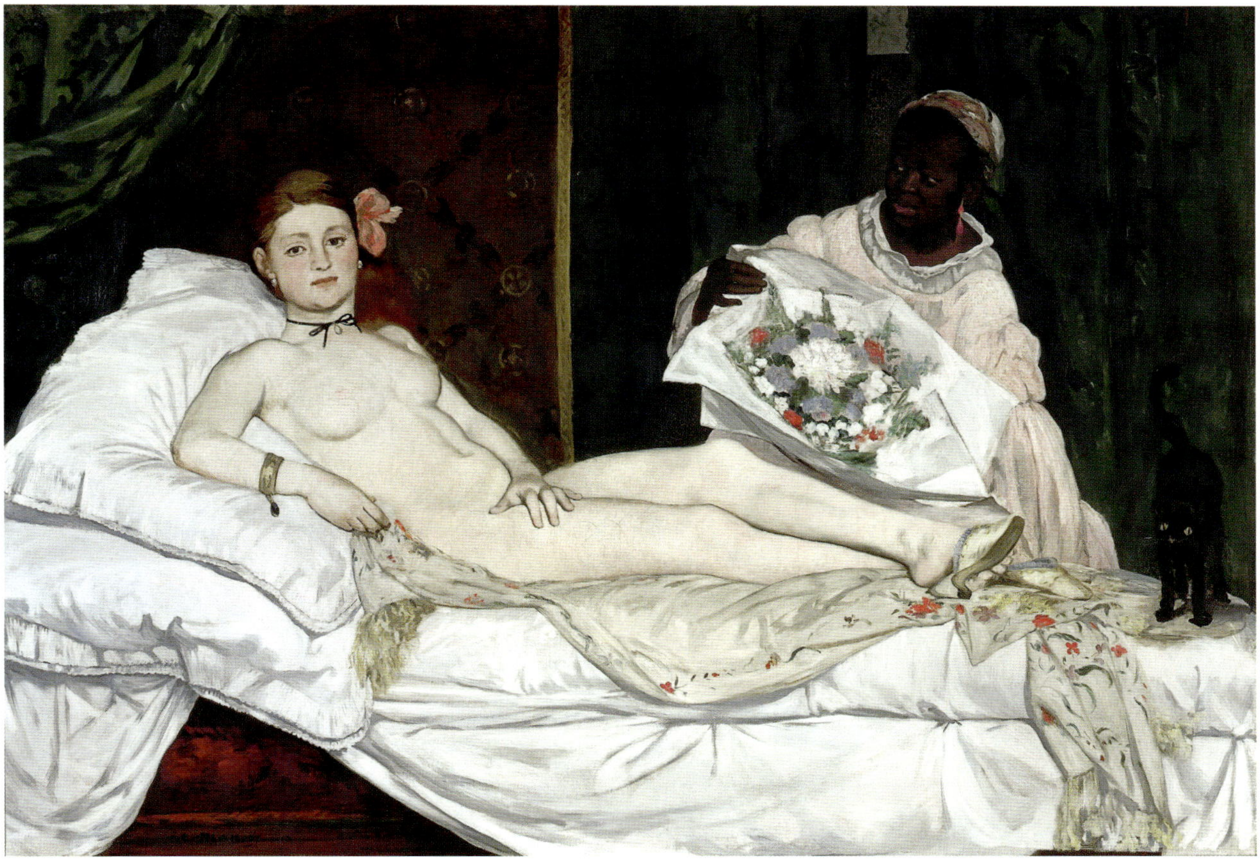

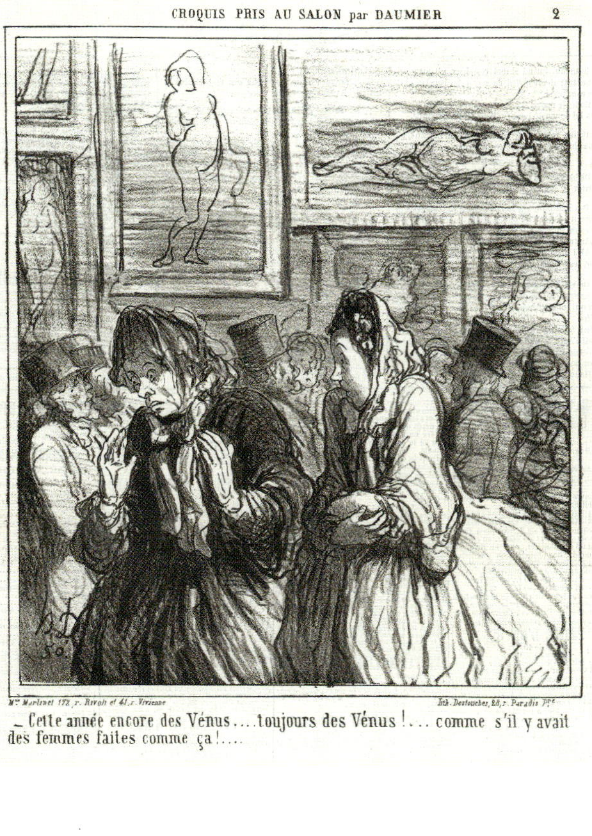
CROQUIS PRIS AU SALON par DAUMIER
2
Mon Martinet 172, r. Rivoli et 41, r. Vivienne
lith. Destouches, 28, r. Paradis Pre
_ Cette année encore des Vénus.... toujours des Vénus !... comme s'il y avait des femmes faites comme ça !....

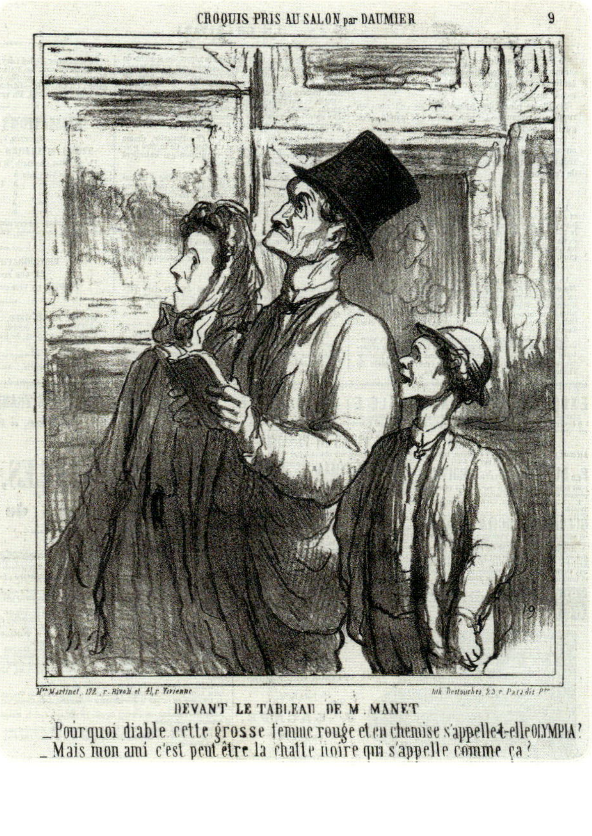
CROQUIS PRIS AU SALON par DAUMIER
9
Mon Martinet, 172, r. Rivoli et 41, r. Vivienne
DEVANT LE TABLEAU DE M. MANET
_ Pourquoi diable cette grosse femme rouge et en chemise s'appelle-t-elle OLYMPIA ?
_ Mais mon ami c'est peut être la chatte noire qui s'appelle comme ça ?

Édouard Manet, *Luncheon on the Grass*, 1863. Paris, Musée d'Orsay

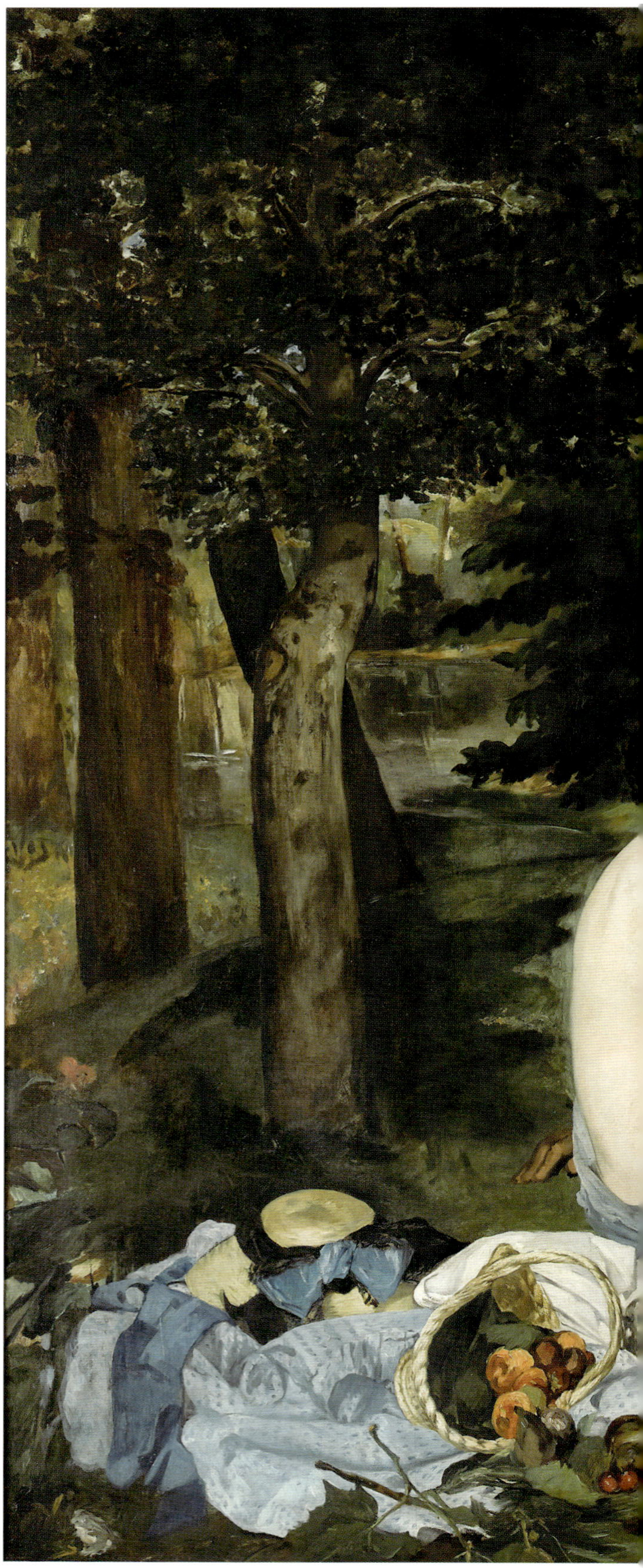

> It was one long succession of gold frames filled with shadow, black, ungraceful shapes, jaundiced-looking nudes in gloomy half-lights, all the paraphernalia of Classical Antiquity, historical subjects, genre paintings, landscapes, each one thoroughly soaked in the train-oil of convention. Every picture oozed unfailing mediocrity; every one showed the same dingy, muddy quality typical of anaemic, degenerate art doing its best to put on a good face.[9]

In 1863, however, the jury was even more severe than usual (3,000 works rejected out of 5,000 presented), stirring up so much agitation in artistic circles that it even reached the emperor's ears. On the afternoon of 22 April, Napoleon III went personally to examine the rejected paintings and, on the 24th, not having found them to be inferior to those that had been accepted, issued a decree establishing that the paintings by the *refusés* would also be submitted to the public's judgement. The Salon, which put them in an annex of the building, thus hosted Manet's famous *Luncheon on the Grass*, which was highly controversial, and two portraits of Spaniards by the same artist, as well as Whistler's *Symphony in White, No. 1: The White Girl.*

We also have an account of this second Salon by Zola, written in a witty, grotesque tone reminiscent of Daumier's satire:

> The laughter, which had sounded very discreet at first, grew louder as he advanced through the various rooms. When he reached the third the women

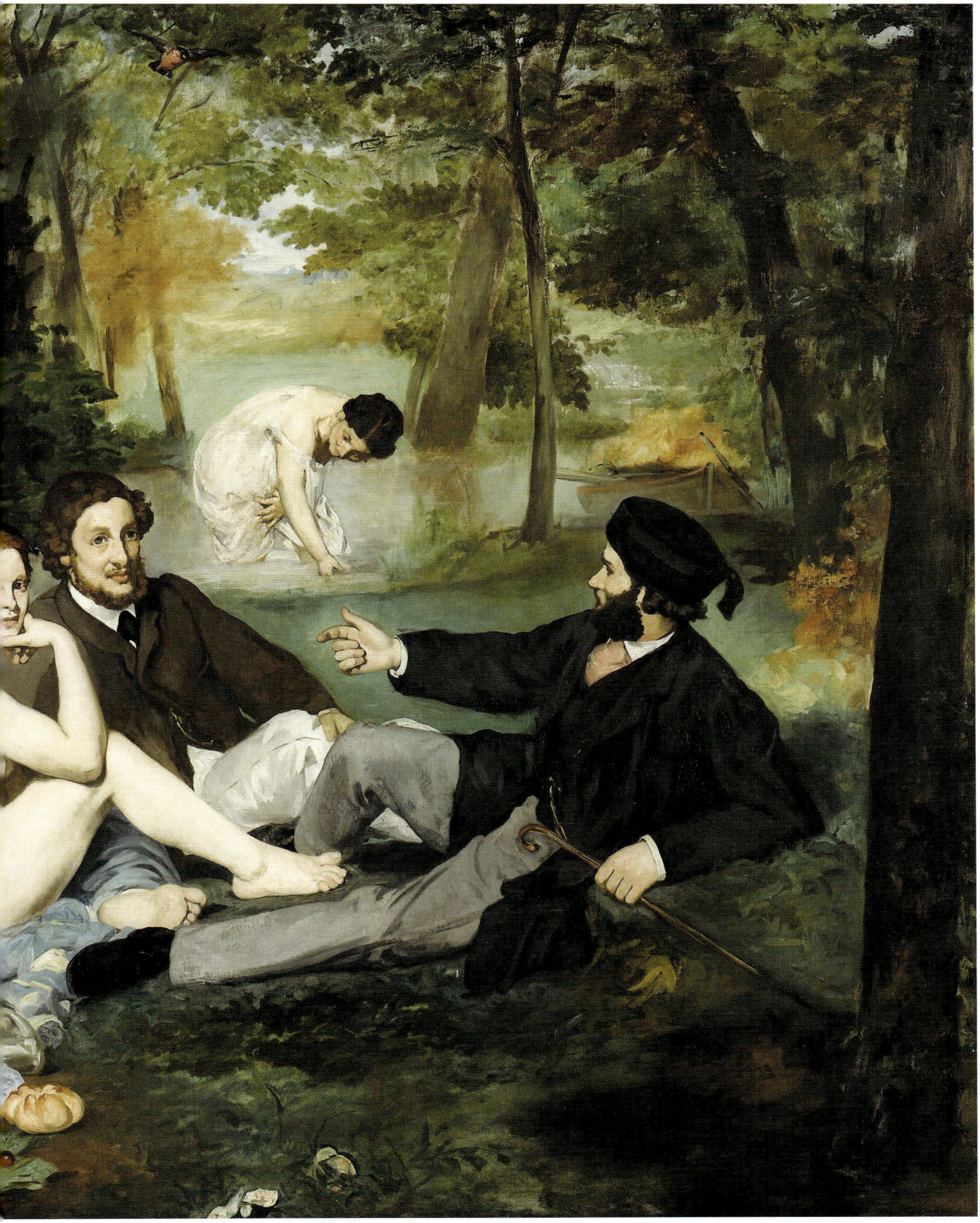

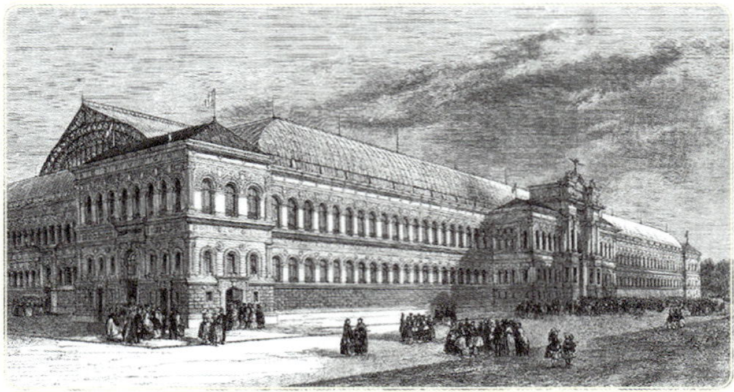

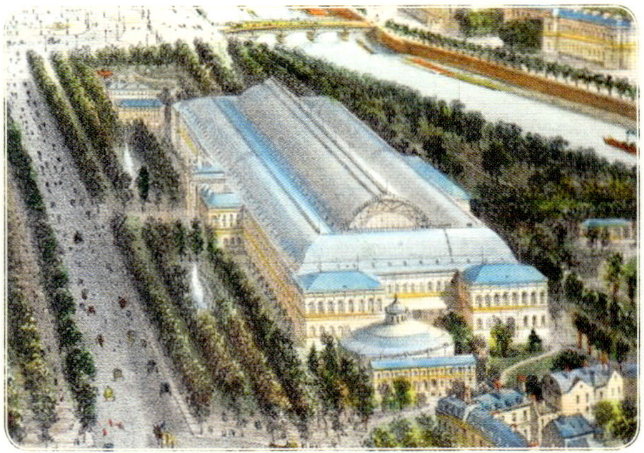

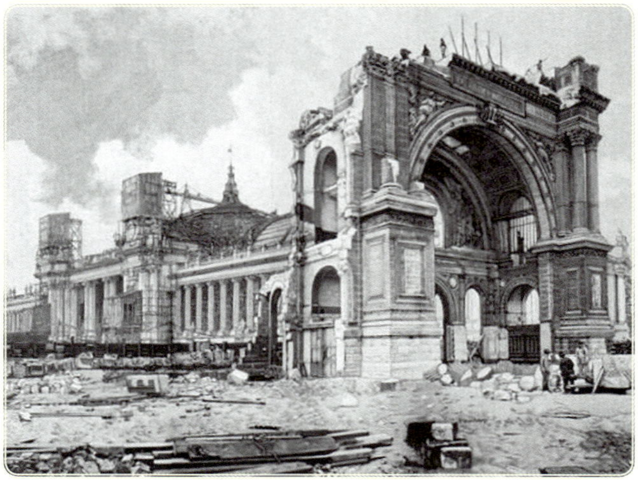

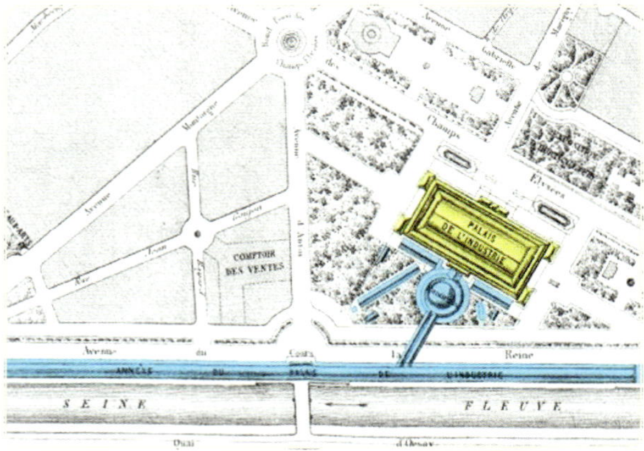

The Palais de l'Industrie. Above, view from the side and from above; below, during the demolition and map

> had stopped stifling their merriment with their handkerchiefs, and the men, completely unrestrained, were holding their sides and roaring with laughter. It was the contagious hilarity of a crowd bent on amusement, gradually working itself up to the point where it would laugh loudly at nothing and be just as convulsed by beautiful things as by ugly ones. Chaîne's *Christ* provoked less laughter than the nude woman whose prominent buttocks, which seemed to stand out from the canvas, were apparently thought to be screamingly funny. The 'Woman in White' provided some amusement, too, for she was rarely without her group of grinning admirers digging each other in the ribs and going off into fits of helpless mirth. Every picture had its peculiar attraction; people would call to each other to come look at this or that, and pithy remarks were heard on every lip.[10]

Episodes like these led writers to start imagining bourgeois obtuseness as a kind of physical deformity, giving physiognomic expression to spiritual vulgarity in the form of the dried-up severity of a conformist's face or the satisfied corpulence of a pleasure-seeking businessman. The tradesperson, firmly rooted in conventional values, was for nineteenth-century literature what the lout had been in courtly texts: the antithesis of all that is noble. And in a certain way, the Palais de l'Industrie, with its speciously sumptuous style, was a mirror in which the triumphalist conventionality of this mercantile spirit could admire itself.

The enormous building survived until 1896, when it was demolished to make way for the Petit Palais and the Grand Palais.

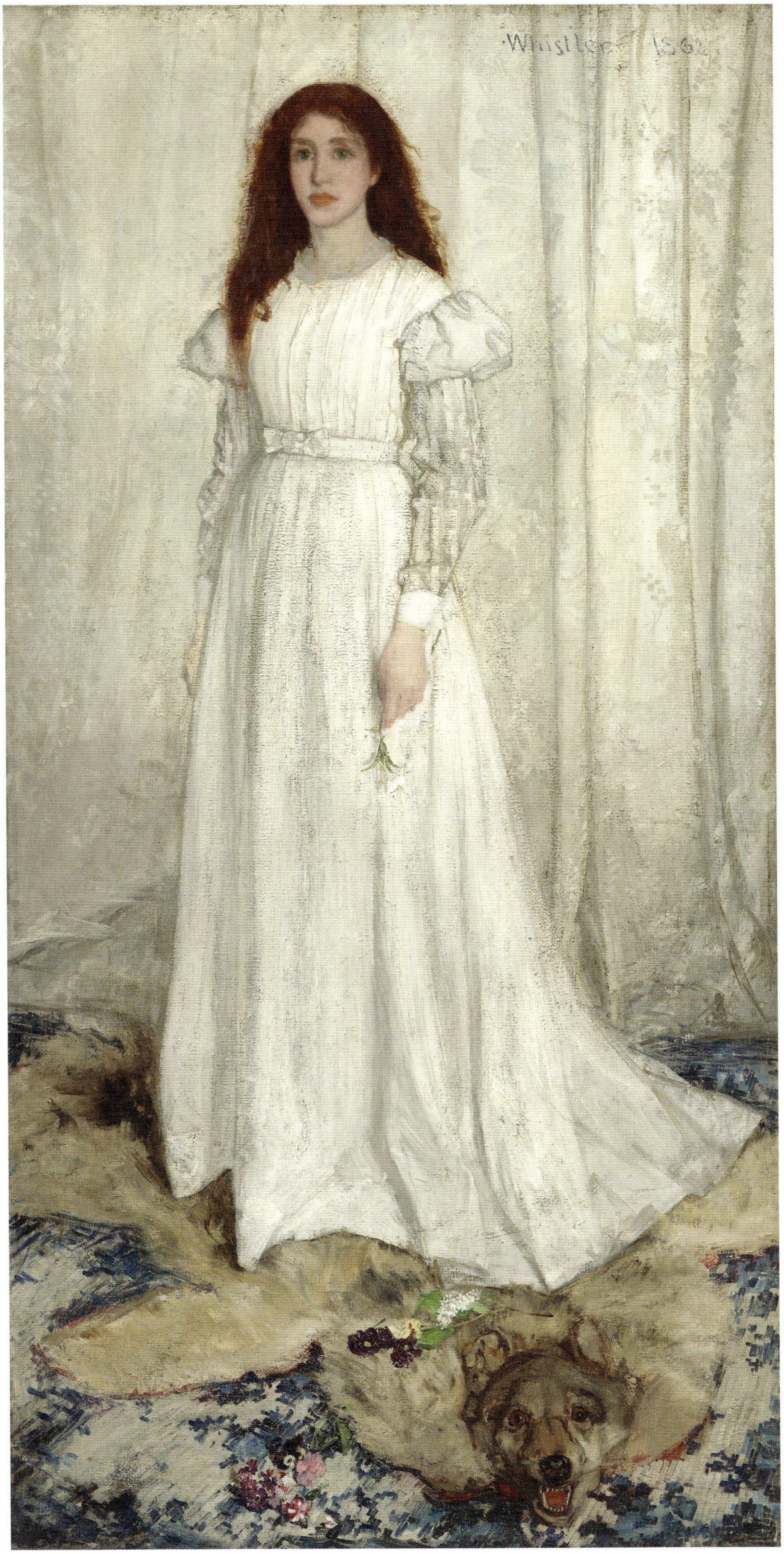

James Abbott McNeill Whistler, *Symphony in White, No. 1: The White Girl*, 1861–1862. Washington, D.C., National Gallery of Art

5. Nadar's Studio

rue Daunou corner boulevard des Capucines

John Rewald described Nadar's studio as a series of large rooms on two floors with red-brown walls that received the light from windows, as in an apartment.[11] When Renoir and his companions decided to organise an exhibition to present their work to the public, the choice fell to this space, one of the advantages of which

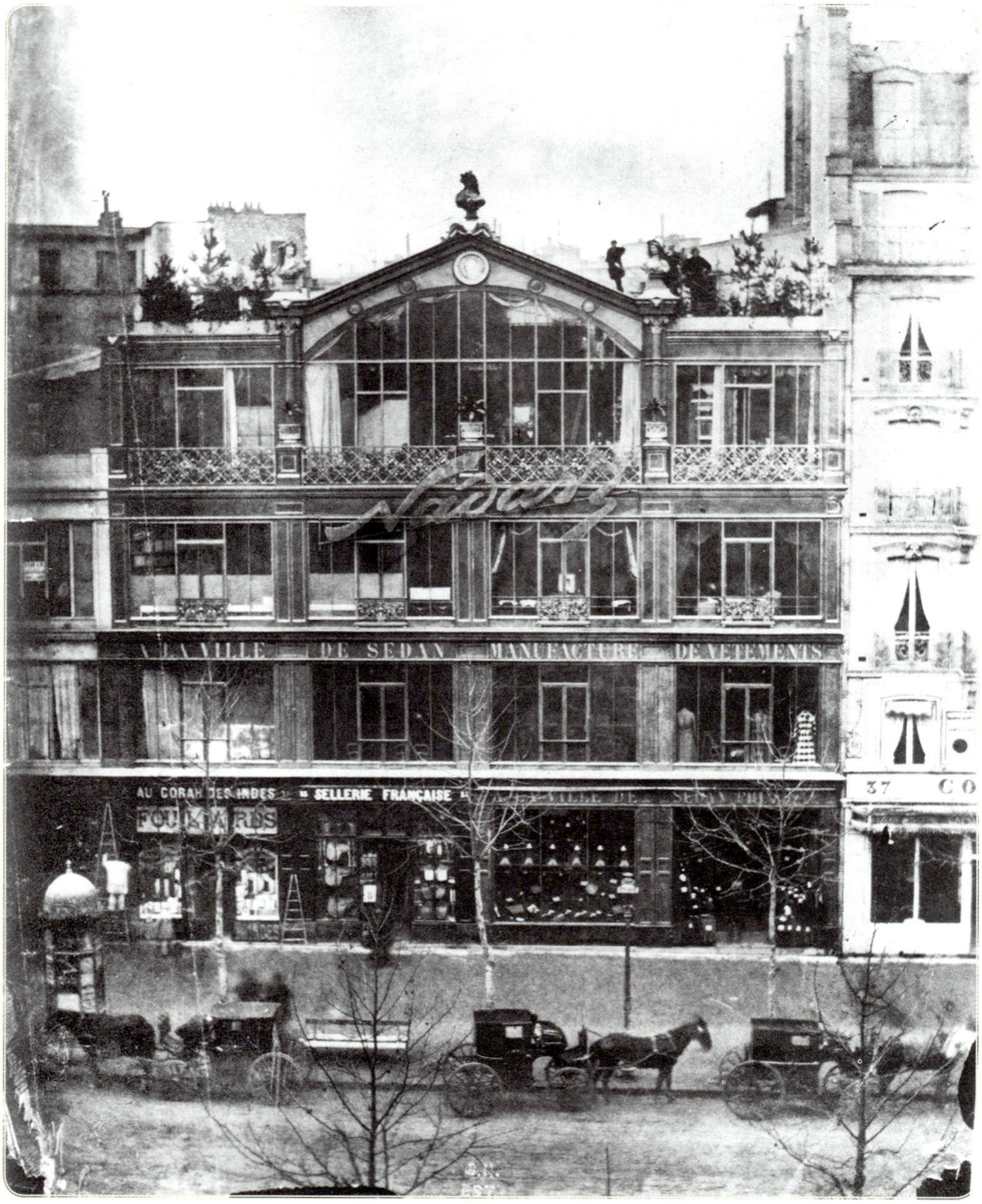

Facade of Nadar's studio at 35 Boulevard des Capucines, *c.* 1855

was its prime location on the corner of the highly central boulevard des Capucines. It seems that Nadar, who was giving up the studio, allowed them to use it free of charge. It was the first time the Impressionists held a group show. They were still being called the 'Batignolles painters', in the same way that people talked about Barbizon in reference to Théodore Rousseau and Jean-François Millet, and although their preference for Delacroix and Corot over the academic painters was known, people were just beginning to distinguish them from the large group of *refusés*. The name 'Impressionists' was also not yet in circulation; if the story told of its origin is true, it was coined in connection with this very exhibition. It seems that Renoir's brother Edmond, who was preparing the catalogue, exasperated by the monotony of the titles of Monet's paintings, complained about it to the artist, who, feeling pressed, renamed one of his works *Impression, Sunrise* right there on the spot. The term was then picked up by the press in a mocking way and, finally, adopted by the painters themselves.

The exhibition opened on 15 April 1874. The artists presented themselves as the *Société anonyme des artistes peintres, sculpteurs, graveurs, etc.* Monet, Renoir, Sisley, Pissarro, Degas and Morisot were among the founding members and each of them brought in other friends. Degas wanted there to be as many as possible and for even painters with a more moderate style to be included, so that the public would not equate them with the Salon rejects. In the end, his vision prevailed. In the interest of fairness, the placement of the works was decided by lots.

Claude Monet, *Impression. Sunrise*, 1872. Paris, Musée Marmottan-Monet

p. 34
Camille Pissarro, *White Frost*, 1873. Paris, Musée d'Orsay

Cover of the catalogue for the first Impressionist exhibition, 1874. Atelier Nadar, Paris, 35 Boulevard des Capucines

Pierre-Auguste Renoir, *The Dancer*, 1874. Washington, D.C., National Gallery of Art

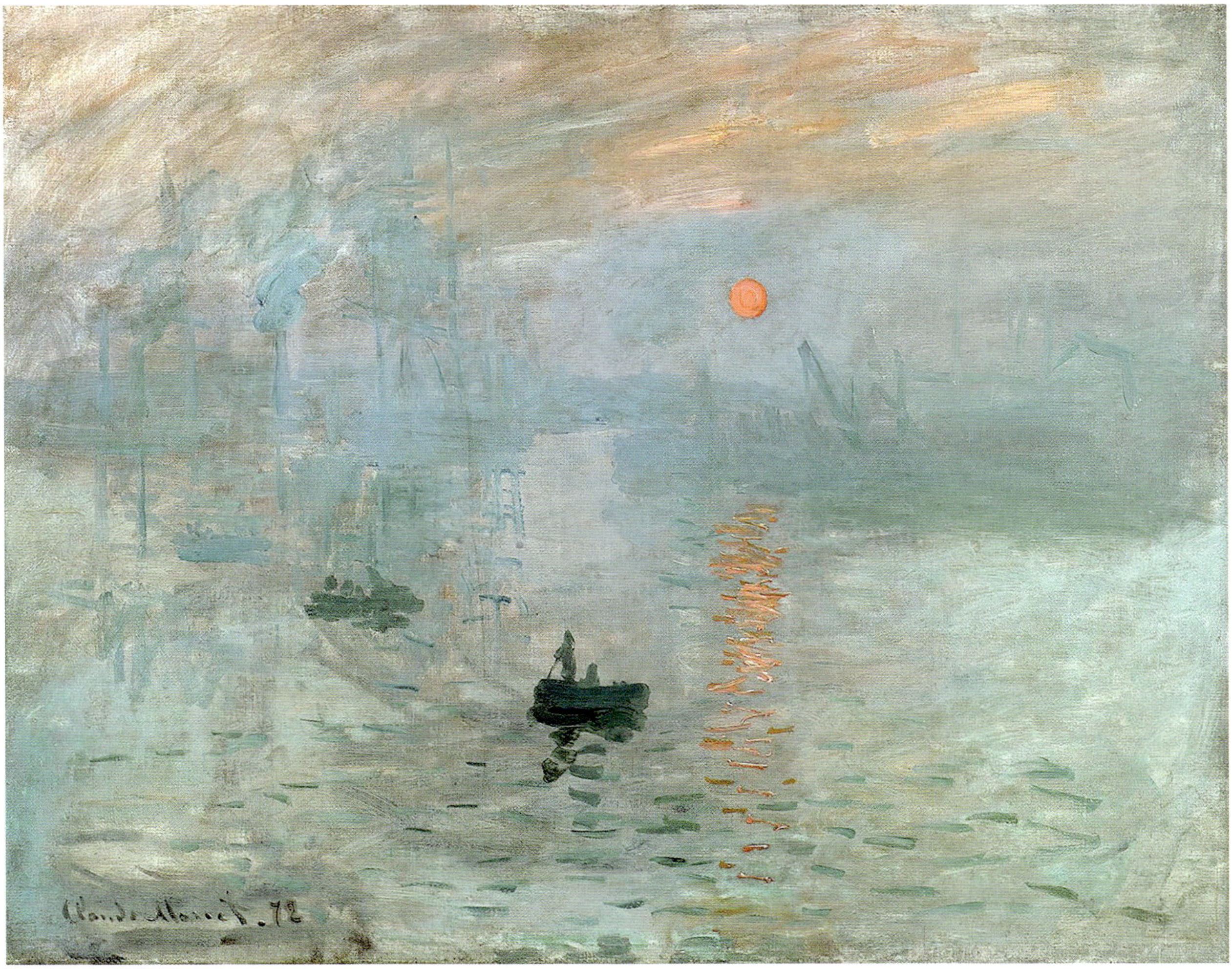

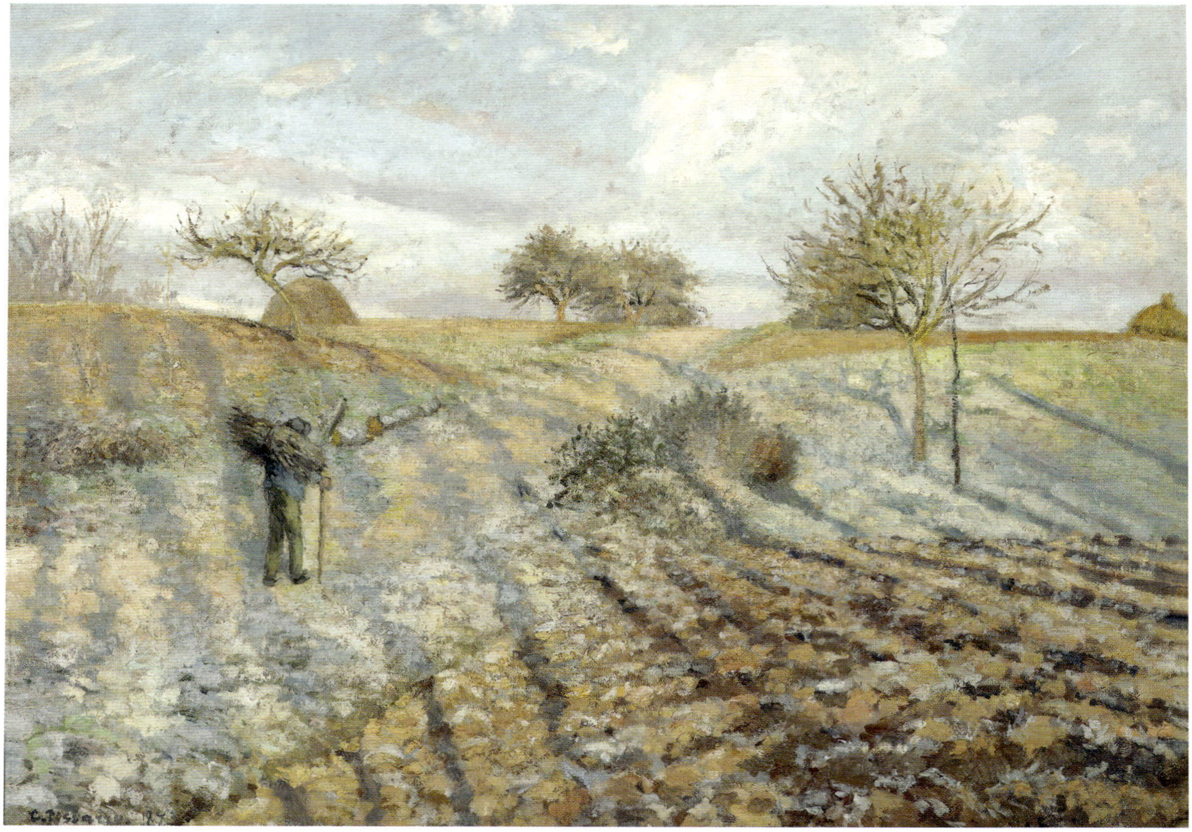

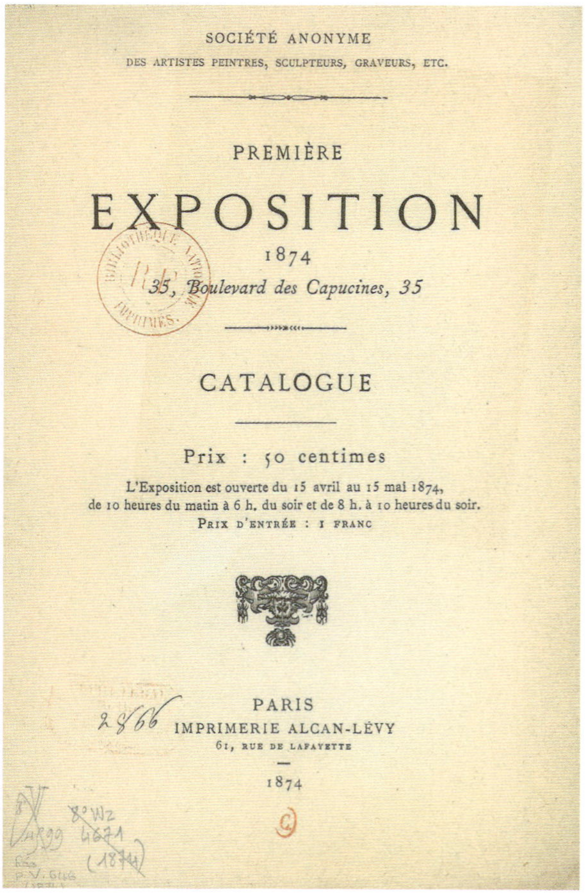

SOCIÉTÉ ANONYME

DES ARTISTES PEINTRES, SCULPTEURS, GRAVEURS, ETC.

PREMIÈRE

EXPOSITION

1874

35, Boulevard des Capucines, 35

CATALOGUE

Prix : 50 centimes

L'Exposition est ouverte du 15 avril au 15 mai 1874,
de 10 heures du matin à 6 h. du soir et de 8 h. à 10 heures du soir.
PRIX D'ENTRÉE : 1 FRANC

PARIS
IMPRIMERIE ALCAN-LÉVY
61, RUE DE LAFAYETTE

1874

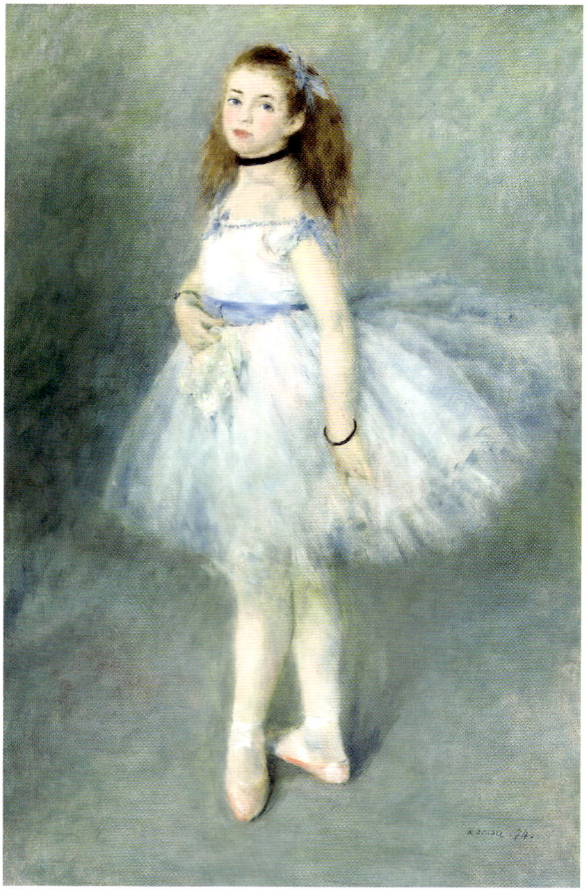

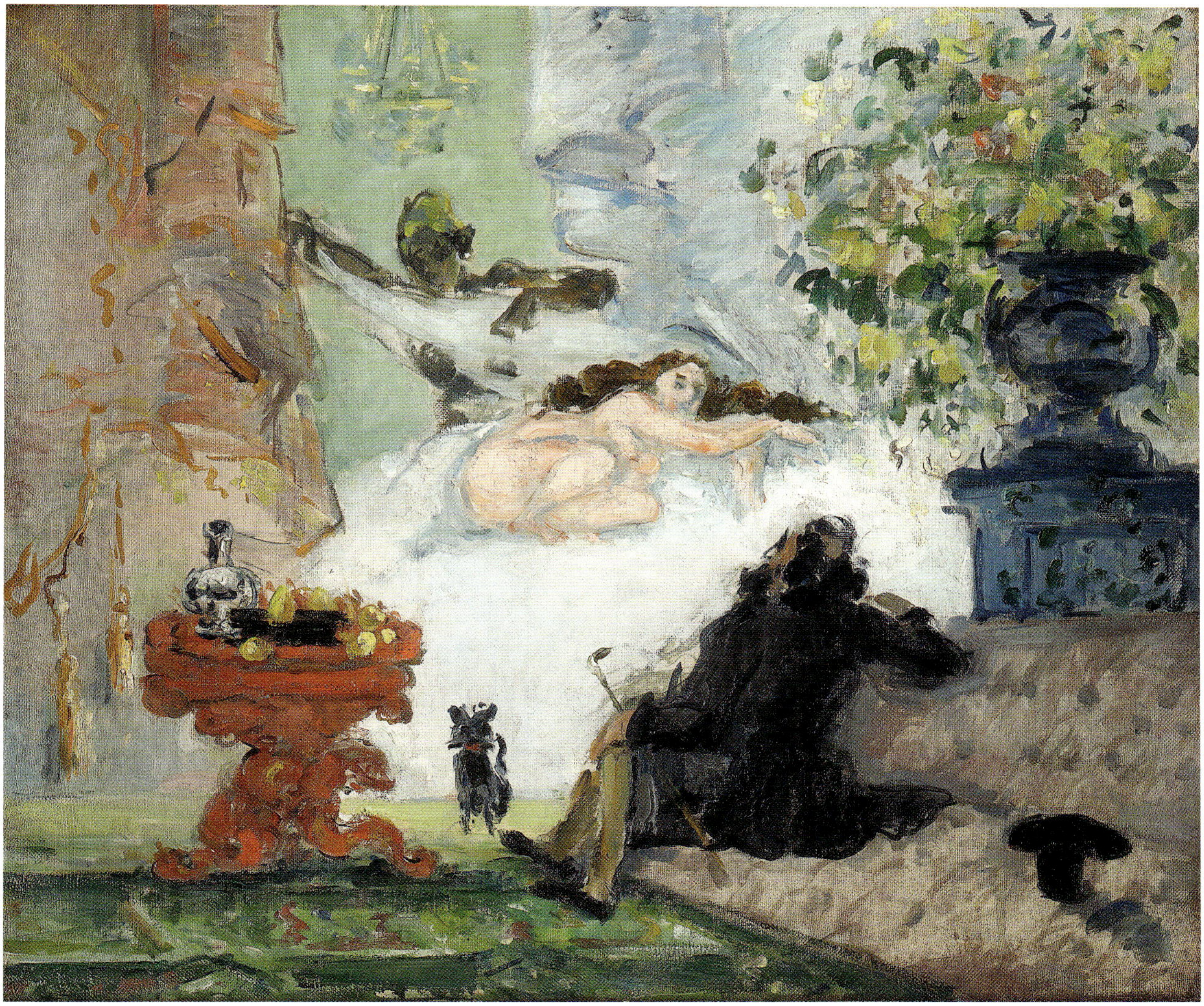

Paul Cézanne,
A Modern Olympia,
1873–1874. Paris,
Musée d'Orsay

There were 165 in all, sent by, among others, Degas, who participated with ten works; Cézanne, three (including *A Modern Olympia* and *House of the Hanged Man, Auvers-sur-Oise*); Guillaumin, also three; Monet, twelve (including the famous *Boulevard des Capucines*), Morisot, nine (including the wonderfully tender *The Cradle*), Pissarro, five (including *White Frost*), Renoir, seven (including two of his most famous: *La Loge [The Theatre Box]* and *The Dancer*) and Sisley, five. But they were not the only ones to present in rue Danou: there were also Boudin, De Nittis, Lepic, Bracquemond and others tied by bonds of partiality to the main members of the group. However, the general public seems to have once again agreed with the academic jury, which had exiled so many of the exhibiting artists among the amateurs, when not among the alienated. And so, the visitors poured in, albeit not in very large numbers, with the attitude of people who go to the circus to see the bearded woman, acrobat dwarves, loquacious parrots and similar bizarrerie, rather than the serious, respectful frame of mind of those who want to learn. One of the most cutting reviews was written by Louis Leroy in *Charivari*: it was nothing more or less than a pyrotechnic display, but it summed up the opinion of most of the viewers. And yet, for the first time, on the walls of the former studio of a famous photographer, people could see the work of the modern school, which had for many years met at Café Guerbois,

Paul Cézanne, *House of the Hanged Man, Auvers-sur-Oise*, 1873. Paris, Musée d'Orsay

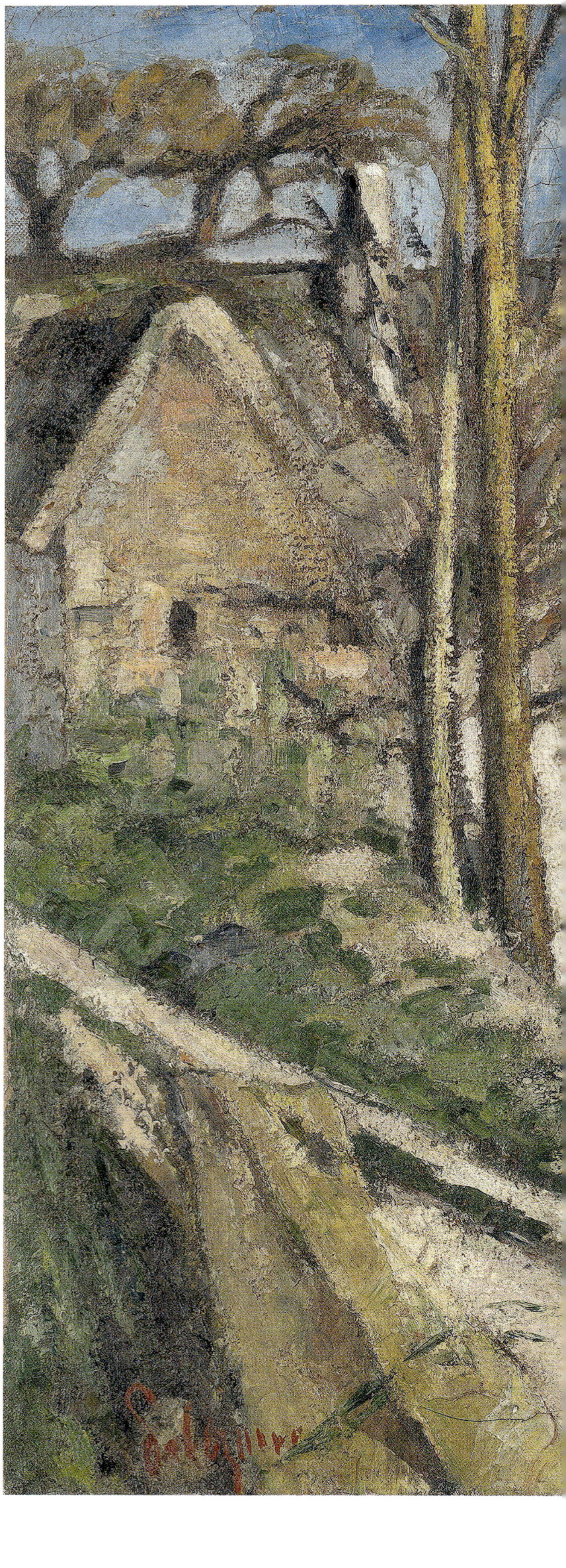

p. 38
Claude Monet, *Boulevard des Capucines*, 1873–1874. Kansas City, The Nelson-Atkins Museum of Art

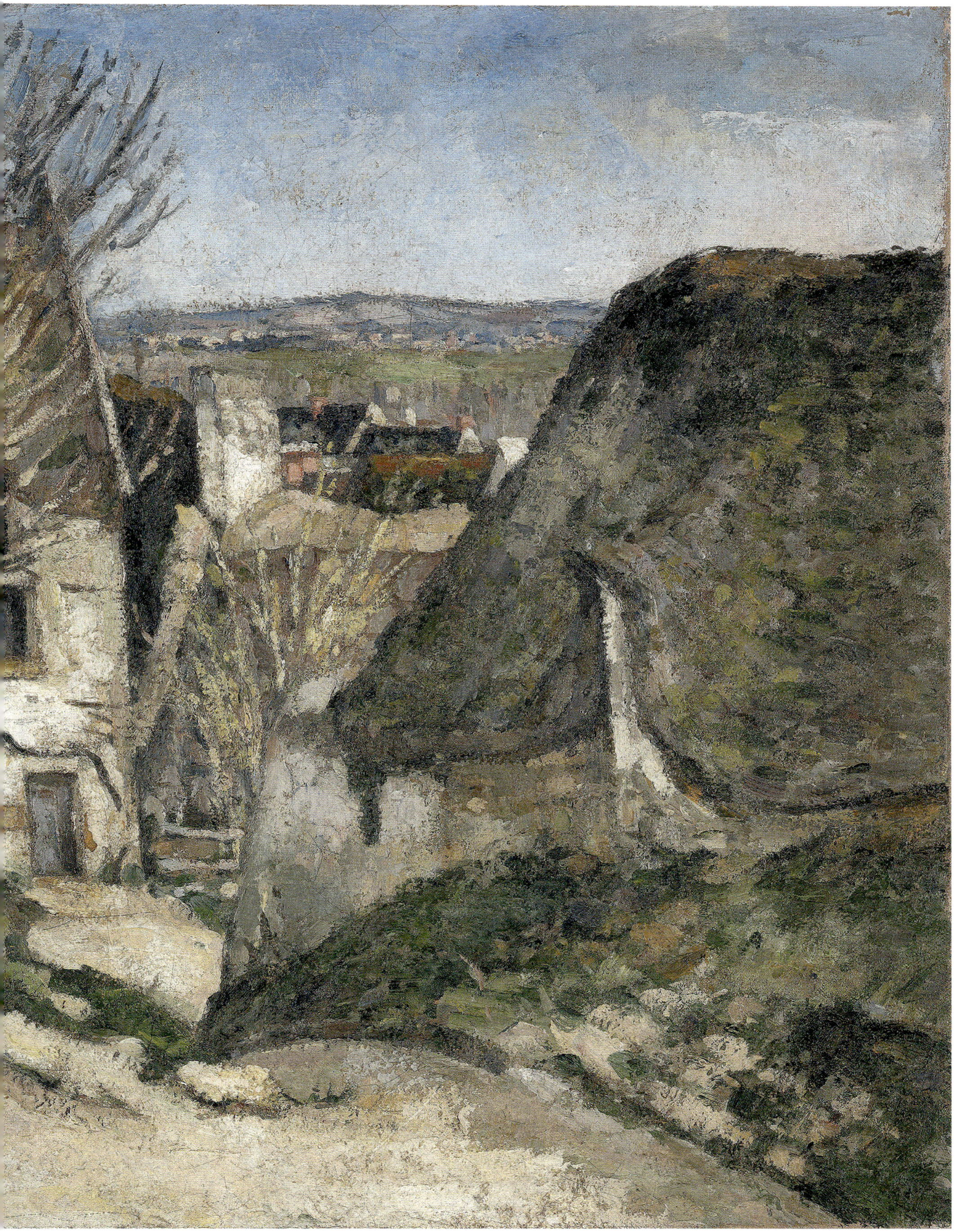

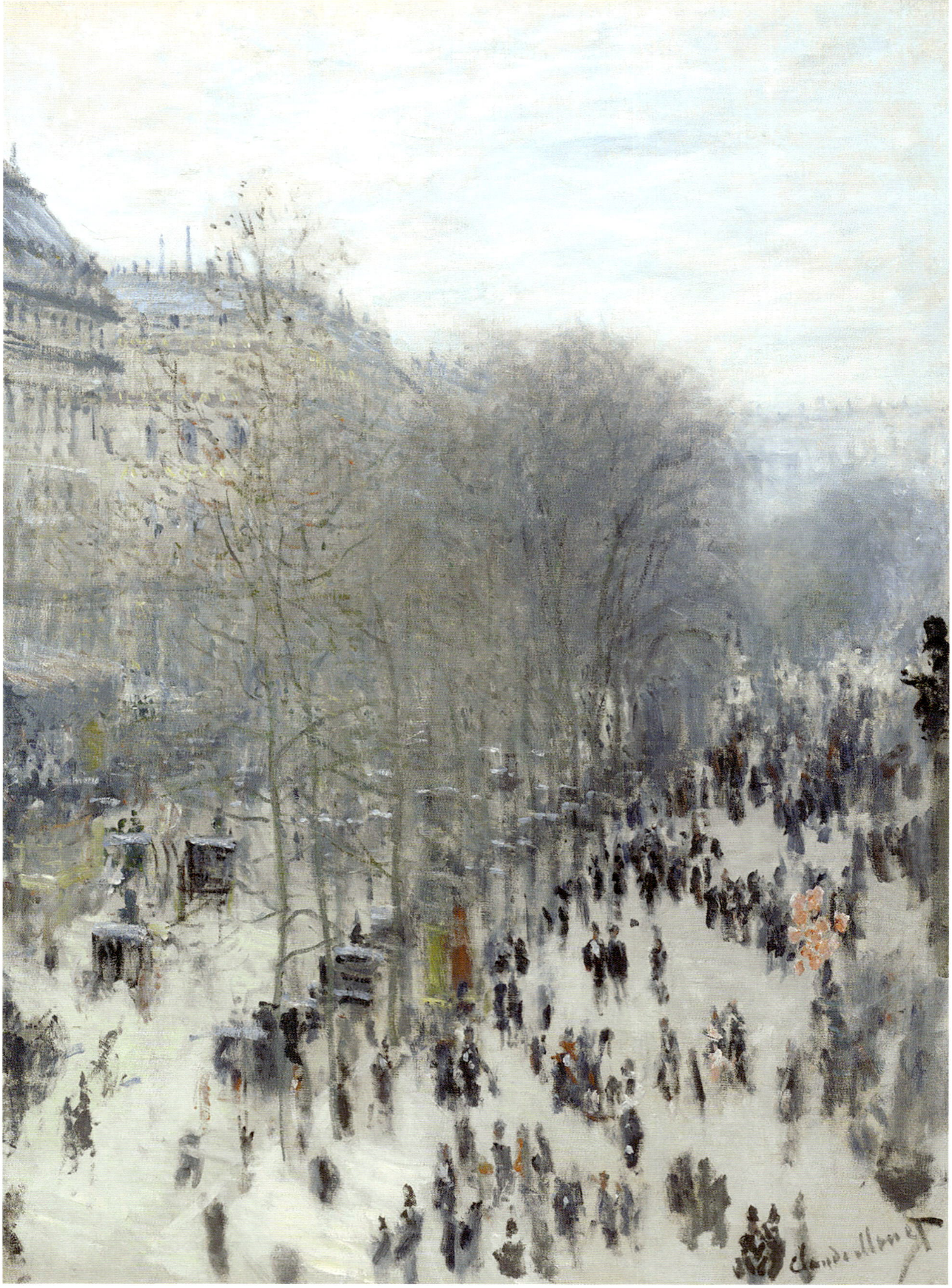

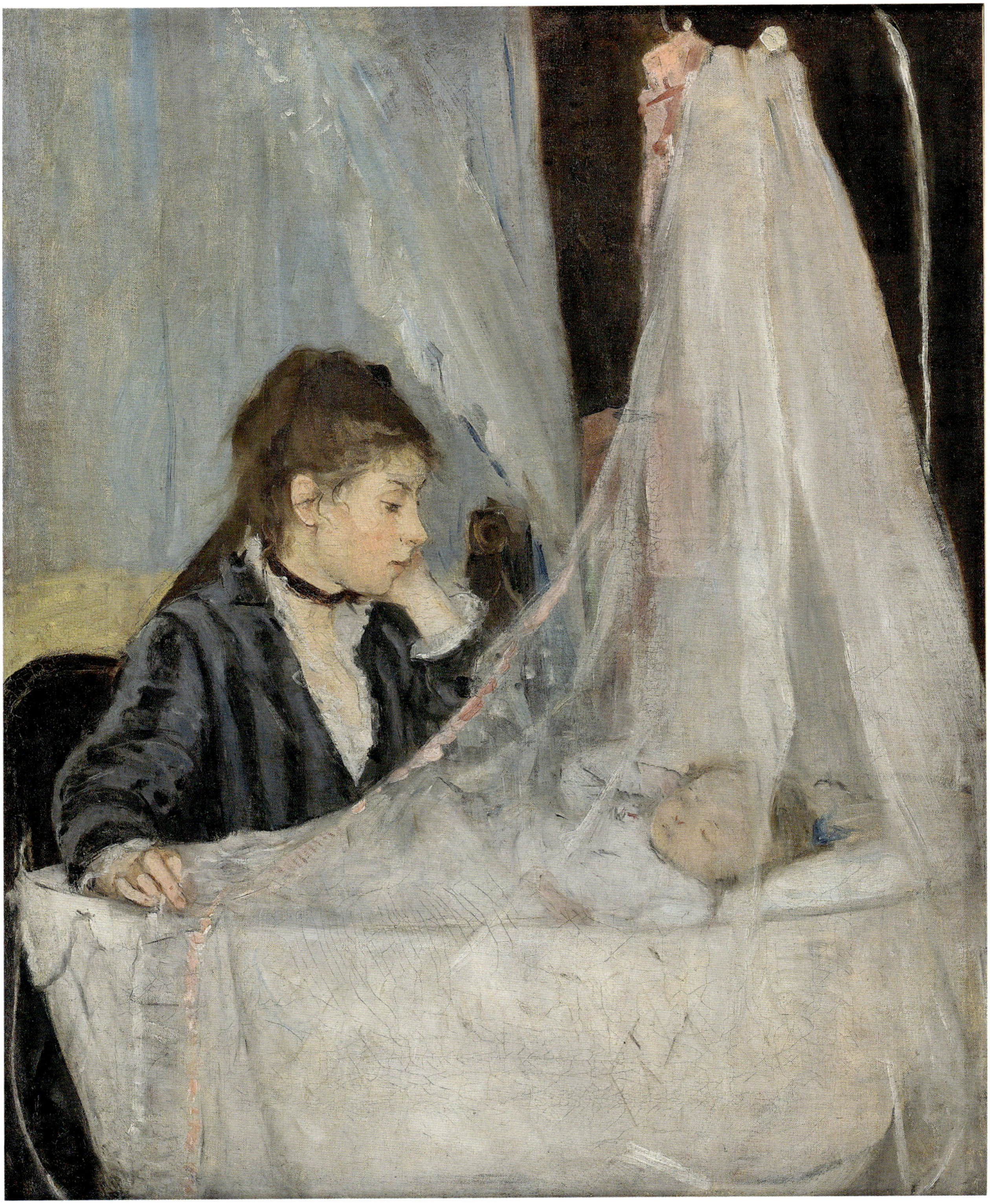

gathered around Manet (who, however, did not participate), to discuss shared problems. No longer mixed up with the others, as had been the case in 1863 at the famous Salon des Refusés, but with the individuality and determination of a new trend.

Berthe Morisot, *The Cradle*, 1872. Paris, Musée d'Orsay

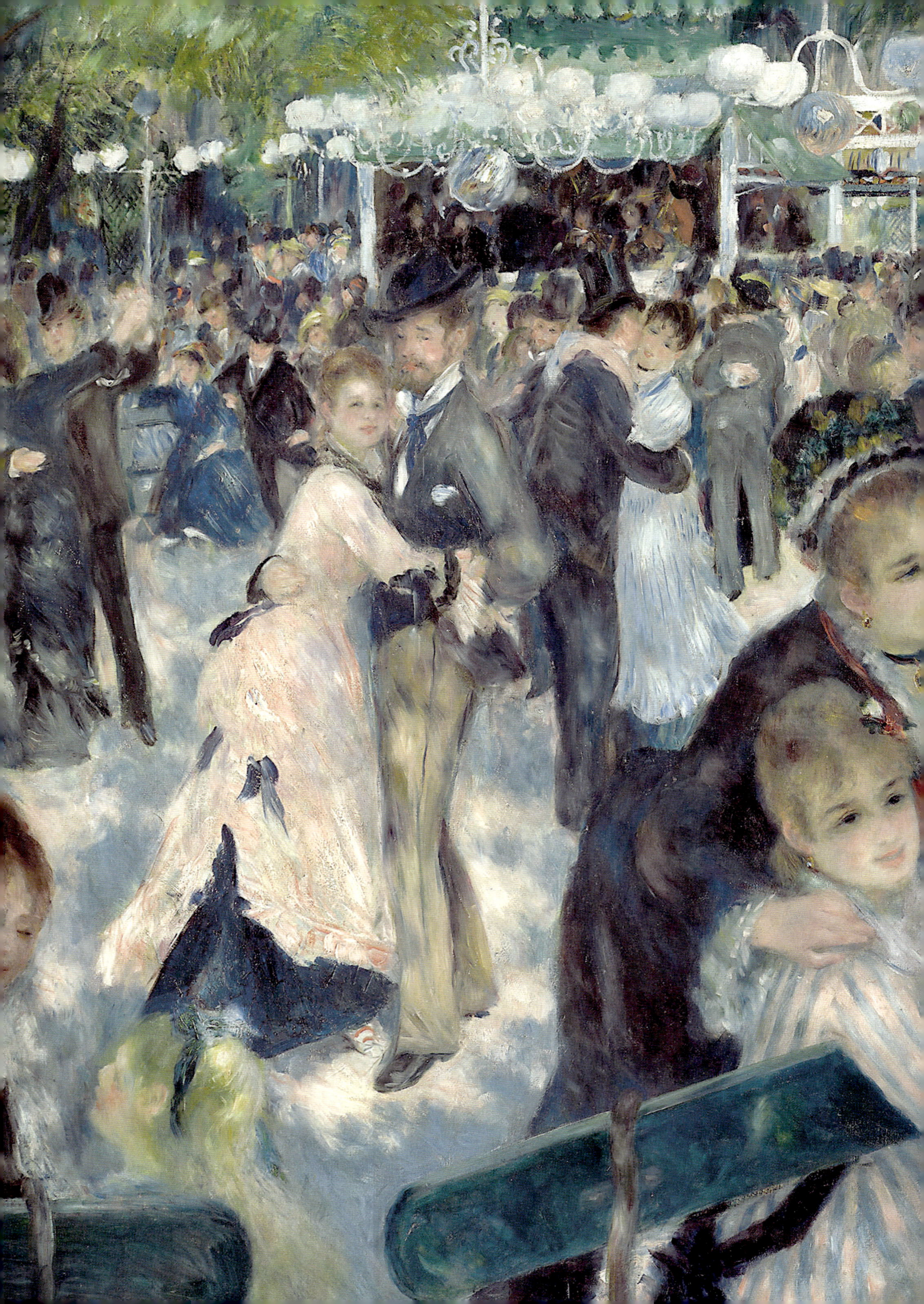

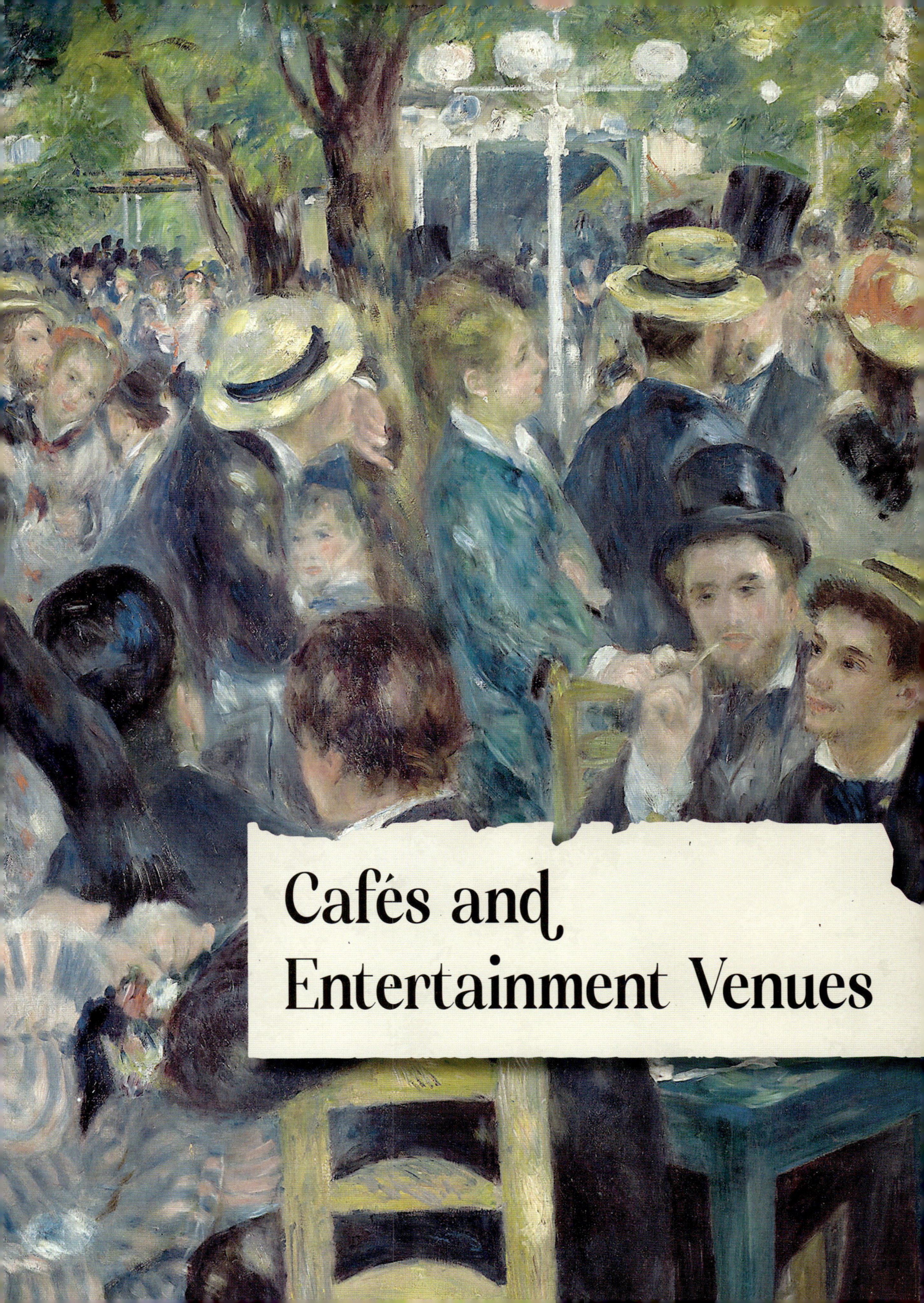

Cafés and Entertainment Venues

6. Café Guerbois

Il rue des Batignolles
today 9 Avenue de Clichy

pp. 40–41
Pierre-Auguste Renoir, *Bal du moulin de la Galette*, 1876. Paris, Musée d'Orsay

Café Guerbois was in Batignolles, next to Hennequin's, where Manet used to buy his paints. It wasn't an elegant place, although its first room, with white and gold walls reflected in a row of mirrors in imitation of what you could see in the cafés on the grand boulevards, aspired to be so. What it achieved instead was an antiquated look. In his story *La double vie de Louis Seguin*, Edmond Duranty notes the provincial air that the heavy Empire furniture (the style that formed the backdrop for Madame Bovary's affairs) could do nothing to attenuate, the cramped spaces and 'irregular windows, some large, some small as skylights'. A small drawing by Manet shows us the row of stocky columns under a too-low ceiling, which gave it the look of a Romanesque crypt. The furnishings were completed by 'five billiard tables, the heavy baptismal fonts of this temple', which showed off

> their green baize in fictive perspective, bathed in a dim light. At the back, a large window takes up the entire wall and reveals a garden with a few young trees around a little building with a portico and columns painted a soft green; a fresh, vivid, intense space behind the oblique, mysterious half-light in the café. It is a singular Dutch scene, far removed from Paris.[12]

Manet discovered Café Guerbois in 1863, but only began to go there regularly sometime later. At the time, the cafés were the academies of the independents (like the Salon des Refusés had been their Salon for a while), for which George Moore's

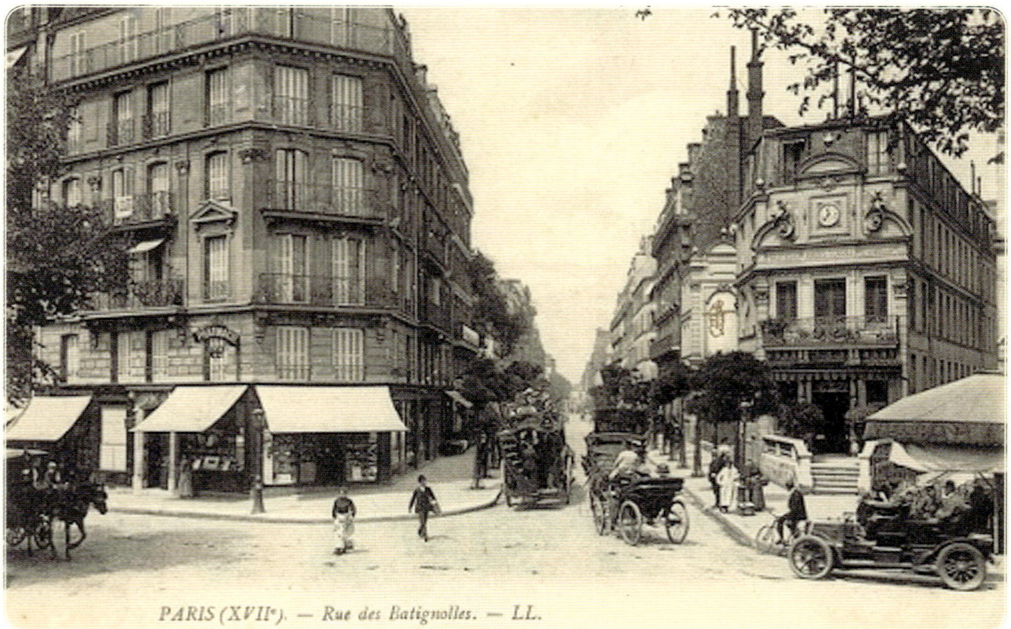

Café Guerbois, 11 grande rue des Batignolles (since 1868, avenue de Clichy 9)

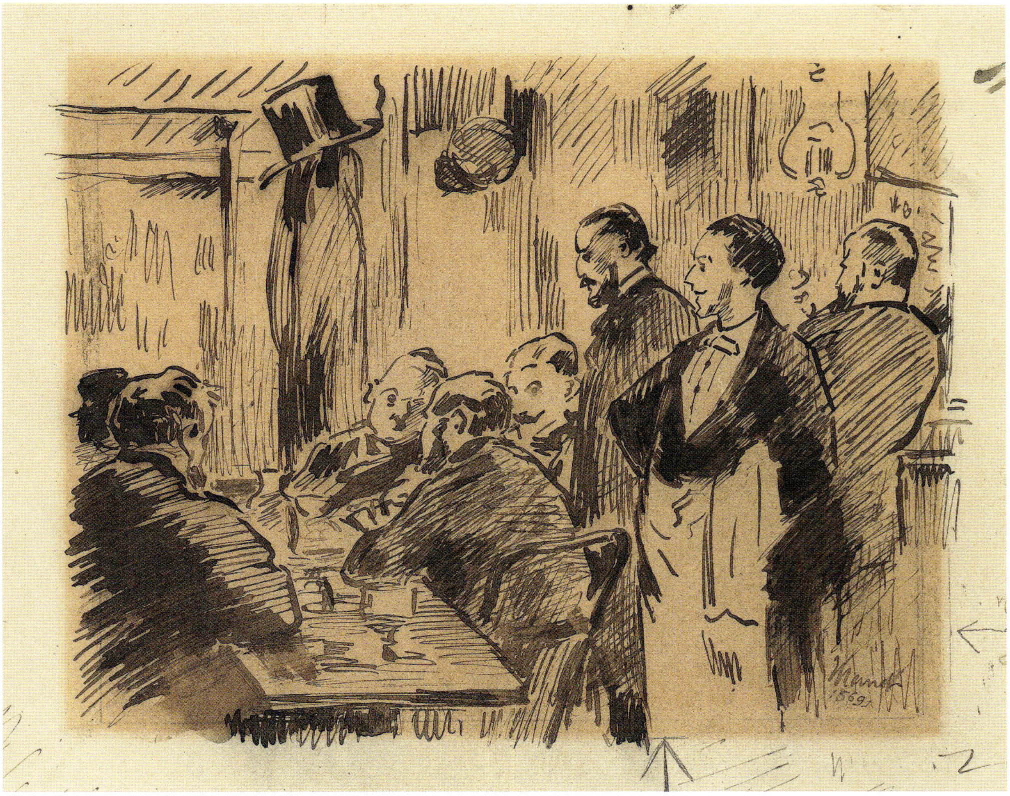

Édouard Manet,
At Café Guerbois, 1869.
Cambridge, Mass.,
Harvard Art Museums/
Fogg Art Museum

declaration that he went to neither Oxford nor Cambridge but to Café Guerbois was more than a simple quip. Between 1868 and 1869, Manet gathered a large number of friends and admirers in the café, who, if not identifying with his technique, at least identified with his independence. The name Batignolles School, foisted onto the non-conformist artists, derived from these meetings. As Monet recalled:

> Nothing could be more interesting than these causeries with their perpetual clash of opinions. They kept our wits sharpened, they encouraged us with stores of enthusiasm that for weeks and weeks kept us up, until the final shaping of the idea was accomplished. From them we emerged with a firmer will, with our thoughts clearer and more distinct.[13]

Many of them almost died of starvation, but their poverty was neither solitary nor desperate. And while Monet ate nothing but lentils, without, however, ever giving up his silk shirt, Degas, Manet and the musician Cabaner erected a firmament of wit above their day-to-day indigence.

We have few visual documents of these meetings. The engraver Émile Bellot was portrayed by Manet in *Le Bon Bock*; the others were, for the most part, depicted with the pen rather than the brush. Writing of Manet, Armand Silvestre recalled that he was

> easily ironic in his speech and often cruel. His words were cutting, capable of wounding and annihilating in a single blow. And yet, he was so witty and there was often so much truth in his ideas! [...] He was the most curious man in the world, with his elbows on the table while he launched his sneering declarations in a voice tinged with the Montmartre accent, similar to the Belleville one. Curious and unforgettable, with his impeccable gloves and a hat that flattened his thin curly hair against his neck.[14]

Édouard Manet, *Le Bon Bock (Portrait of Émile Bellot)*, 1873. Philadelphia, Philadelphia Museum of Art

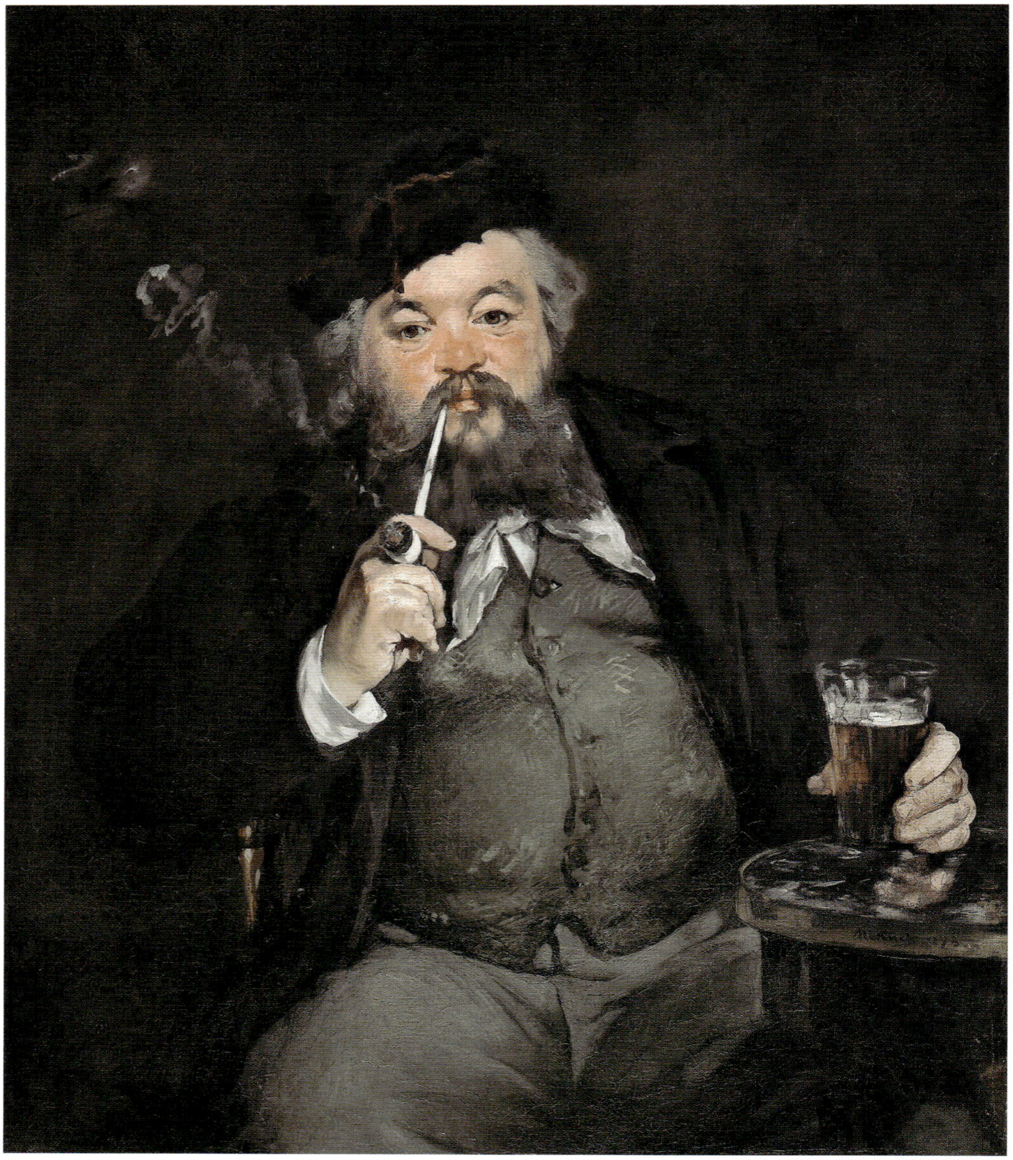

Manet, like Degas, had a bit of the eighteenth-century spirit. The former was as caustic as Voltaire, while the latter's wit had a tartness that could have recalled Chardin. Cézanne, who was described by Zola as 'tall, thin, with knotty joints, bearded with a big head, a thin nose hidden in the bristly wilds of his moustaches, narrow, light eyes ... and deep in his eyes, a great tenderness', usually sat to the side.[15] He only occasionally took part in the conversation, and when he did he would flare up, acting like a good savage whose rusticity was a little bit affected. However, these gatherings, in which Sisley, Pissarro, Zola, Fantin, Renoir and Nadar also participated, were no less peppered with displays of intelligence than an eighteenth-century salon, although, when it was time to say goodbye, the attendees were a good deal less presentable than the guests of Madame du Deffand or Madame de Lespinasse.

Today, Café Guerbois is no more: first transformed into a pub, it ended up being demolished.

7. Café de la Nouvelle Athènes

9 place Pigalle

When Café Guerbois's clientele began to change after the Franco-Prussian War and the Commune, shifting to a new, more anodyne and vulgar set, the Impressionists moved to Café de la Nouvelle Athènes, which was located in place Pigalle, not far from the Cirque Fernando. In truth, not many from the old guard spent their evenings there regularly, since only Manet, Degas and Renoir still lived in Paris, while Sisley, Pissarro, Monet and Cézanne only visited occasionally. However, there were a few new artists to make up for their absence, for the most part from the circle of Degas, like Jean-Louis Forain, Jean-François Raffaëlli and Federico Zandomeneghi, as well as many men of letters and bohemians. The most colourful among the latter was unquestionably Marcellin Desboutin, the man with a pipe and hat sitting at a café table next to Ellen André in Degas's famous painting *The Absinthe Drinker*. He was an unusual character, Desboutin. Heir to a large fortune, he spent it all on a princely lifestyle in Florence, and after he had singed his wings, flying too close to the flame of aristocratic luxury, this rare moth left, bringing along his poetic heap of ashes and no regrets, to be a painter and engraver in Paris, taking a small studio in rue des Dames.

Manet and Degas showed up at the café in well-cut suits, in almost impertinent contrast to its chaotic atmosphere. Villiers de l'Isle-Adam sported the moustaches

Café de la Nouvelle Athènes, 9 place Pigalle, *c.* 1890

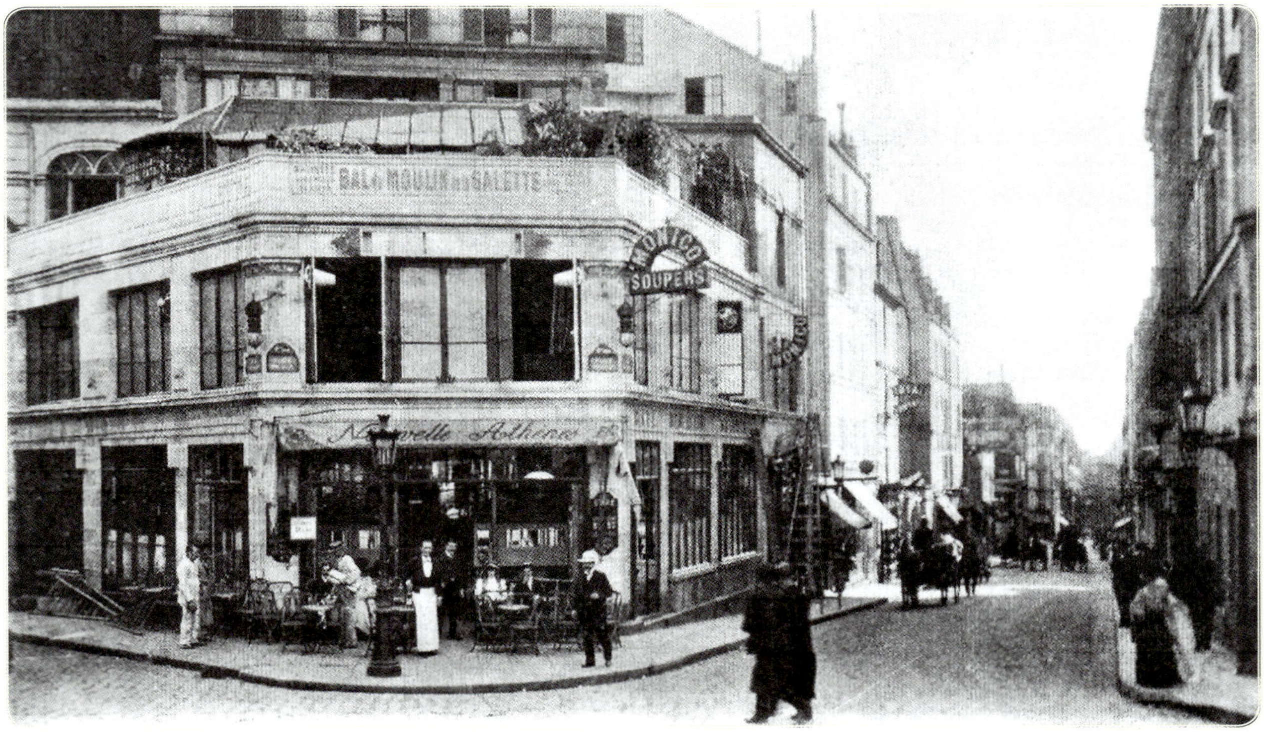

and hair of a musketeer from the time of Louis XIV, an age he longed to live in. Among the poets, you could also find Catulle Mendès, loquacious, attractive, with a long mane of hair that came down over his shoulders and gave him the vague air of a disheartened ancient divinity, an Apollo come down into the smoke of the kitchens. Many of the café's customers, for that matter, corresponded to Baudelaire's caricature of the artist Pinelli, with 'his big gnarled stick, his hair falling in long tresses over his cheeks, the tavern, evil company, the affectation of destroying, with extravagant abandon, works he was not offered enough for'.[16] All of this, the poet concluded, was part of their prestige, but also, one could add, of their perpetual youth: and *Confessions of a Young Man* is in fact the title of one of the two memoires in which the writer George Moore recalls the years of his friendship with Manet, long after having left Paris.

> With what strange, almost unnatural clearness do I see and hear—see the white face of that café, the white nose of that block of houses, stretching up to the Place, between two streets. I can see down the incline of those two streets, and I know what shops are there; I can hear the glass door of the café grate on the sand as I open it. I can recall the smell of every hour. In the morning that of eggs frizzling in butter, the pungent cigarette, coffee and bad cognac; at five o'clock the fragrant odour of absinthe; and soon after the steaming soup ascends from the kitchen; and as the evening advances, the mingled smells of cigarettes, coffee and weak beer. A partition, rising a few feet or more over the hats, separates the glass front from the main body of the café. The usual marble tables are there, and it is there we sat and aestheticised till two o'clock in the morning.[17]

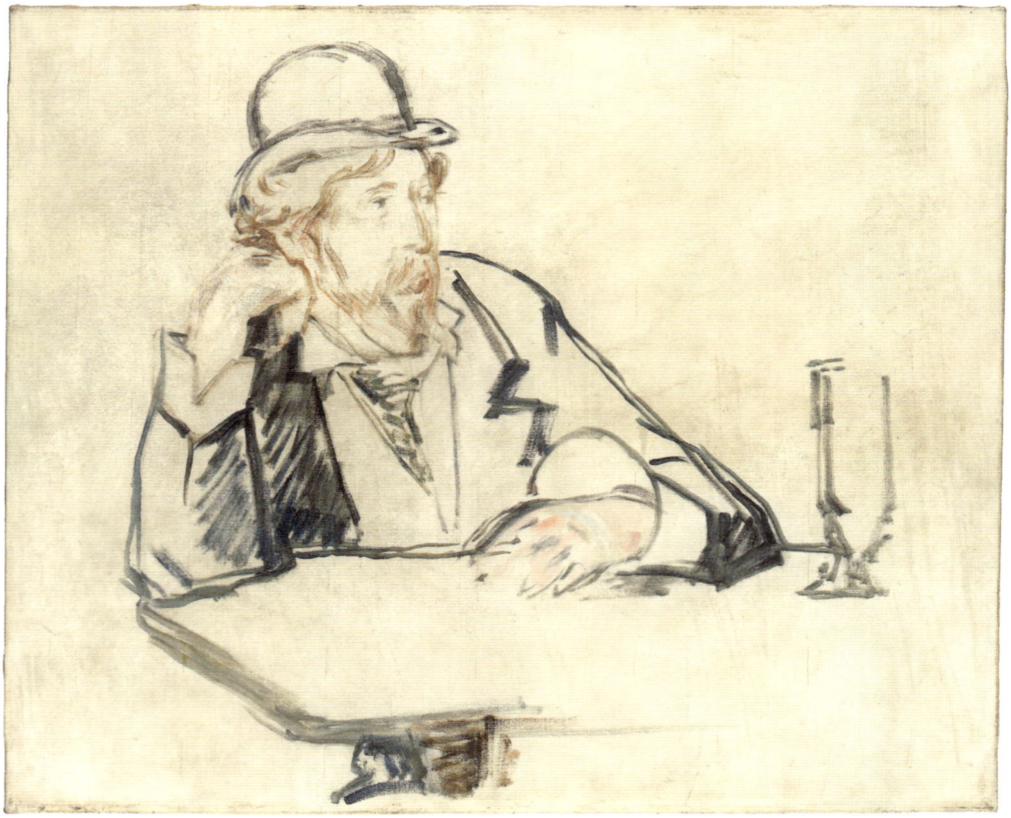

Édouard Manet, *George Moore at the Café de la Nouvelle Athènes*, 1879. New York, The Metropolitan Museum of Art

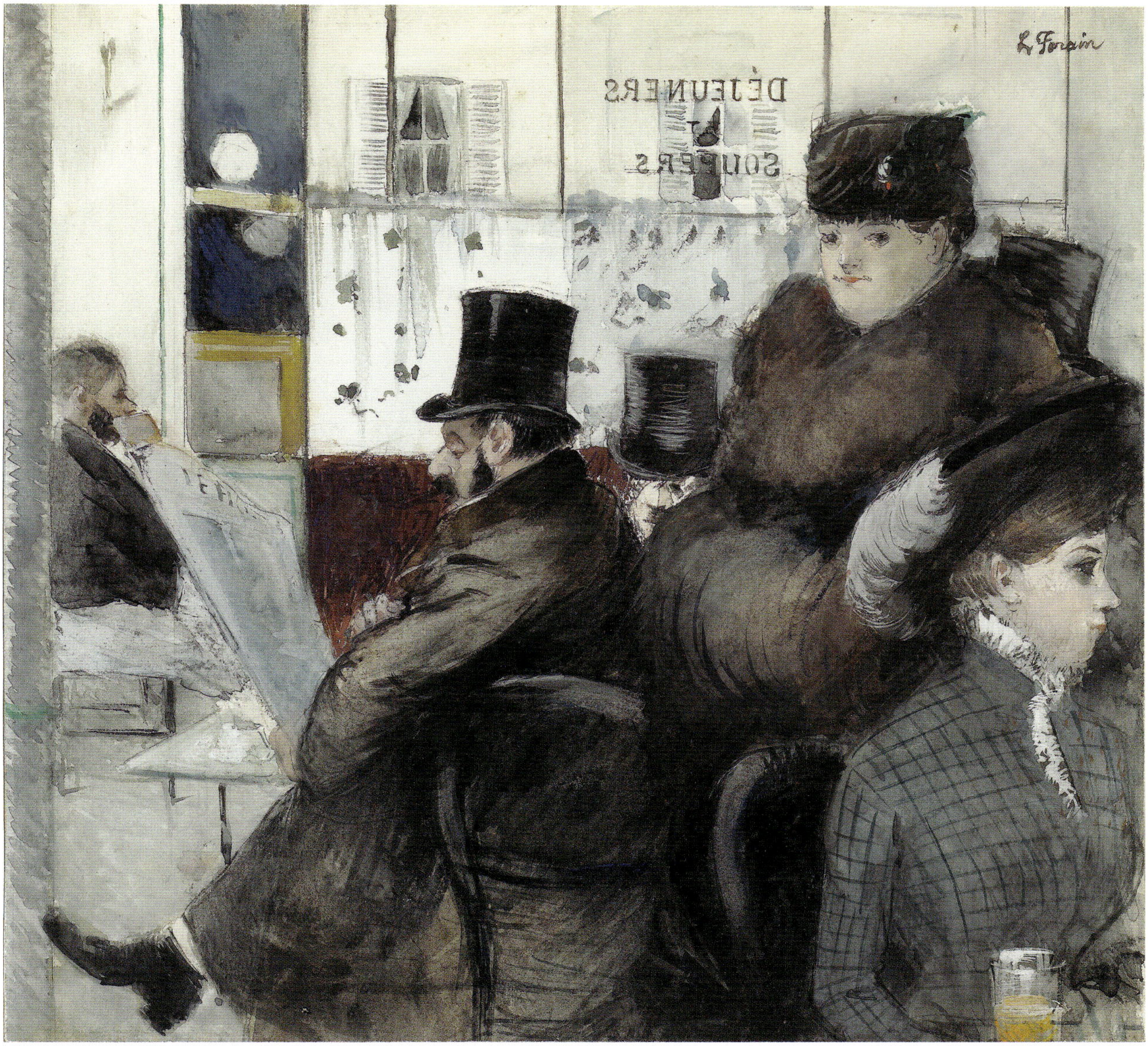

At the first light of dawn, the café closed its shutters. The last regulars, shown the door, continued to natter about aesthetics through the streets of Montmartre, but by now it was drunkenness rather than subtlety that supported their aphorisms, which, for that matter, were mostly simple jokes, when not total nonsense.

Like Café Guerbois, Café de la Nouvelle Athènes gradually lost its lustre when its old patrons began to abandon it after Manet's death. In the 1940s, it changed name and became a meeting place for prostitutes. After the war, it changed name again, and was destroyed by a fire at the end of the century.

Jean-Louis Forain, *At the Café de la Nouvelle Athènes*, 1879. Paris, Musée du Louvre

p. 48
Edgar Degas, *In a Café (The Absinthe Drinker)*, 1875–1876. Paris, Musée d'Orsay

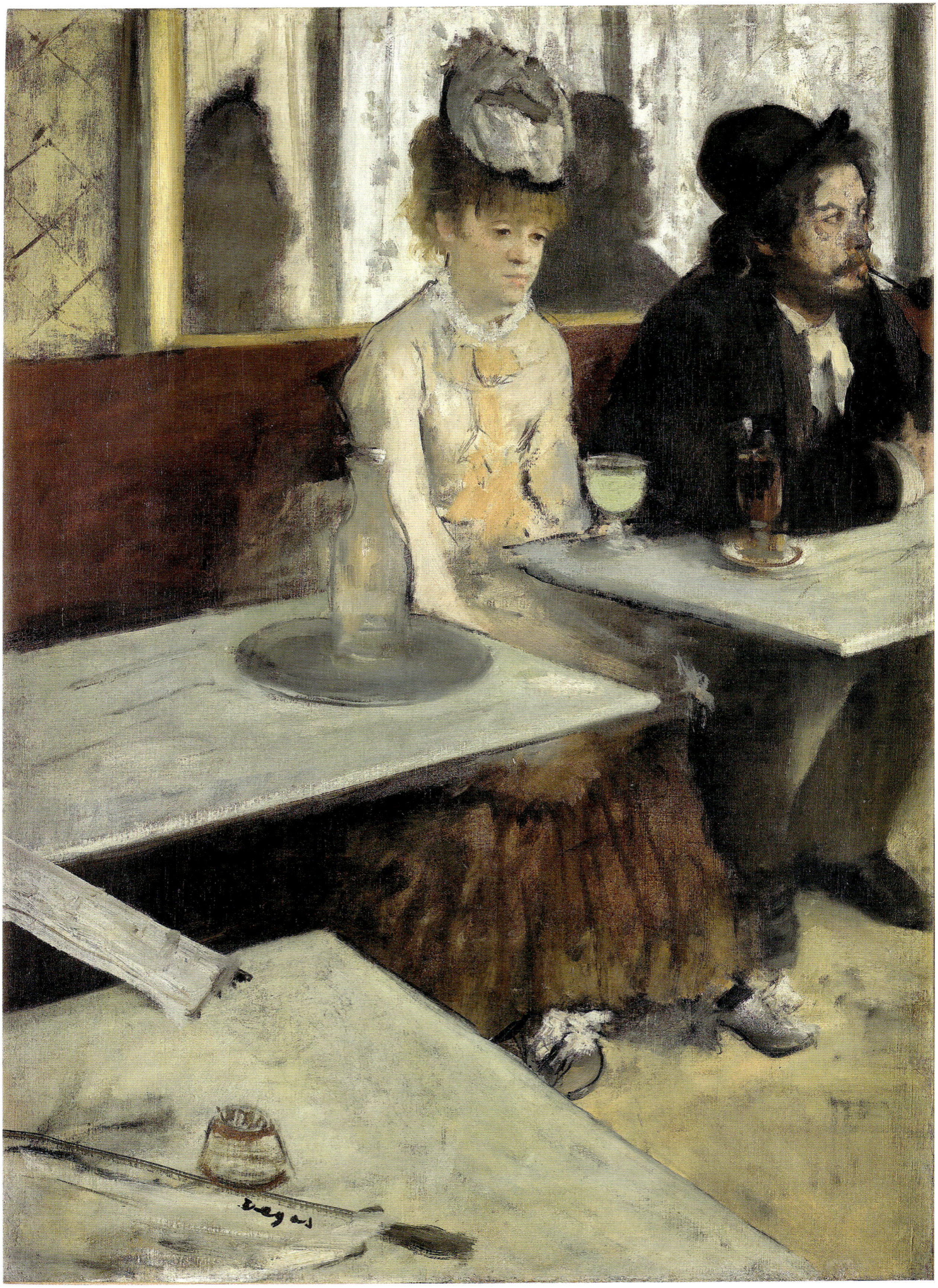

8. The Moulin de la Galette

rue Lepic

The landscape of Montmartre had long been dotted with mills. Their vanes could be seen from the city and covered the crest of the hill, amidst rows of grapevines and labourers' hovels. The mills remained active until the factories entirely took over the grain fields of Saint Denis. And then, the big vanes stopped turning and many of these giant structures, now impotent, were reduced to the decorative duty of sign bearer, like sad kings that were now just for show. One of them, however, the Blute, had made it in time to honour the ancient name of the quarter, Mons martyrum, which means 'hill of martyrs', serving as the implement for the torture of a miller by the name of Debray, who had heroically fought against the Cossacks in 1814. According to legend, the poor wretch was torn apart and his limbs were nailed to the arms of the mill. But the Moulin de la Gallete, which was built next to it, bore no trace of this sadistic wickedness. Built of a light material, it was nothing more than an open-air dance floor, where the good people of the place came to dance and be merry. Renoir was one of its most loyal *habitués*. He loved those still tortuous and precipitous roads, spared Haussmann's formal zeal, the cracked low walls and the little gardens near the ruins of ancient villas, the only remaining distinction of which being a faded cartouche. These were the vestiges of the old France of Louis XV, the solid graces of which he had painted as a young man on porcelain, when he worked as a decorator. It was the shadow of the gardens of Watteau. The artist rented

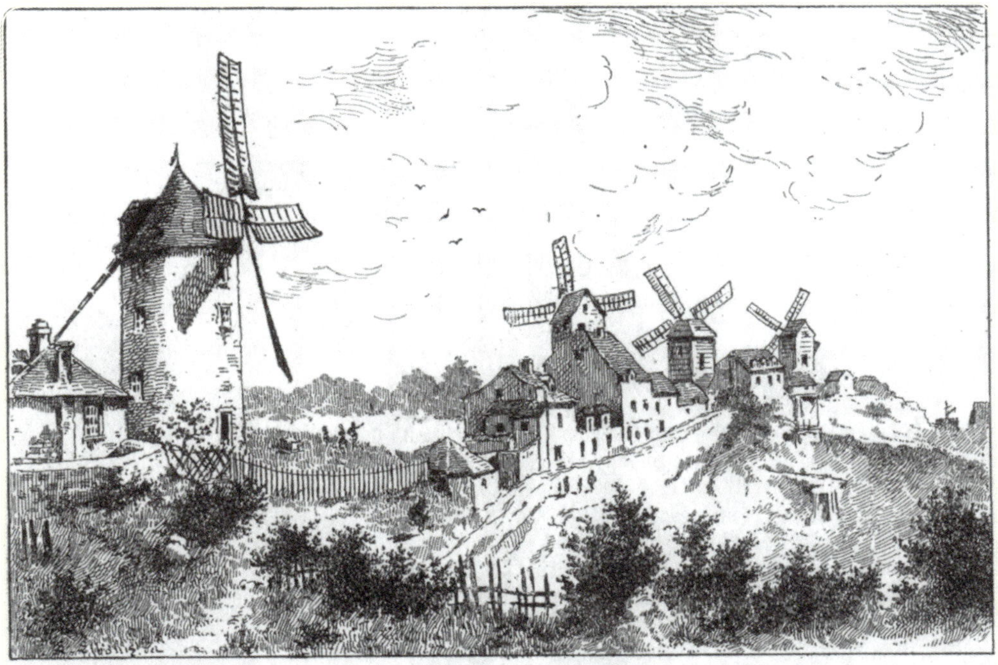

LES MOULINS DU VIEUX MONTMARTRE. (Commencement du XIXe siècle.)

The windmills of old Montmartre at the beginning of the 19th century

The Moulin de la Galette, view from the back and side

one of these hovels, from which he could go to the Moulin de la Galette and work, with the idea of portraying the men and women from life, dancing under the cantilever roof amidst globes of white light. They were simple people, even a bit vulgar, but vulgarity was one of the attractions of Montmartre. Renoir was intensely moved by this everyday joy, expressing it in the frothy, magical atmosphere of *Dancing at the Moulin de la Galette* (pp. 40–41): possibly the most exquisite portrayal of the douceur de vivre in French painting since the time of Jean-Honoré Fragonard.

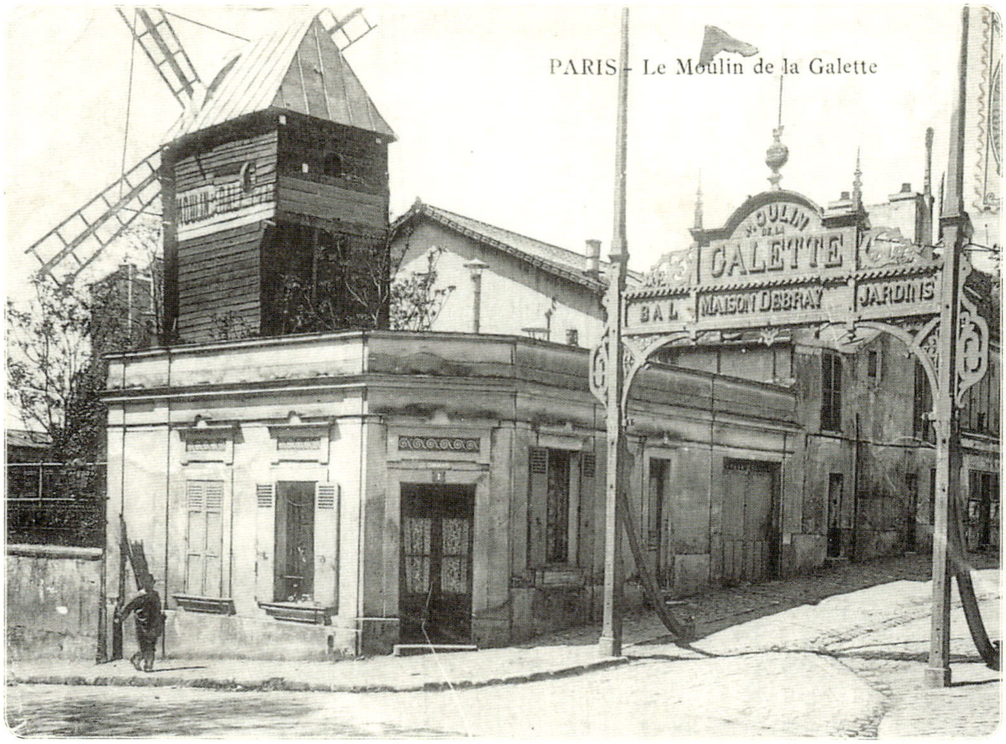

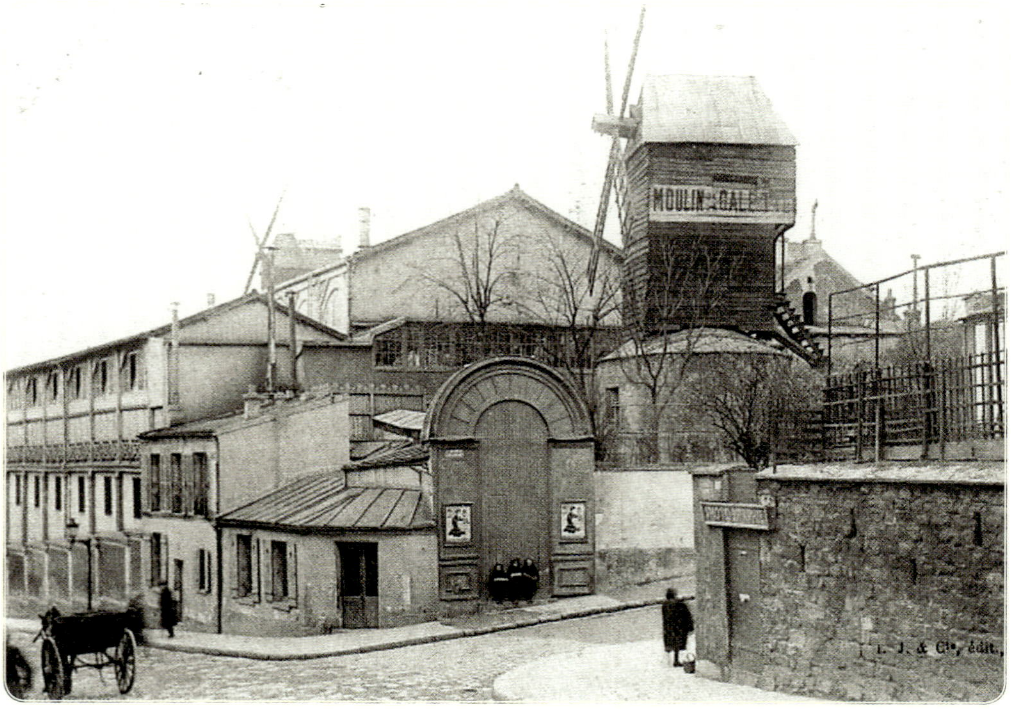

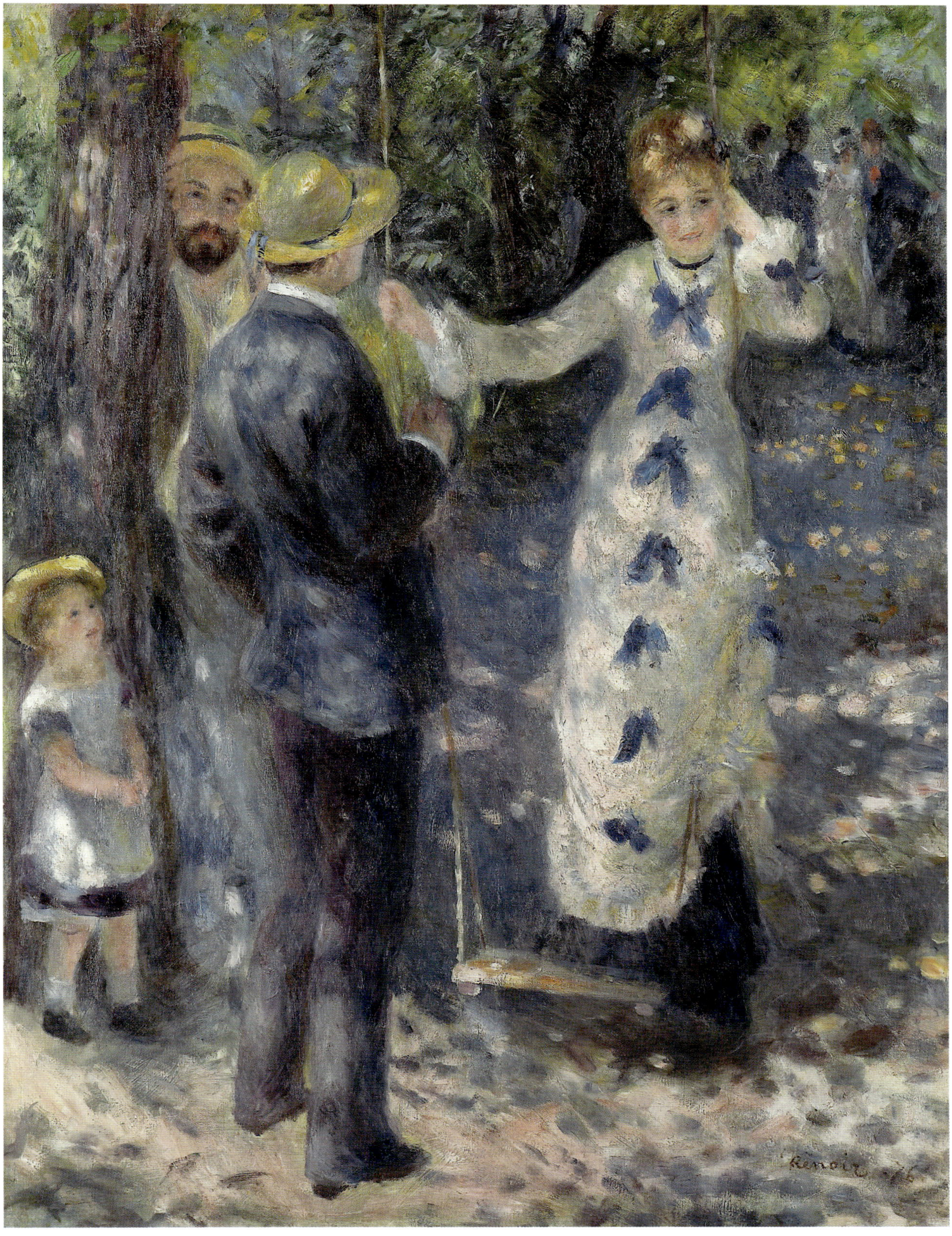

Pierre-Auguste Renoir, *The Swing*, 1876. Paris, Musée d'Orsay

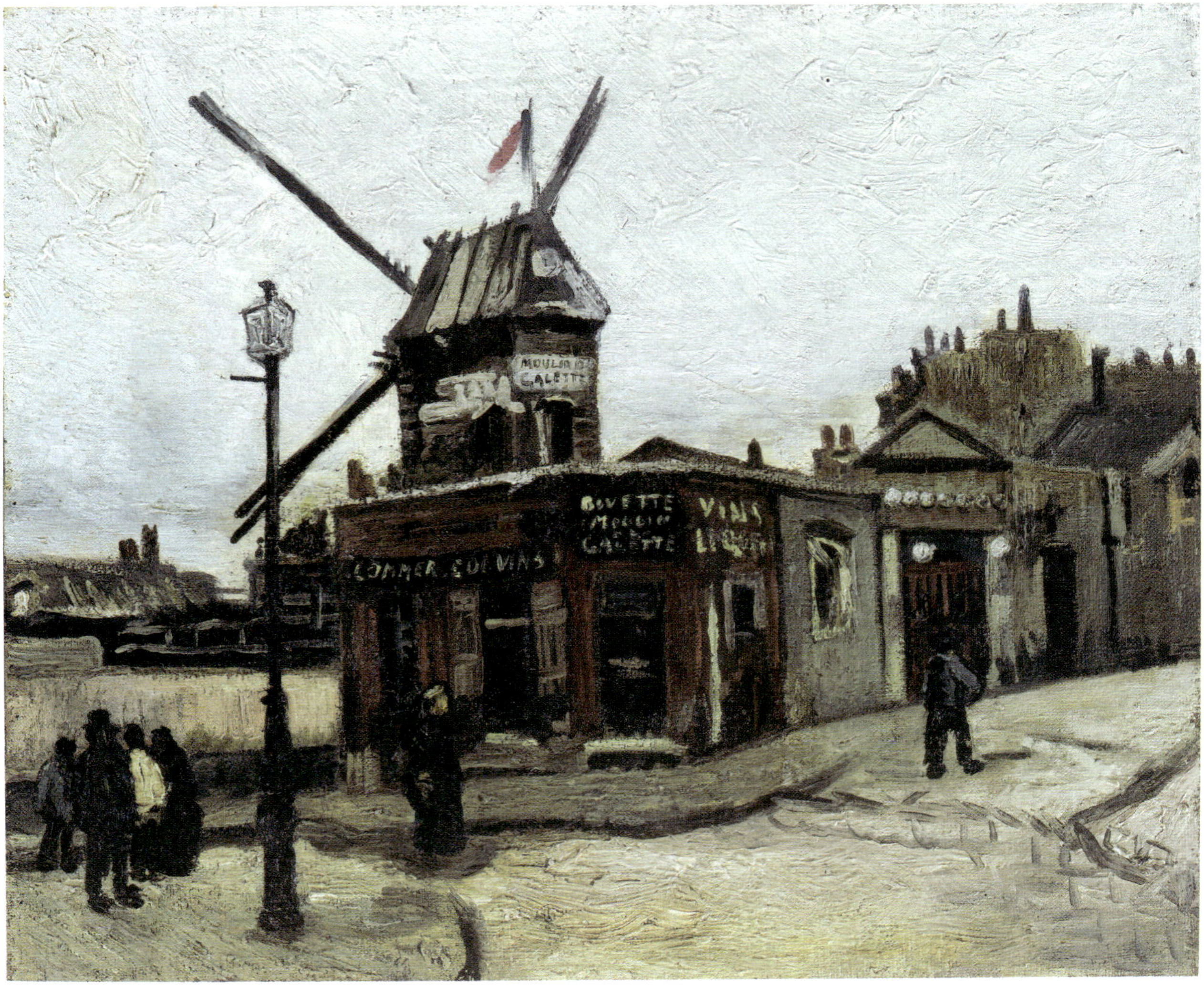

Vincent van Gogh,
The Moulin de la Galette,
1876. Berlin,
Neue Nationalgalerie

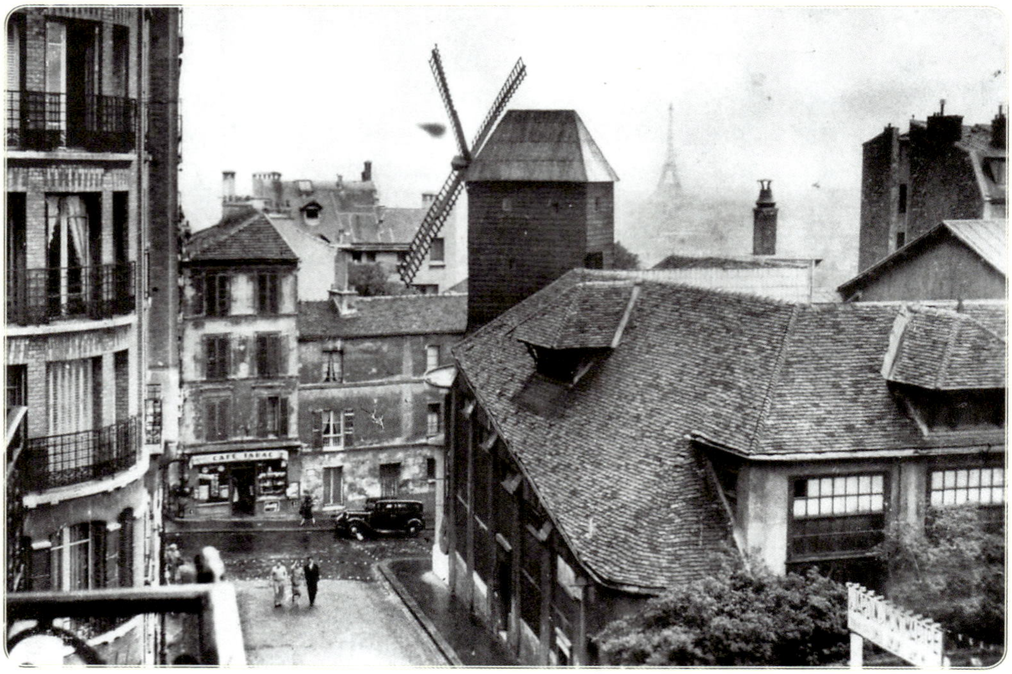

The Moulin de la Galette
seen from rue Girardon

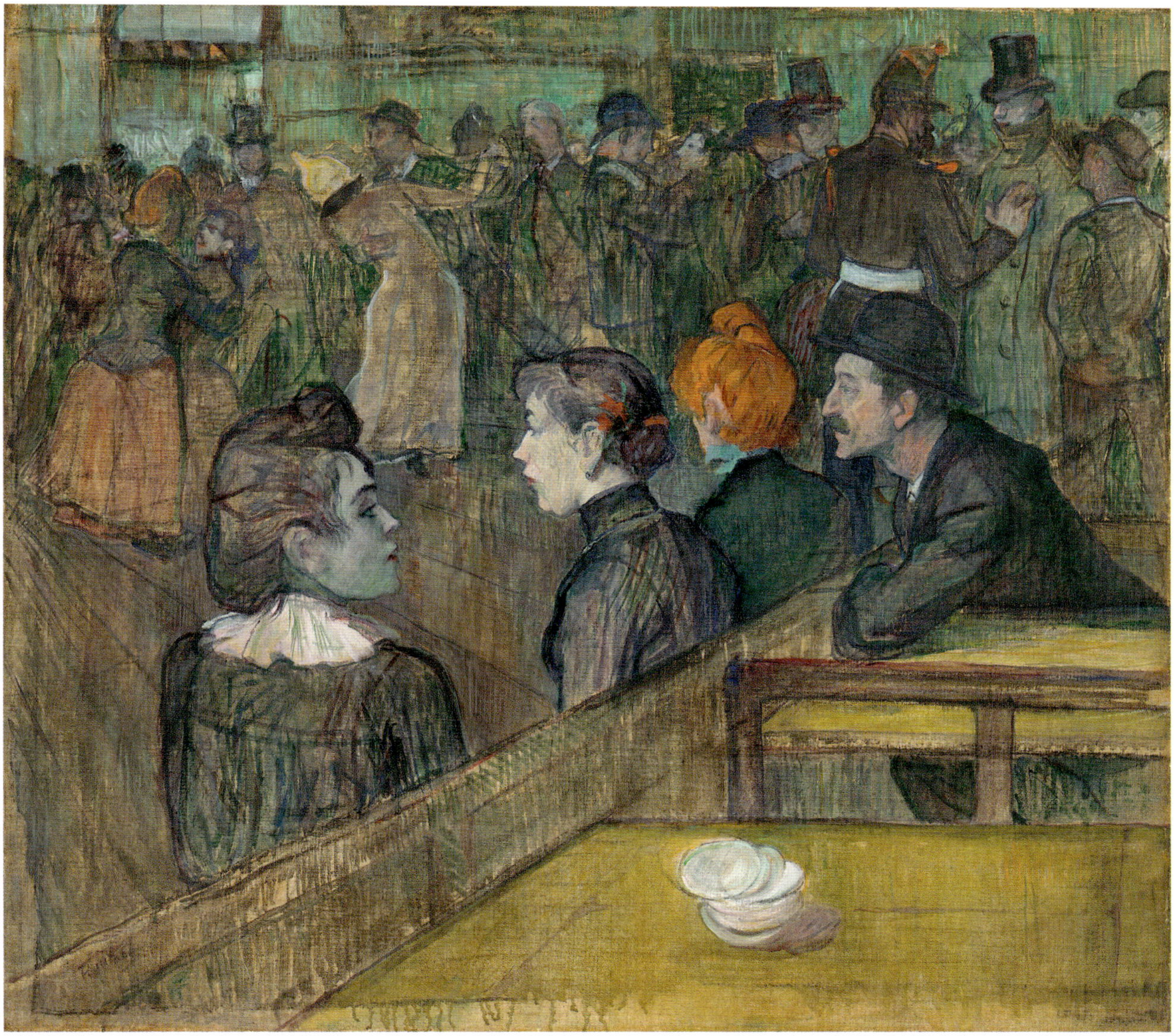

Henri de Toulouse-Lautrec, *Moulin de la Galette*, 1889. Chicago, Art Institute of Chicago

The rusticity of the furnishings and bright hues of the clothing stand out in the painting, the latter worlds away from the mauves, whites and greys worn by De Nittis and Tissot's models. Satin dominated, along with elaborate hairstyles and bijouterie, the dazzle of which seemed to transport the musical sparkle of the orchestra. Many of his friends posed for the large painting: Georges Rivière, Eugène Pierre Lestringuez and Henri Gervex are the young men sitting at the little café table; Estelle is the girl sitting on the bench in the foreground, while her friend Margot is dancing in the middle with the Cuban painter Pedro Vidal de Solares. The two girls were Renoir's models, as was Jeanne, who danced at the café and posed for *The Swing*.

The activities at the Moulin de la Galette remained above board, in contrast to Le Chat noir and similar, and the café was also portrayed by artists from the subsequent generations, like Toulouse-Lautrec and Van Gogh.

9. Le Folies-Bergère

32 rue Richer

Le Folies-Bergère (named after the pleasure halls, called *folies*, that were particularly popular during the Regency) was probably one of the best-known cafés concerts of its time. Designed by the architect Plumeret and inaugurated in 1869, it was one of many halls of this type that were built after the passing of an edict in 1867 that deregulated their construction. They offered variety shows, circus performances and dancers. The profusion of cocottes sitting at the tables lent a slight stench of licentiousness to a place where the dancers' legs were lifted just a little too high. If we are to believe a small volume published in 1867—and why not believe those books that, having no ambitions of timelessness, have no reason to lie, either?—the success of the café concert was

> a fever the character of which results from all the common passions without deriving directly from any, that draws its deprivations from eroticism, its youthful enthusiasms from love of art, its joys from love of life, its sensual pleasure from leisure, its languor from drunkenness. [...] They are blessed effusions, irrepressible joys, bestial ecstasies, delights that verge on sickness—and the man who stirs up and directs all this is a self-important

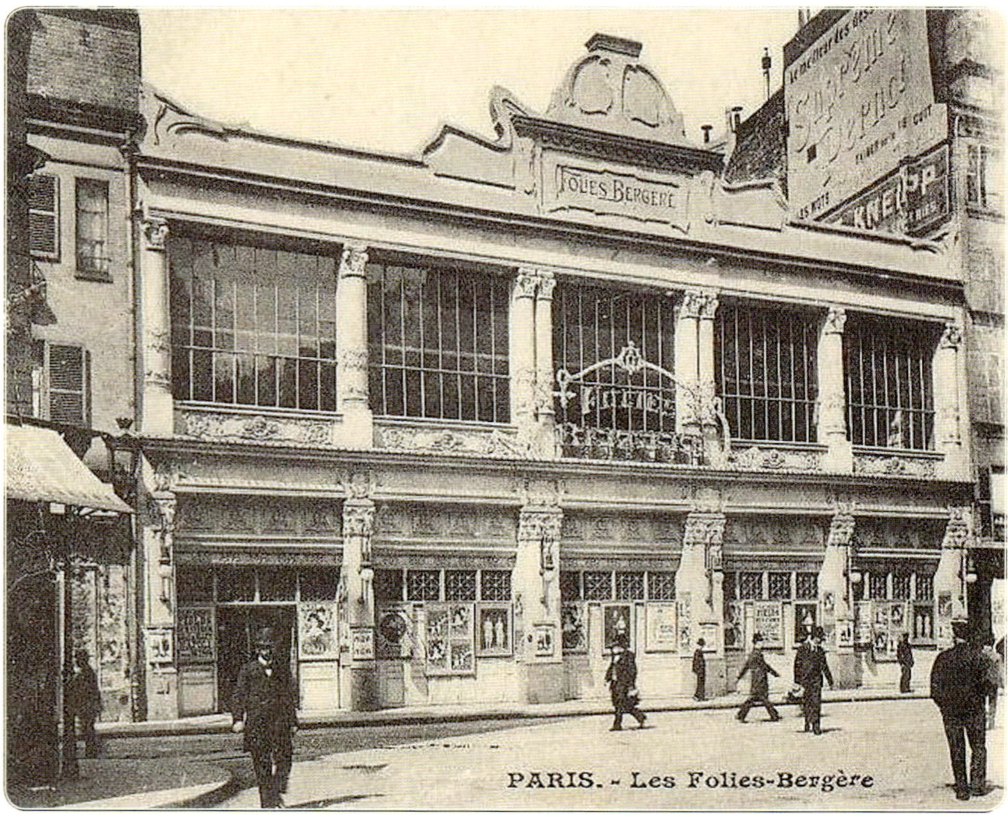

Le Folies-Bergère in rue Richer

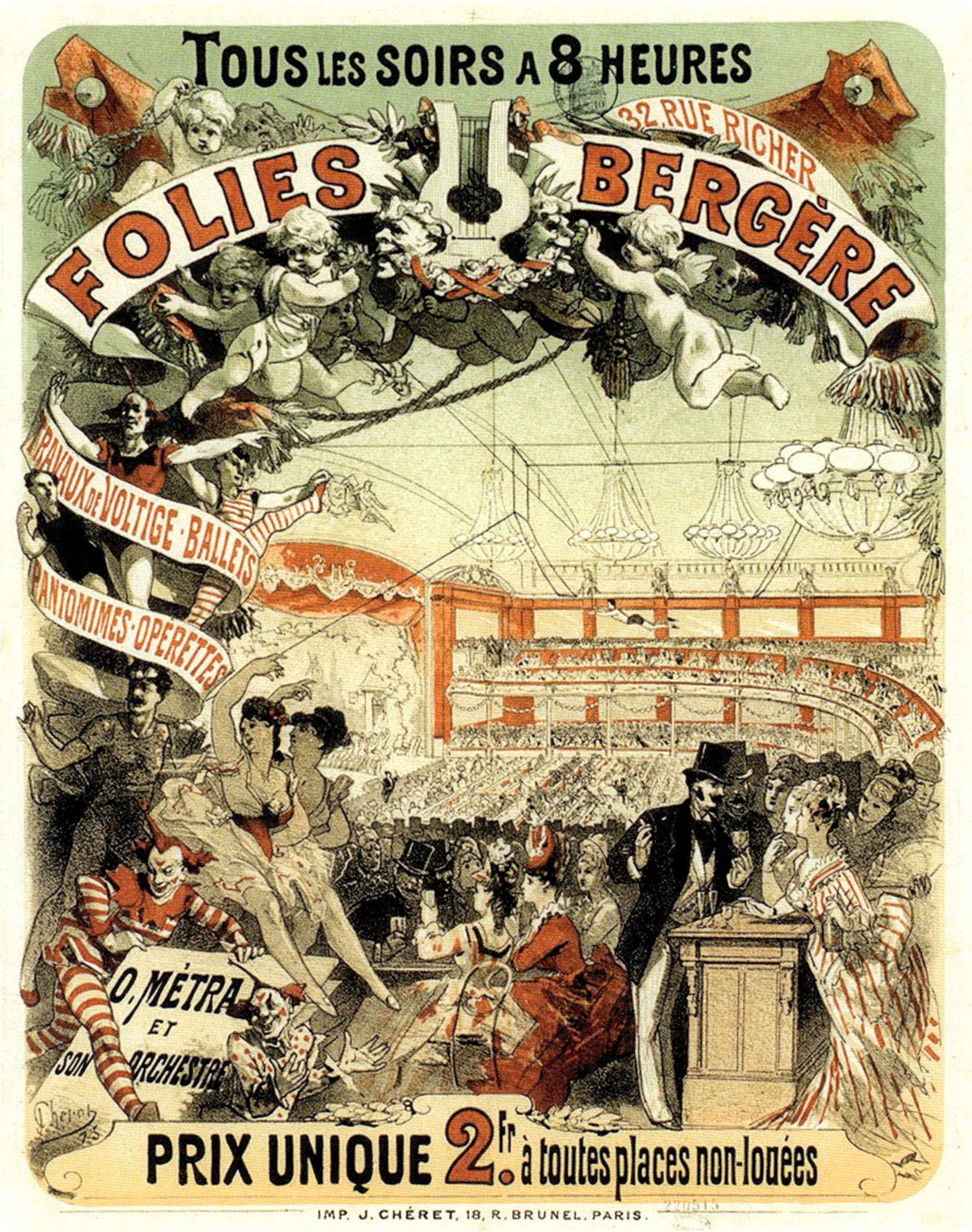

Poster for a show at the Folies-Bergère, featuring acrobats, dancers, pantomime and light opera

pedant in a white apron, escaped from the kitchen, who smokes while watching his marionettes writhing on the stage.[18]

Jean Lorrain is more caustic, seeing in the café concert

all the squalor of a public of bourgeois and low-level employees who applauded, titillated by the ambiguity of the cross-dressers. The grotesque spectacle of men in women's clothing excited them as much as seeing the buttocks of the beautiful girls squeezed into hussar costumes. And the abject flock of walk-ons crossed and recrossed over all this flesh offered in theatre frills, over the fumes of the armpits of the blondes and the amber necks of the androgynous brunettes, more scantily clad with each passing scene, increasingly naked from one act to the next, in an exhibition of moving fat and bone, assimilated by the mixing of make-up and sweat.[19]

Édouard Manet, *A Bar at the Folies-Bergère*, 1881–1882. London, Courtauld Gallery

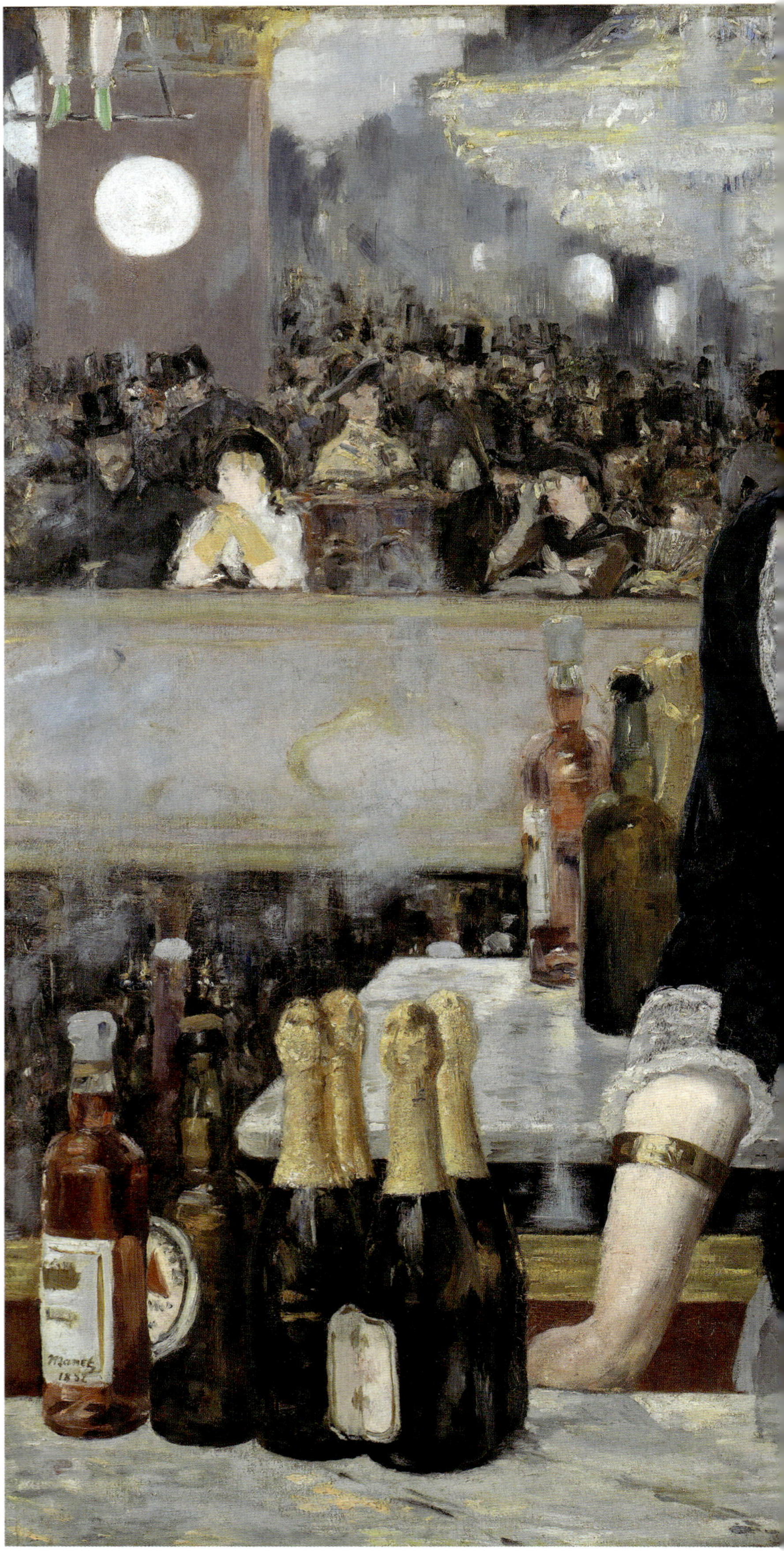

p. 58
Louise Weber, known as La Goulue, wearing a cancan costume and in the 'port d'armes' pose, *c.* 1890

Henri de Toulouse-Lautrec, *Moulin Rouge*, 1891. Houston, Museum of Fine Arts

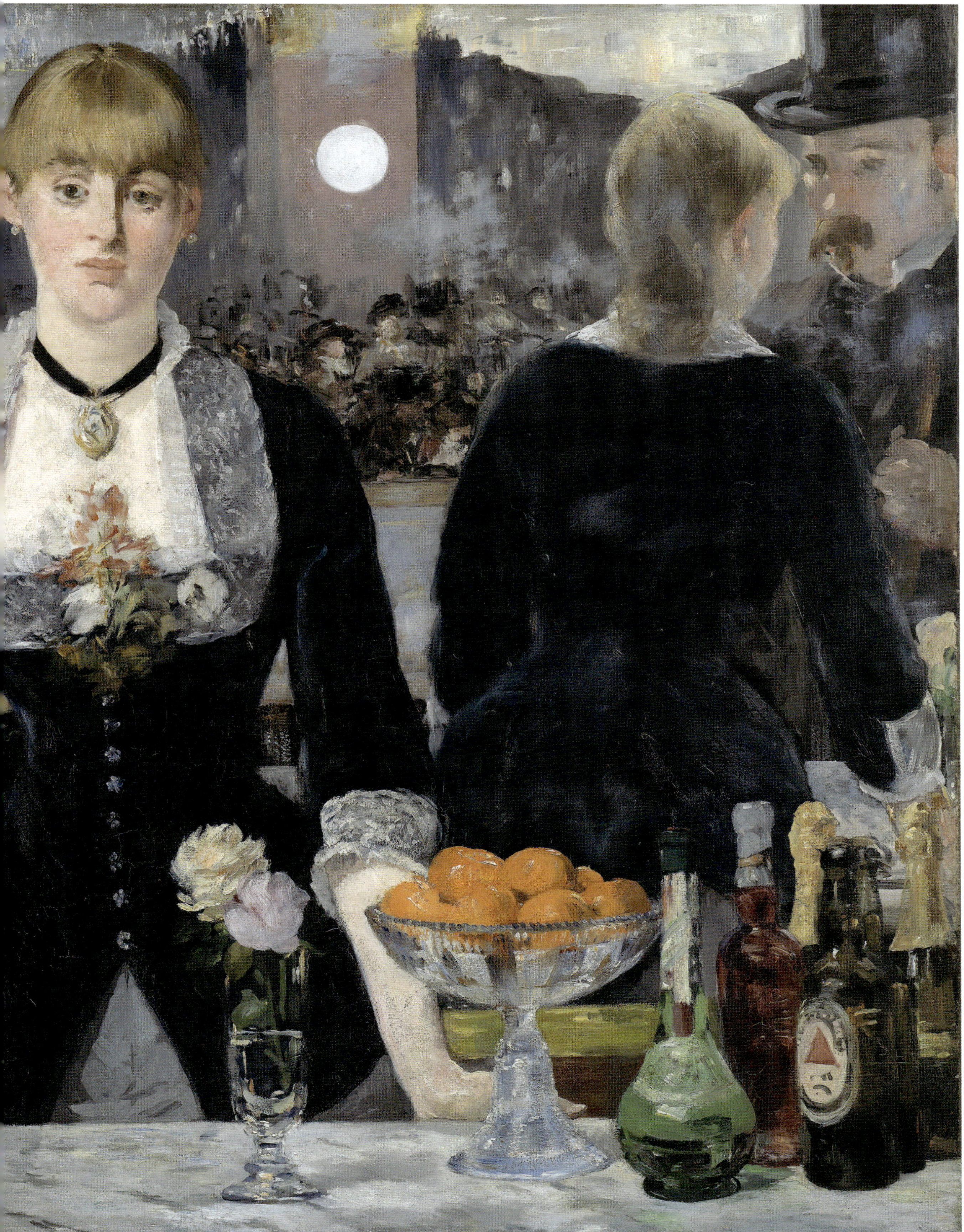

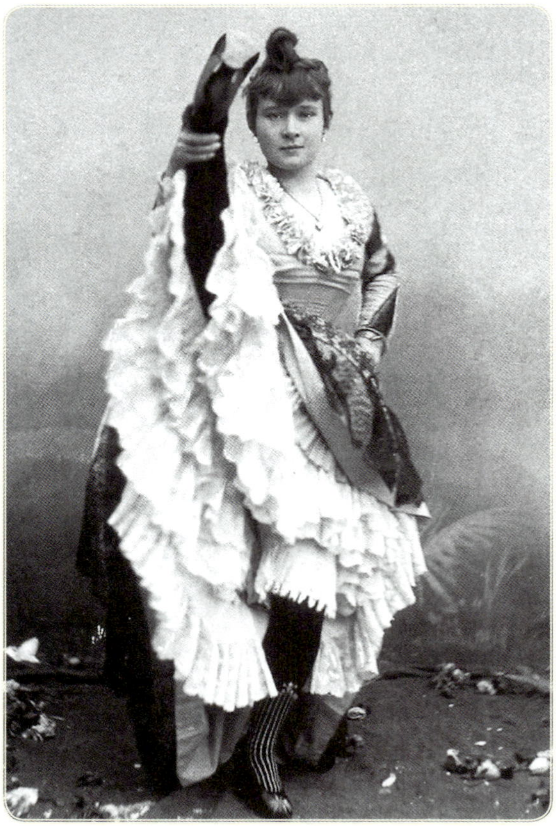

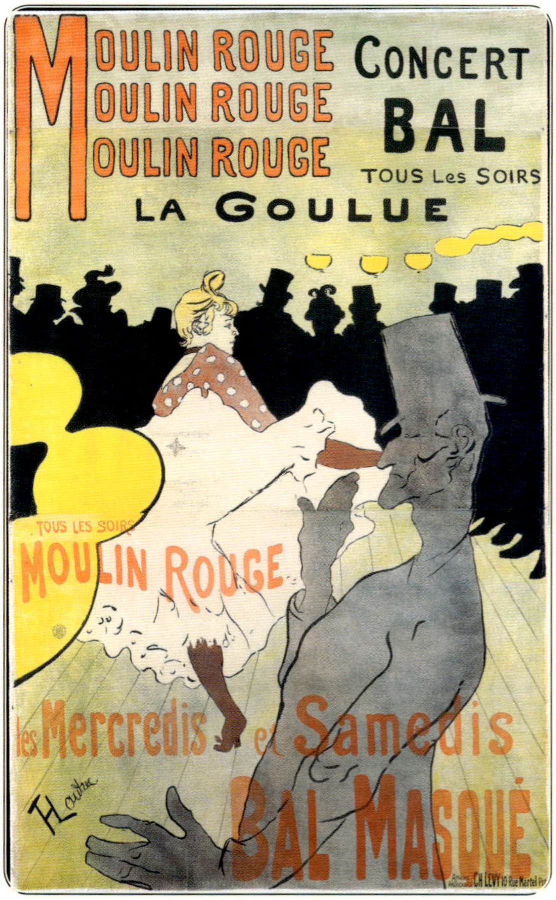

Although Lorrain's prose is not without the same defects that he so fiercely condemns, not all the details in his account can be put down to his personal decadent taste. Behind the screen of gaiety—and *Gaîté parisienne* was the name of a dance to the music of Jacques Offenbach that was often played in this type of venue—there was much misery. More gentlemanly and less petulant than Lorrain, George Moore, in *Memoirs of My Dead Life*, writes of Marie Pellegrin, an actress in another café concert, the Élysée Montmartre, and friend of the Goulue portrayed by Toulouse-Lautrec, with all the sensibility of a Victorian writer, quite similar to Dickens. Here is the description of her flat:

> A bottle of absinthe stood on a beautiful Empire table that her prince had given her, and Bijou, Clementine's little dog, slept on an embroidered cushion. [...] She was going to have puppies, and I was stroking her silky coat thinking of her coming trouble, when I suddenly heard Clementine's voice raised above the others, and looking up I saw a great animation in her face; I heard that the cards had not been fairly dealt, and then the women threw their cards aside, and La Glue told Clementine that she was not wanted, that *elle ferait bien de débarrasser les planches*, that was the expression she used. I heard further accusations, and among them the plaintive voice of Marie begging of me not to believe what they said. The women caught each other by the air, and tore at each other's faces, and Marie raised herself up in bed and implored them to cease; and then she fell back crying.[20]

Splendour and misery! The divas of the café concert alternated lavish parties with prolonged privations, prawn soup with bread and sausages: a diet that led them in the span of a few years from the stage to the morgue. Gifts from their admirers, the fruits of intemperate nights, were lost the next morning at the game. Their faces betrayed the intensity of the strain, their compromised health their attendance. Big stars also passed through the Folies-Bergère, but most of them did not live long: like real stars in the sky, when their splendour was at its most intense, they were already dead or close to it.

Although Manet immortalised it in his famous painting *A Bar at the Folies-Bergère*, the Impressionists spent less time there than at Café Guerbois and Café de la Nouvelle Athènes. Le Folies-Bergère was instead the favourite café concert of Toulouse-Lautrec, its best possible bard, and it was also preferred by the great poster artist Jules Chéret.

0. The Cirque Fernando

63 boulevard Rochechouart

It was located between rue des Martyrs and boulevard Rochechouart, at the edge of the Montmartre quarter, not far from the famed Élysée-Montmartre dance hall. The circus of Ferdinand Beert (stage name Fernando), as it was known to Degas and his friends, was no longer the modest tent with simple wooden benches that Parisians saw rise up one day in 1873 with such unexpected speed that the writer Jules Claretie said it was like a weed that sprouted in a single night after heavy rain. Indeed, the new building, designed by Gustave-André Gridaine, had something of the bold liveliness of temporary encampments in its otherwise graceful Corinthian elegance. The two concentric domes, with their slender iron columns topped by a lantern, were what gave it this slightly gypsy-like air. The interior was instead quite spartan, divided in rows of tiered rustic benches with no divisions between them, so that the audience, all muddled together, must have looked like the perfect subject for a pointillist painting. The painters went there often, no less than the poets, who perhaps identified a bit with the acrobats, twirling above the amused crowd. Hadn't

Gustave Gridaine, *Plan for Cirque Fernando*, 1874. Paris, Bibliothèque nationale de France

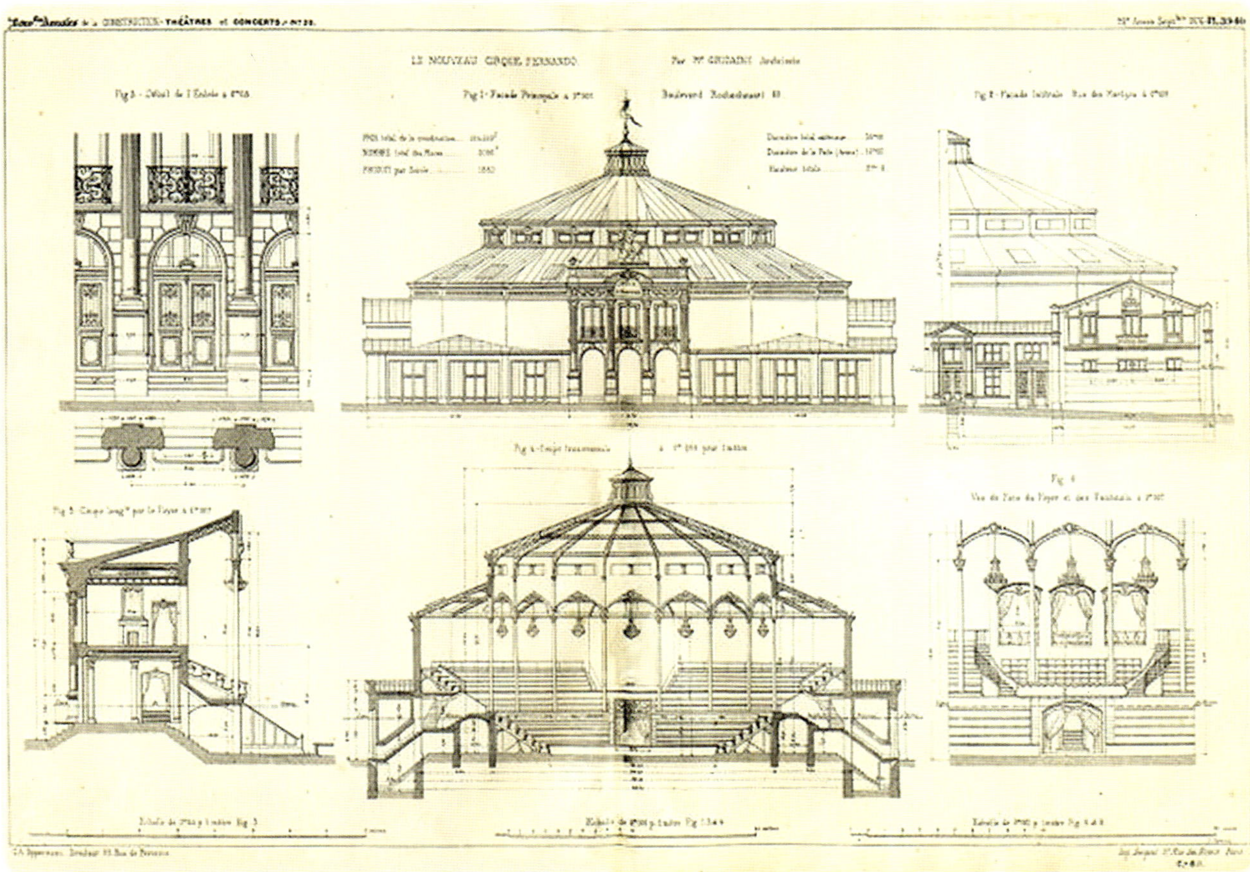

Baudelaire compared the artist to the albatross mocked by the crew? The Parisians went into raptures over the clowns Foottit and Chocolat, who were often portrayed by Toulouse-Lautrec and performed at the Nouveau Cirque, as well as Cha-U-Kao,[21] part clown, part acrobat, whose Amazonian legs could be admired in the fair pavilions and at the Moulin Rouge; but not all these pastimes were so innocent. The equestriennes immortalised by Toulouse-Lautrec excited the masochistic fantasies of the more perverse spirits, already introduced to algolagnia by Algerton Swinburne's poem *Dolores*, inspired by Adah Menken. It is also possible that, as insinuated by Jean Lorrain in one of his stories, some of the regulars went to these shows with the secret hope that an accident would transform the farce into tragedy, as happened at the end of Edmond de Goncourt's *Zemganno Brothers*. And it is in that novel that we find one of the most accurate descriptions of the time's circus performances:

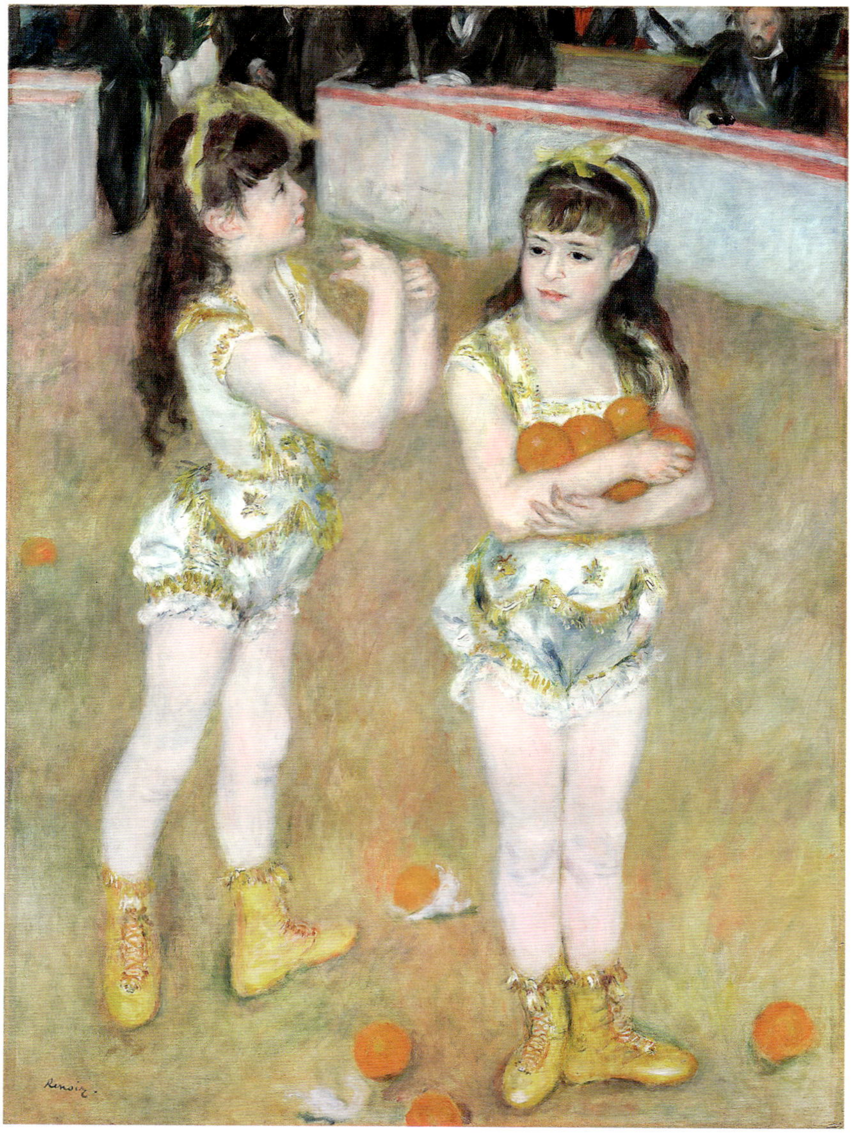

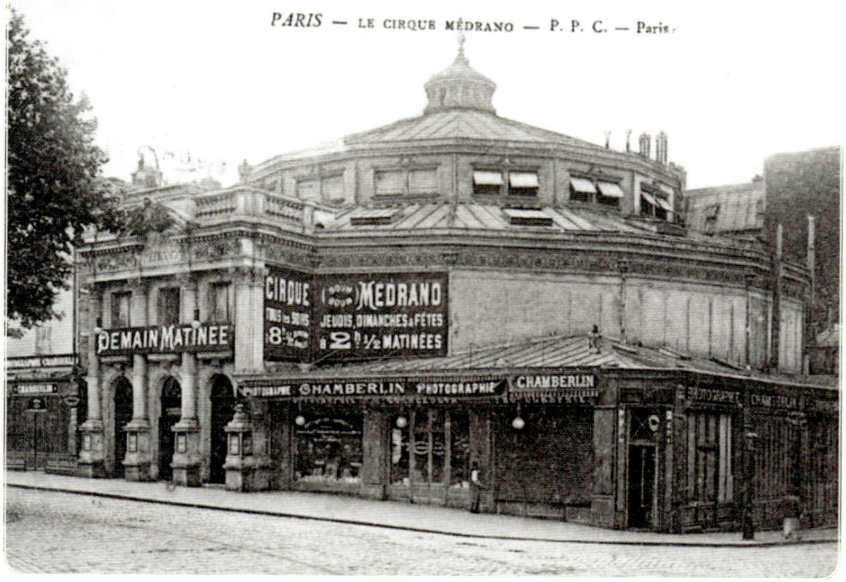

> In one second, at the top of the big pole, studded with pegs at intervals so that it could be climbed, the sylph was on the tightrope, skirt puffed out, waving the swinging balance over her head with her arms forming an arc. She advanced with gliding steps, alternating her feet, which seemed like wires underneath, and touched the void as if on the curved end of a branch. She walked on the pliant, elastic wire lowering and

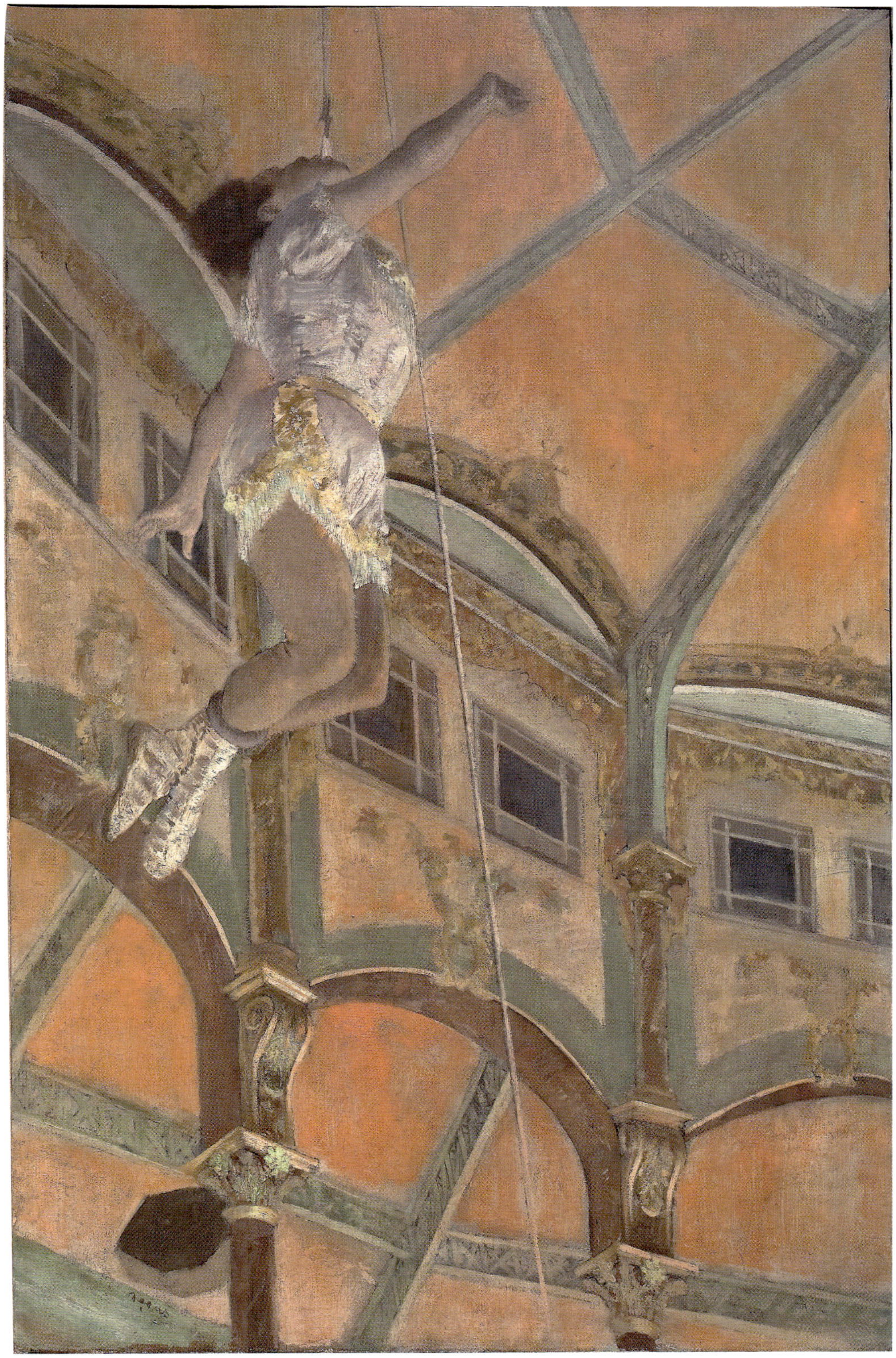

p. 60
Pierre-Auguste Renoir, *Acrobats at the Cirque Fernando*, 1879. Chicago, Art Institute of Chicago

The Cirque Medrano, which replaced the Cirque Fernando in 1898

Edgar Degas, *Miss La La at the Cirque Fernando*, 1879. London, National Gallery

p. 62
Jean-Louis Forain, *Tight-Rope Walker*, *c.* 1885. Chicago, Art Institute of Chicago

Henri de Toulouse-Lautrec, *At the Cirque Fernando*, 1887. Chicago, Art Institute of Chicago

raising herself, as if with each step she were going up or down a step ... Then she returned to the middle of the tightrope with small quick steps, with one foot behind the other, curving, bending and crouching on her legs, folded beneath her. And then, flipping backward, she stretched out on the invisible wire, with the immobility of someone sleeping: head resting on her shoulder, hair strewn, feet resting one on

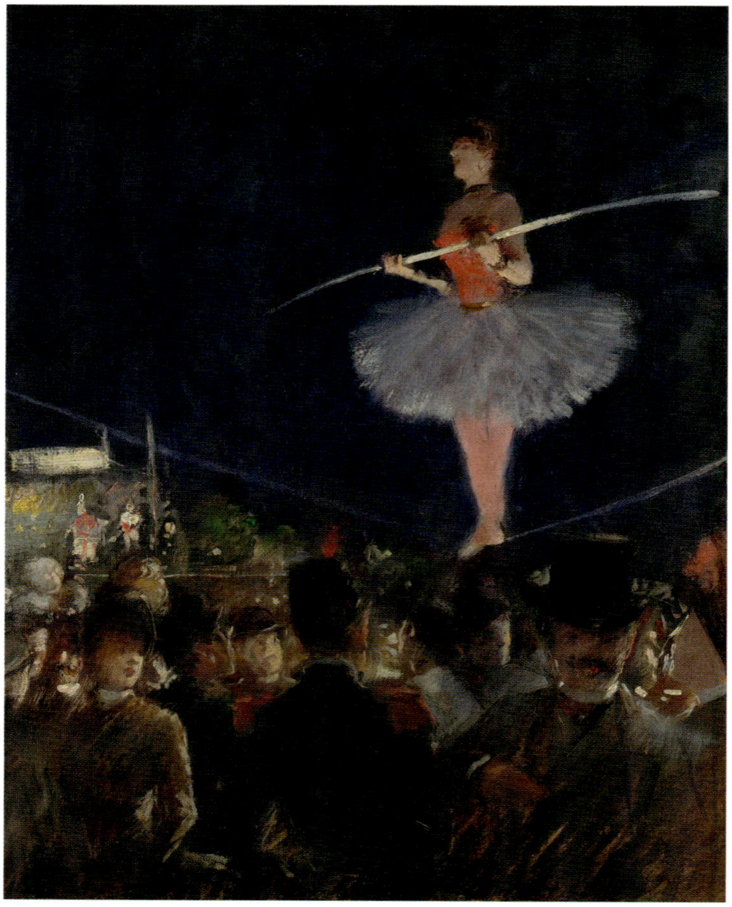

the other, with something of the trembling rest of two birds tucked under the same wing.[22]

Renoir, who always leaned towards the tender, painted two small acrobats from the Circus Fernando, almost lost amidst the roars of the crowd, while Degas preferred to portray the famous trapeze artist *Miss La La*, with an agile play of limbs that exalts the animal prowess of her body. Seurat, whose studio was not far away, at the *passage de l'Élysée des Beaux-Arts*, also often went to these shows, which provided him with the subject of one of his most famous paintings, *The Circus* (1890–1891). The history of the Circus Fernando lasted until 1897, when it was taken over by Gerónimo Medrano, and has survived under this name to the present day; but the spirit of the travelling troupes was transmitted, tinged with melancholy, in the works of Picasso of the Rose Period, in Stravinsky's *Pulcinella* and in Charlie Chaplin's comedies.

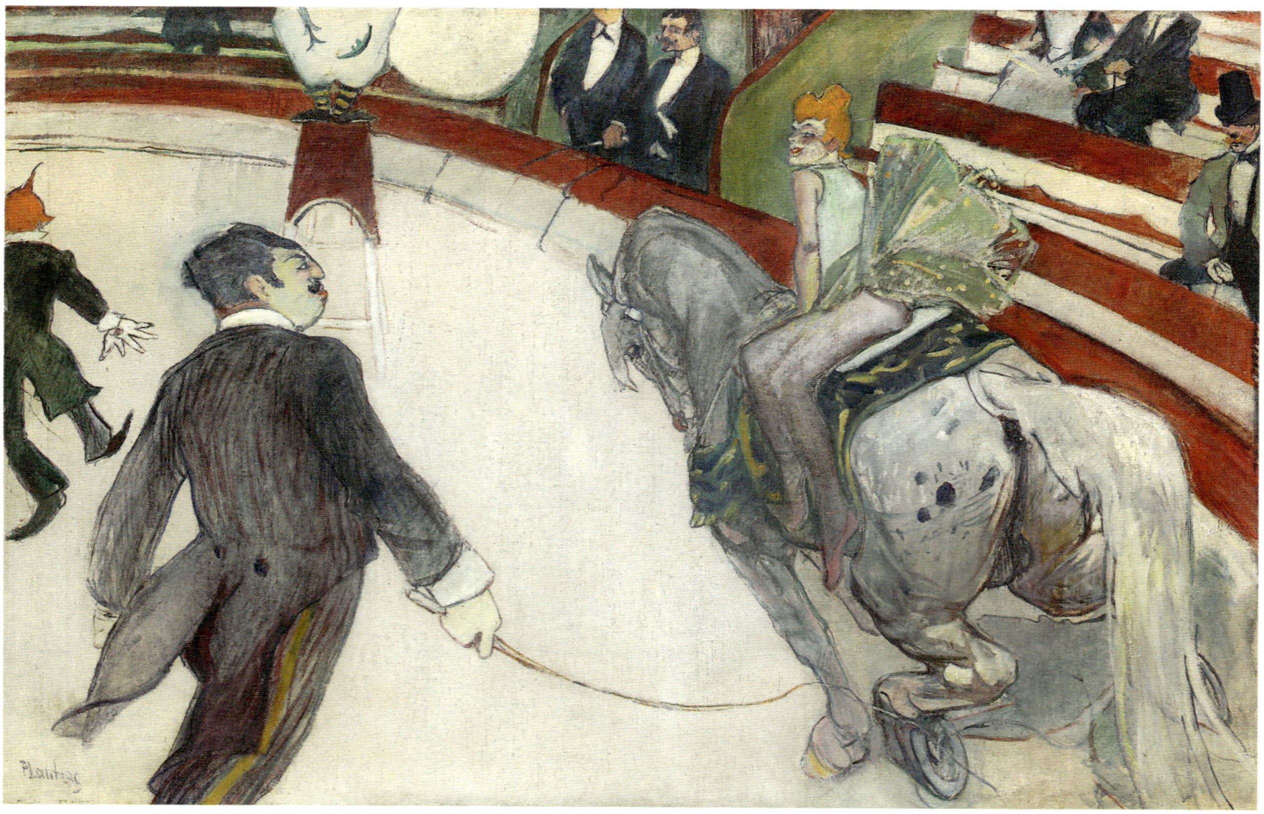

11. The Opera

Opéra Le Peletier, 12 rue Le Peletier
today Opéra Garnier, place de l'Opera

The Opéra Le Peletier was designed and built by François Debret in 1821 in rue Le Peletier, from which it took its name. There, one found a famous *passage*, called passage Le Peletier or passage de l'Opéra, that was popular with the artistic *bohème* of the time and a simple restaurant that catered to the same clientele, Divan Le Peletier. The guides to the city described it as 'the most surprising of all the Paris theatres, for the magnificence of its ornamentation and the sumptuousness of its interiors'. Indeed, the engravings and paintings from the time show it as a grand space luxuriously hung with lights, the festive purpose of which must have been exalted each time the stage and orchestra were removed to create a single, enormous room, as we see in Manet's *Masked Ball at the Opéra.*

L'Opéra Le Peletier: facade and interiors

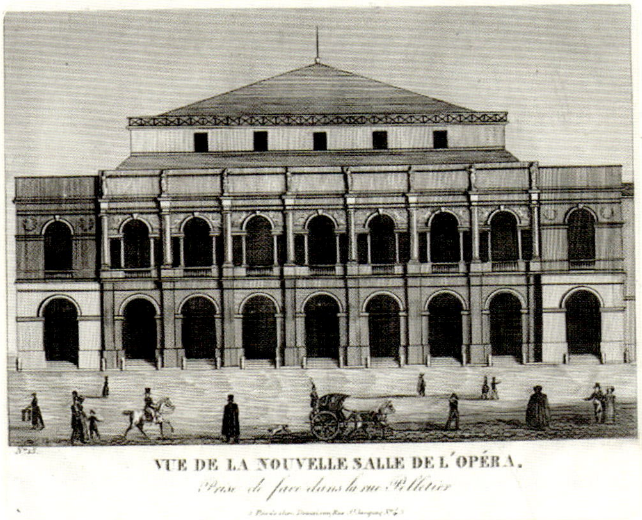

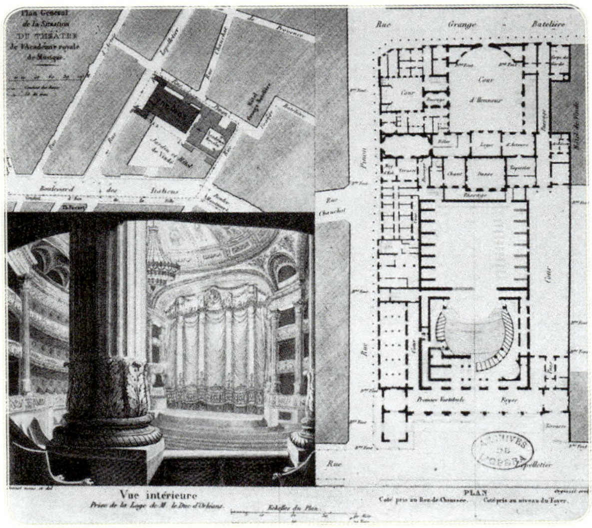

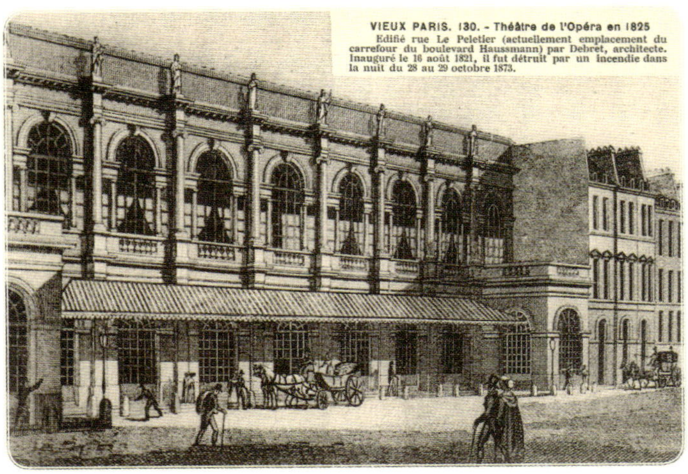

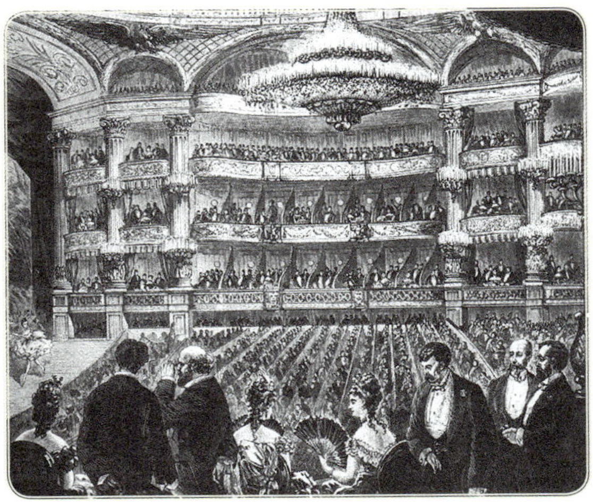

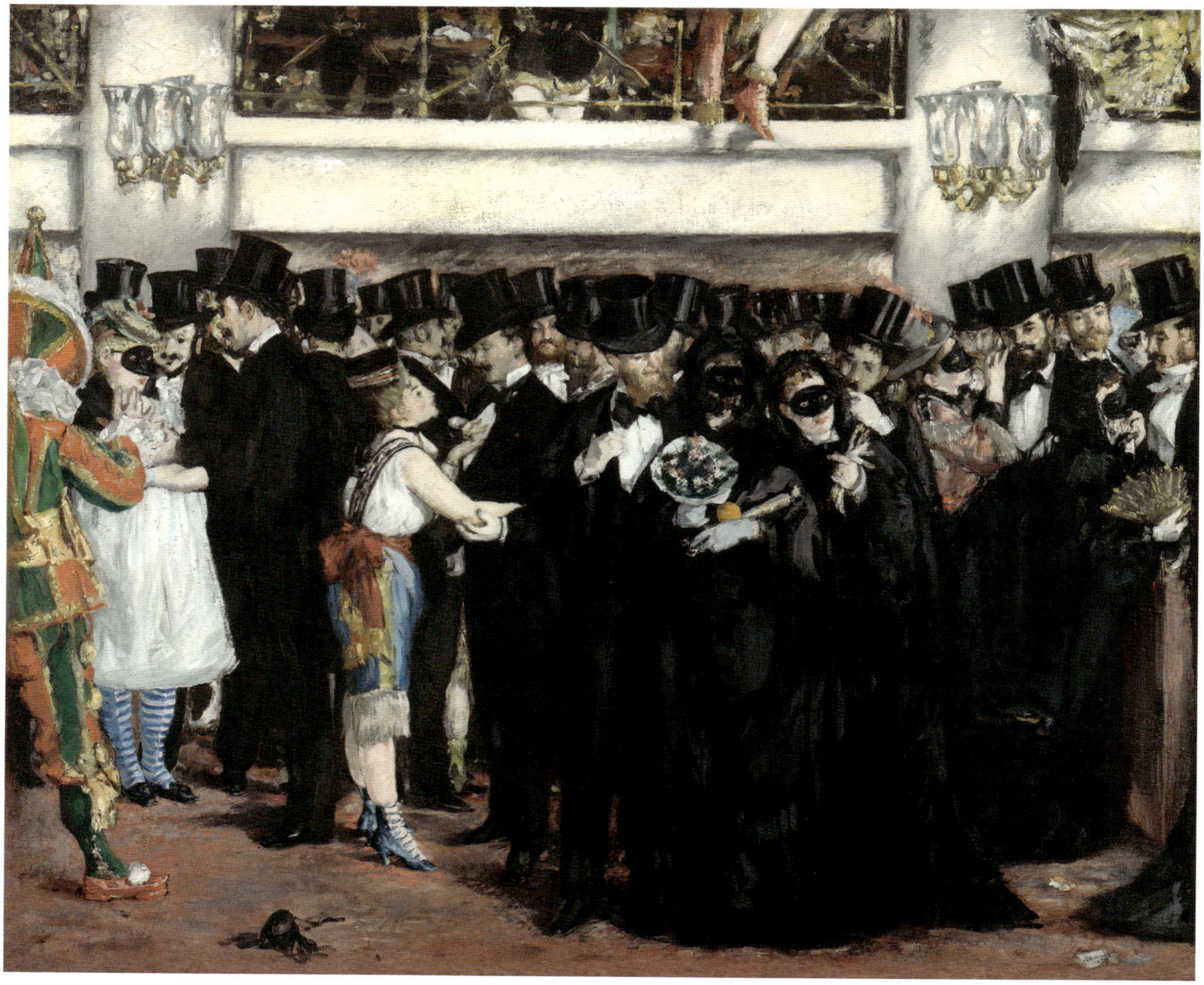

Édouard Manet, *Masked Ball at the Opéra*, 1873. Washington, D.C., National Gallery of Art

The spectacles were made even more enchanting by the depth of the sets and the possibilities offered by the new gas lighting, the prodigious variety of effects of which was experimented with for the first time in 1822 for Nicolas Isouard's *Aladin, ou la Lampe merveilleuse.* Romantic fabulosity expressed through the most modern and sophisticated technical systems, a few decades before the invention of film. It was in this atmosphere of shadowy, rarefied opalescence, where even tragedy was haloed with *féerie*, that Rossini's *William Tell*, Meyerbeer's *Robert le Diable* and Verdi's *Don Carlos* debuted. Degas (who painted a scene of Meyerbeer's *grand opéra* with his friend the musician Désiré Dihau in the foreground) loved to depict ballerinas under the artificial light, to the point that we can say that it played the same role in the development of his artistic technique as the sparkles on the water of the Seine at Argenteuil had for Monet. When, however, the ballerinas removed their satin slippers and massaged their aching legs, Degas took his inspiration from the Japanese artist Utamaro's engravings. He was the painter of the stage and its mirages, to be sure, but also the world behind the scenes, rehearsals and practices, during which his anatomical and ferocious eye stripped the dancers of allure and embellishment (which was for Baudelaire the very essence of feminine charm). And so, they really became *petits rats* or 'little monkey girls' as Goncourt described them with his usual pungent wit. Degas was aware of this, and indeed confessed: 'Women can never forgive me; they

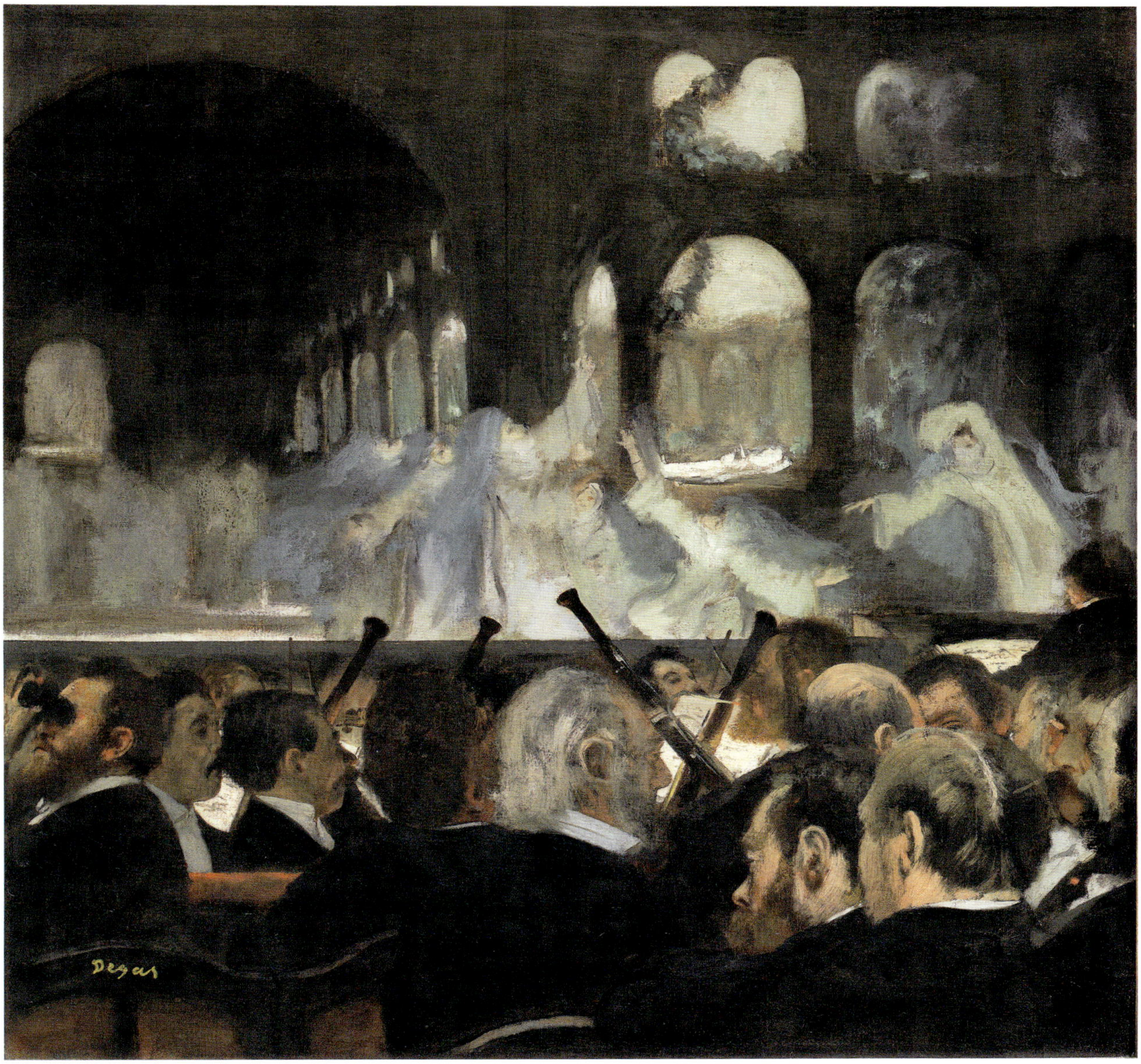

Edgar Degas, *The Ballet Scene from 'Robert le Diable'*, 1871. London, Victoria & Albert Museum

hate me, they feel that I am disarming them. I show them without their coquetry, like animals cleaning themselves'.[23]

Although most of the audience was swept up in transports of rapture, we mustn't imagine that the reverent silence of today also reigned in the theatres of the time, and where it was required, as in the case of Wagner at Bayreuth, this was an exception. It was more typical for the intermissions to be filled with witty, light operettas or, as happened in France, for people to spend them playing cards. In the dressing rooms, the female artists could entertain themselves with bored dandies, for whom they were just lovers of the day. Nor was this an infrequent occurrence, since the poor girls of the ballet corps were more socially akin to Germinie Lacerteux than the proud Faustin in Goncourt's novel. The dancers, like the painters' models, mostly came from the demi-monde of Montmartre: so, one could say that the Opéra truly embraced all the strata of the population.

Degas was not the only one in his crowd who went to the theatre in rue Le Peletier, although he was the only one to get access to the areas reserved for rehearsals. Both

Edgar Degas, *The Dance Foyer at the Opéra*, 1872. Paris, Musée d'Orsay

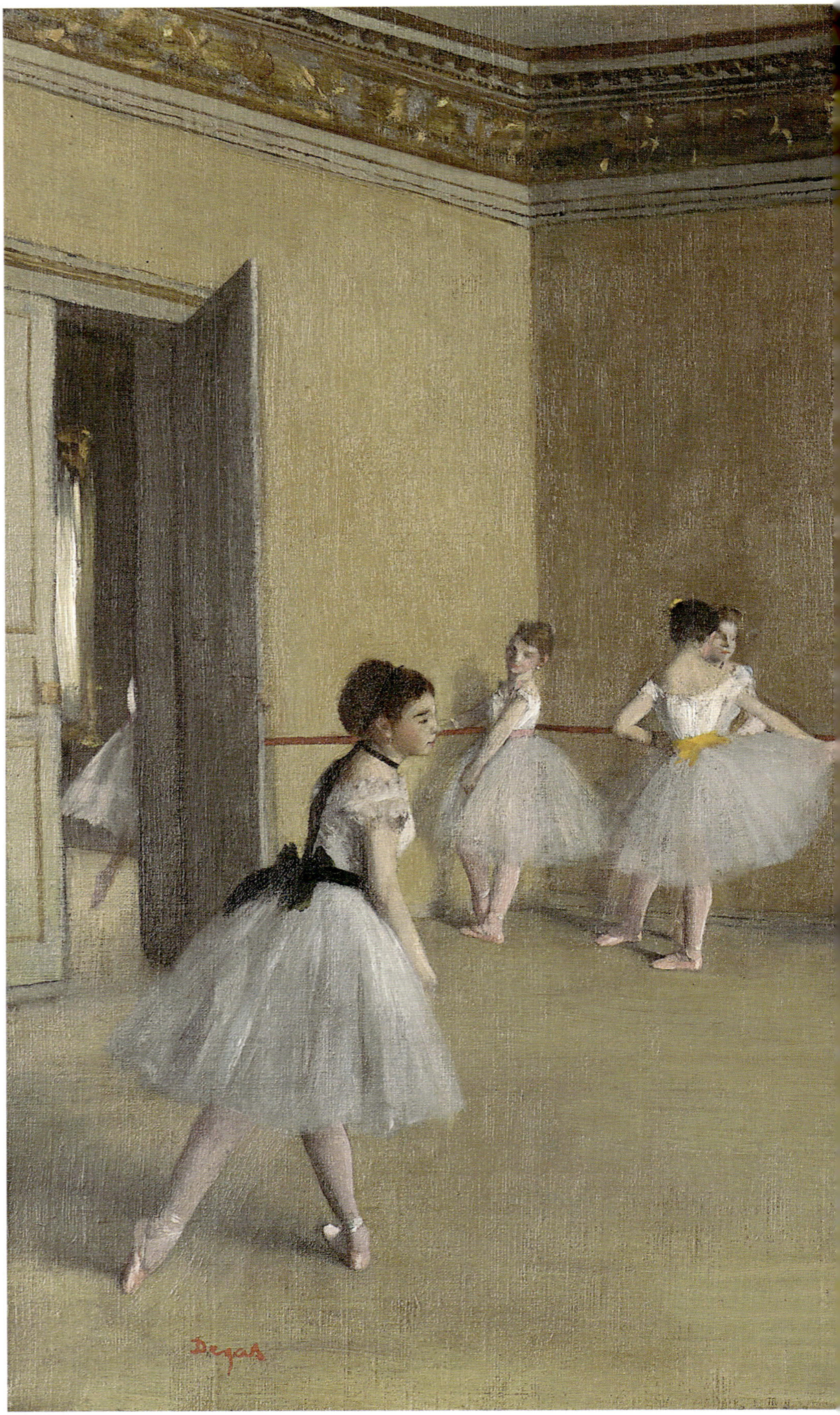

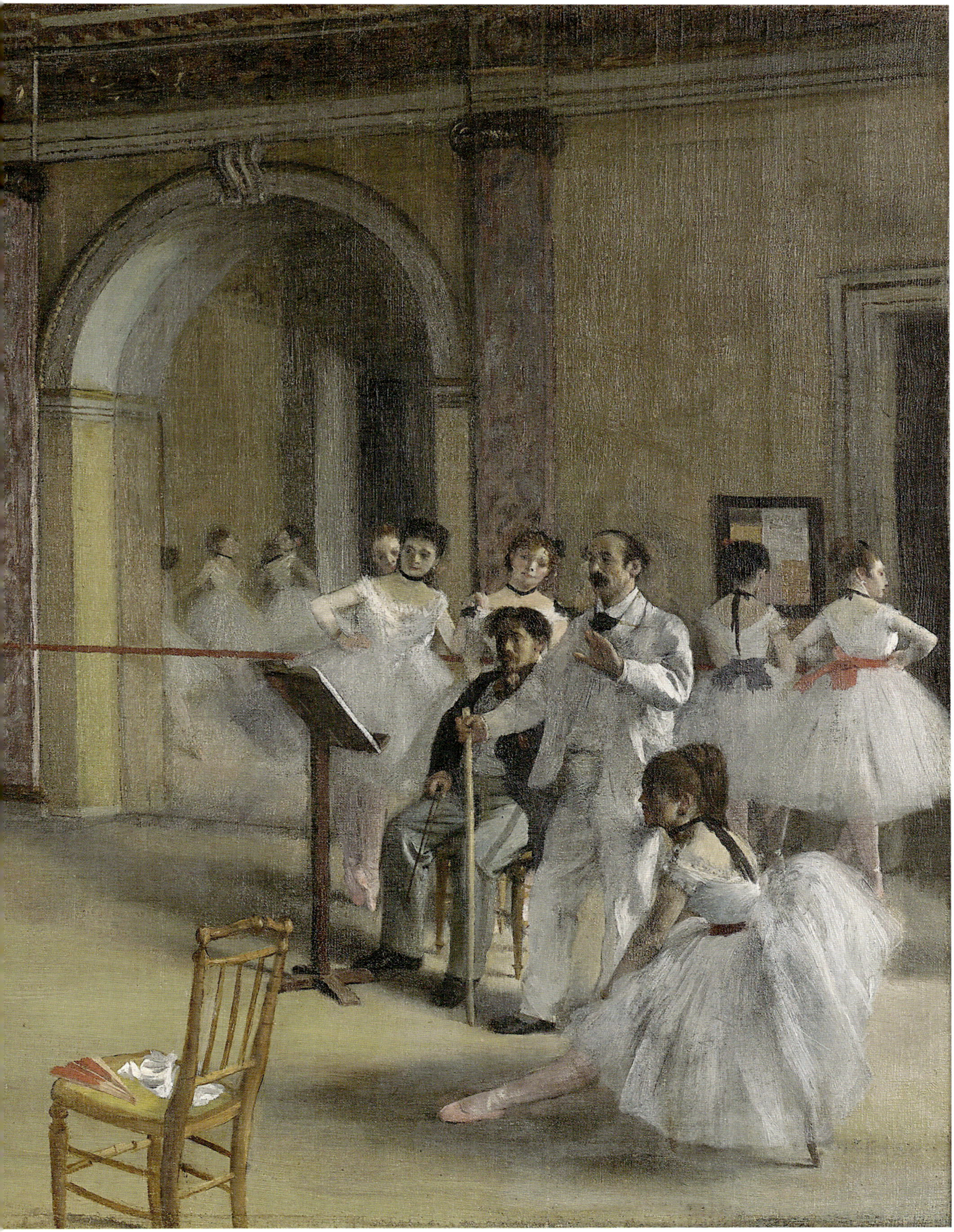

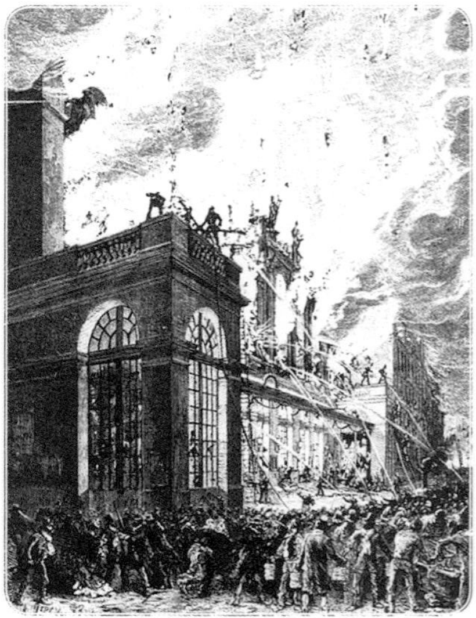

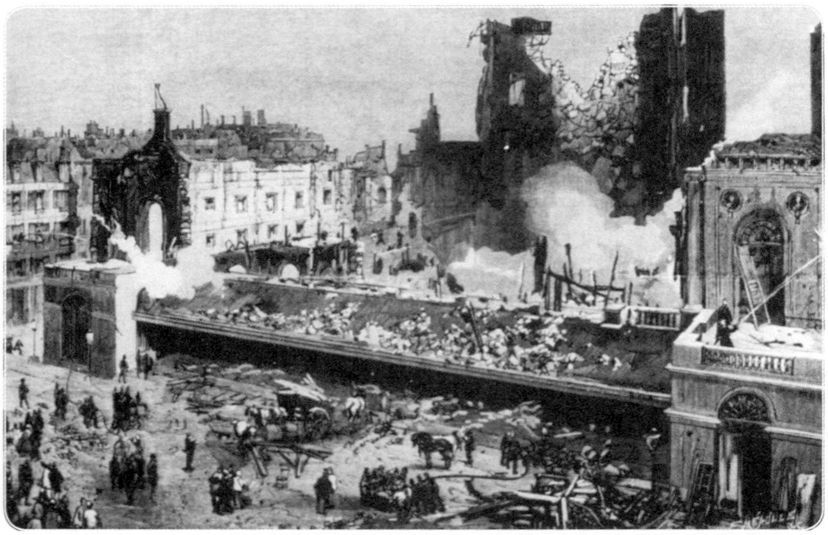

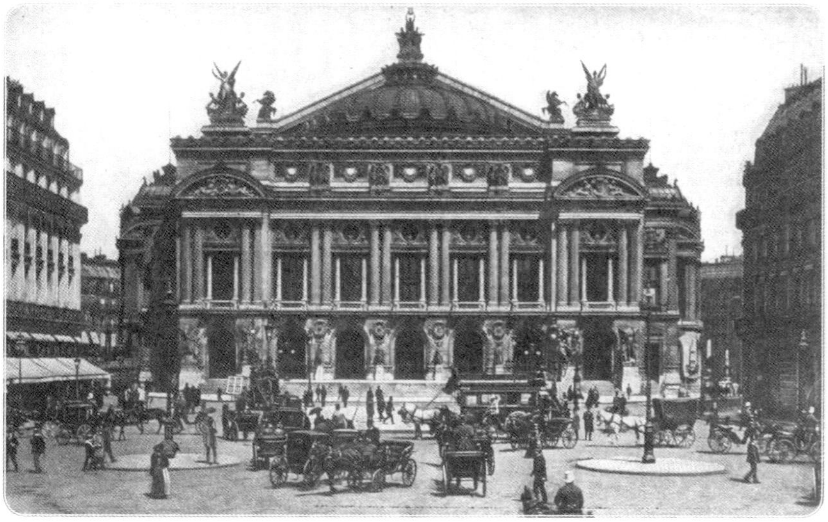

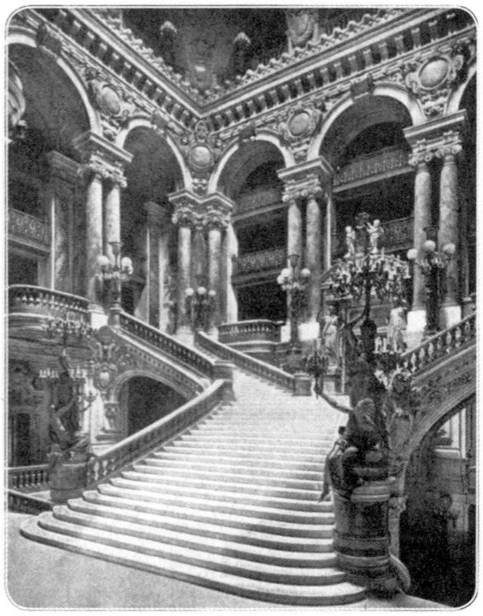

Above: The fire at the Opéra Le Peletier, 1873. Below: The Opéra Garnier, 1875. Facade, grand staircase and foyer

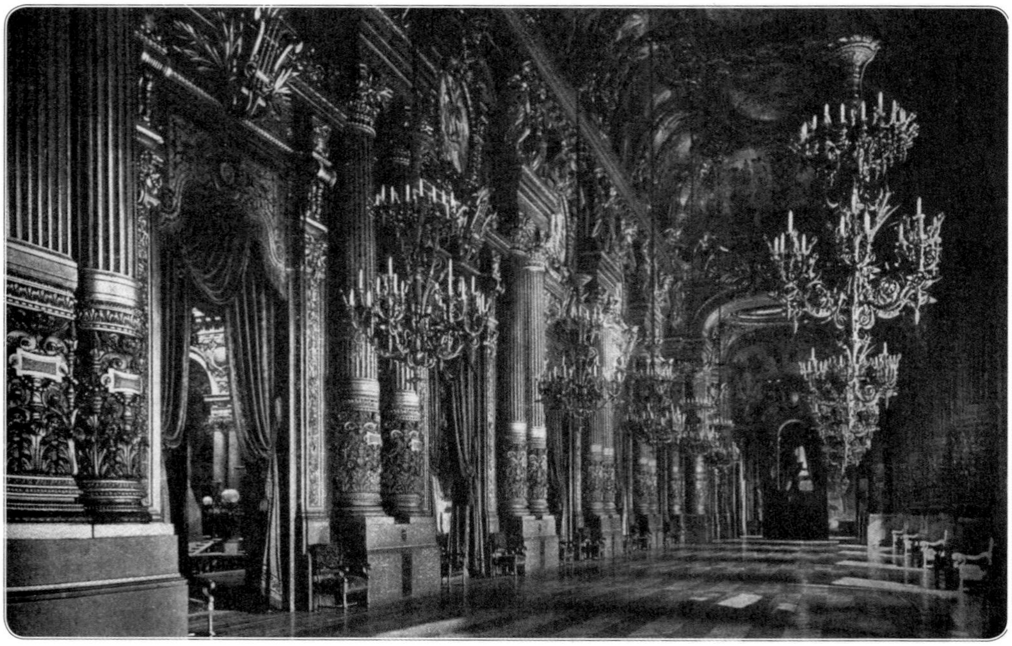

p. 69
Edgar Degas, *The Star*, 1876. Paris, Musée d'Orsay

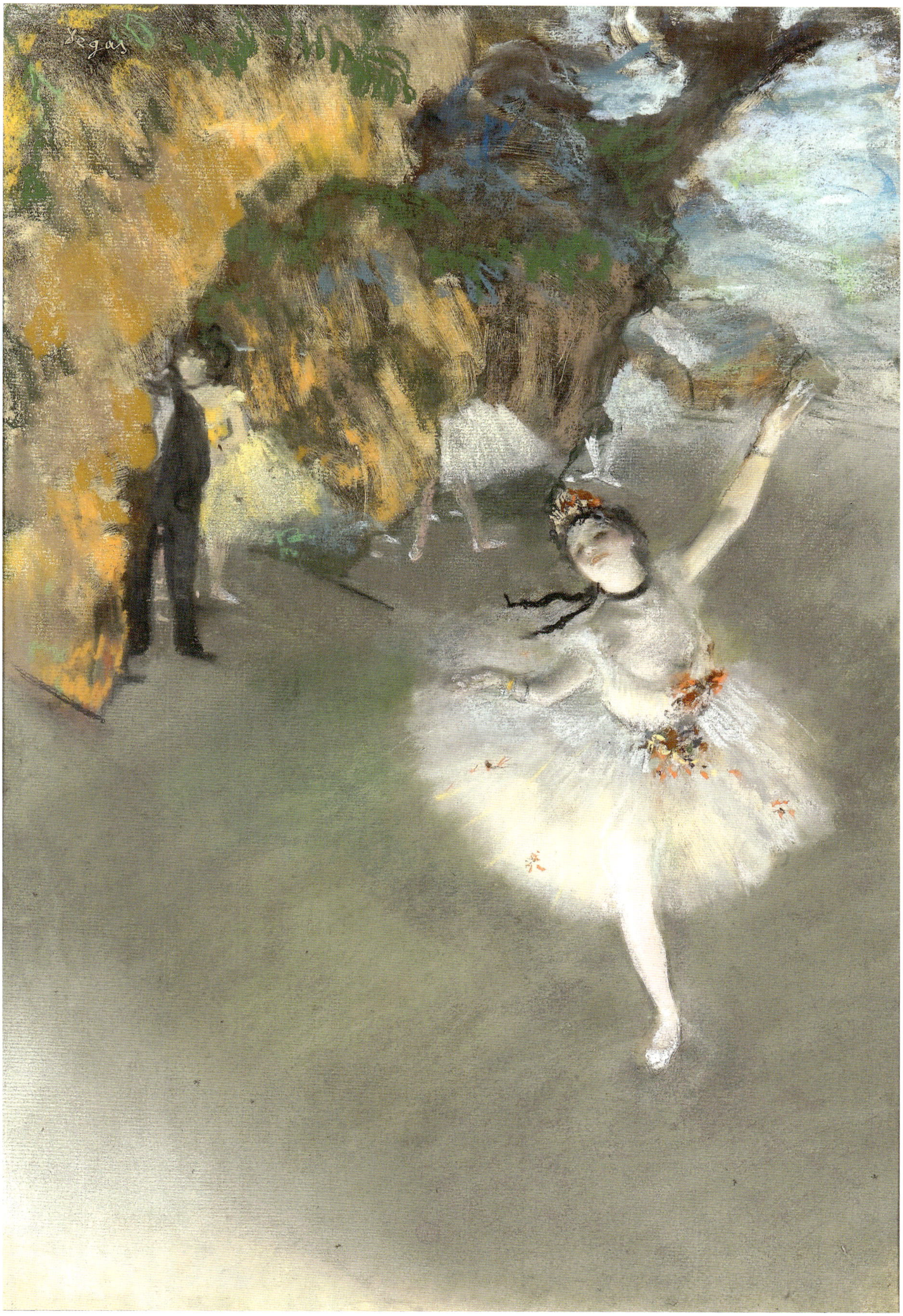

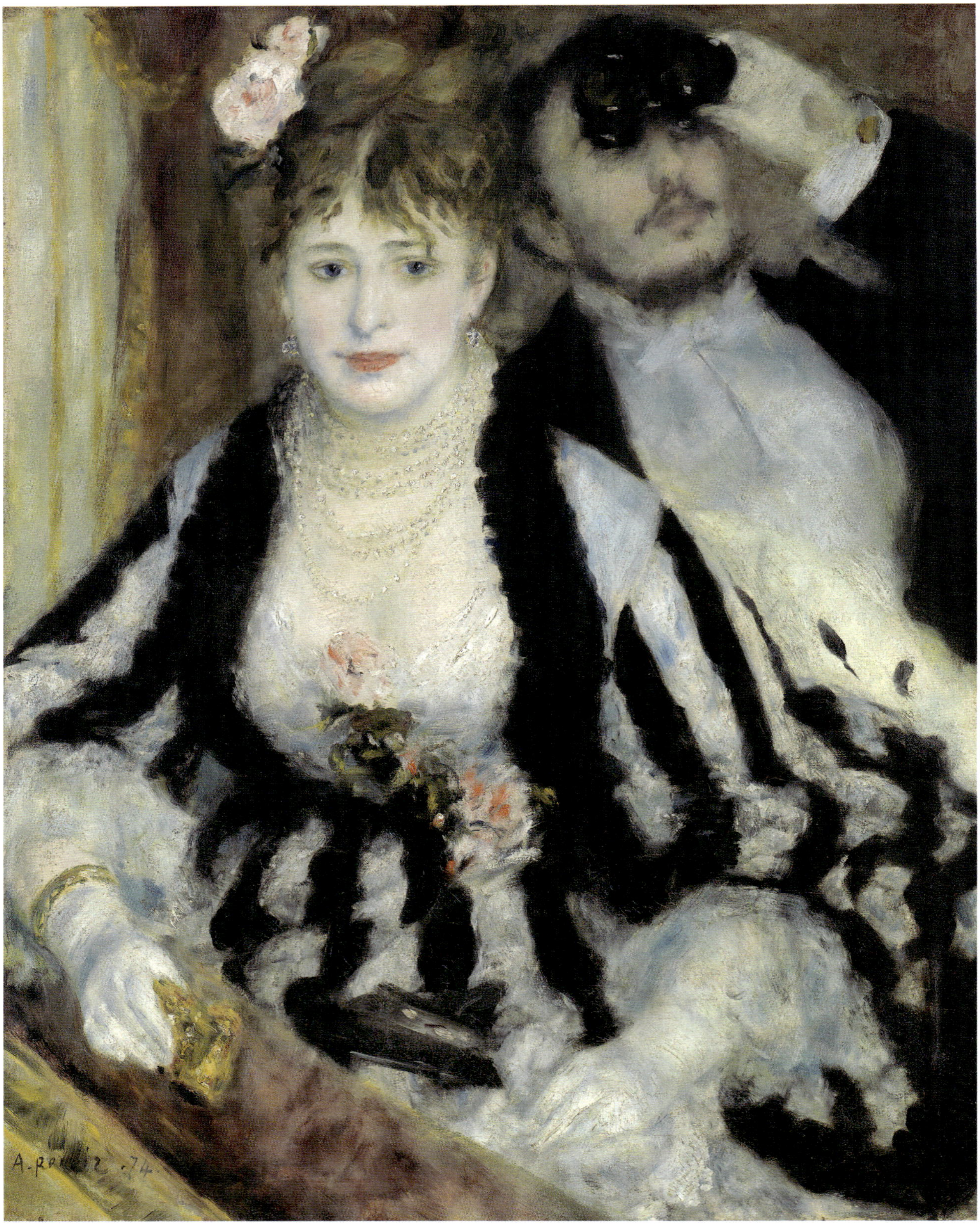

Pierre-Auguste Renoir,
La Loge (The Theatre Box),
1874. London, Courtauld
Institute

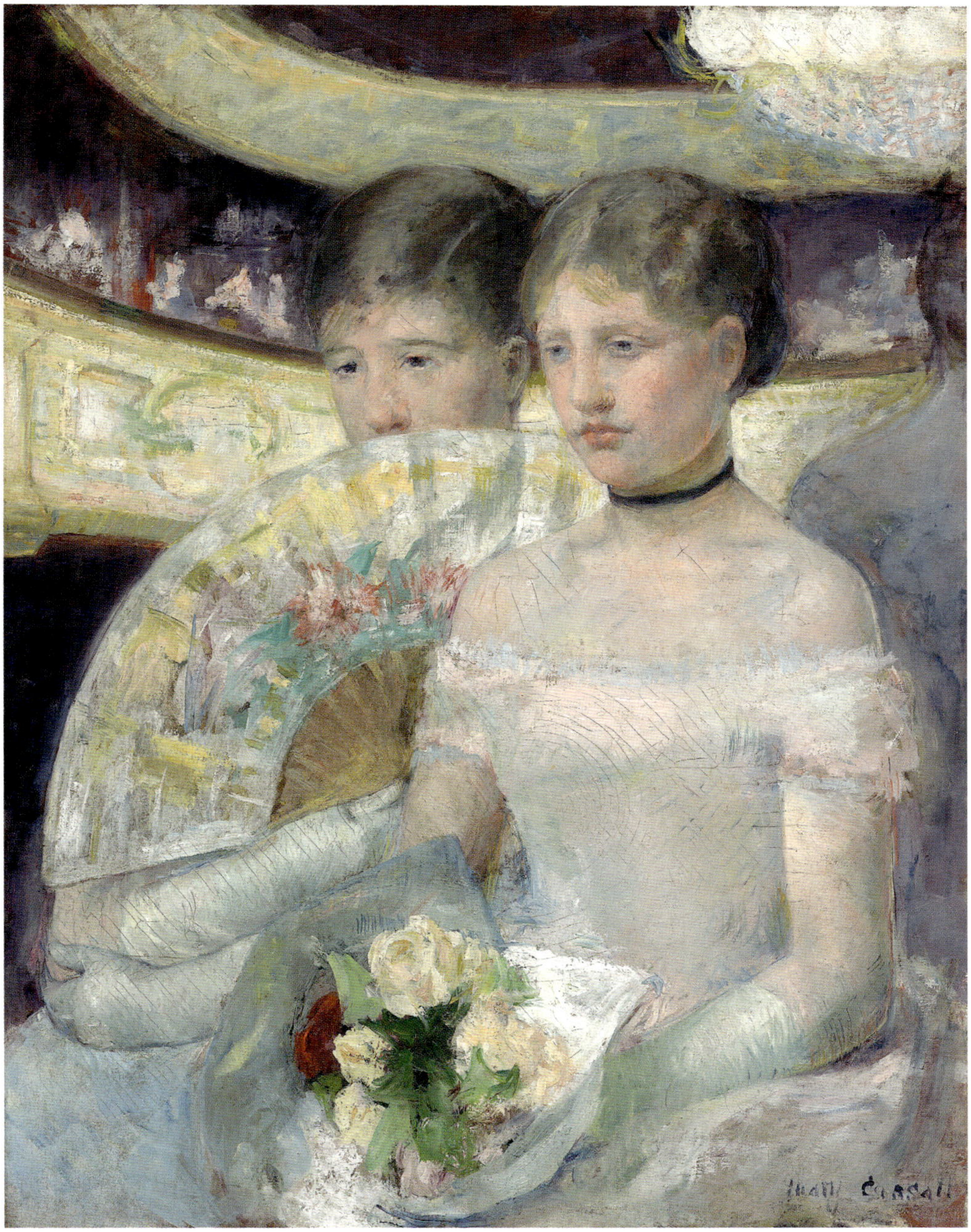

Mary Cassatt, *The Loge*, 1882. Washington, D.C., National Gallery of Art

Renoir and Mary Cassatt left us paintings of men and women looking out onto the stage. However, in these works the backdrop is not the Opéra Le Peletier but the Opéra Garnier, which replaced the former when it was destroyed by a fire. Built as it was of wood and plaster, it was made to perish and it was just a matter of time, like the fine, delicate beauties in the novels of the time. And the time came on 28 October 1873, when fire consumed it and all its fascination dissipated in the smoke-darkened sky.

12. The Longchamp Racecourse

Bois de Boulogne

Built on the insistence of the duke de Morny at the edge of the Bois de Boulogne, the Longchamp Racecourse was inaugurated in 1857 by Napoleon III and Empress Eugénie. Although the pastime of going to the races was imported from England—and both the winning horse of the first Grand Prix, instituted in 1863, and the liveliest description of the atmosphere at the event (in the novel *Esther Waters*, by the Irish writer George Moore) were English too—it spread quickly through France. All the society painters went, including those, like De Nittis, who tended to dilute the innovations of the Impressionist group to be more palatable: his *Races at Longchamp from the Grandstand* is the perfect reverse shot paired with

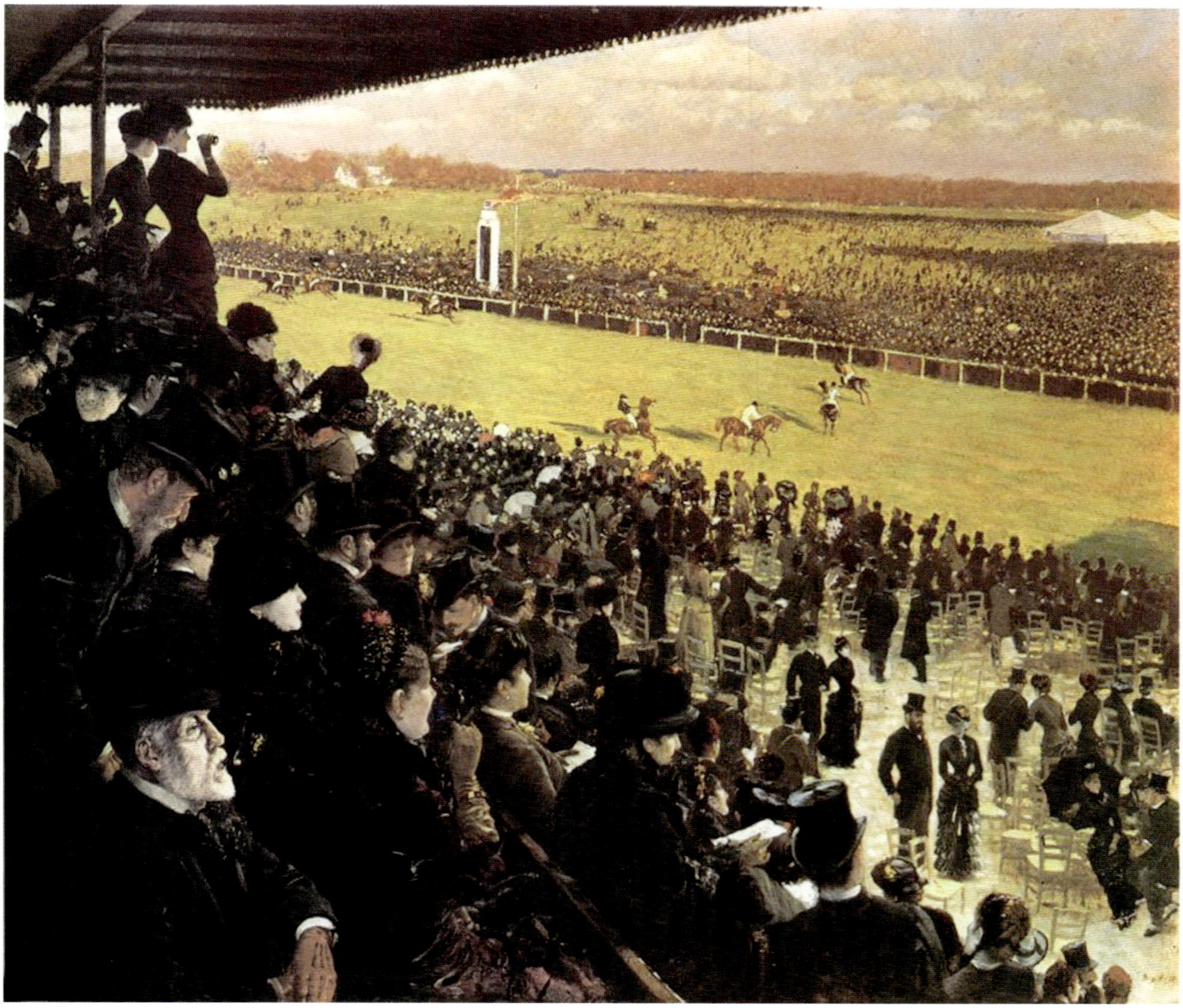

Giuseppe De Nittis, *The Races at Longchamp from the Grandstand*, 1882. Private Collection

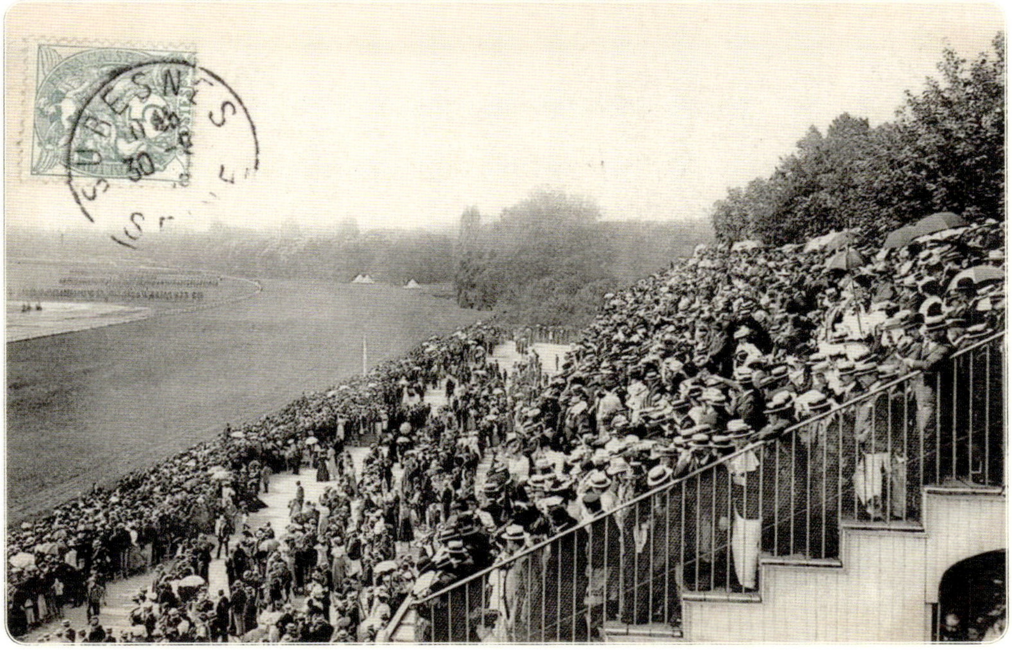

The Stands at Longchamp

Manet's *The Races in the Bois de Boulogne* and Degas' *Racehorses in Front of the Stands*, because it portrays what the other two leave out. As at the Opéra, the static conventionality of the public, the subject of De Nittis' painting, was of far less interest to Degas than the main characters of the event. Here, one could have said of him that, like certain excessively continent sovereigns, he preferred horses to ladies.

There is a highly detailed account of one of these events in Chapter 11 of *Nanà*:

> A long shiver ran through the crowd, while a fresh peal from the bell announced the arrival of the horses upon the racecourse. At this Nana got up and stood on one of the seats of her carriage so as to obtain a better view. [...] At this last feverish moment the course was empty and closed by gray barriers, between the posts of which stood a line of policemen. [...] In the middle landscape, as she lowered her eyes, she saw the field swarming with vast numbers of people, some on tiptoe, others perched on carriages, and all heaving and jostling in sudden passionate excitement. Horses were neighing; tent canvases flapped, while equestrians urged their hacks forward amid a crowd of pedestrians rushing to get places along the barriers. When Nana turned in the direction of the stands on the other side the faces seemed diminished, and the dense masses of heads were only a confused and motley array, filling gangways, steps and terraces and looming in deep, dark, serried lines against the sky. [...] Suddenly a cheering influence warmed the hundred thousand souls who covered this part of the plain like insects swarming madly under the vast expanse of heaven. The sun, which had been hidden for about a quarter of an hour, made his appearance again and shone out amid a perfect sea of light.[24]

Both women and men liked to put themselves on display at these events; many of them found their ruin there. Longchamp conveys a bit of both the grandeur and the wretchedness of the second Empire.

Edgar Degas, *Racehorses in Front of the Stands (The Parade)*, 1866–1868. Paris, Musée d'Orsay

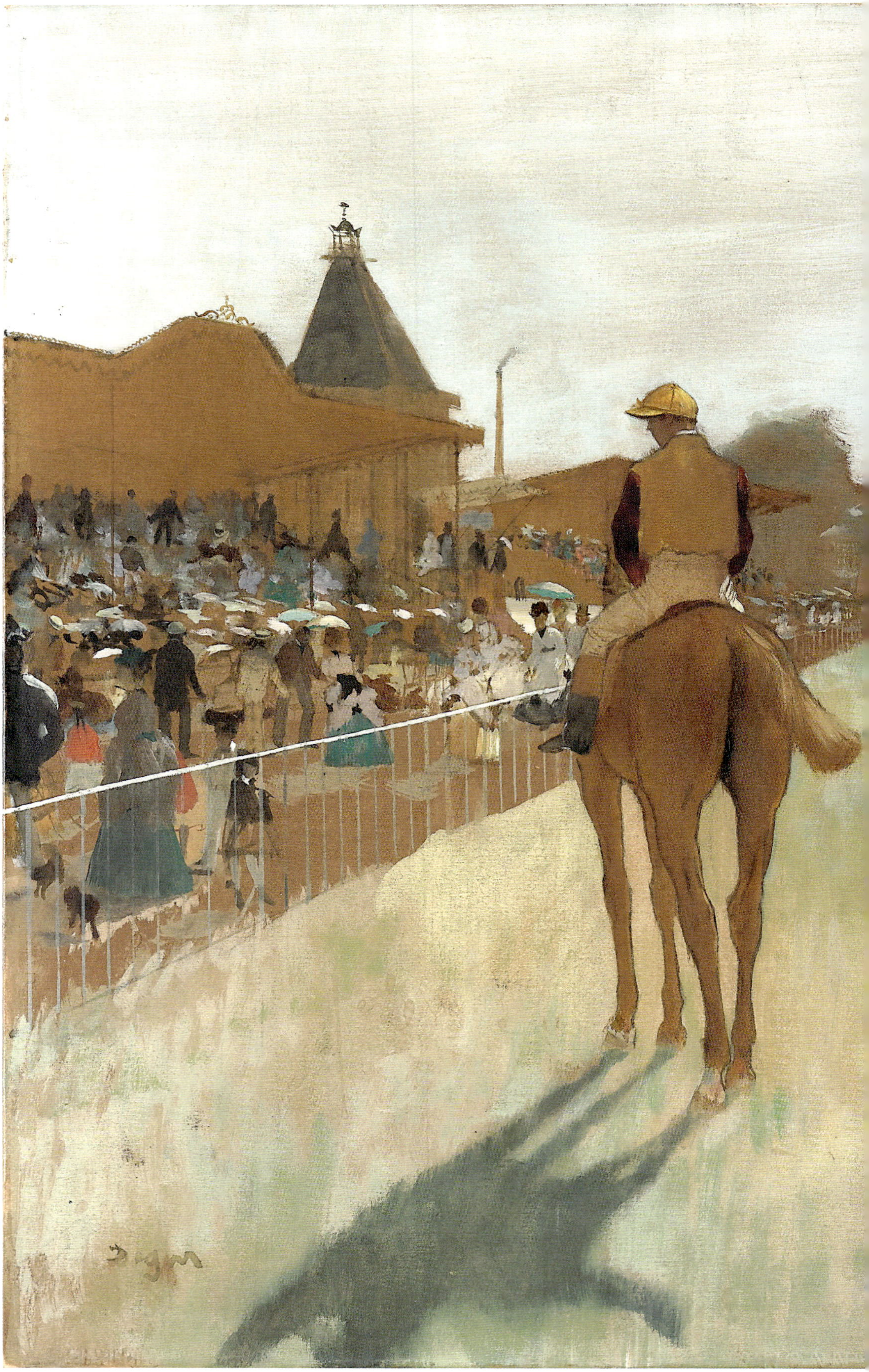

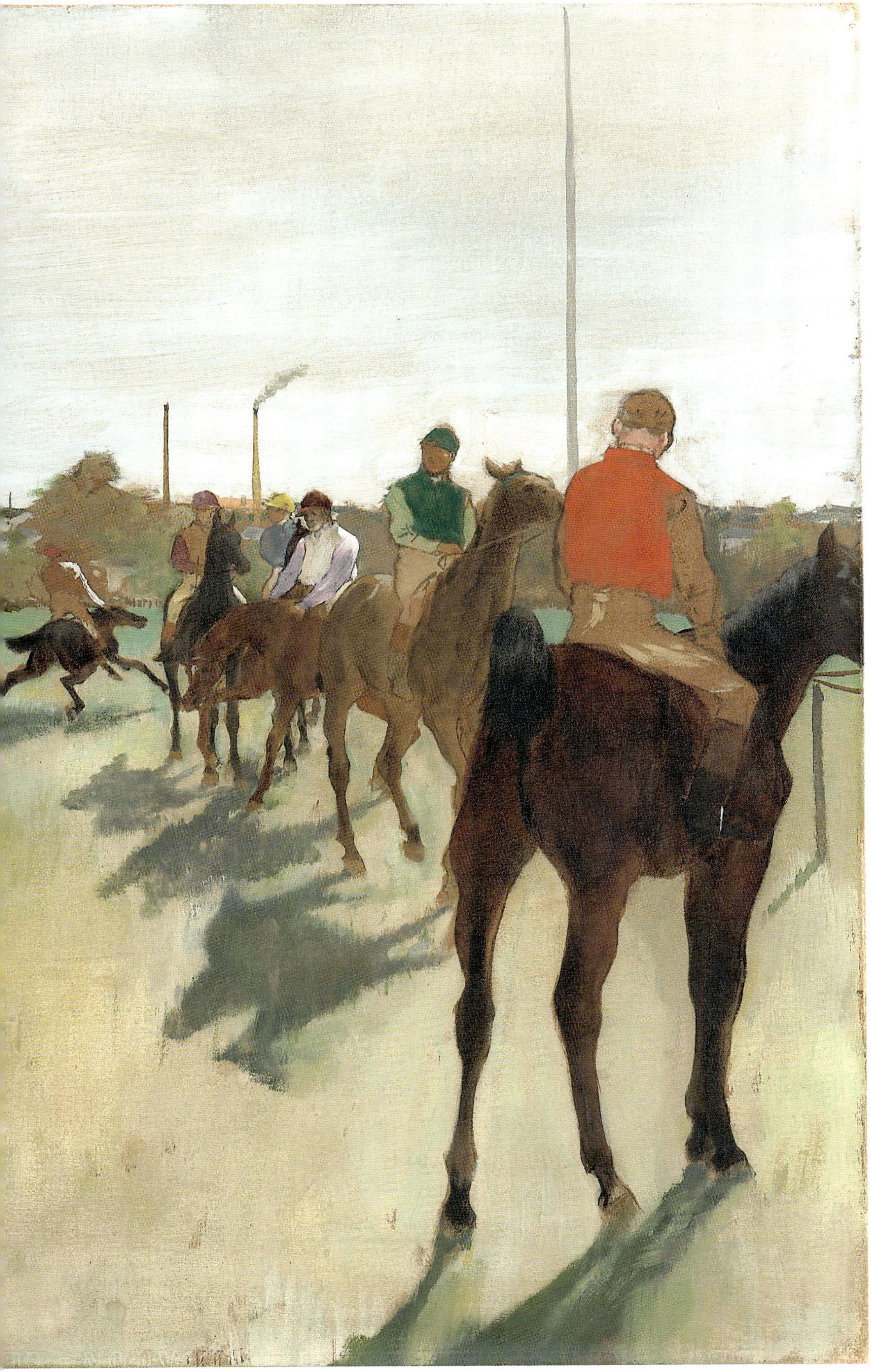

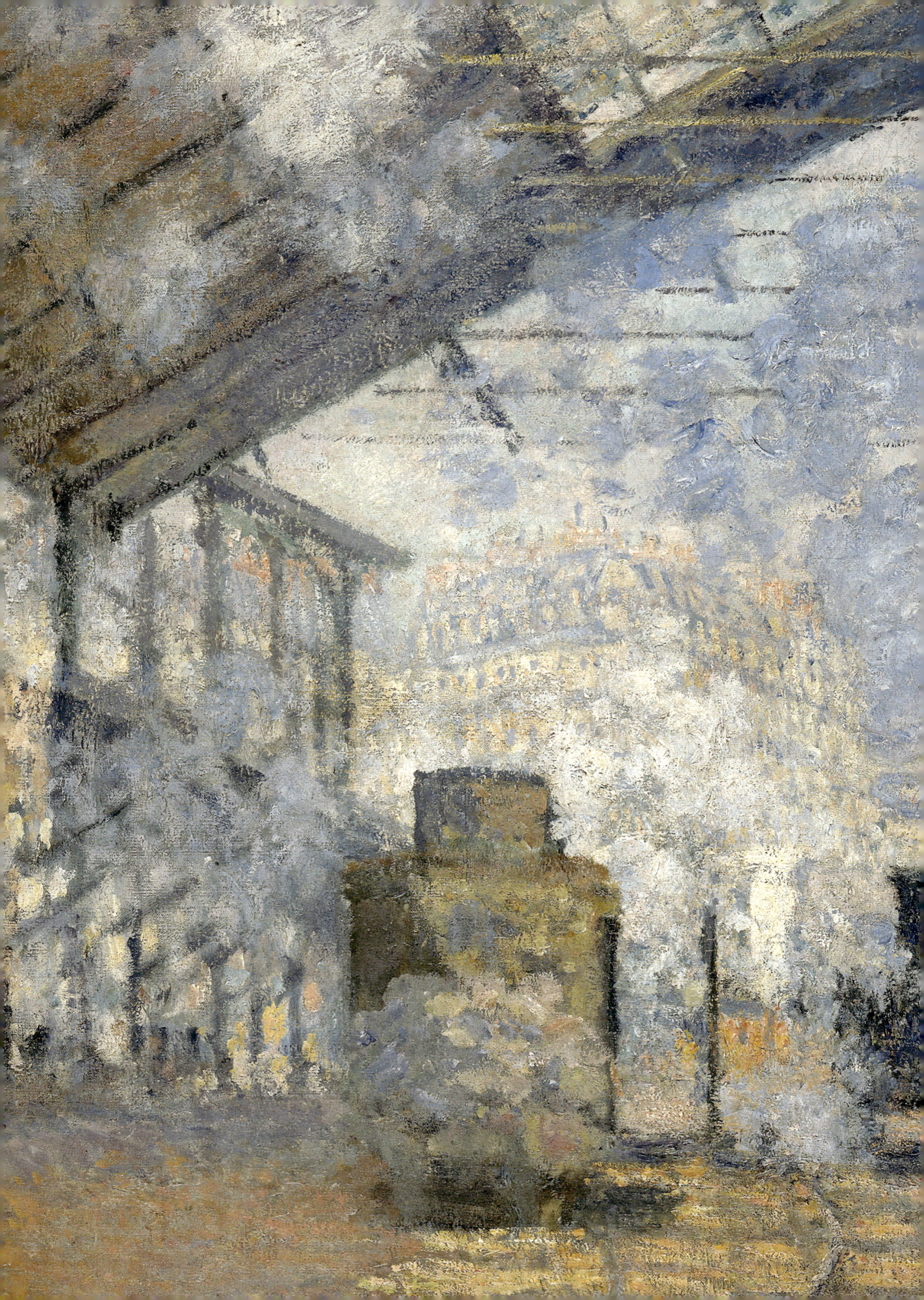

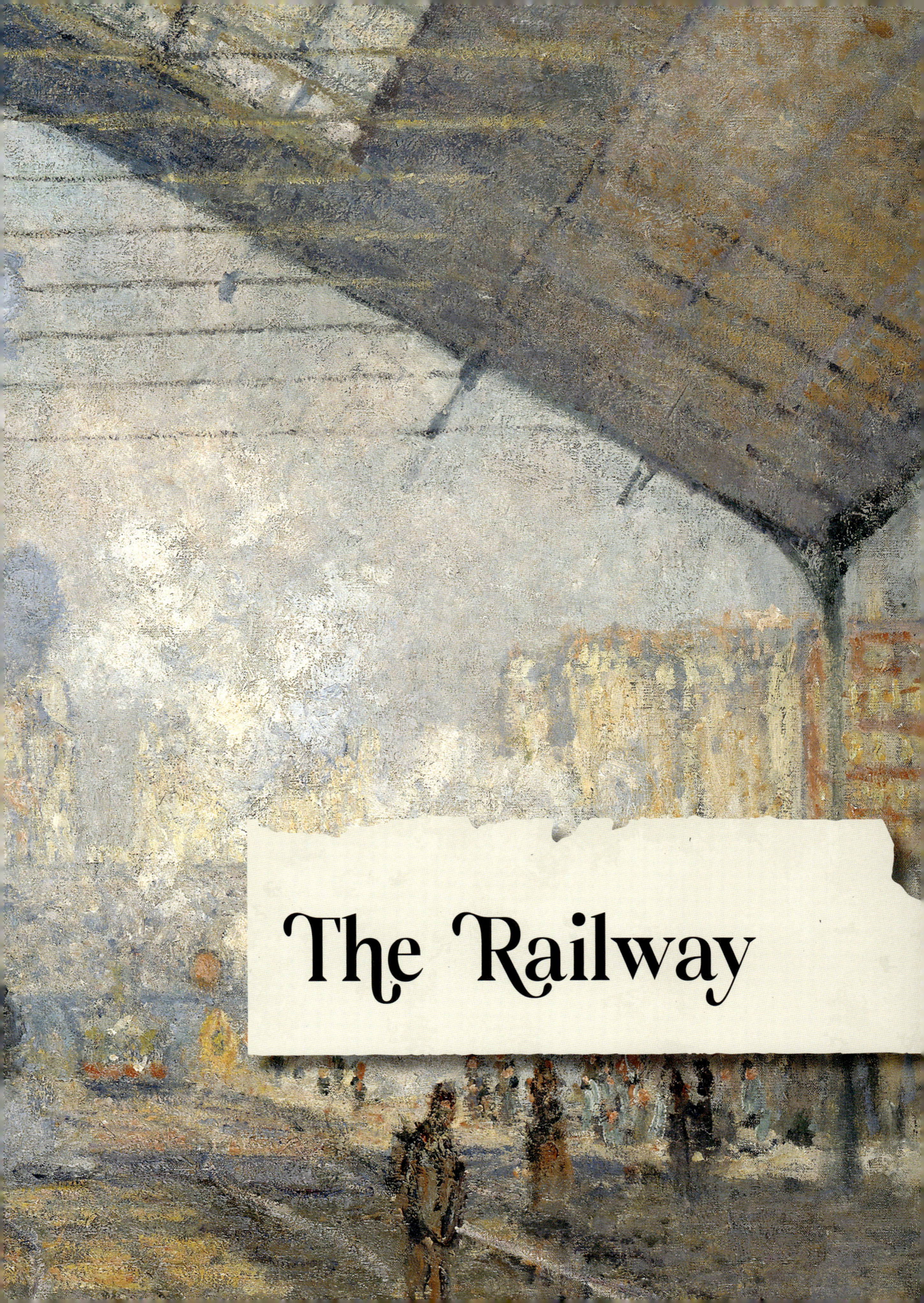

The Railway

13. The Saint-Lazare Station

13 rue d'Amsterdam

Impressionist art would not be what it was without the invention of the locomotive: it presupposes it, no less than it presupposes Corot, Delacroix and the Barbizon School. The railways, which were massively expanded under the Second Empire, allowed Bougival, Argenteuil, Marly-le-Roi and countless villages and little places along the Seine to turn themselves into holiday destinations, which attracted the brushes of the Impressionists with their moving spectacle of a vague and colourful crowd. Neither La Grenouillère nor Maison Fournaise, favourite subjects of Monet and Renoir, would have existed without the railway. Wherever the train passed, up popped cafés, restaurants, terraces and everything else for bourgeois Parisian pastimes and amusement. Following the tracks, you could also go to Fontainebleau for a picnic and Normandy for a beach holiday. Modern life now spilled over far beyond the Île-de-France. One of the most enchanting journeys was the one from Dieppe to Paris, which was described by George Moore in *Memoirs of My Dead Life*:

> We moved along the quays, into the suburbs, and then into a quiet garden country of little fields and brooks and hillsides breaking into cliffs. The fields and the hills were still

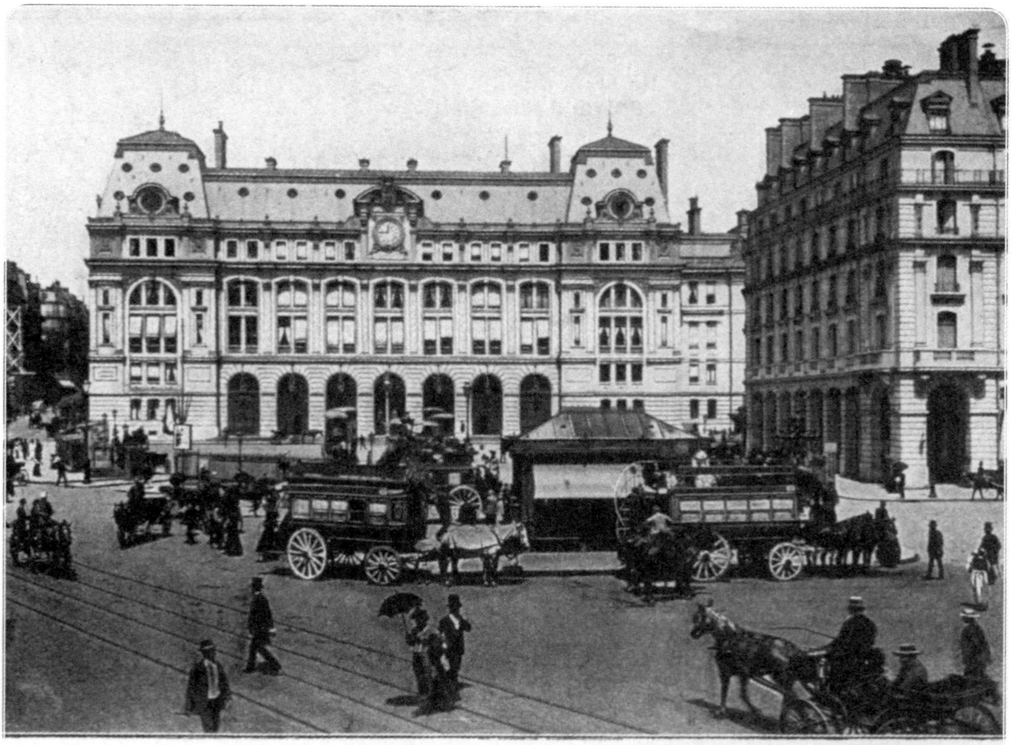

Phot. Neurdein.

FAÇADE DE LA GARE SAINT-LAZARE (BATIMENT OUEST).

pp. 76–77
Claude Monet, *The Gare Saint-Lazare*, 1877. Paris, Musée d'Orsay

Facade of Saint-Lazare Station

shadowless and grey, and even the orchards in bloom seemed sad. But what shall I say of their beauty when the first faint lights appeared, when the first rose clouds appeared above the hills? There is no such journey in the world as the journey from Dieppe to Paris on a fine May morning. [...] the river winding about islands and through fields in which stood solitary poplar-trees, formerly haunts of Corot and Daubigny. I could see the spots where they had set their easels: that slight rise with the solitary poplar for Corot, that rich riverbank and shady backwater for Daubigny. [...] and at every moment the river grew more serene, more gracious, it passed its arms about a flat, green-wooded island, on which there was a rookery; and sometimes we saw it ahead of us, looping up the verdant landscape as if it were a gown, running through it like a white silk ribbon, and over there the green gown disappearing in fine muslin vapours, drawn about the low horizon.[25]

Artists took the train as well: their pilgrimage in search of interesting subjects was by rail; the train ticket their scallop shell. When inspiration or economic need required it, they could disperse to all the regions of France: from Gare Saint-Lazare or Gare du Nord, Monet could visit his friends Boudin and Jongkind in Le Havre or Honfleur, Bazille in Montpellier, Cézanne in Aix, Renoir in Cagnes. But the railway did not just give the group a way of finding interesting subjects, it provided one as well: the swarming crowd and the thick steam coming out of the smokestack were also new pictorial themes. The one who got the most from it was Monet, who portrayed the Saint-Lazare station in a series of paintings. It seems that one day he went to the director of the train station all dressed up and introduced himself as simply a 'painter'. The director, struck by his aristocratic manner, agreed at once to stop all the trains and fill the machines with coal, to give the artist all the steam he liked. Monet painted various views of Saint-Lazare; one of the most famous is now in the Musée d'Orsay.

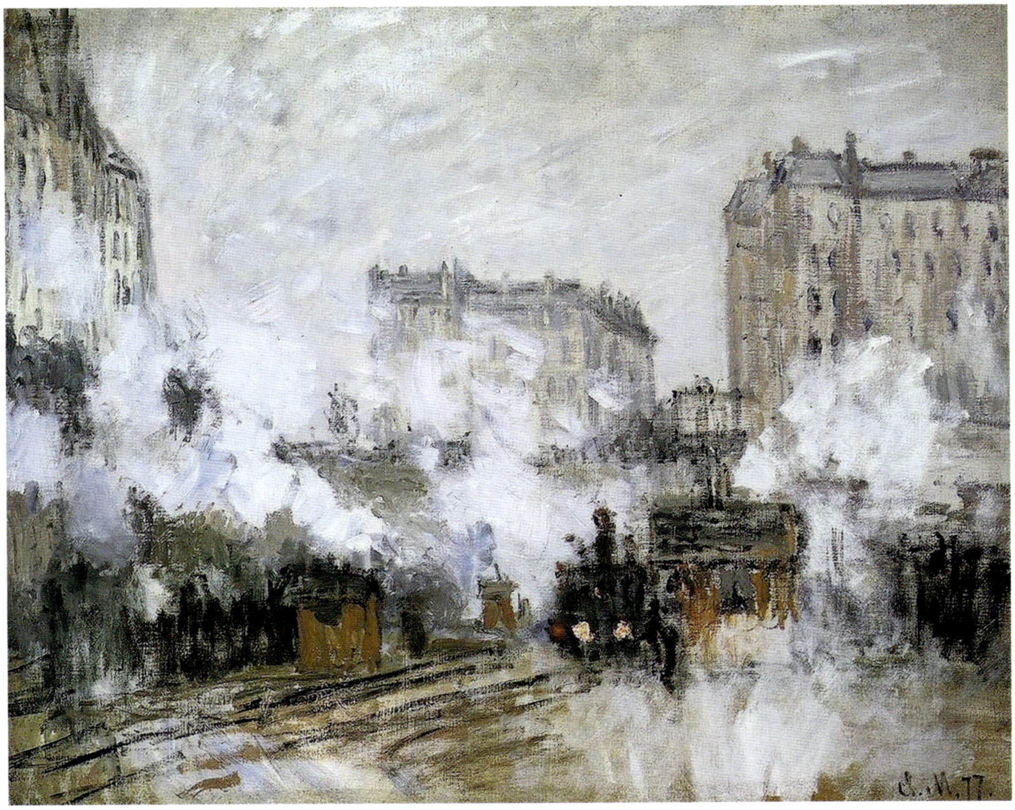

Claude Monet, *Arrival of a Train at the Gare Saint-Lazare*, 1877. Private Collection

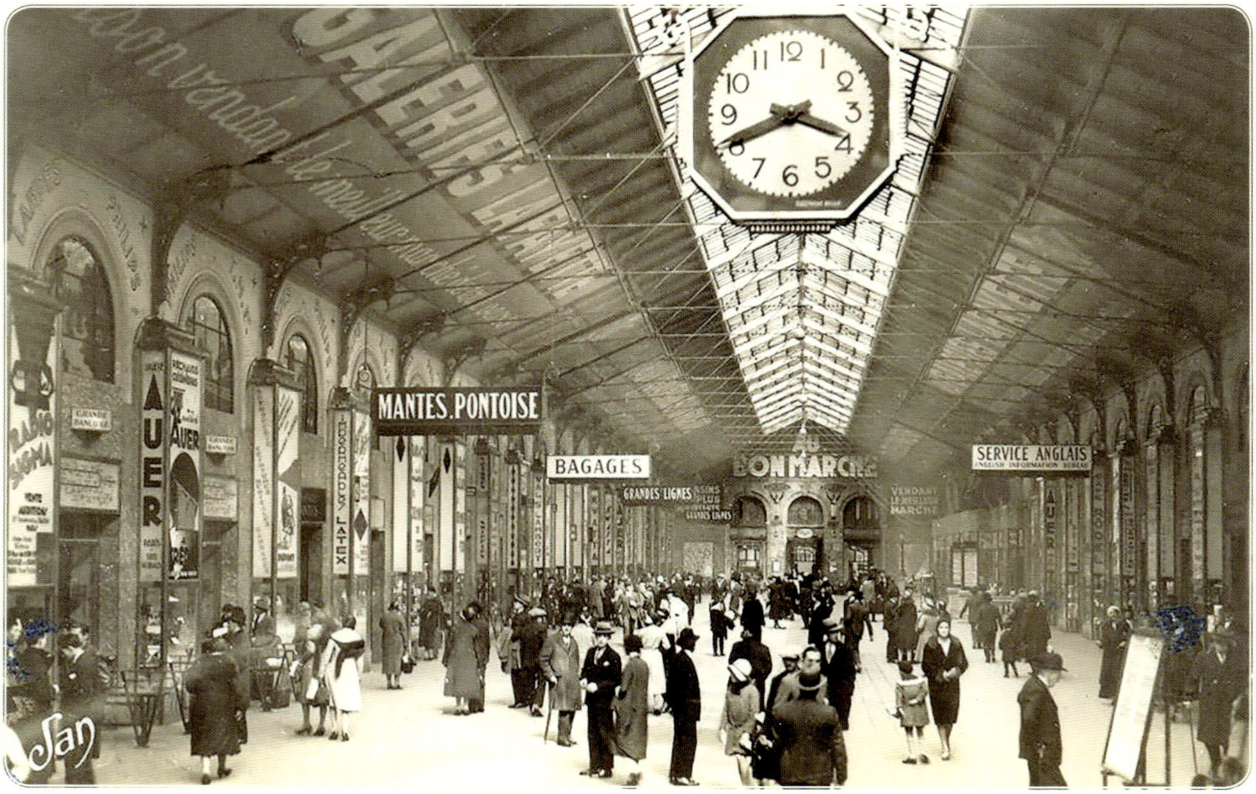

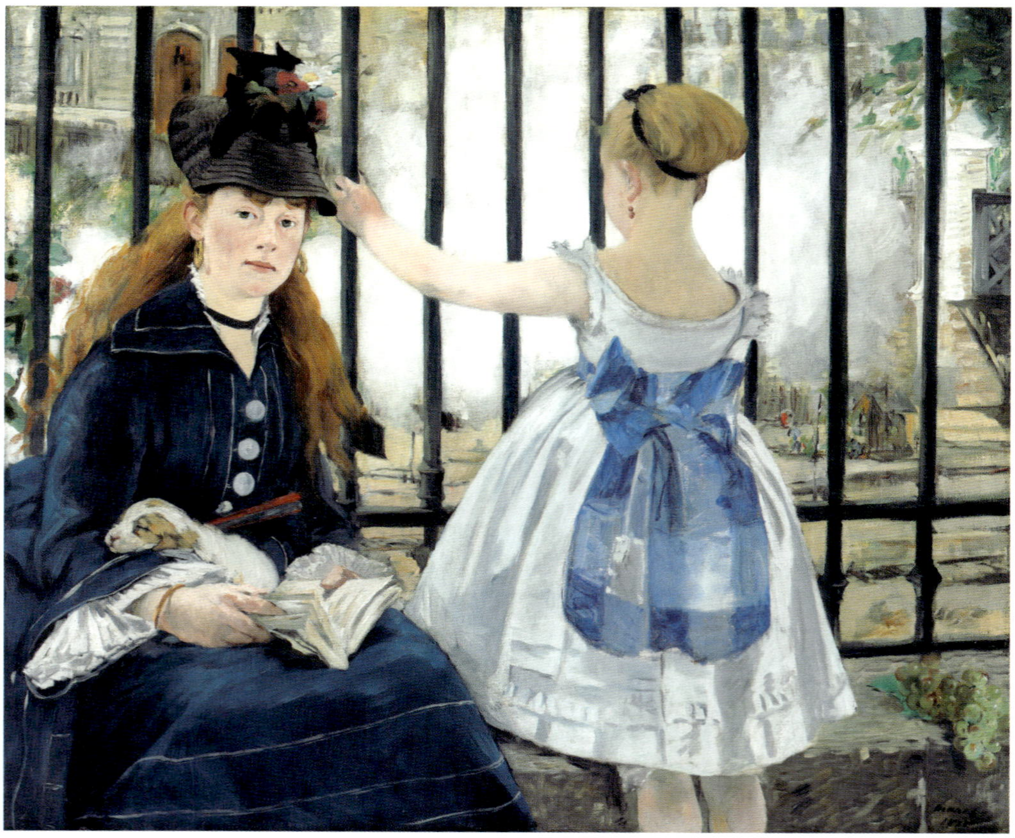

Saint-Lazare State, Salle des Pas Perdus (Lobby)

Édouard Manet, *The Railway*, 1873. Washington, D.C., National Gallery of Art

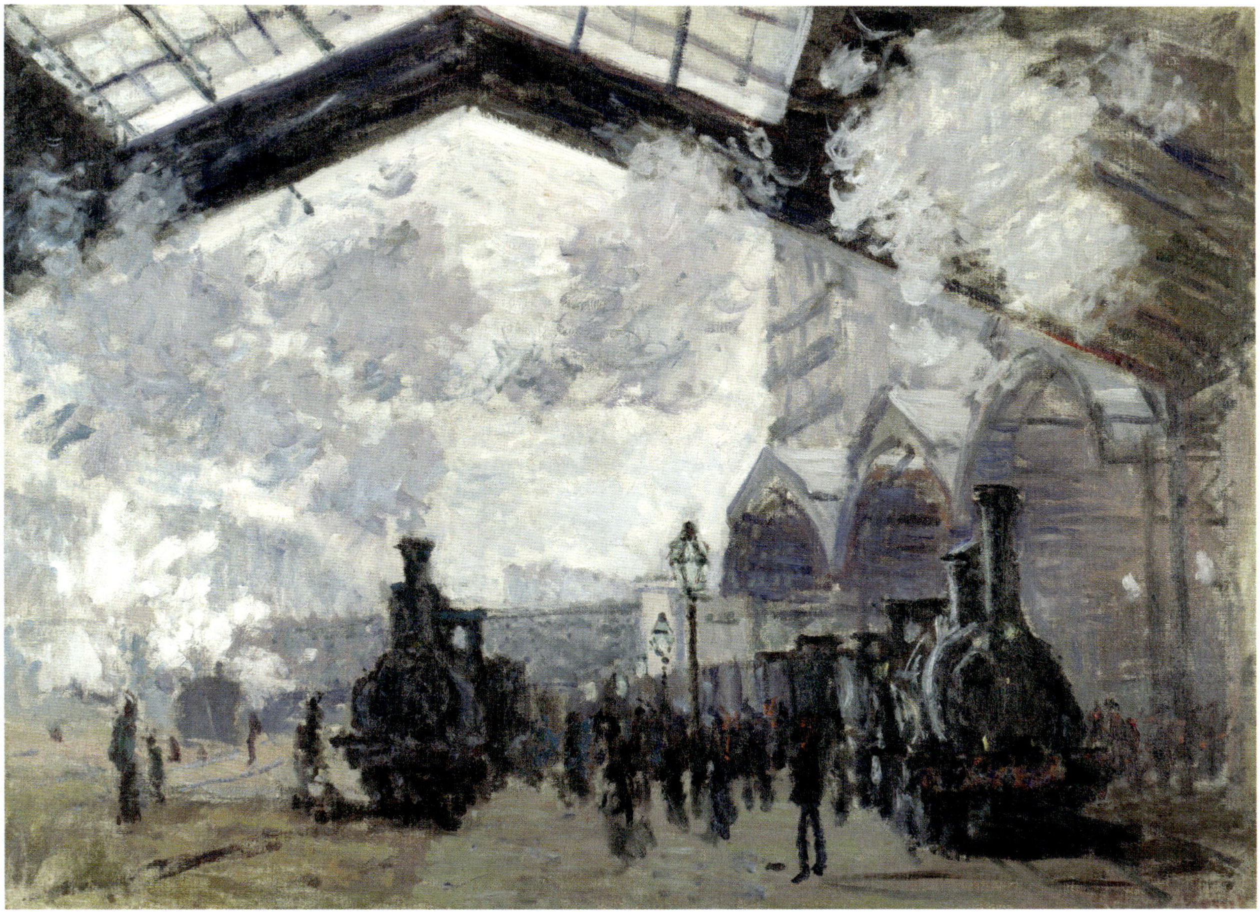

Claude Monet,
The Gare Saint-Lazare,
1877. London, National Gallery

Train stations were magnificent buildings at the time and so overflowing with an eclectic mix of pinnacles, frescoes, Neoclassical pilasters and slender columns as to justify the expression coined by Théophile Gautier, 'cathedrals of modern humanity'. And at base, cathedrals they were, but of a new hard-working, industrial society, temples containing all the opulence once reserved for the house of God. Like emblems of contemporary life, they were as loved by Impressionist painters as by novelists like Zola, who set one of his most famous works there, *The Beast Within*, in which he describes the tumultuous movement between the tracks:

> A newsvendor was valiantly trying to persuade people to buy his last remaining copies of the evening paper; a few passengers still stood on the platform, finishing their cigarettes. All of a sudden everyone got into the train. Two inspectors walked along it from each end, closing the doors with a bang ... The train was ready to leave. A fine drizzle had begun to fall. Trains continued to thread their way through the rain-swept night; all that could be seen were moving row of lights from the carriage windows. Green lights shone through the gloom; here and there a lineman's lamp bobbed and curtsied close to the ground. All else was darkness, a vast impenetrable darkness, save for the two train sheds of the mainline station, illumined by the pallid glow from the gas lamps.[26]

Paris in 1840

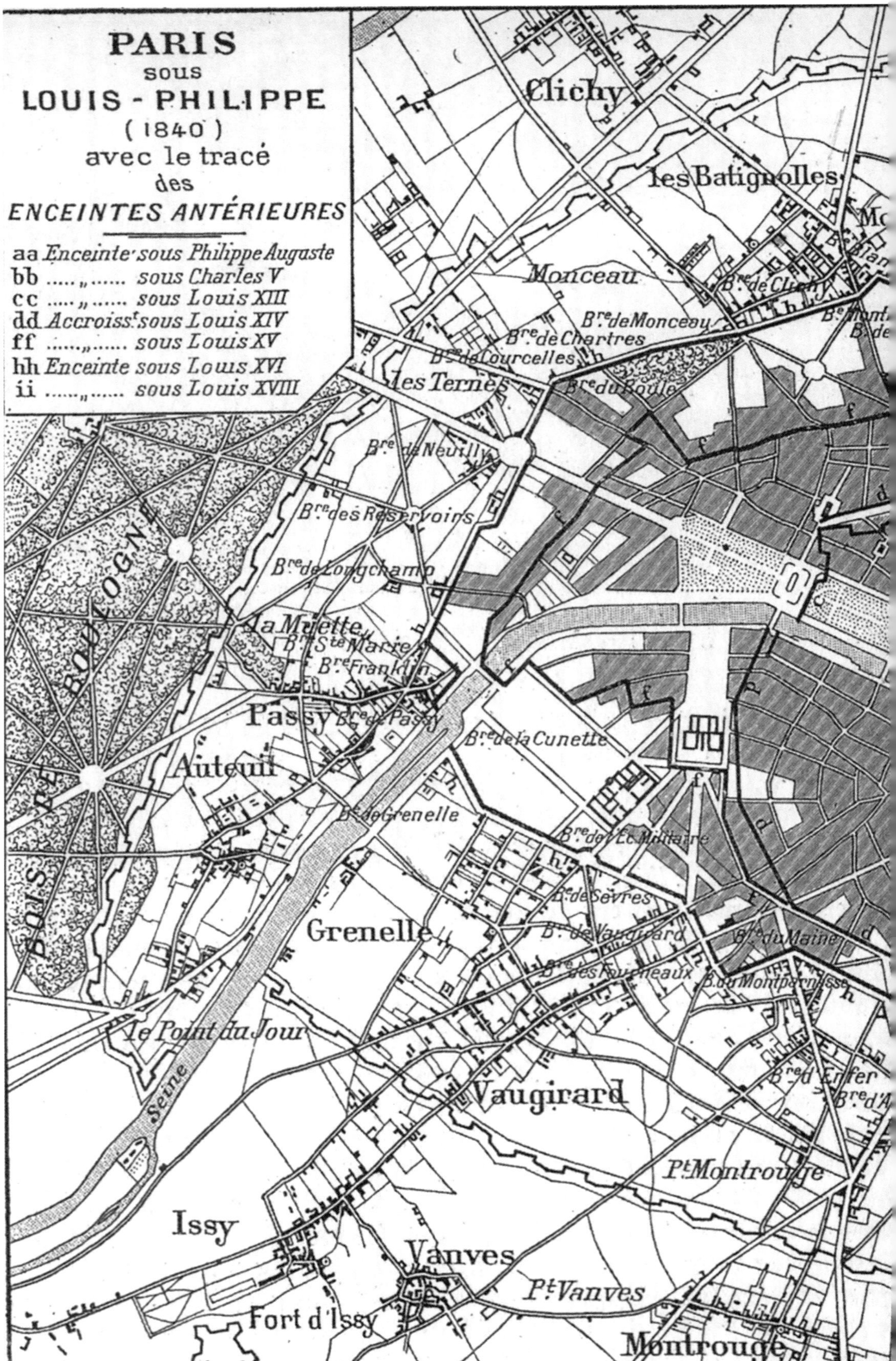

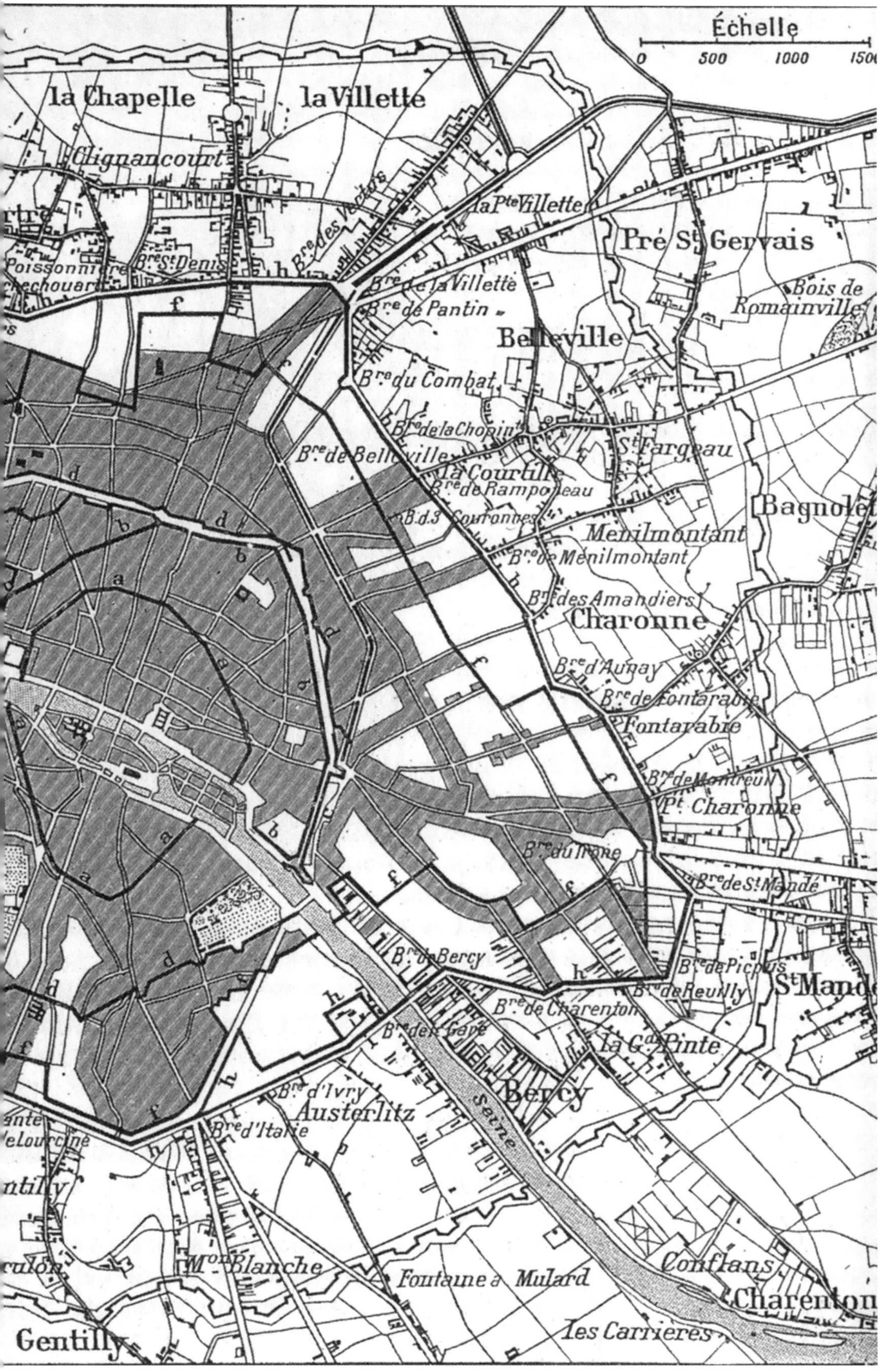

pp. 84–85
Claude Monet, *Chailly Road in the Forest of Fontainebleau*, *c.* 1865.
Paris, Musée d'Orsay

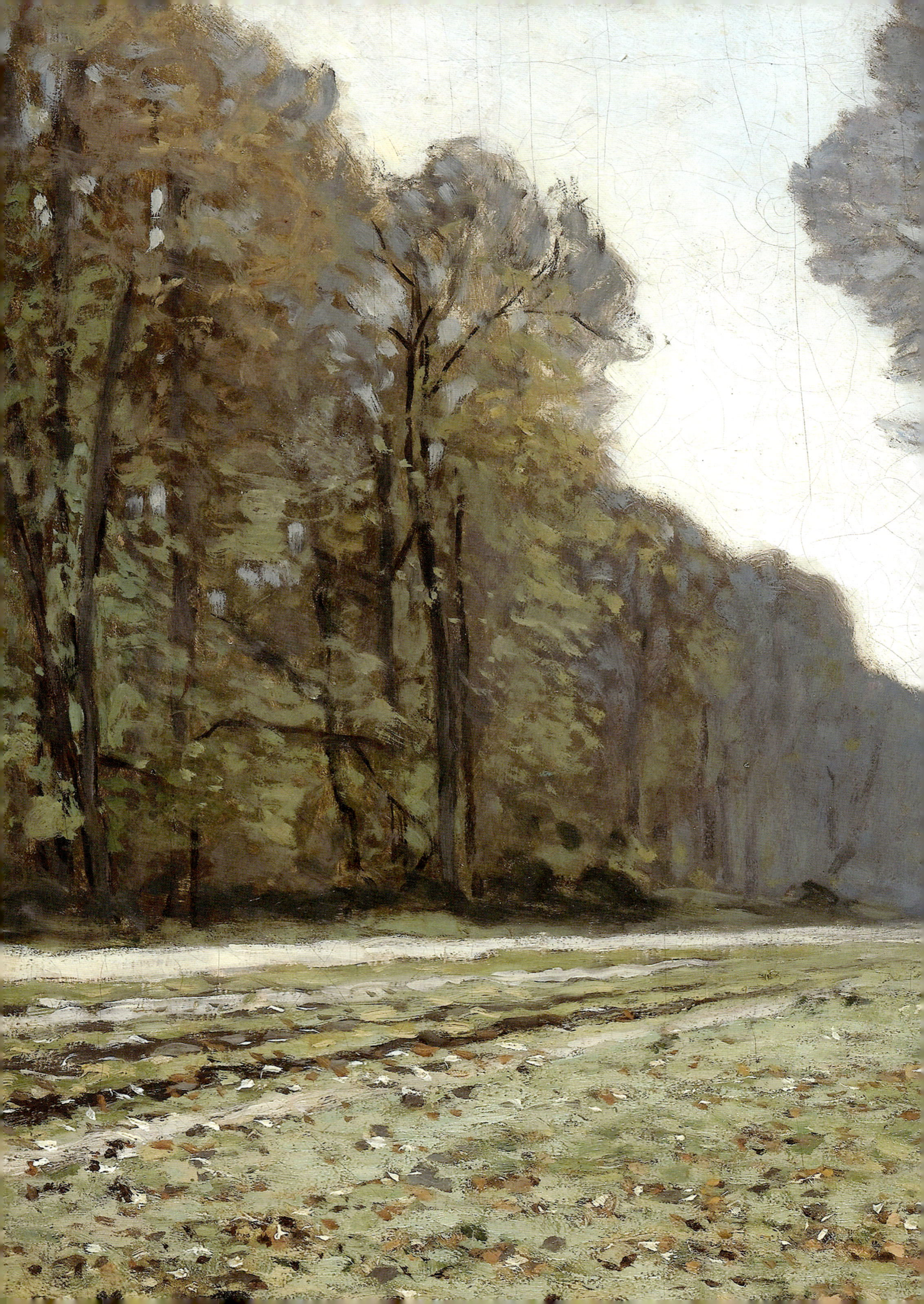

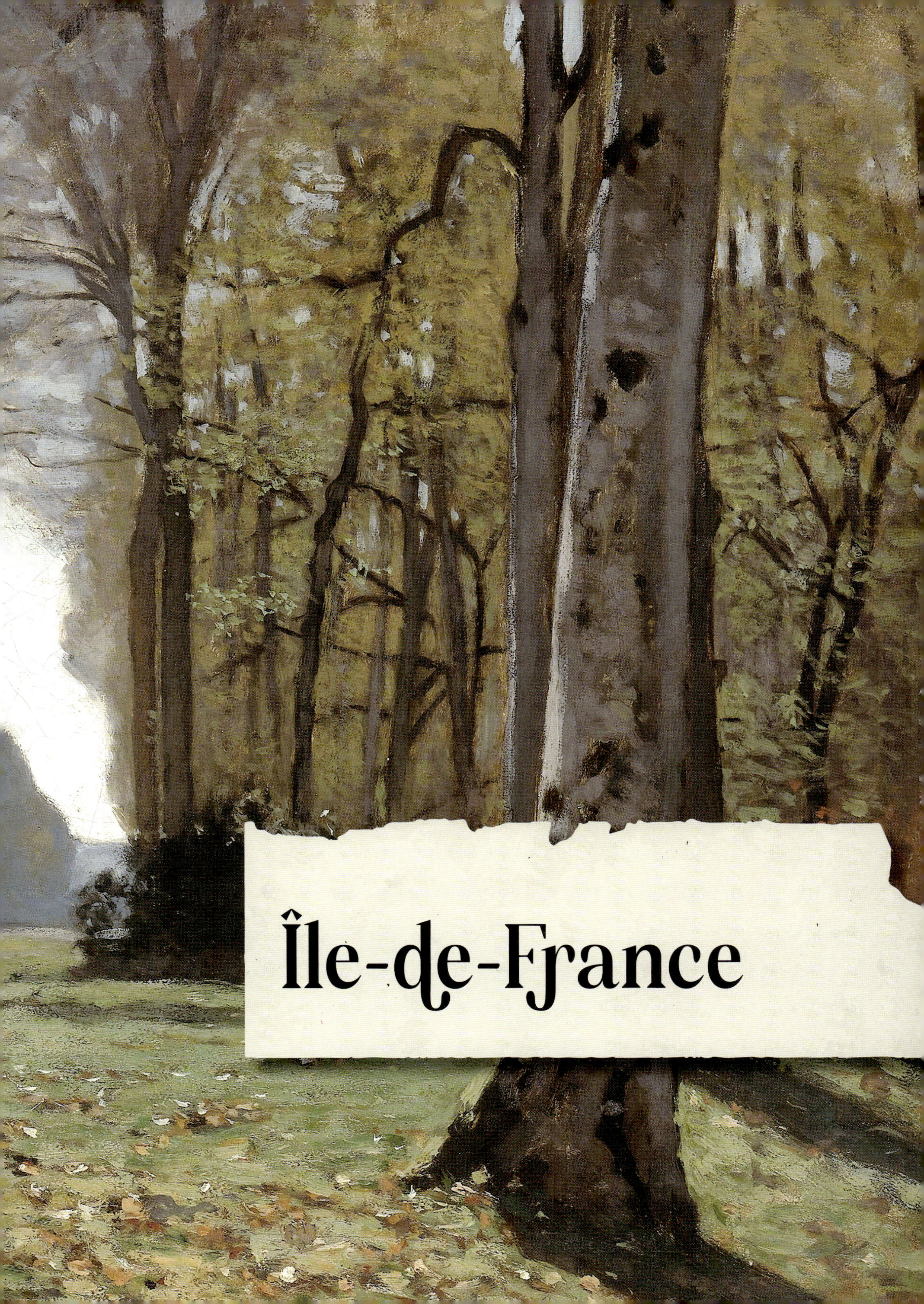

Île-de-France

14. The Banks of the Seine: Argenteuil, Bougival, Marly-le-Roi

In 1837, the construction of the track connecting the Saint-Lazare station to that of Saint-Germain-en-Laye made the banks of the Seine the perfect destination for Sunday outings. There, one could dance, swim and row. All of Paris swarmed there: the masses were joined by junior government employees and modest shopkeepers with their families, who went there every week to break up the particular monotony of daily life that so many nineteenth-century writers, from

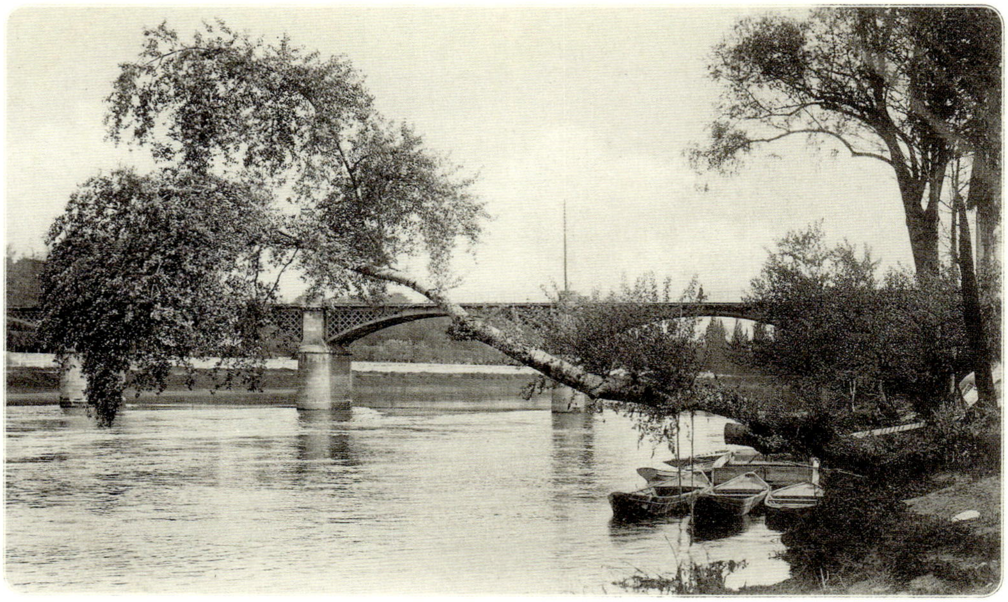

The bridge over the Seine at Chatou

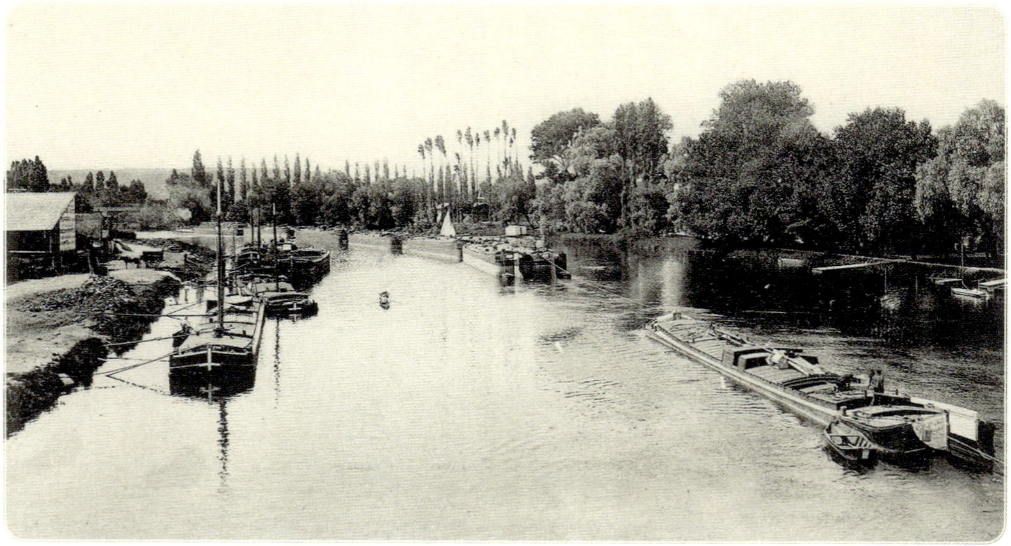

Boats towed along the Seine

p. 87
Claude Monet, *The Bridge over the Seine at Argenteuil*, 1874. Paris, Musée d'Orsay

Maupassant to Dostoevsky, elevated to a subject of art. For its regular visitors, this section of the river, where the current split around a series of delightful islets, had the poetic air of a rustic idyll, albeit a bit modest and flat. The first village that one came to along the railway was Argenteuil, which was almost a suburb, still rural, of Paris, brightened by a riot of sails and bridges that delighted the eye and helped one forget the conformist, grey backdrop of the city. Monet, who moved there in 1871, went to live in a cool little house with a beautiful garden, in which he had his portrait made by both Renoir and Manet. The friends were soon joined by Sisley and Pissarro as well.

It was in Argenteuil that the Impressionists discovered Impressionism. All they had needed was a problem with a solution that would allow them to develop and clarify their technique: and they found it in the quick flicker of light on the water, demeaned in paintings made in the academic tradition. The study of reflections confirmed their idea that all subjects presented themselves to the eye with colours that varied according to the environment and atmospheric conditions. In translating the fleeting nature of the flashes of light, their brushstrokes took on the elastic, vibrant character that, although differing from individual to individual, typified the entire group. Monet pushed himself further, to the point of having a miniature studio built on a boat (there is a portrait of him by Manet that shows him using it: *Monet Painting on His Studio Boat*), from which he could more easily observe the coming and going of the boats and the agile dance of

p. 88
Claude Monet, *The Artist's Garden in Argenteuil*, 1873. Washington, D.C., National Gallery of Art

Édouard Manet, *The Monet Family in Their Garden at Argenteuil*, 1874. New York, The Metropolitan Museum of Art

p. 89
Chatou seen from the 'Island of the Impressionists'

Édouard Manet, *Monet Painting on His Studio Boat*, 1874. Munich, Neue Pinakothek

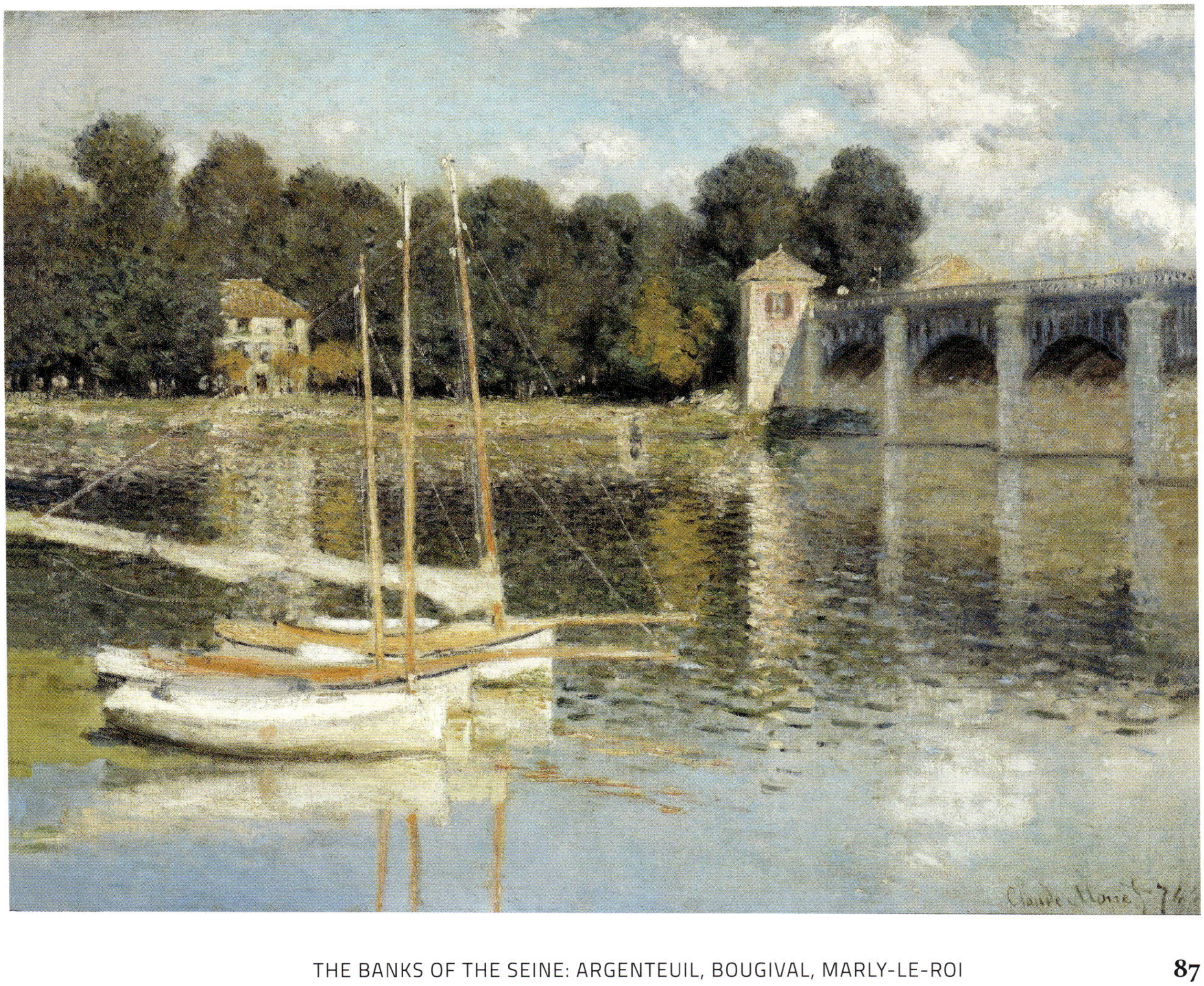

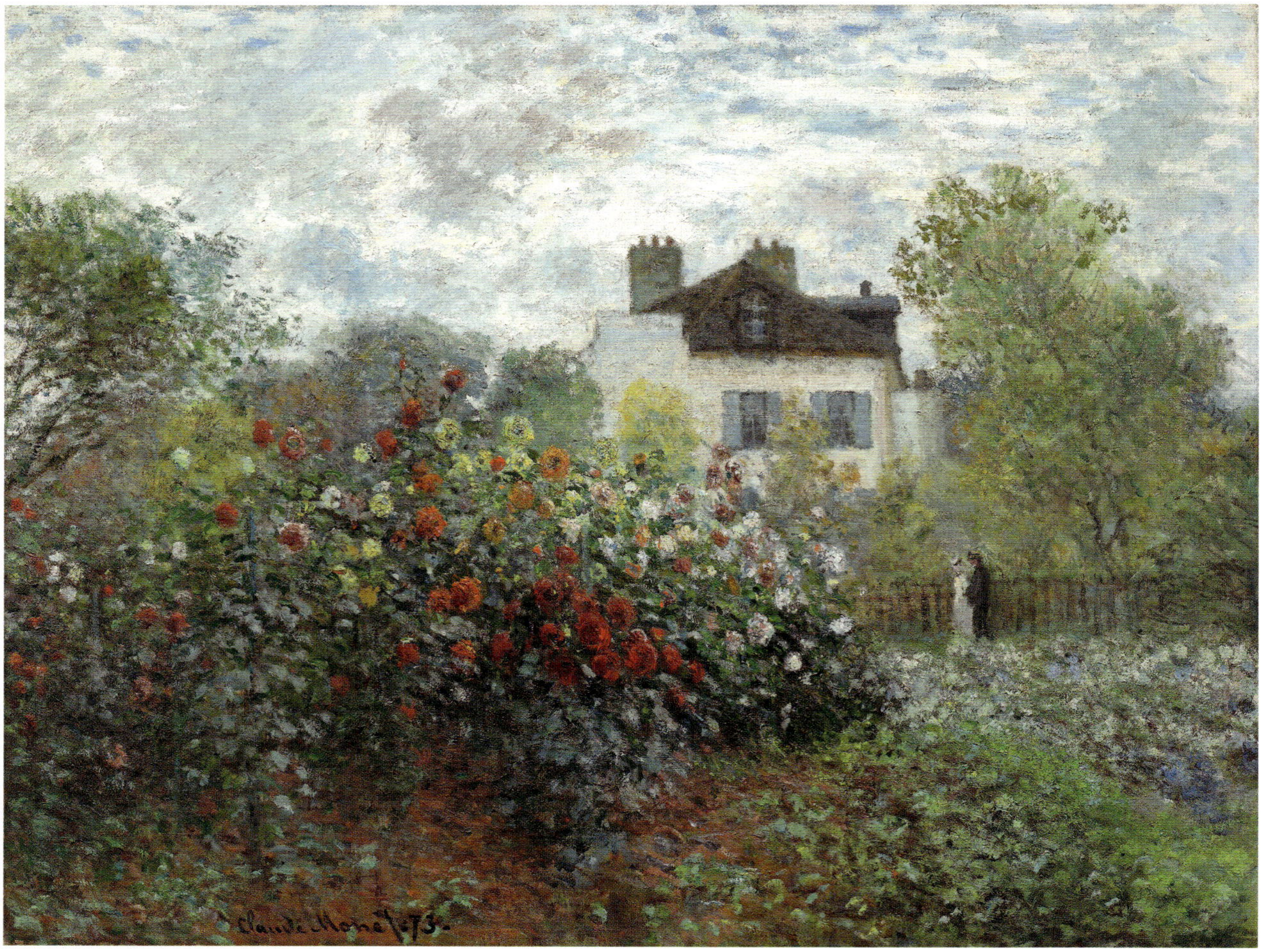

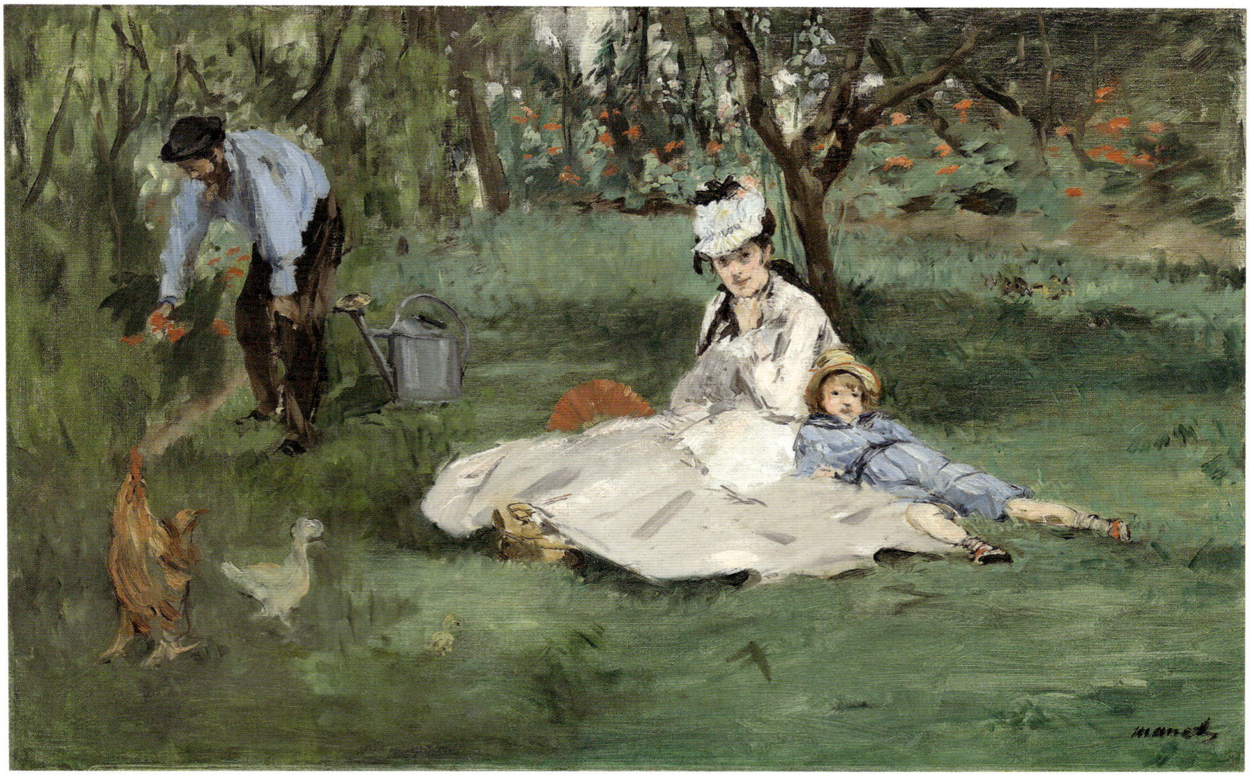
manet

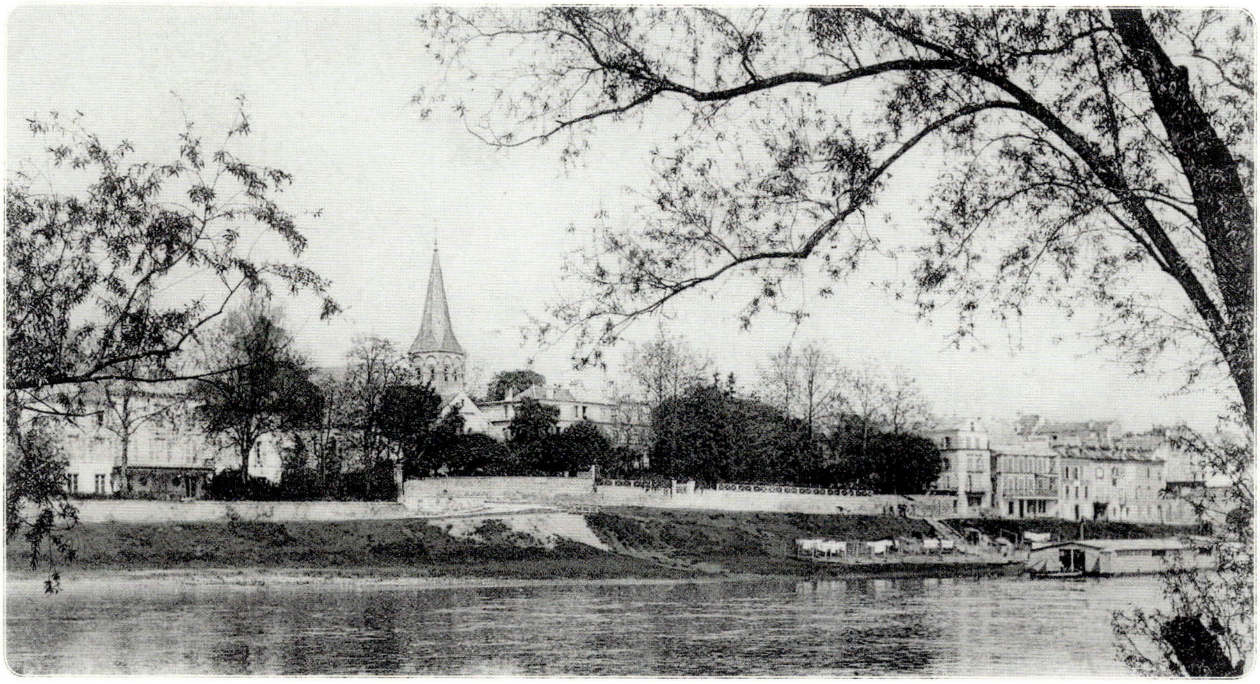

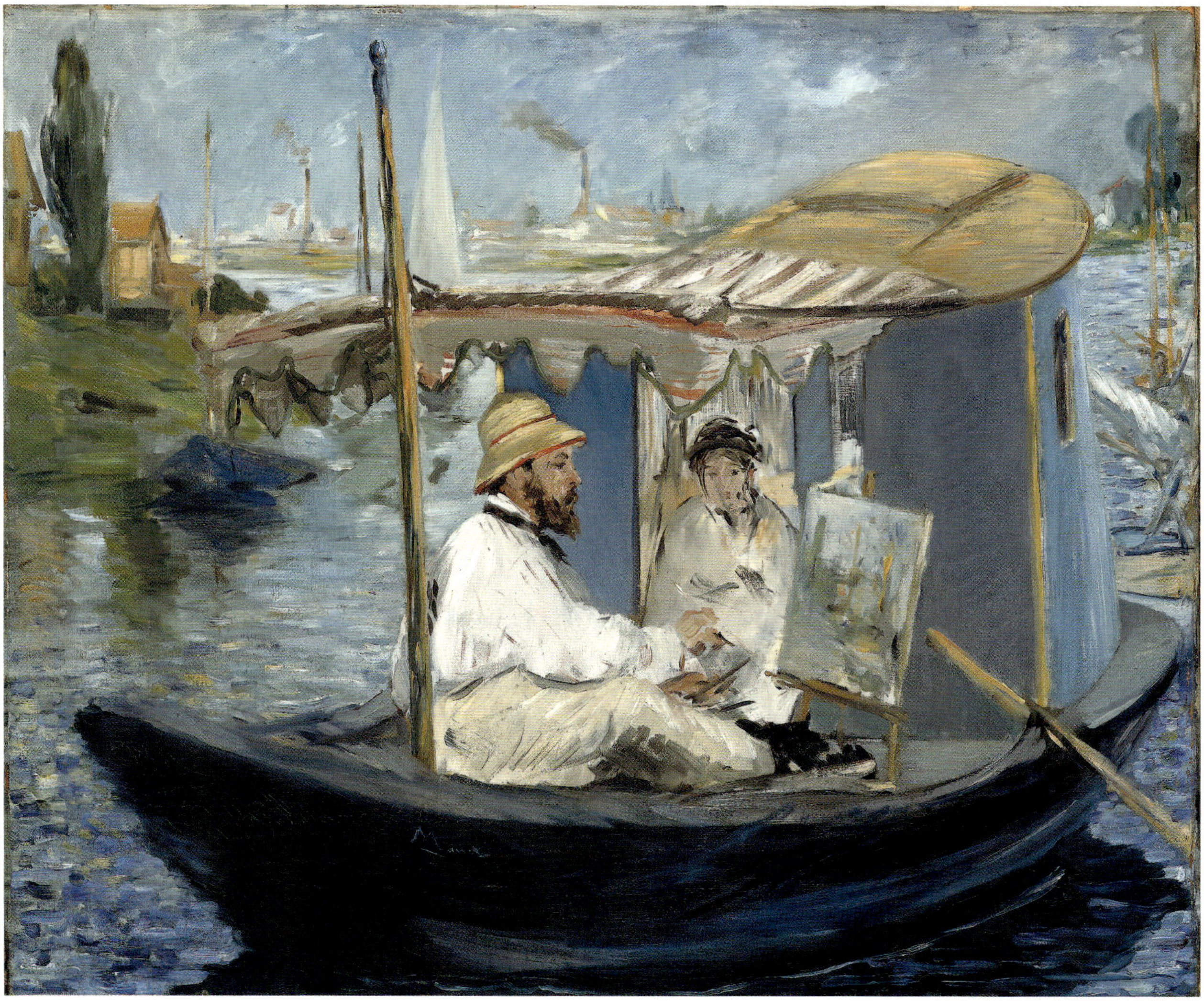

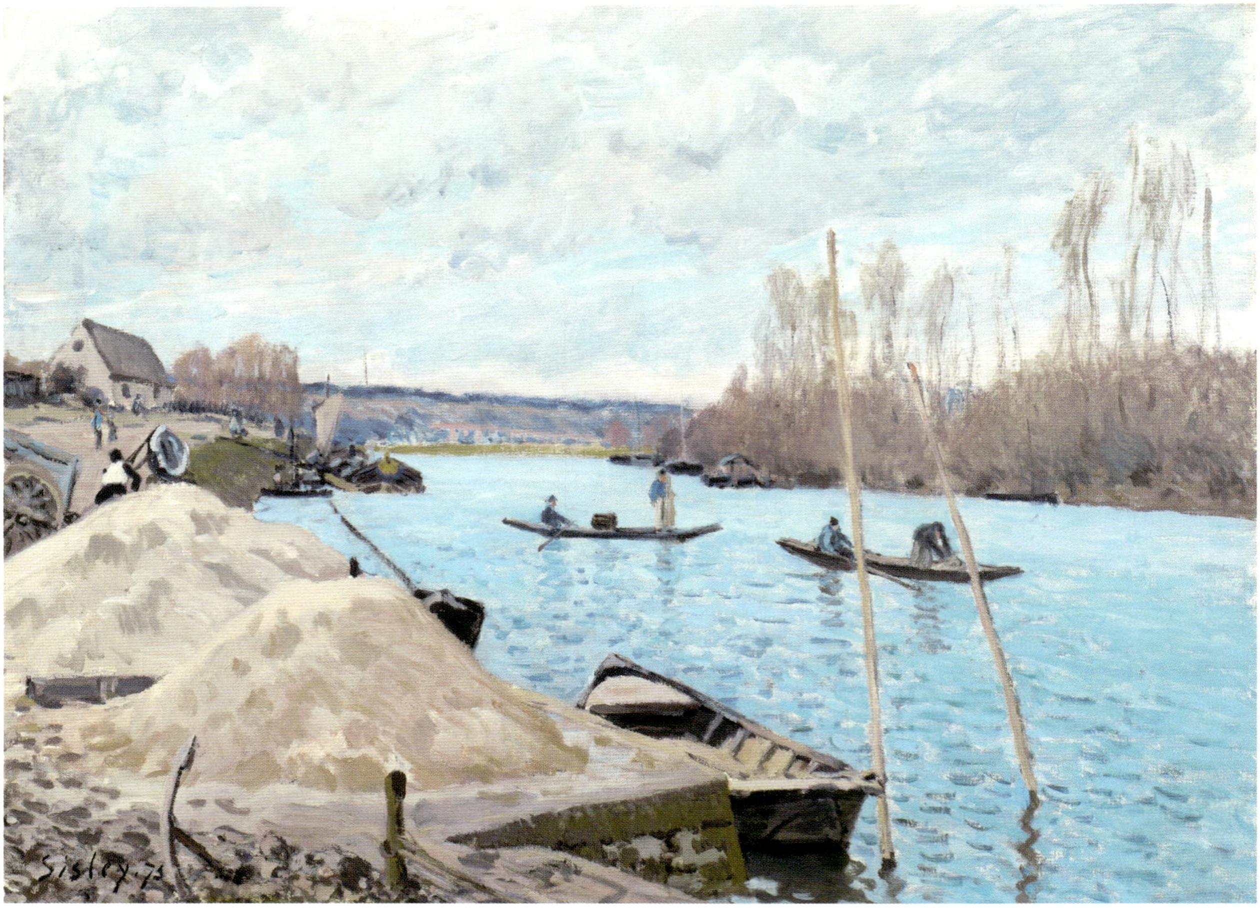

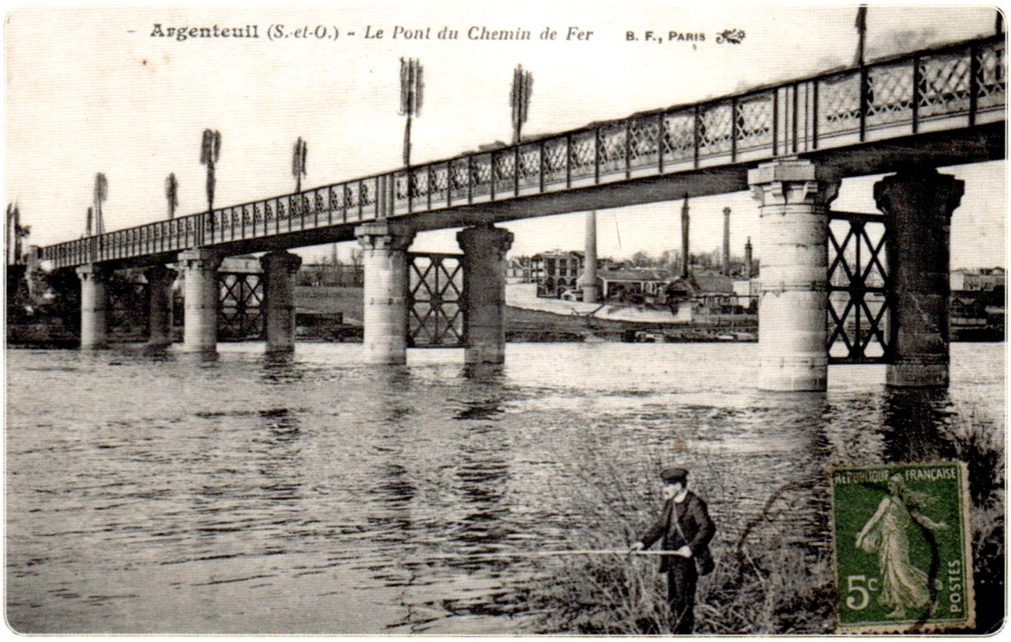

Alfred Sisley, *The Seine at Port-Marly, Piles of Sand*, 1875. Chicago, Art Institute of Chicago

The rail bridge at Argenteuil

p. 91
The locks on the Seine at Bougival

The Grande Rue at Argenteuil

Alfred Sisley, *The Grand-Rue at Argenteuil*, 1872. Norwich, Norwich Castle Museum

Alfred Sisley, *Footbridge at Argenteuil*, 1872. Paris, Musée d'Orsay

light on the water. This oddity, which seemed made to confirm the bathers' idea that genius usually goes hand in hand with some degree of eccentricity, was made with the help of the painter Gustave Caillebotte, a patron and friend of the Impressionists.

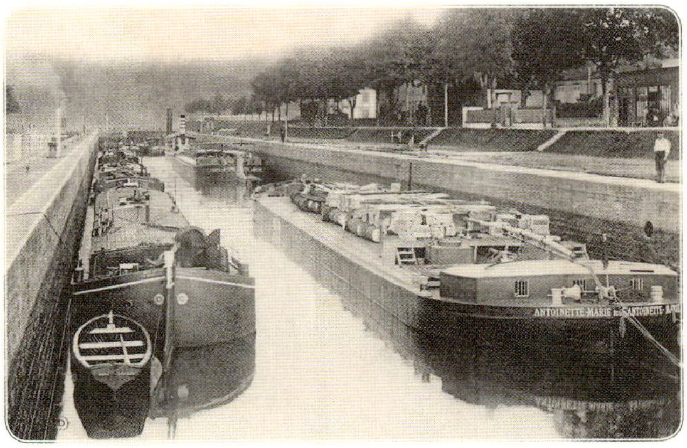

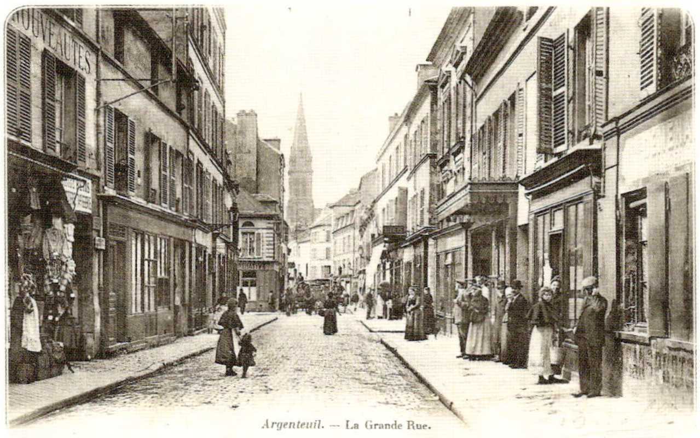
Argenteuil. — La Grande Rue.

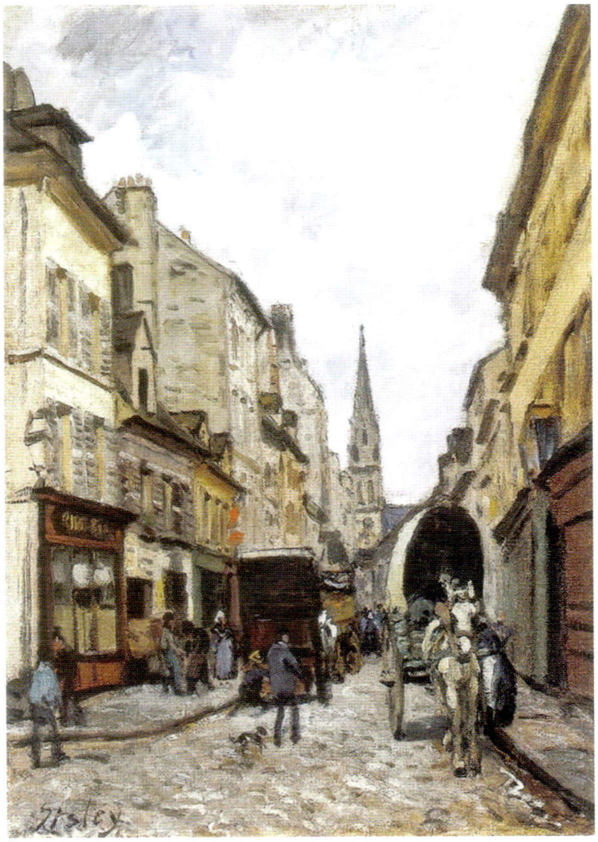

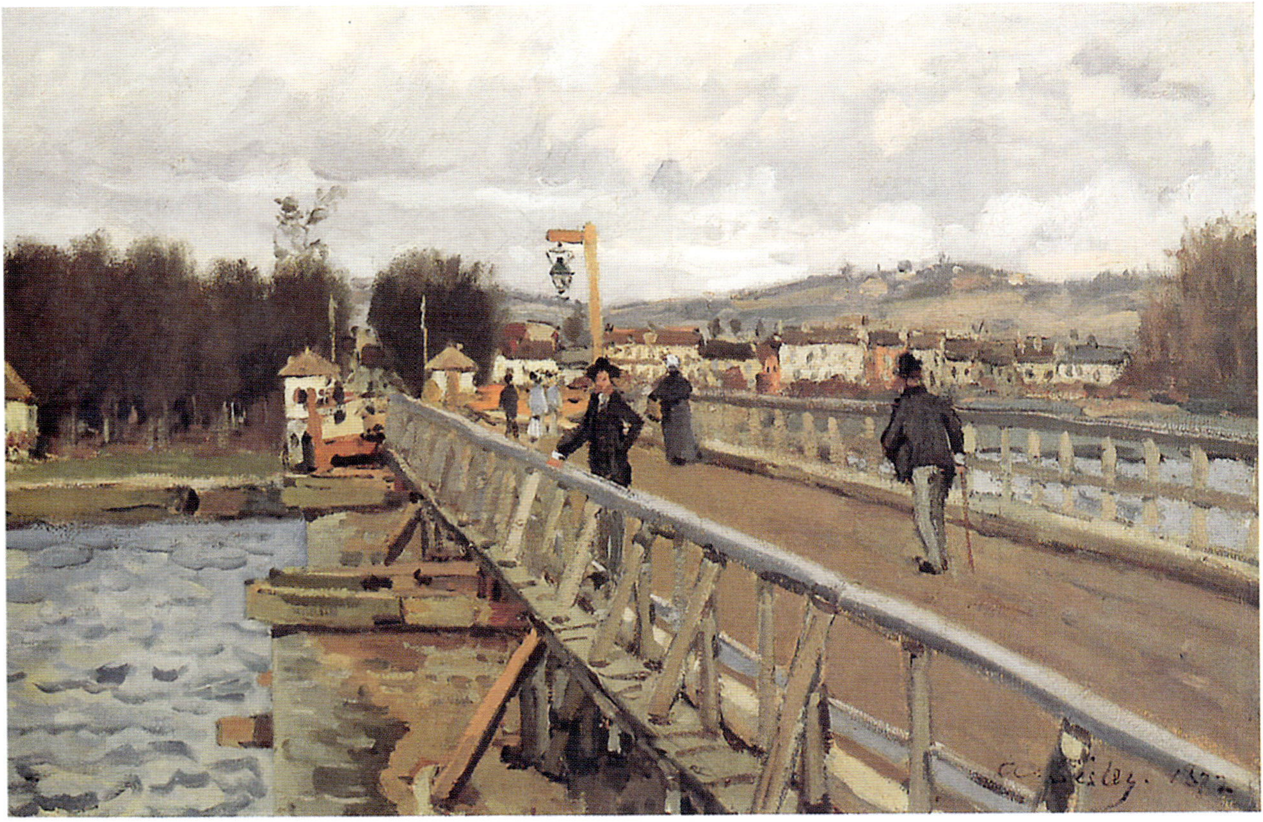

The Chatou Bridge with the 'Island of the Impressionists'

La Grenouillère at Bougival

p. 93
Claude Monet, *La Grenouillère*, 1869. New York, The Metropolitan Museum of Art

Holiday on the Seine at Bougival

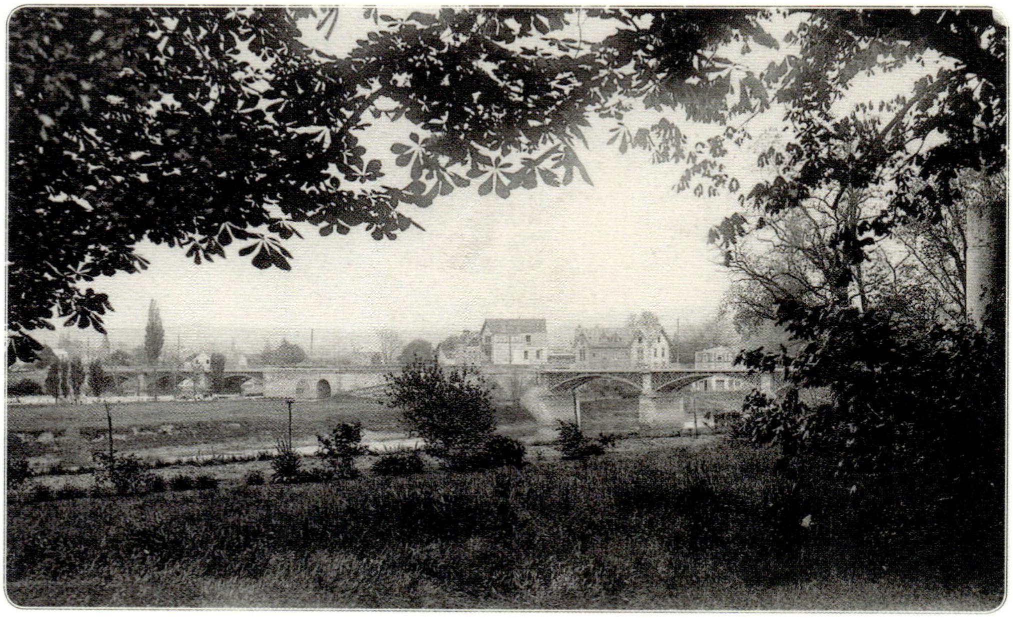

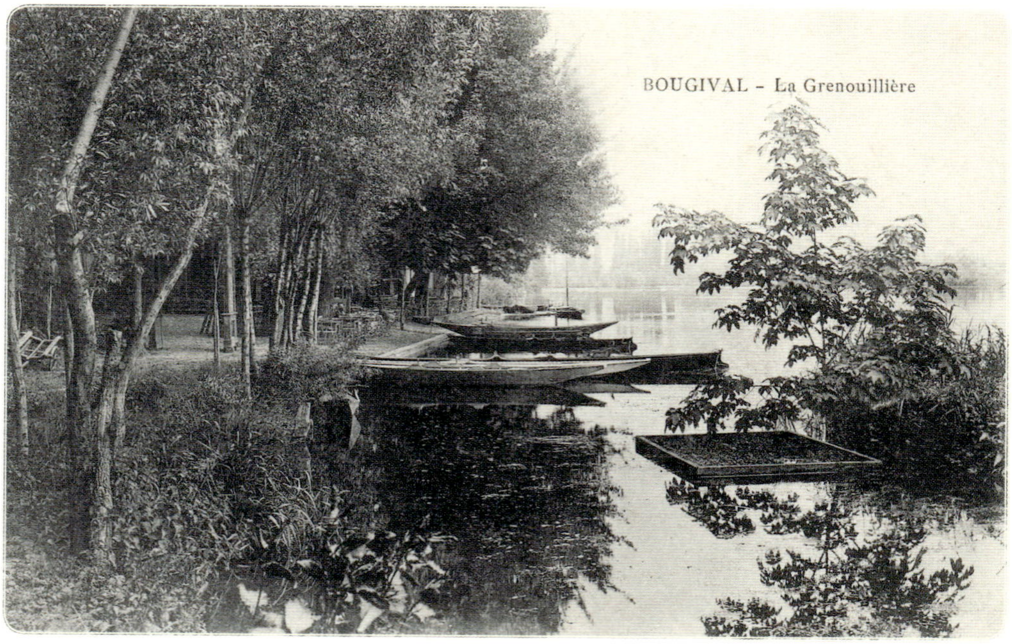

Further on, following the river, one came to Bougival, 'a delightful place on the shore bathed by the Seine and dotted with enchanting country residences', as one guidebook from the time put it. The closest station was Chatou/Chailly, where there was also a spot where one could leave their horse and gig, while carriages were parked along the road. When they went there for the first time, in 1869, Monet and Renoir were both in severe financial straits, but their dark mood quickly dissipated as they set to work. They painted briskly, with a certain predilection for floating establishments like La Grenouillère, which was opposite the islet of Croissy, and restaurants like the nearby Maison Fournaise, which was made of brick and had a cheerful terrace. We have a description of La Grenouillère written by Maupassant:

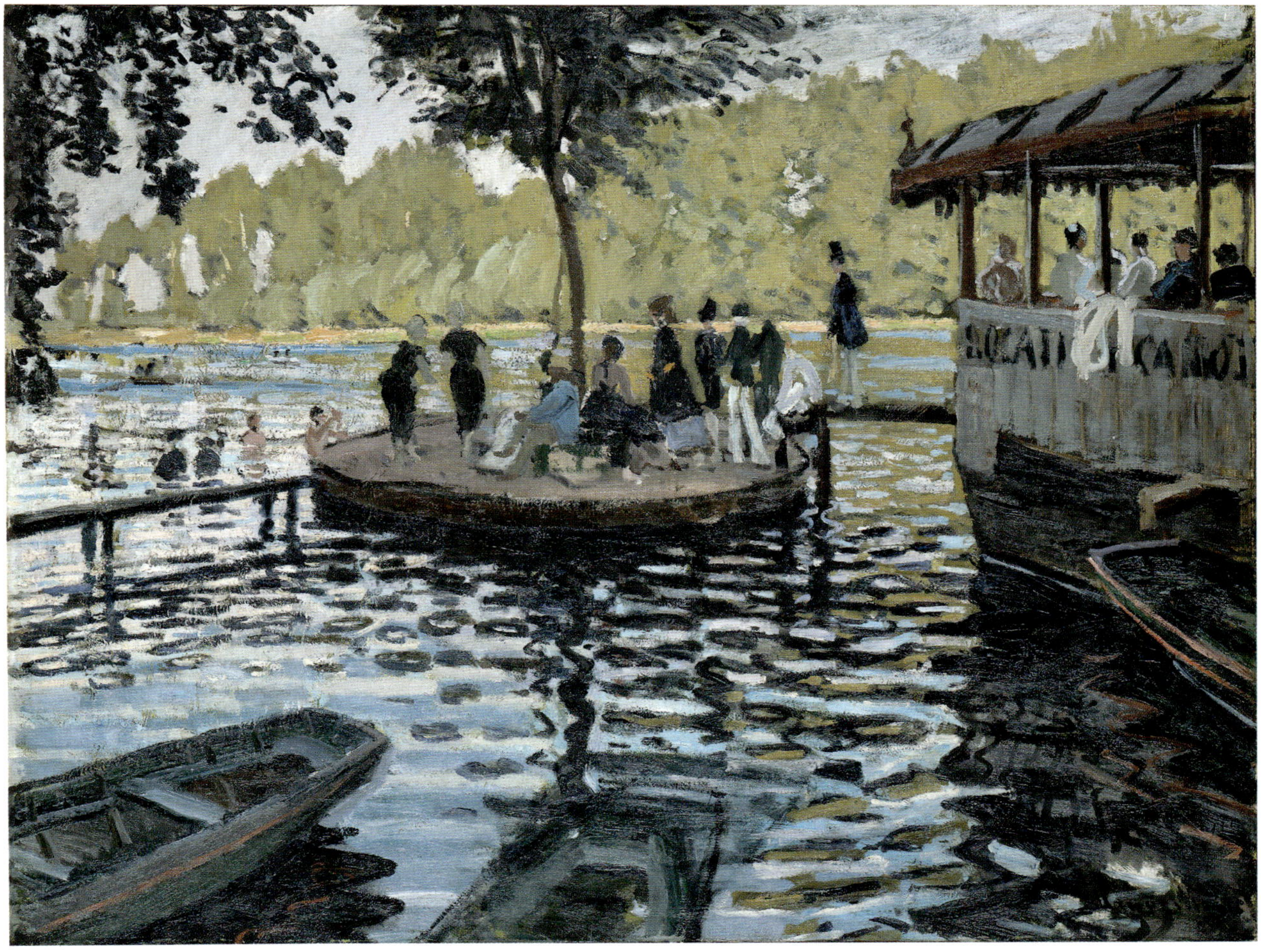

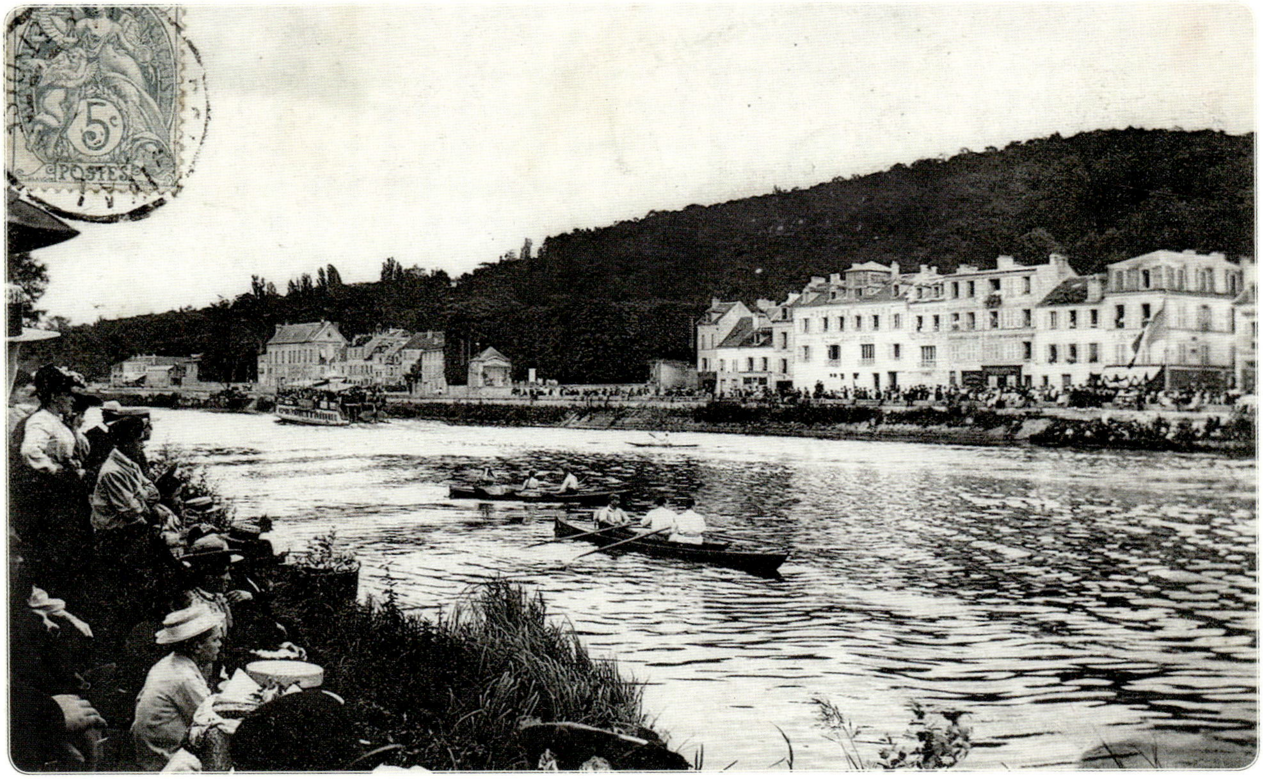
5c
POSTES

Pierre-Auguste Renoir, *Luncheon of the Boating Party*, 1881–1882. Washington, D.C., Phillips Collection

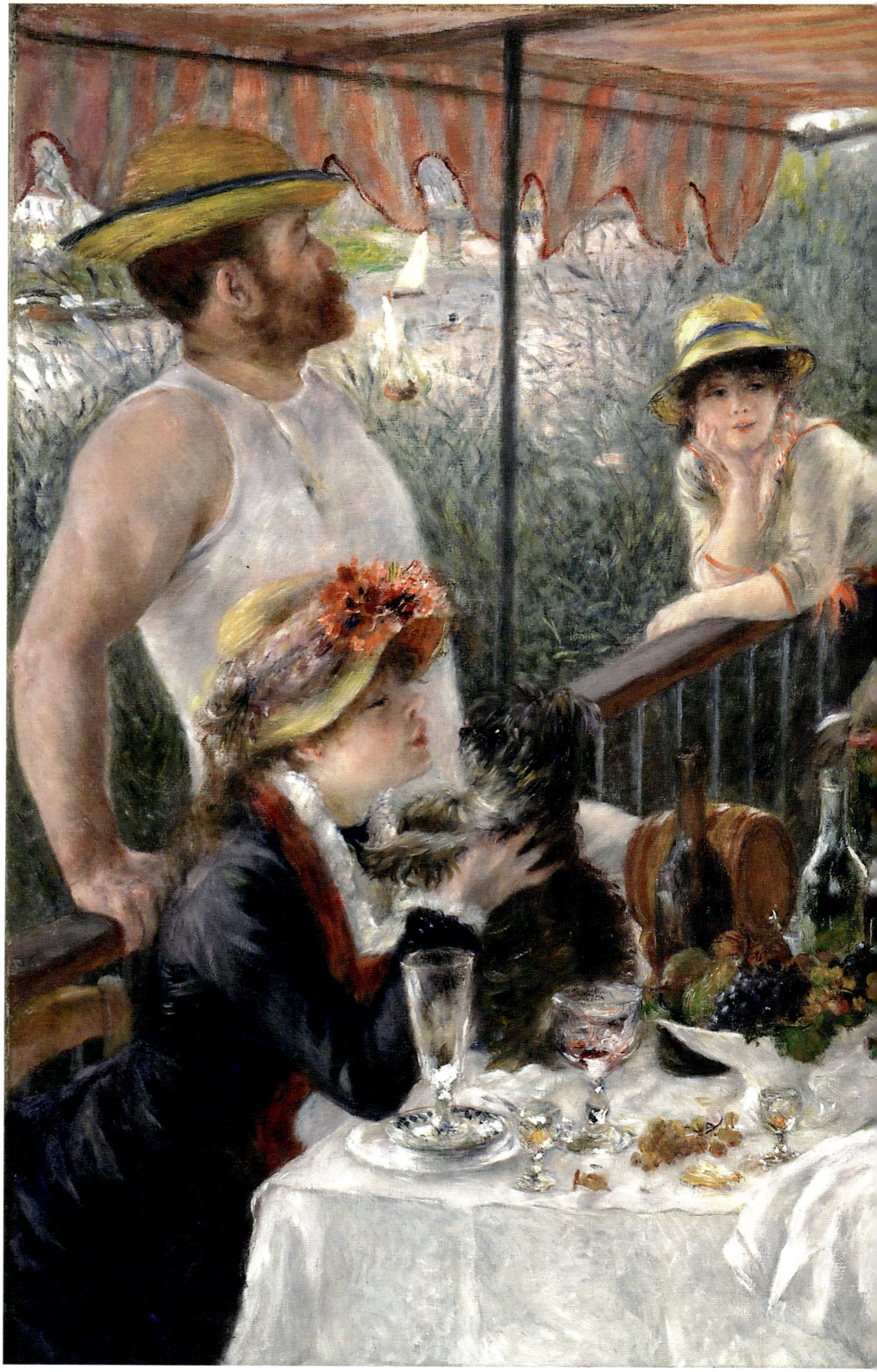

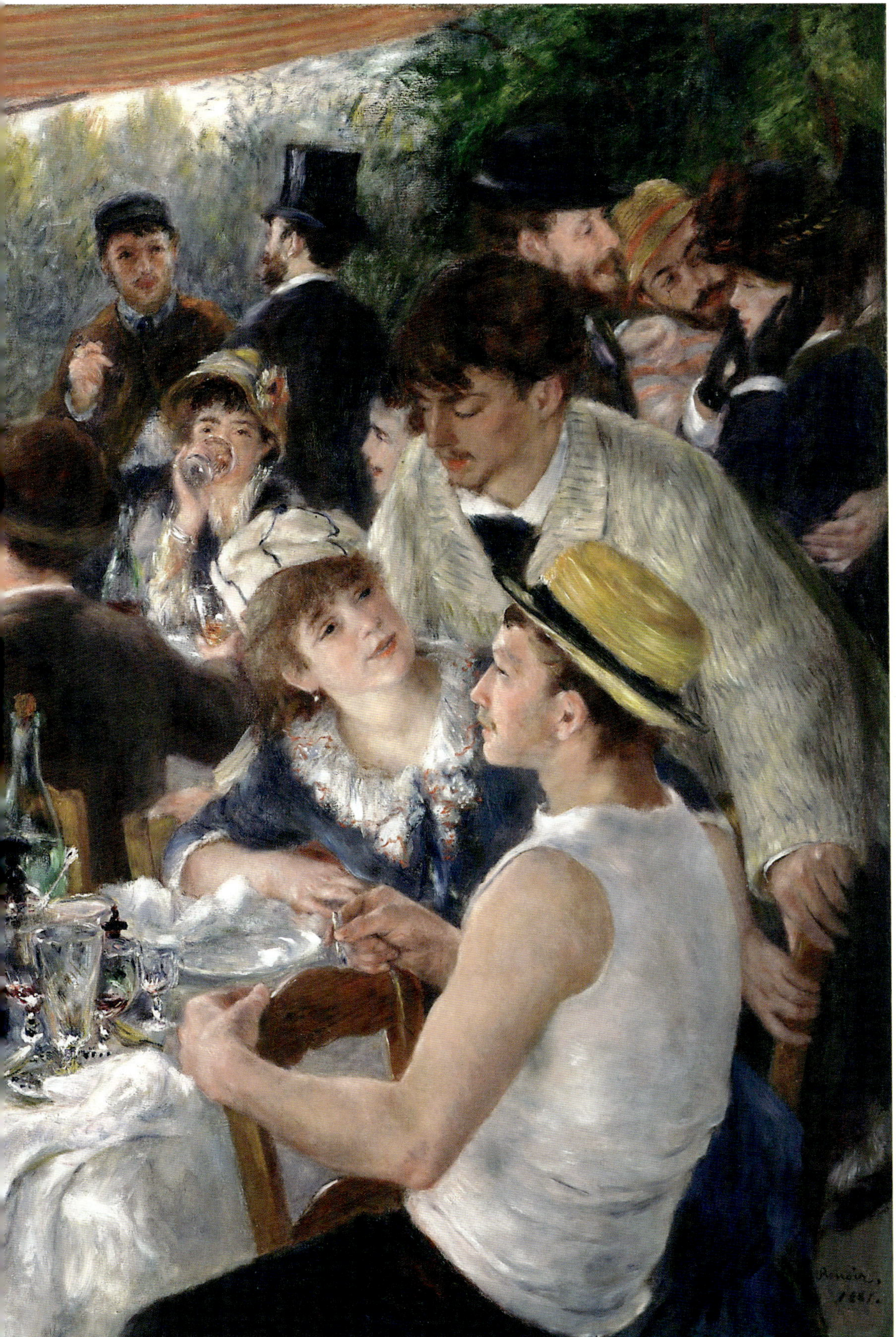

Pierre-Auguste Renoir, *La Grenouillère*, 1869. Stockholm, Nationalmuseum

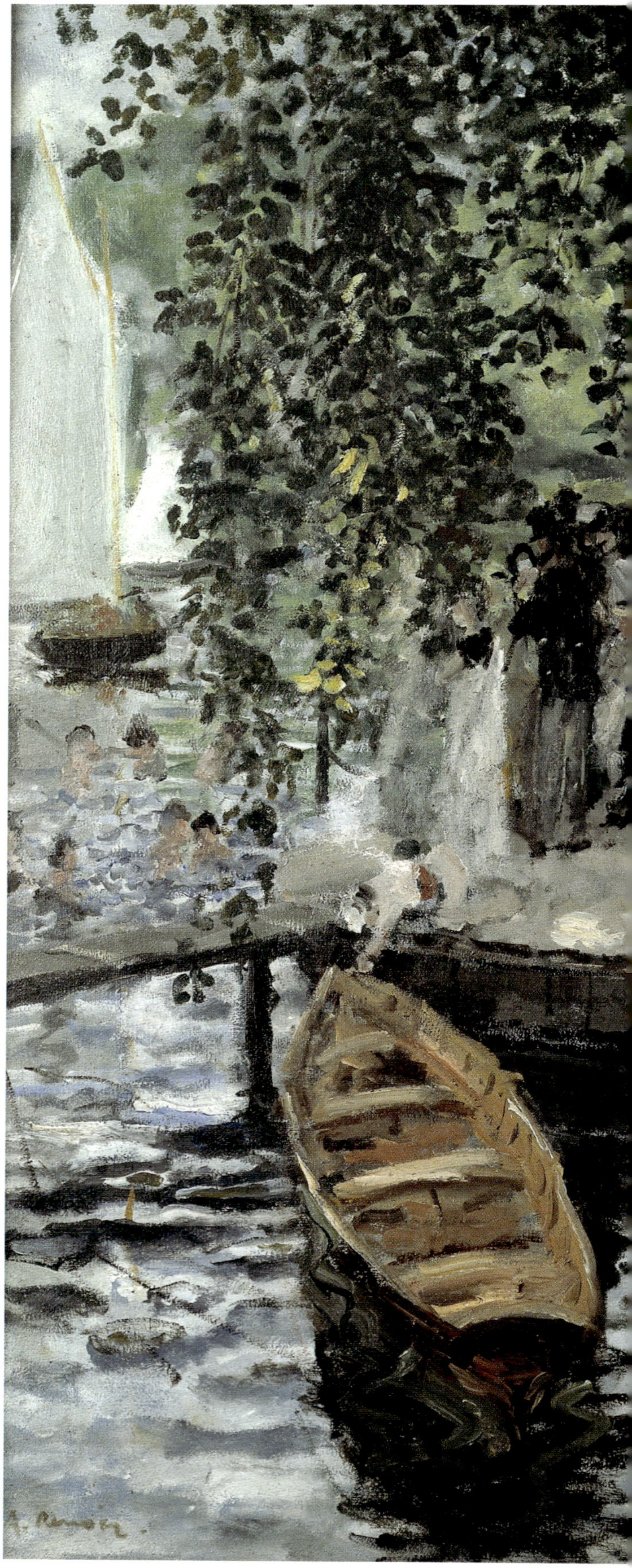

The immense raft, sheltered by a tarpaulin roof, is attached to the charming island of Croissy by two narrow foot bridges, one of which leads into the center of this aquatic establishment, while the other unites its end with a tiny islet planted with a tree and surnamed 'The Flower Pot,' and thence leads to land near the bath office.[27]

The name *grenouillère*, 'frog pond' alluded to the type of young women who went there: *demi-mondaines*, for the most part, as one used to say at the time, using an expression borrowed in the *pièce* by the same name written by Dumas, fils to describe women of ambiguous morals, neither aristocratic nor bourgeois, with a slightly garish elegance and yielding manner. Renoir, with his usual bonhomie, considered them nice girls, rash and high spirited, and he depicted them as such in the paintings *La Grenouillère* and *Luncheon of the Boating Party*, elevating them at least a handbreadth above the censure of the conformists. In his paintings, even more so than in those by Monet, Croissy looks like a mini-Cythera, and Renoir its Watteau. The ways of the Regency, for that matter, would not have been much more chaste.

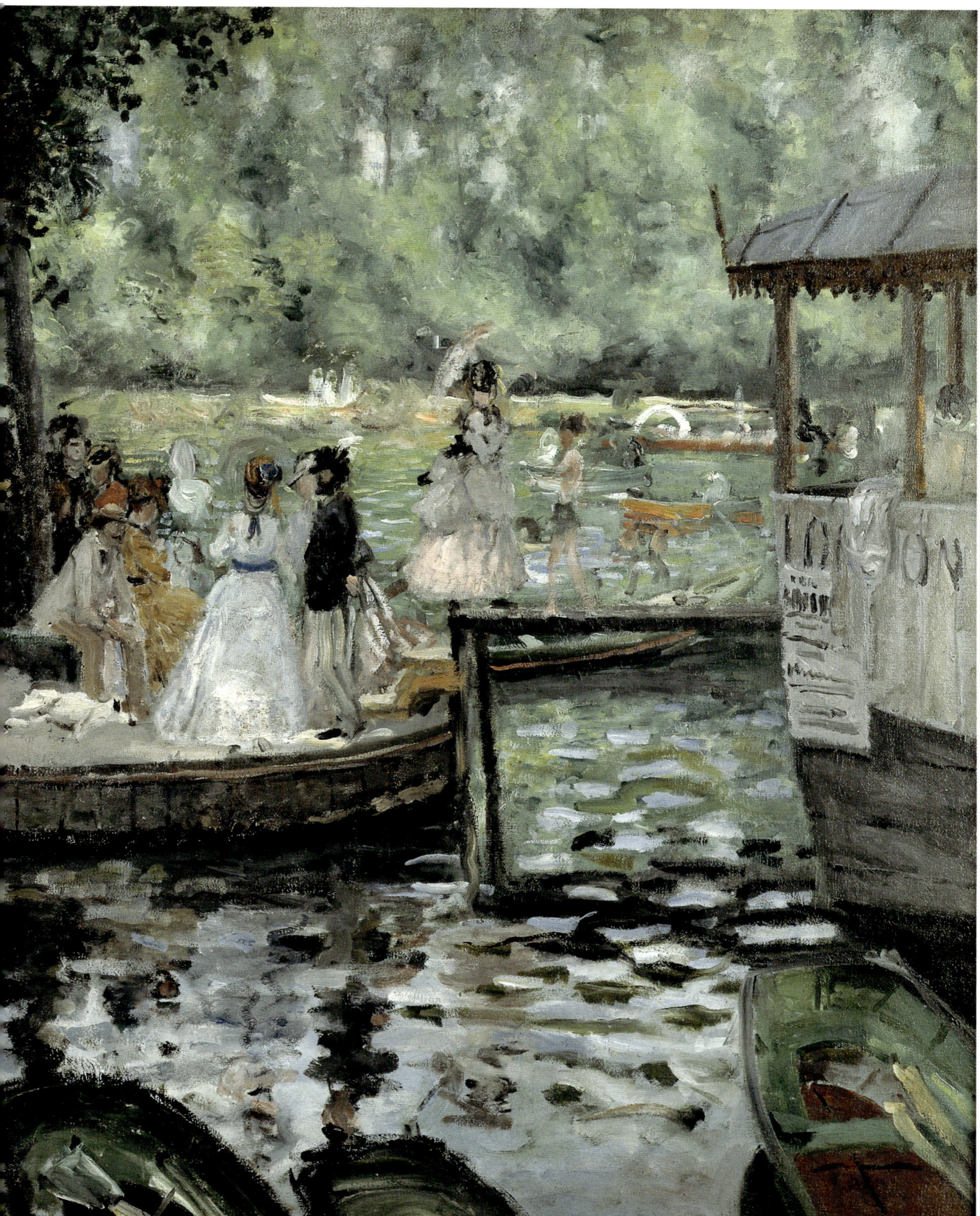

When the bend of the river turned, Bougival gave up its place to Marly-le-Roi, where Sisley went to live at the end of 1870. Once the summer residence of Louis XIV, the vast park had lost much of its grandeur, despite the prodigious efforts of Le Nôtre in designing its gardens, and now it instead called to visitors' minds the first lines of a poem by Victor Hugo: 'It was a big castle from the time of Louis XIII. At dusk the sun bathed that forgotten palace in red'.[28] The 'trough', a curious construction used to collect the plentiful water available in the environs to water the horses, now looked like a modest pond, and while, a little further on, one could still see, until the middle of the nineteenth century, the ruins of the giant machine

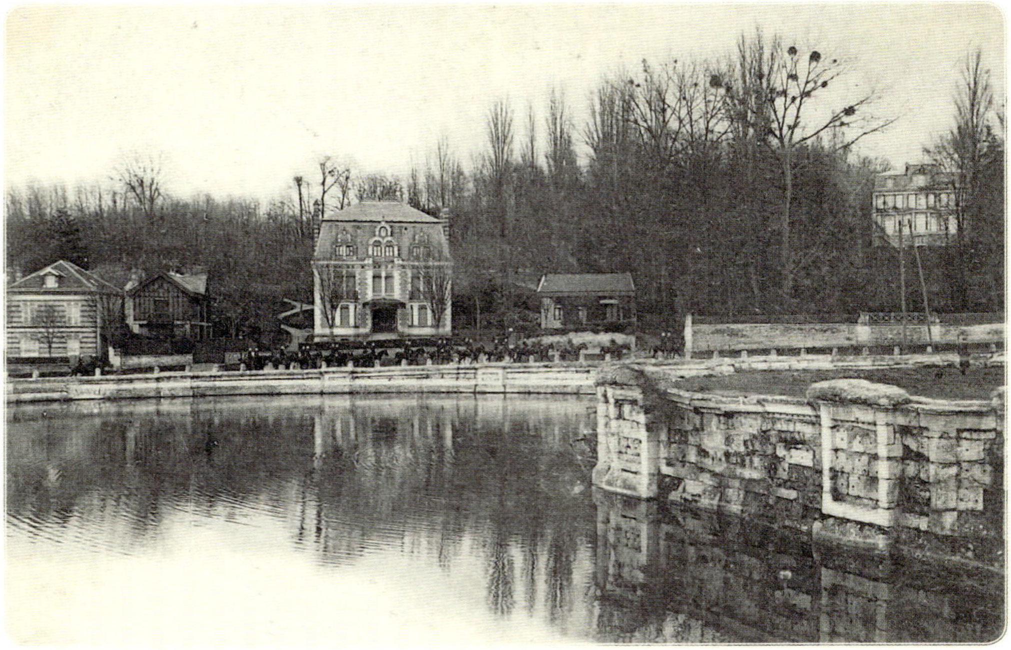

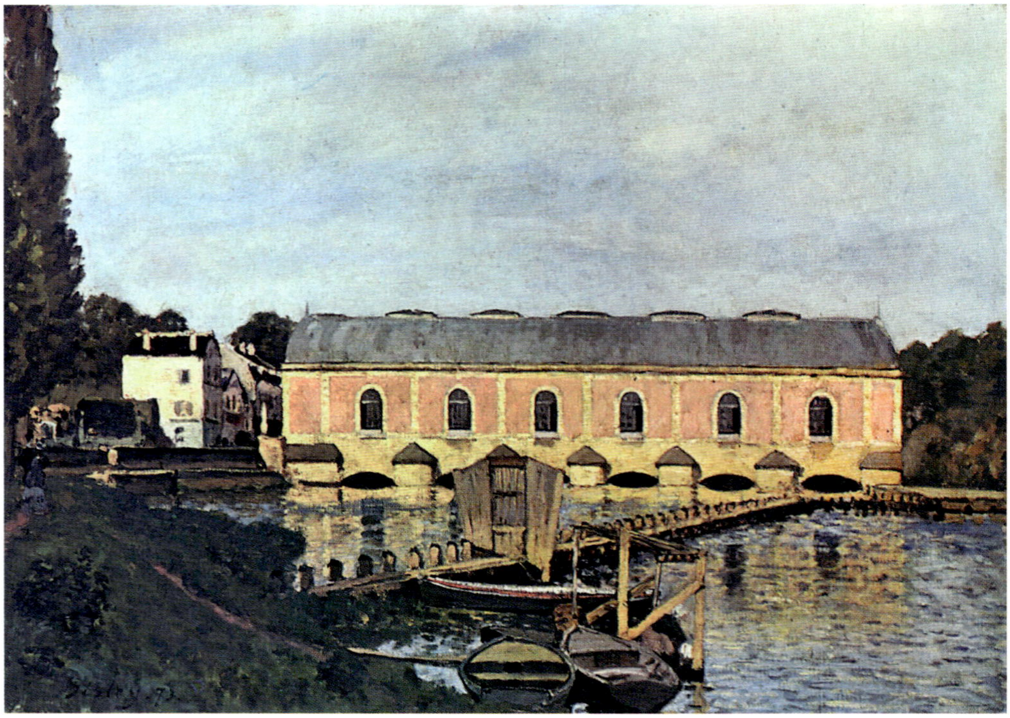

Trough at Marly-le-Roi

Alfred Sisley, *The Machine at Marly*, 1873. Copenhagen, Ny Carlberg Glyptotek

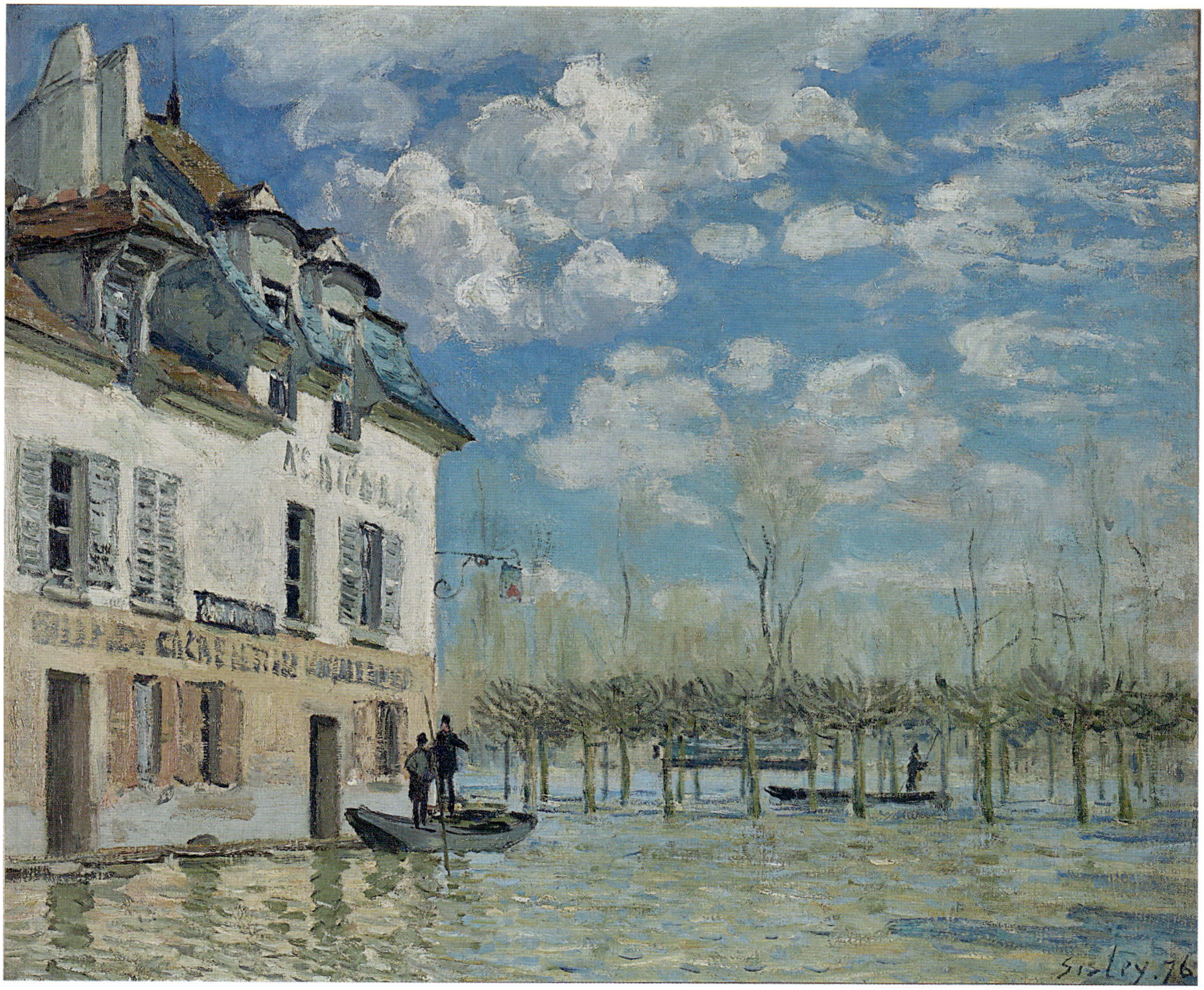

Alfred Sisley, *Boat in the Flood at Port Marly*, 1876. Paris, Musée d'Orsay

used to bring the waters of the Seine to Versailles, they were now reduced to a sorrowful skeleton.

Sisley deeply loved the village of Marly-le-Roi and its picturesque surroundings, probably even more so than Mary Cassatt, who stayed there a few years later with her family. When Port-Marly flooded, Sisley depicted the countryside submerged in water. The melancholy notes and silence of the landscape, the squalid appearance of the land, faintly enlivened by a few meagre glints of light, inspired some of his best paintings, which are indeed among the most beautiful of the entire Impressionist movement: perhaps because, in the limited range of hues, necessitated by the cloudy skies reflected in the muddy density of the water, he had found the perfect subject for his muted, gauzy art, made up of just a few, mostly dull and finely modulated tones, with an airiness permeated with a hint of musicality.

15. Louveciennes

Not far from Marly-le-Roi lay the village of Louveciennes, the surroundings of which were painted on more than one occasion by Sisley and Renoir, the latter of whom went there to see his parents. Monet also visited this quiet little village in the winter, far from the noisy banks of the Seine, where life remained

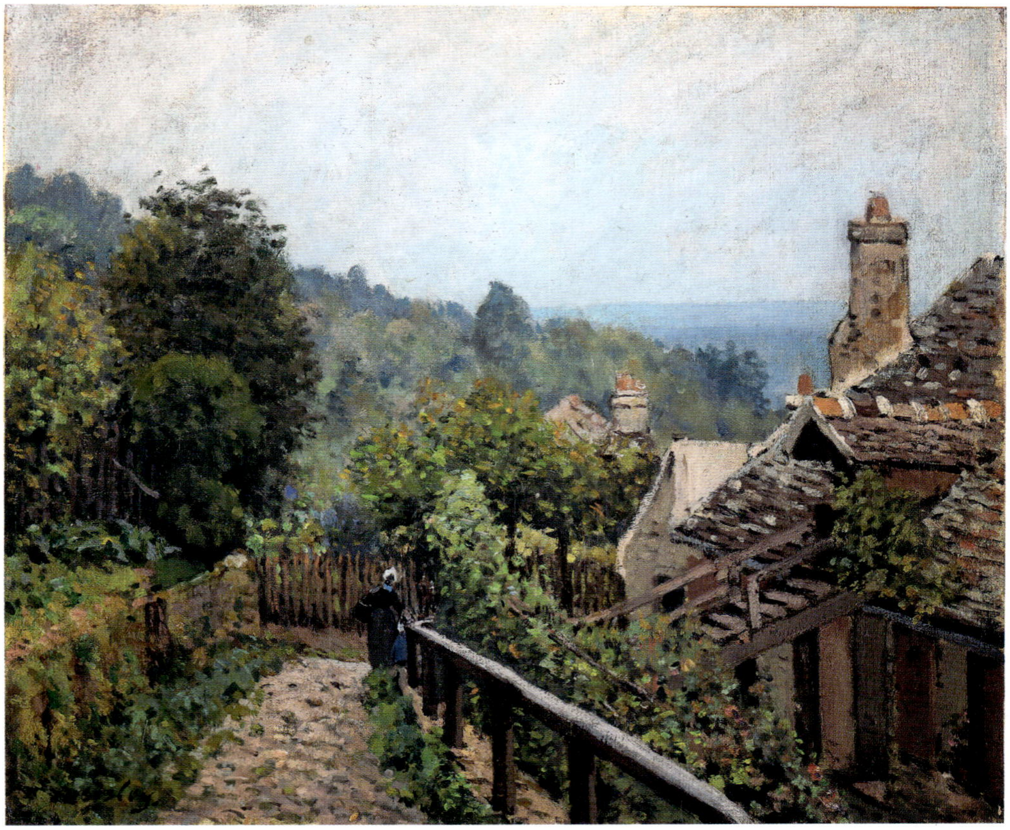

Alfred Sisley, *Hillside Path in Louveciennes*, *c.* 1873. Paris, Musée d'Orsay

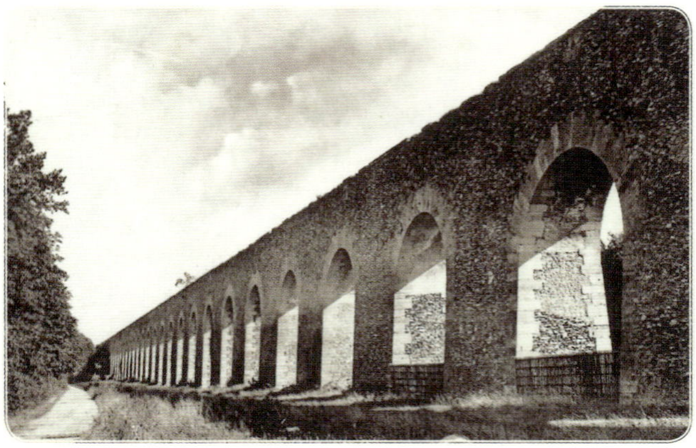

The Marly Aqueduct

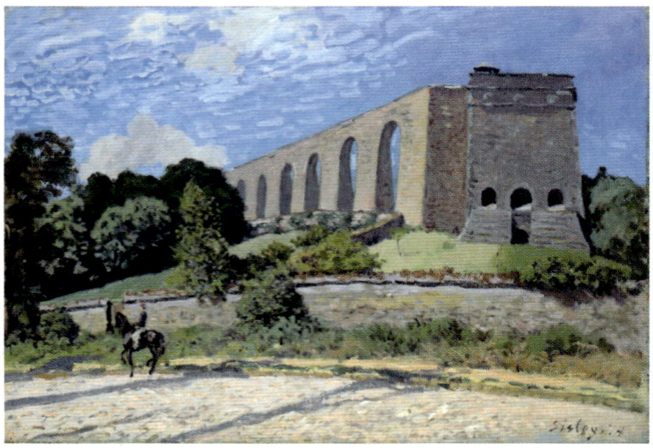

Alfred Sisley, *The Aqueduct at Marly*, 1874. Toledo, OH, Toledo Museum of Art

the same as it had been for centuries. Like Marly-le-Roi, Louveciennes also offered the neglected allure of past royal splendour, along the trails that led from the castle of Madame du Barry to the river across the hill. The little paths, however, quickly slipped away from all form of opulence to wind amidst well-cultivated vegetable gardens and orchards. Renoir's *A Road in Louveciennes* shows us its typical rural, green, sunny landscape. When snow fell, the little houses in the village, packed tight within the low walls, the rows of trees and the whole landscape, its lines simplified by the white blanket embroidered with splendid golden or light blue accents, gave painters a magnificent subject. Sisley appreciated its gentle melancholy in autumn and winter, as shown in *Hillside Path in Louveciennes* or *Snow in Louveciennes*, as did Pissarro, who moved there in 1869 and often painted its rustic, peaceful roads.

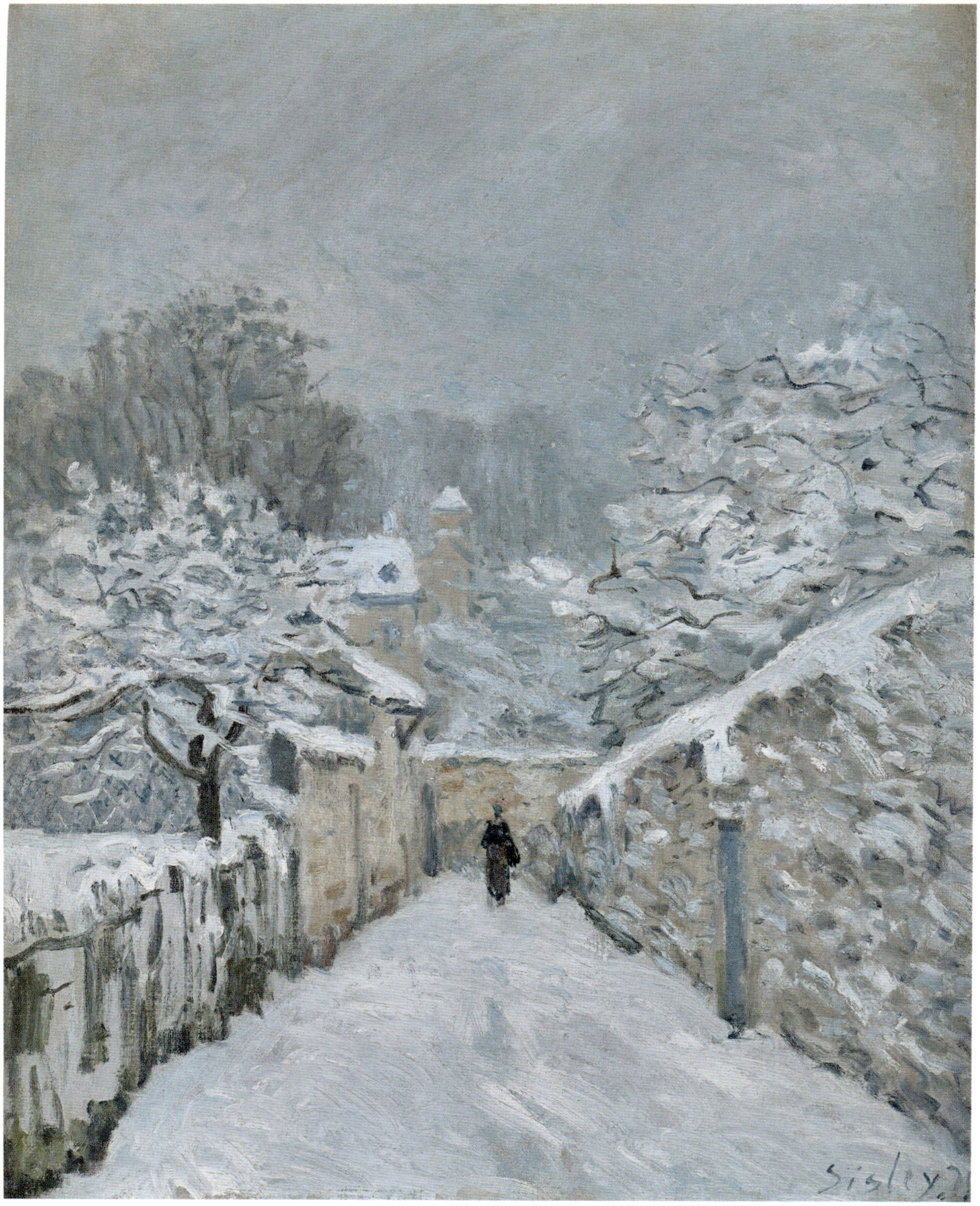

Alfred Sisley, *Snow in Louveciennes*, 1873. Paris, Musée d'Orsay

16. The Forest of Fontainebleau

The ancient game reserve of the kings of France had been depicted by artists long before the new romantic doctrine imposed pristine nature as the ideal subject for painting. Jean-Baptiste Oudry's cartoons of the royal hunt for the tapestries woven at Gobelins in fact date to the first part of the eighteenth century. In these cartoons, the most civil of courtly gatherings is shown against a backdrop of the trees of Fontainebleau raised to the wind, amidst precipitous ravines and roughly squared rocks, a tousled, uneven crown that calls to mind the ravaged landscapes of Salvator Rosa. Oudry's gentlemen boldly ride out of thick, dark woods, like their paladin ancestors emerged from enchanted forests. The trunks are sometimes powerful, sometimes dry and sturdy like trigs, while the paths twist in sinuous labyrinths. This is the same forest visited by Frédéric and Rosanette in Flaubert's *Sentimental Education*, a counter to Le Nôtre's rigid Versailles, with its paths marked out and symmetrical like alexandrine verse:

Théodore Rousseau, *At the Edge of the Forest at Fontainebleau, Setting Sun*, *c.* 1849. Paris, Musée du Louvre

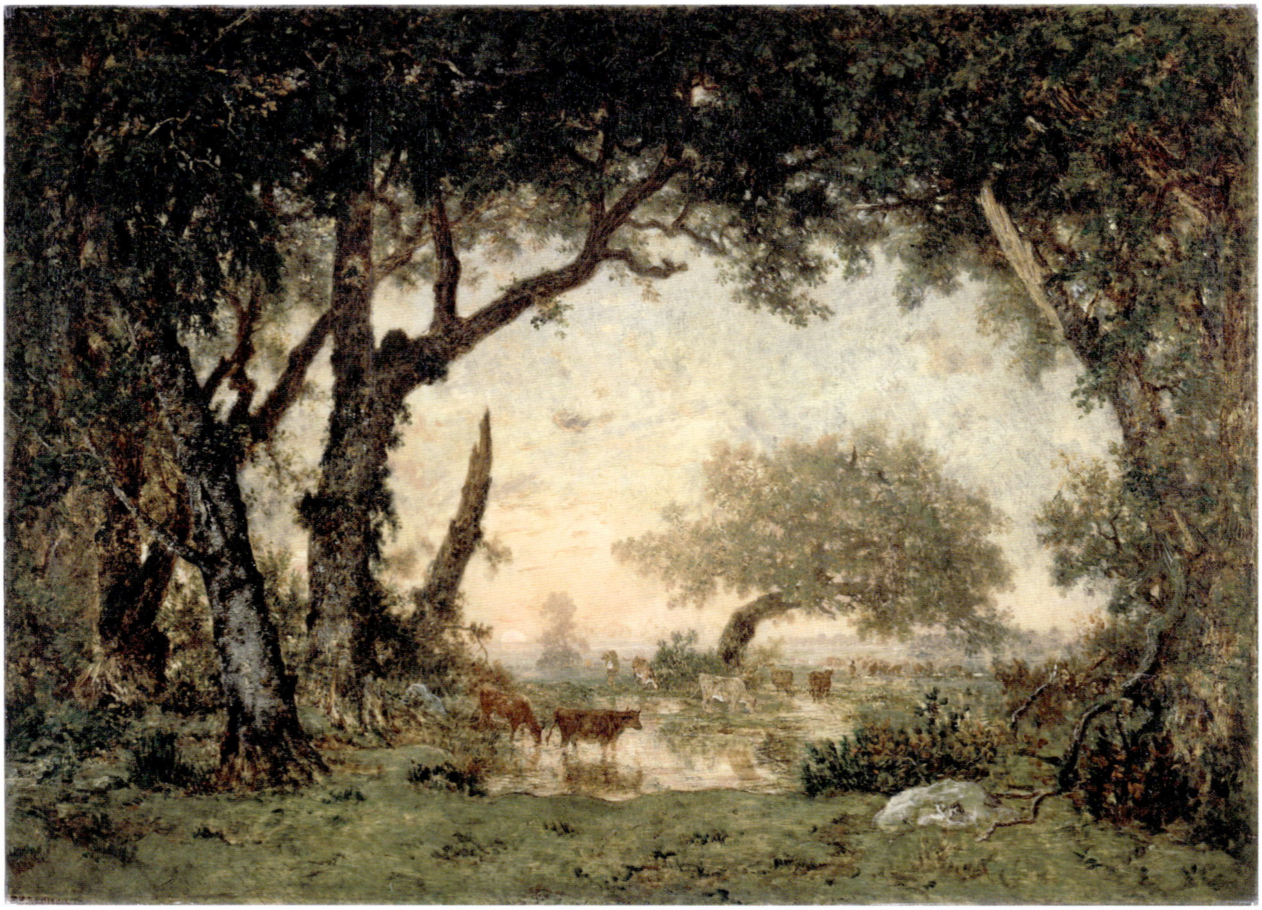

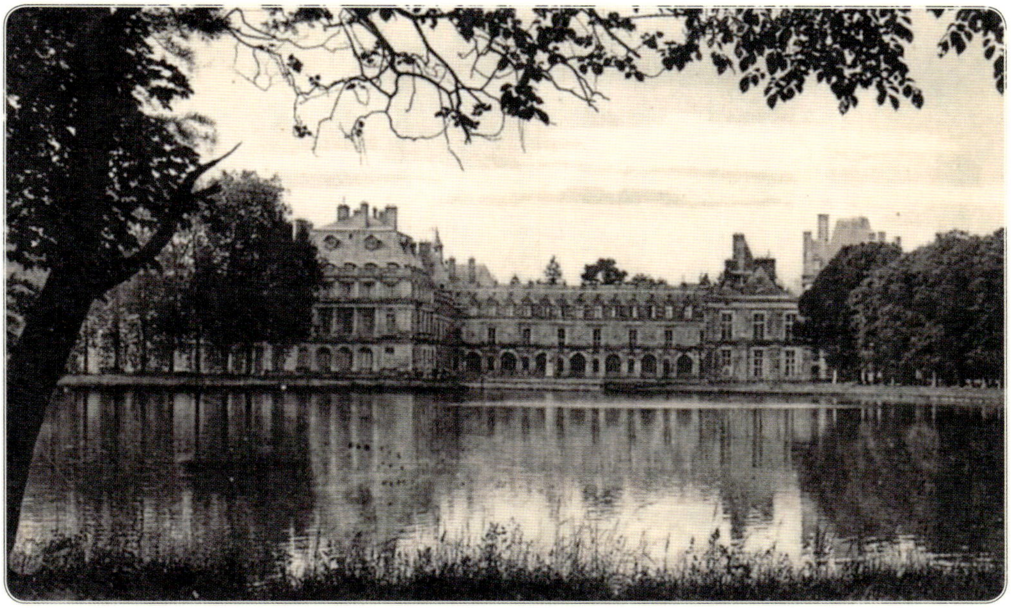

Fontainebleau Castle with the Carp Pond

They entered the Franchard forest [...] soon coming to the bottom of the gorge. It was covered, on one side, by heaps of sandstone and juniper, while on the other, the almost bare earth sloped down to the hollow of a valley where a path traced a pale-tinted line through the heather; and they could see, in the distance, a cone-shaped hill with a flat top, and a telegraph tower behind it. A half hour later, they got out of the carriage again to climb the heights of Aspremont. The path zigzagged through dwarf pines, beneath rocks with jagged edges; this whole corner of the forest seemed somehow muffled, wild, and secret. It made one think of hermits, companions to the great stags of bygone eras with fiery crosses between their horns, who would have welcomed, with paternal smiles, the fine old kings of France when they came to kneel before their caves. The smell of resin permeated the warm air; tree roots interlaced on the ground, looking like live veins.[29]

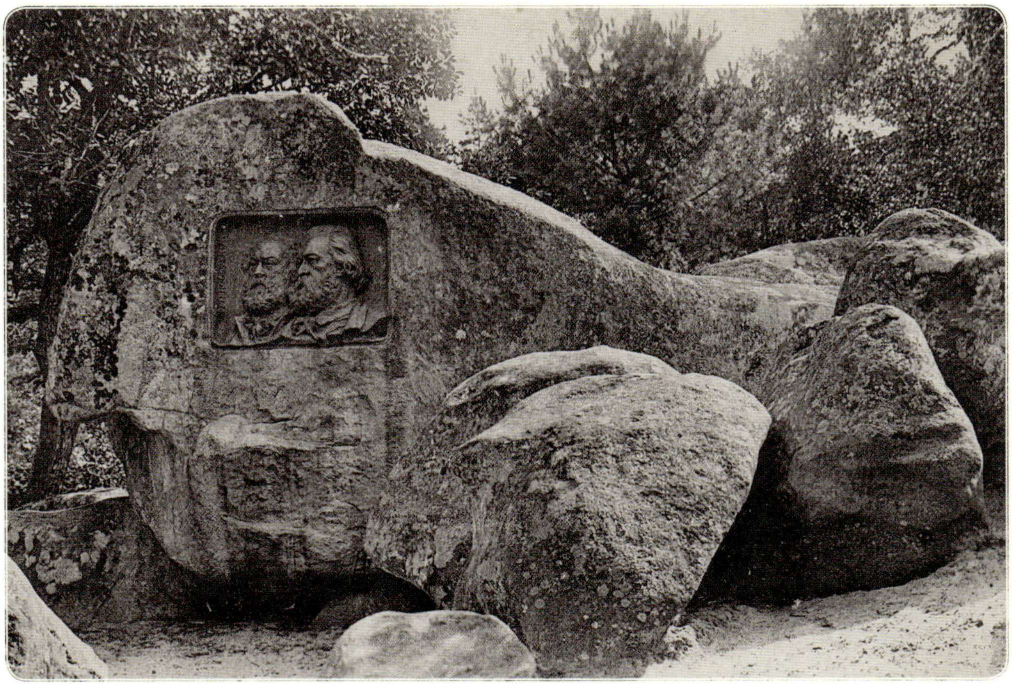

Henri Chapu (1833–1891), *Monument to Jean-François Millet and Théodore Rousseau*, 1884. Barbizon, forest of Fontainebleau

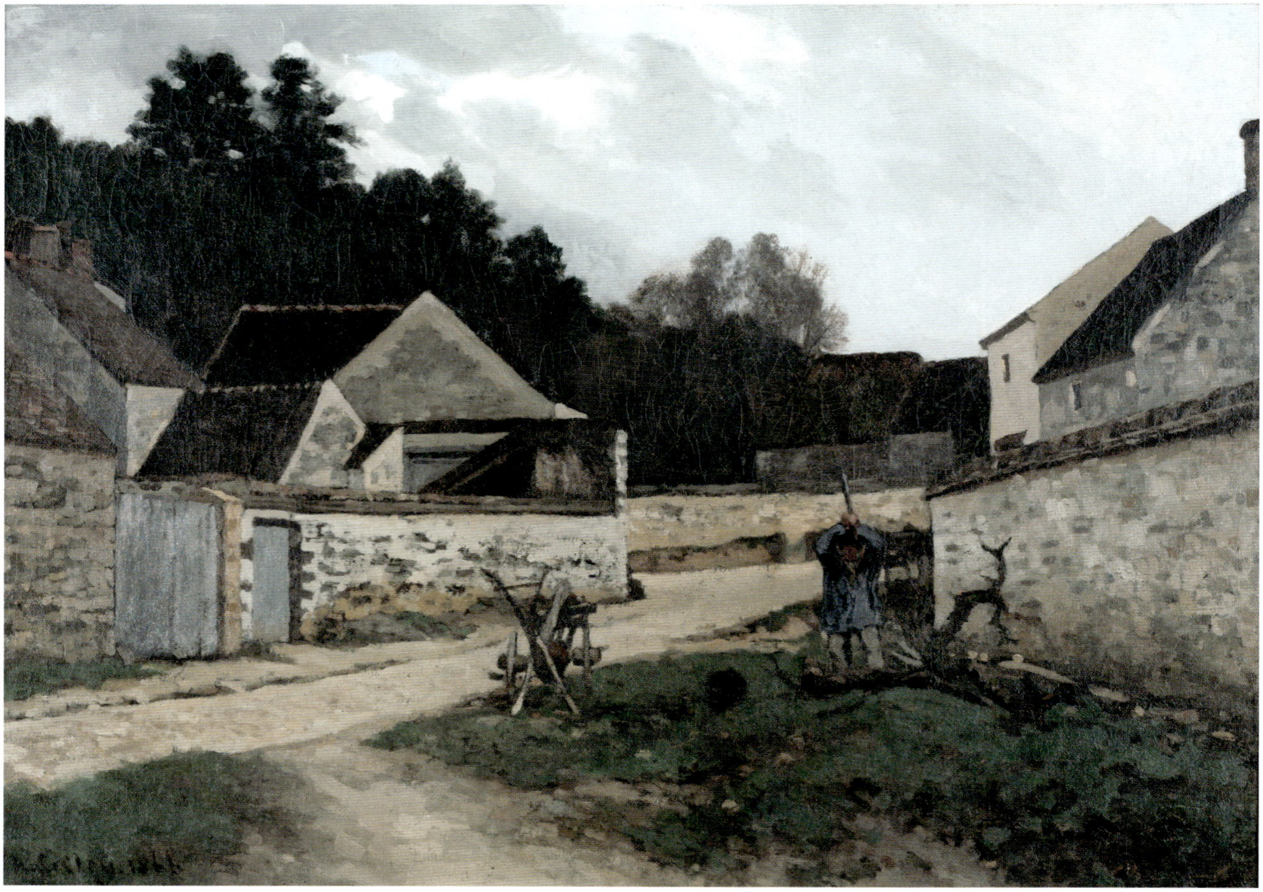

Alfred Sisley, *Village Street in Marlotte*, 1866. Buffalo, Albright-Knox Art Gallery

p. 105
Pierre-Auguste Renoir, *Mother Anthony's Tavern*, 1866. Stockholm, Nationalmuseum

All of this is what made Fontainebleau the realist painters' Arcadia. You could find them scattered everywhere in the forest, attempting to reproduce, as faithfully as possible, the dark shadow of a tree, the splendour of the grass and the reflections of the clouds, their stance similar to that of Virgil's shepherd-poets, inspired by the rustle of the tamarisk or the gurgle of a brook. Sometimes, there were fugitive republicans hiding amidst those leafy meanders, who, dressed as wandering landscape artists, could spend months there safe from the police; and this only increased the picturesque allure of the place.

Artists like Jean-François Millet, Camille Corot and Théodore Rousseau usually met in Barbizon, a small village on the northern edge of the forest, but the Impressionists preferred Marlotte, where life was more pure. According to Renoir, some of the farmers in Barbizon had begun adopting the air of the subjects of Millet, who, in paintings like *The Gleaners* or *The Potato Harvest*, worked the earth with the solemn resignation of a bunch of Jobs. From his son, the director Jean Renoir, we learn that the village of Marlotte was

> composed of only a dozen or so houses and properties, clustered about a little crossroads leading from Fontainebleau and Montigny to Bourron. The actual forest came almost to the first group of houses on the northern side. Those on the south side looked out towards the valley of the Loing, a delightful little river, with tall, graceful trees shading its banks.[30]

After the war, you could still see the big porches of the farms with yards covered with sandstone cobbles stolen from the king's paving during the Revolution. The

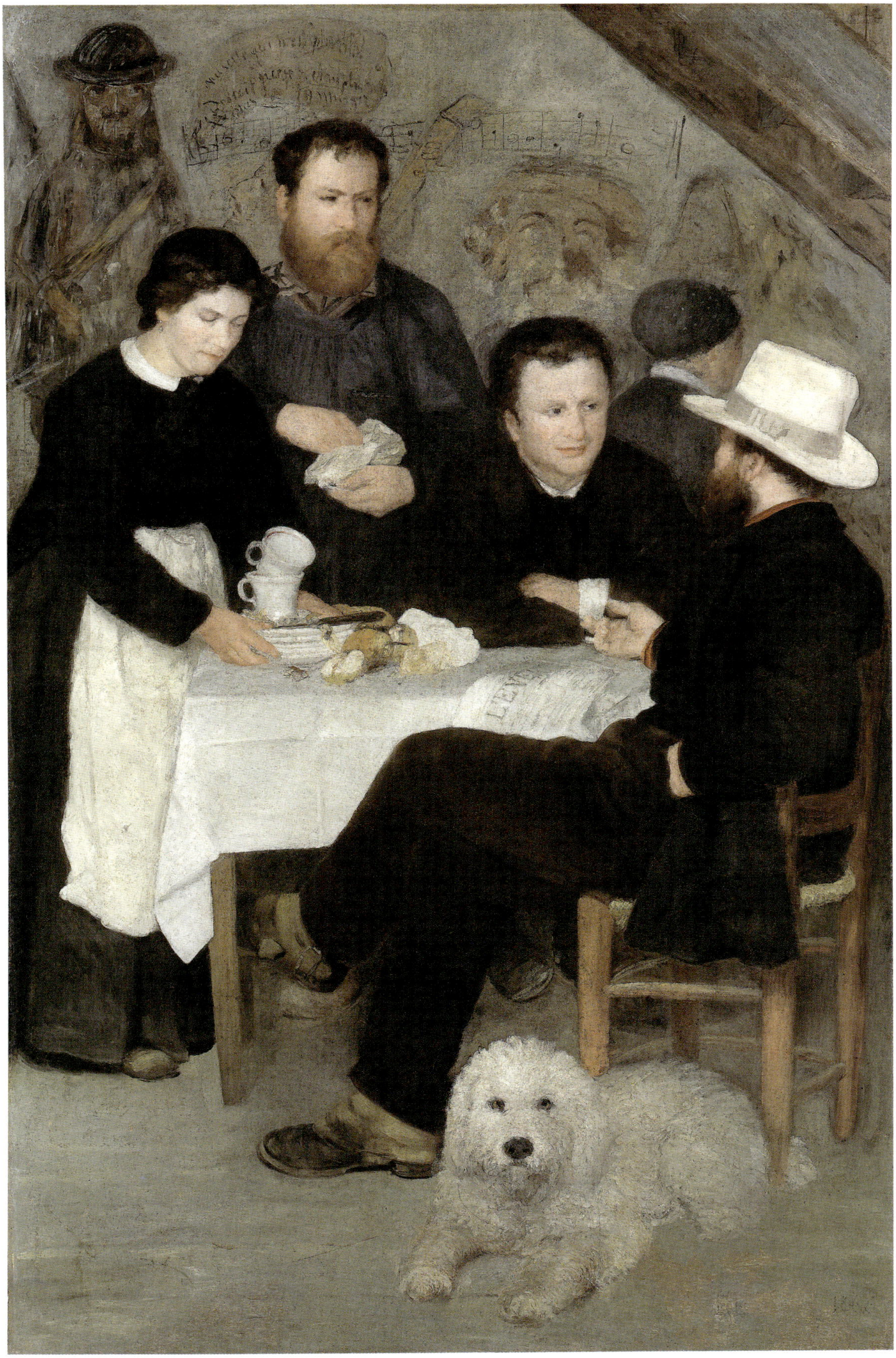

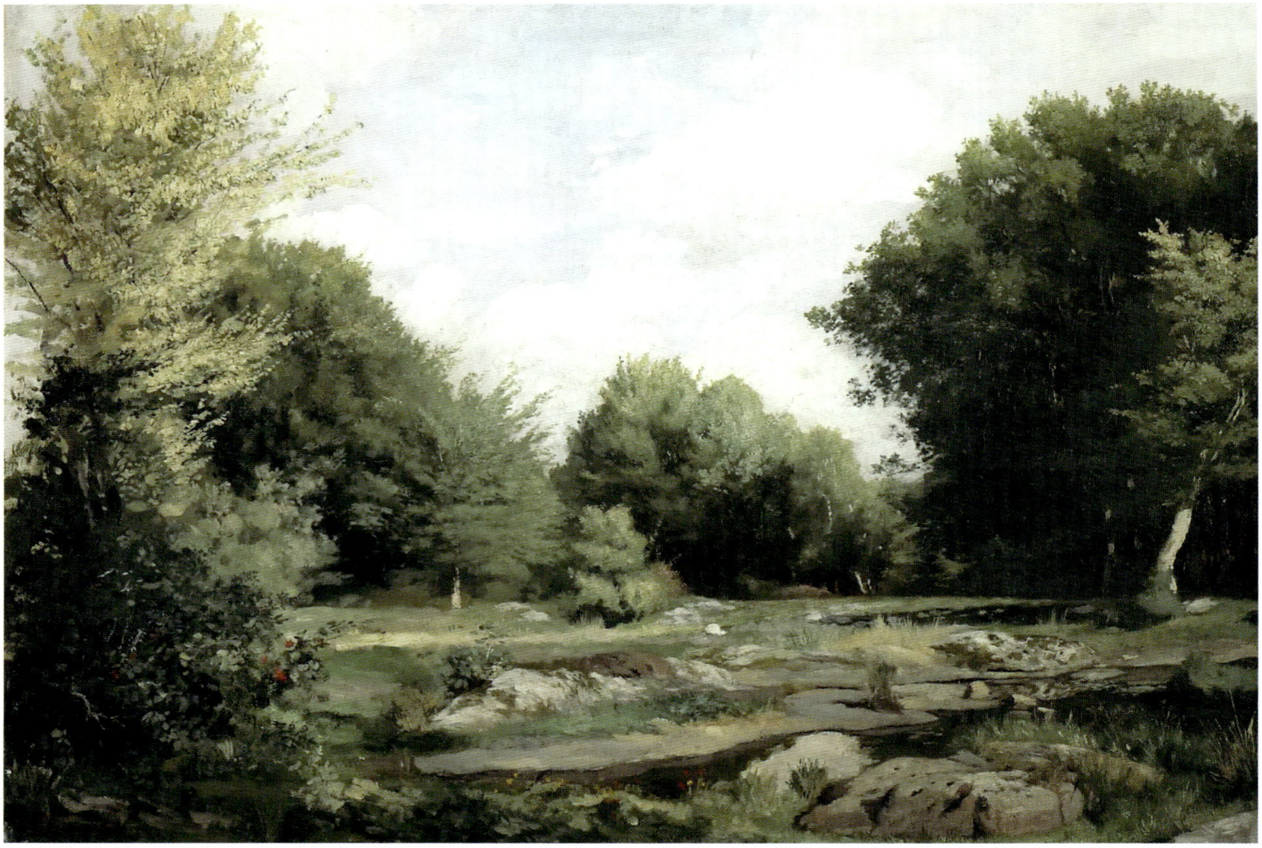

Pierre-Auguste Renoir, *Clearing in the Woods*, 1865. Detroit, Detroit Institute of Arts

The Cheval Blanc Inn in Chailly-en-Bière

facades were instead a distinctive pink or pale blue hue because, those cobbles being easily breakable, when they were used to build houses they were carefully covered with plaster.

In 1863, Monet and Bazille spent the Easter holiday in Chailly-en-Bière; the next year, Monet brought Renoir and Sisley there as well. They stayed in the inns of Mrs Mallet and Mother Anthony, the latter of which was depicted by Renoir in *Mother Anthony's Tavern*. This is one of his early paintings and among the sitters we find

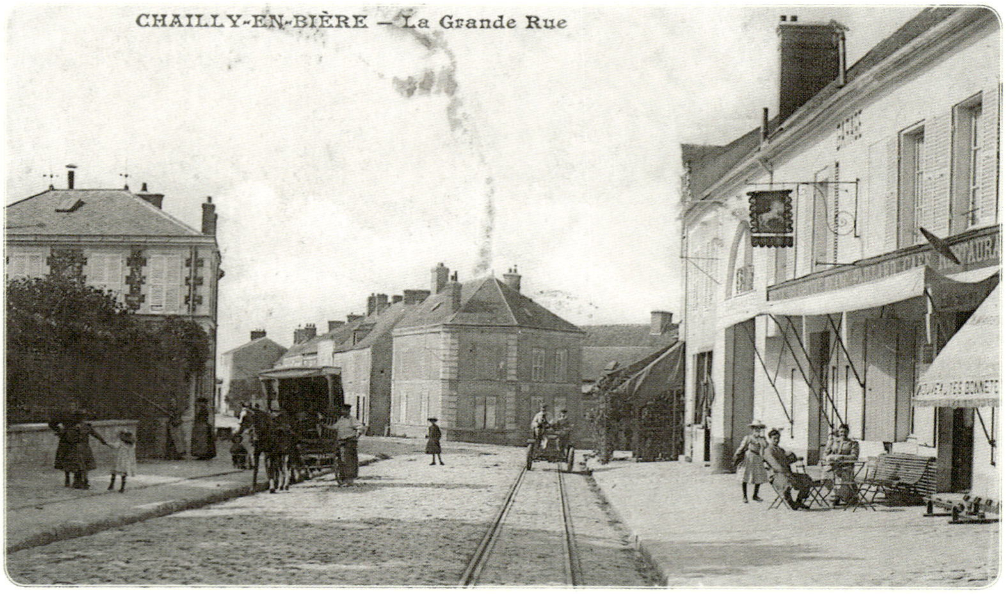

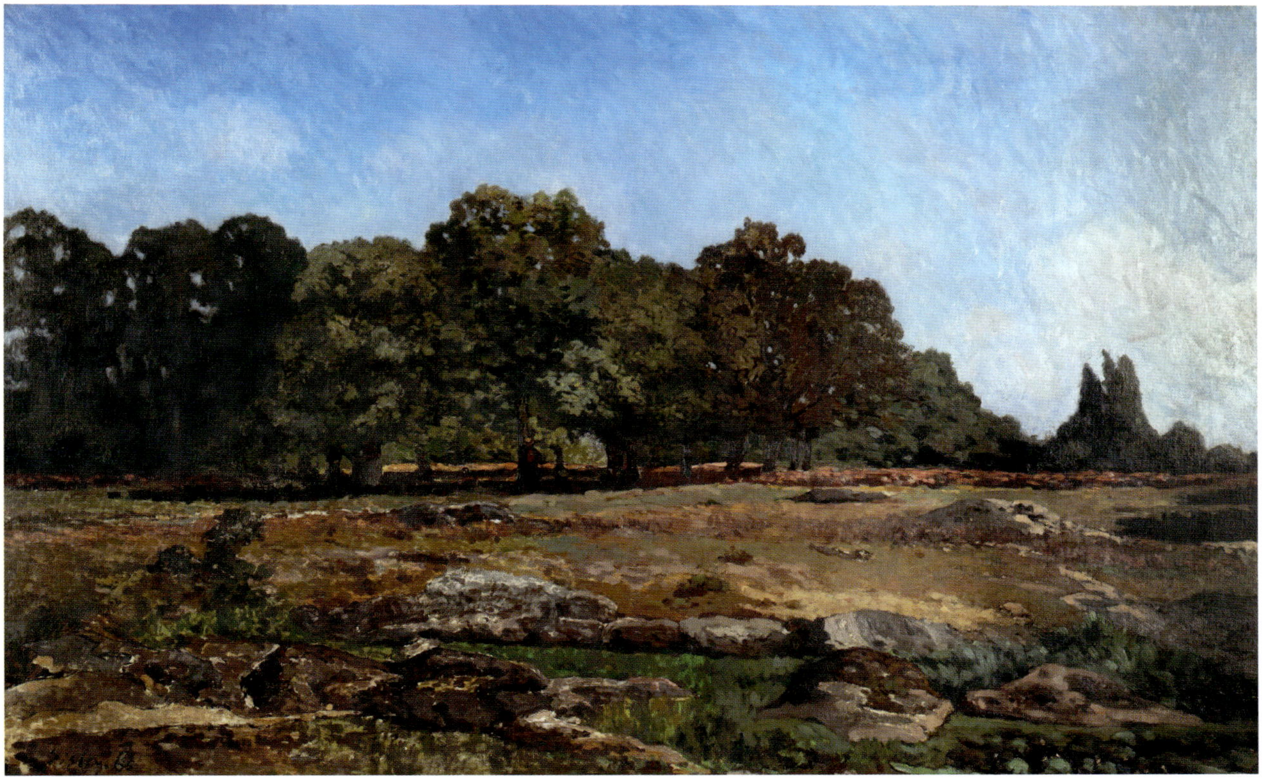

Alfred Sisley,
At the Edge of Fontainebleau Forest,
1865. Petit Palais, Musée des Beaux-Arts de la Ville de Paris

Jules Le Cœur, who was the guest of Sisley and Renoir. There were also other places where artists could find reasonably priced food and lodging, like the Cheval Blanc or the Lion d'or. Thanks to the railways that made it possible to get to Fontainebleau from Paris in a short time, the Impressionists went there often. Sometimes, weary of the same subject, they would pick up their canvas and easel and start rambling. For the city dwellers who went on Sundays, they must have looked like local gods, similar to the satyrs and sileni of ancient mythology. These were the years of Renoir's *Clearing in the Woods*, Monet's *Chailly Road in the Forest of Fontainebleau* and Sisley's *At the Edge of Fontainebleau Forest.*

Fontainebleau was the paradise of artists until art was asked to equal, rather than reproduce, nature. People started to believe that the flowers in the field, no matter how fresh and vivid their hues, paled before the complicated floral decorations that man could reinvent artificially. As Huysmans has the exacting Des Esseintes declare in *Against Nature*, there is

> no moonlit Forest of Fontainebleau that cannot be reproduced by stage scenery under floodlighting; no cascade that cannot be imitated to perfection by hydraulic engineering; no rock that papier-mâché cannot counterfeit; no flower that carefully chosen taffeta and delicately coloured paper cannot match![31]

Les fleurs du mal are at base hothouse flowers. Fallen in the eyes of Symbolists to the level of monotone background created by a set designer devoid of imagination, the trees of Fontainebleau disappeared from canvases to be replaced by stylised copies, on the model of the stained-glass windows of the churches of Rouen or tapestries from the time of Henry III.

17. The Oise Valley: Pontoise, Auvers-sur-Oise

The Oise Valley was undoubtedly one of the Impressionists most cherished places: its brown earth and low houses with sloping roofs were as much a part of their world as the cafés of Montmartre and the sparkling waves of the Seine. Both Pissarro and Cézanne found the serenity there that they needed to refine their technique. The two artists, who had not been fully in their element in the unstable river environment or the lively din of night spots, found themselves in these isolated, industrious provincial villages, where muddy roads travelled by carts, crossing through flower and vegetable gardens, connected the countryside to the market square, located near the old Gothic cathedral. The habit of walking while mulling over the same motifs led them to simplify their volumes and lighten their palettes.

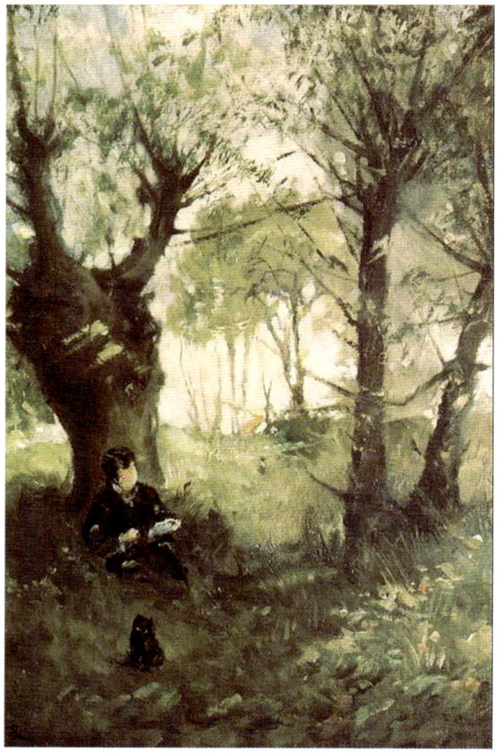

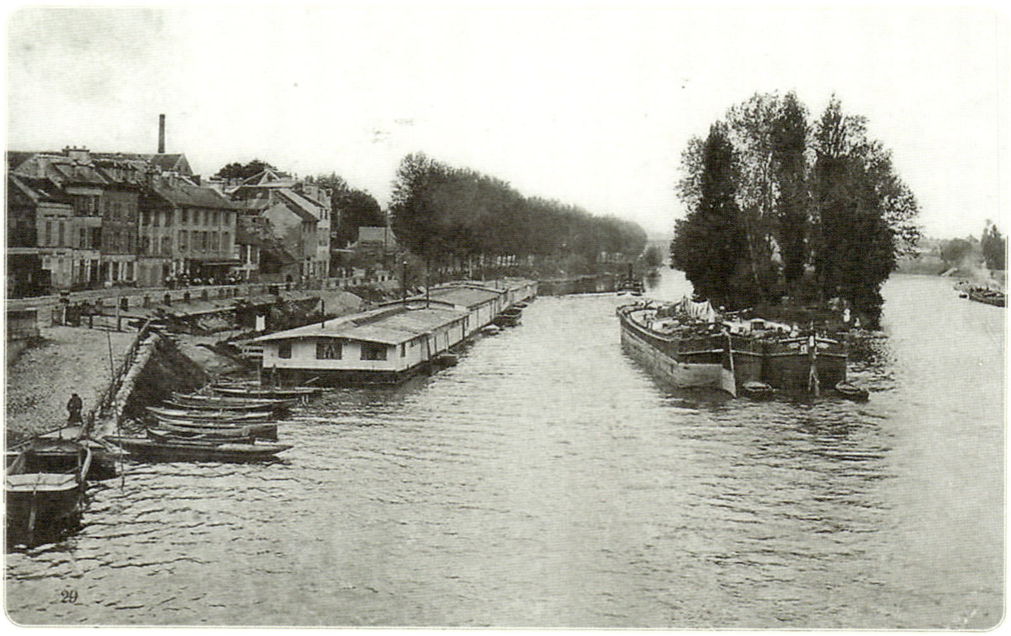

Berthe Morisot, *Old Road to Auvers*, 1863. Private Collection

The Oise River in Pontoise

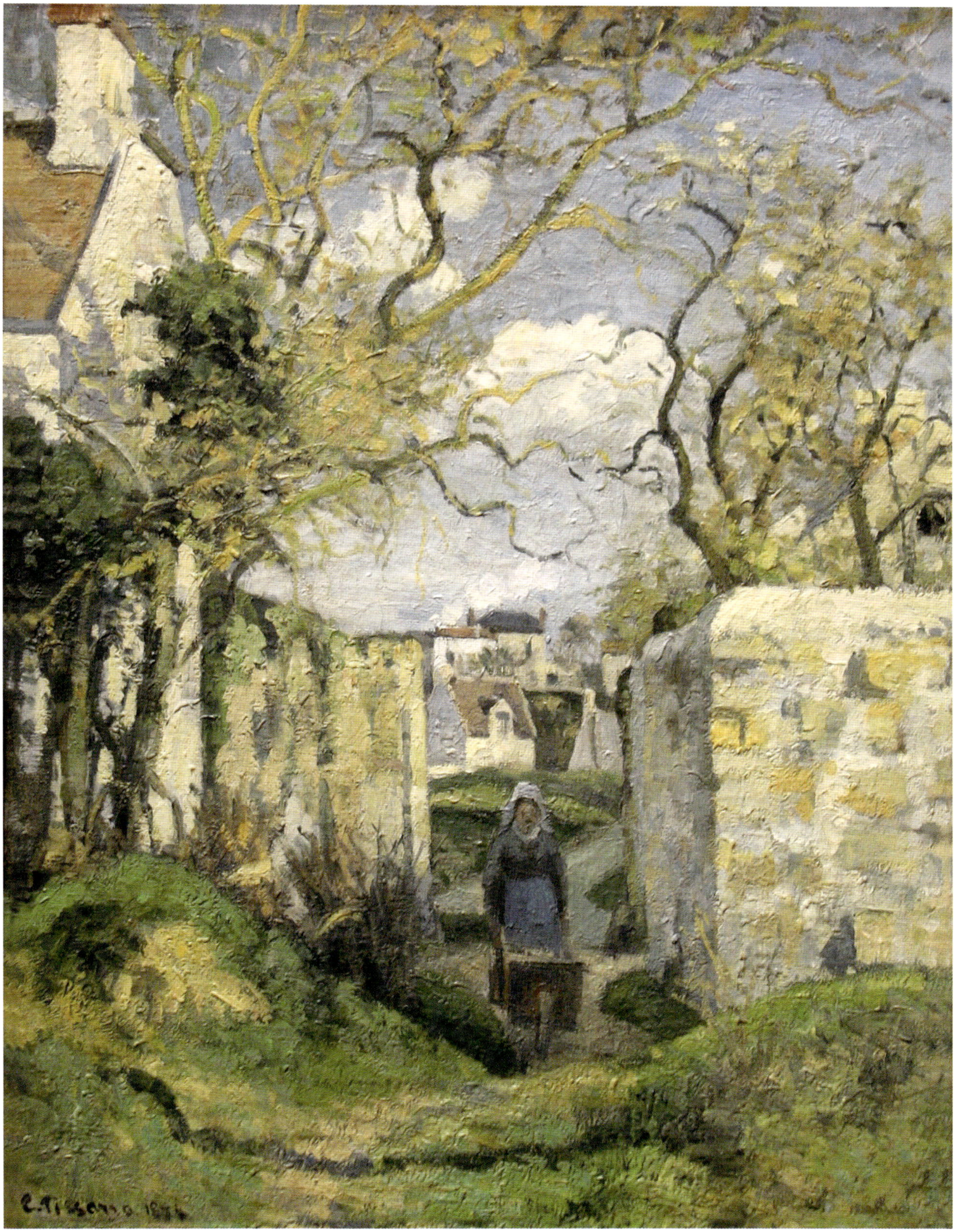

Camille Pissarro, *View of Pontoise*, 1874. Stockholm, Nationalmuseum

Amidst this calm and through their constancy, their vision was clarified, and their impressions were translated onto the canvas more simply and directly. The first to visit the region were, however, the Morisot sisters: in 1863, on the advice of Corot,

Camille Pissarro, *Rue de l'Hermitage*, 1866. Private Collection

The main street in Pontoise

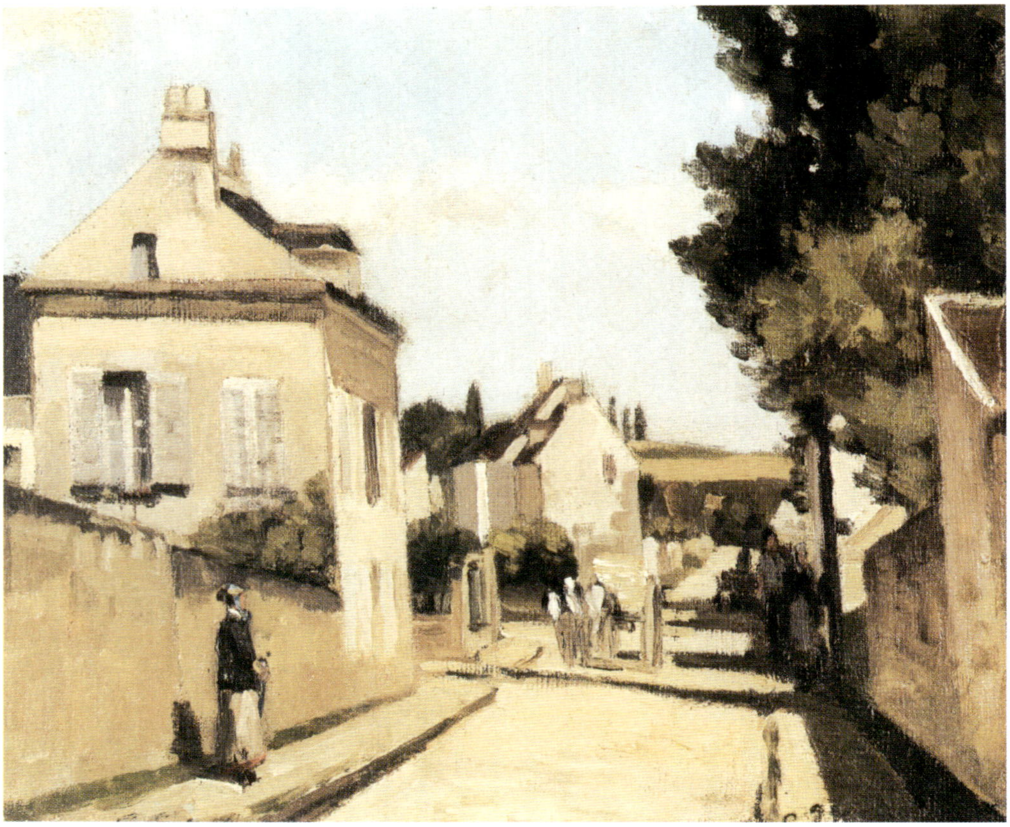

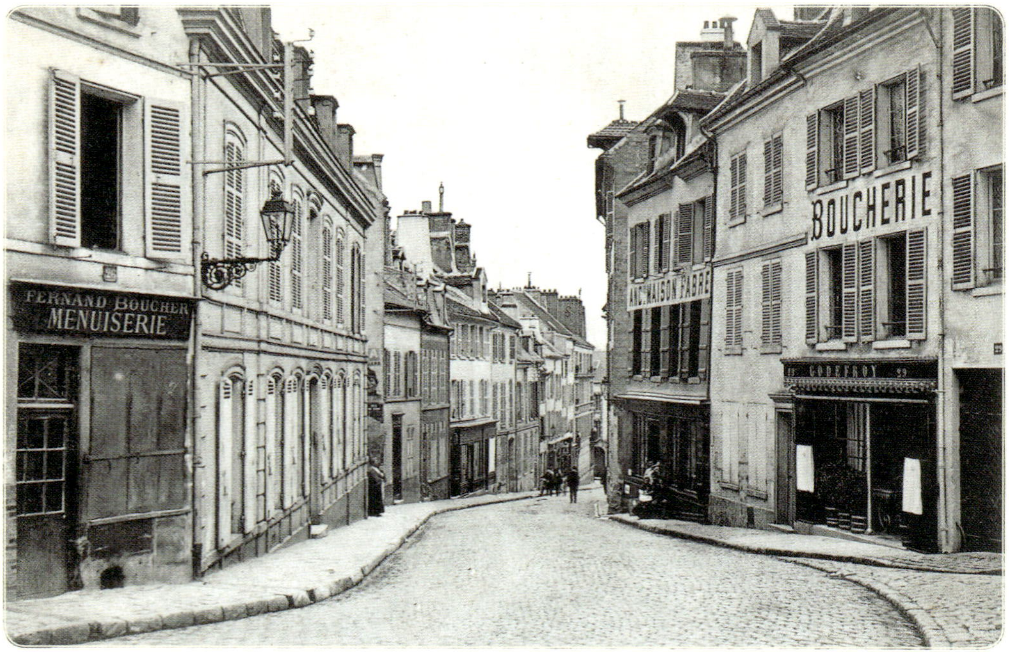

they rented a house in Le Chou to take lessons from the painter Achille Oudinot, who lived in the area. Berthe completed a few delightful landscapes there that year, including *Old Road to Auvers*, with its fine balance of just a few shades of green and light brown. But the Morisot sisters did not link their name to the Oise Valley in the same way as Pissarro, who moved to Pontoise in 1867. At first, he lived in rue

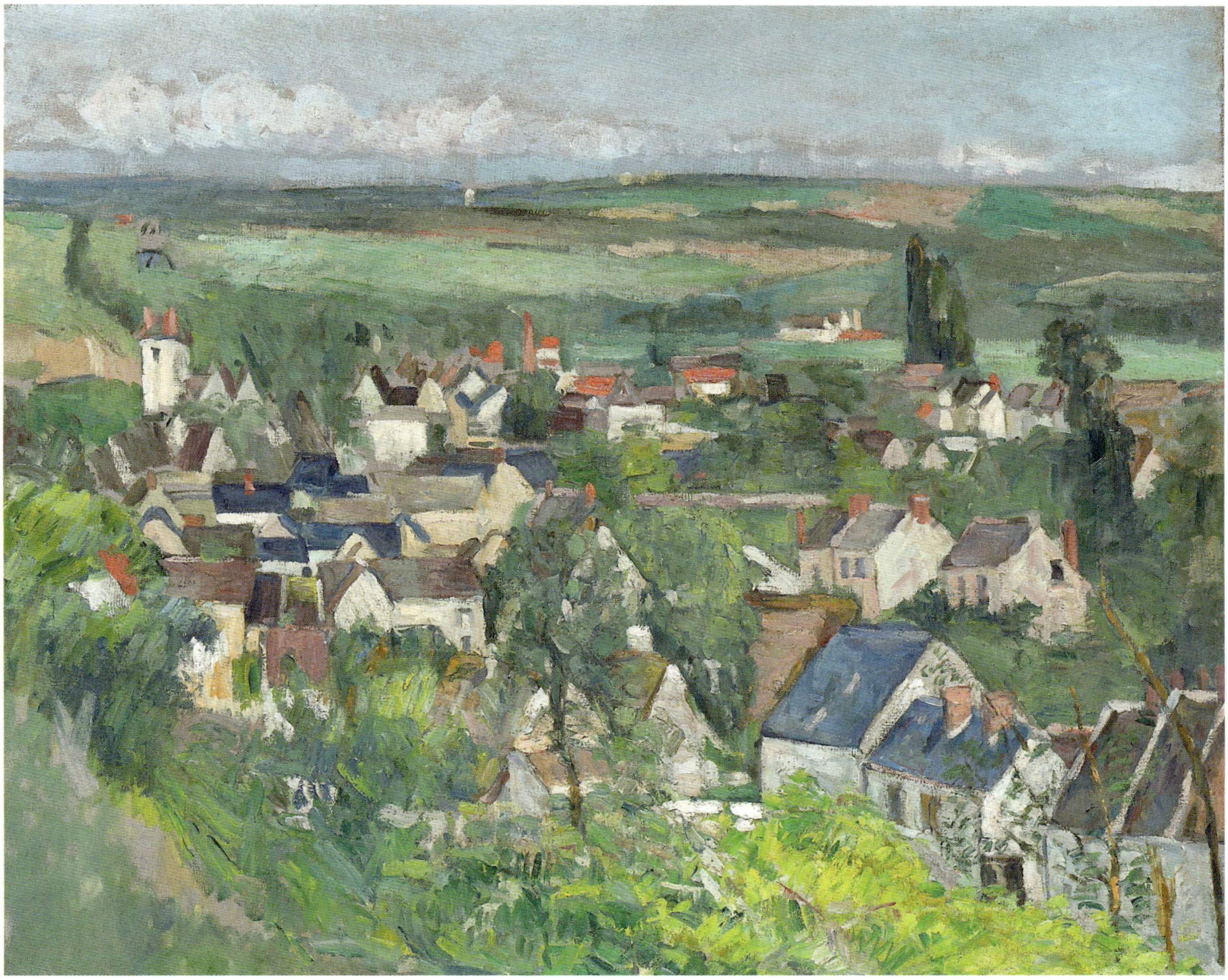

Paul Cézanne, *View of Auvers*, 1874. Chicago, Art Institute of Chicago

du Fond de l'Hermitage with his lover Julie Vellay and their children, then, in 1872, at 16 rue Malebranche, after a stay in London during which he discovered the art of Turner. He often went for walks beyond the village, to Le Chou or Auvers, where he found his beloved straw roofs, or all the way to Ennery, Montgeroult, Le Valhermeil or Chaponval. He led a simple life, like that of the farmers, getting up at dawn and returning at dusk, wearing the tall boots and felt hat he was photographed in alongside his friend Cézanne in 1874. After moving there in 1872, the latter began to slowly mature his style, gradually eliminating its more unchecked and impetuous aspects. He was extremely docile, imitating Pissarro, who in those years grew a long flowing beard, taking on the appearance of a benign patriarch. By dint of following Pissarro's suggestions, Cézanne finally managed to go along with nature, which he had at first bent with his own impetus. We can see the results in *View of Auvers*, the nearby town where he had recently moved. In 1881, Pissarro was followed by another young painter, the still inexpert Gauguin. He then resumed moving from village to village, until, after having explored all of Oise Valley, he settled in Éragny-sur-Epte.

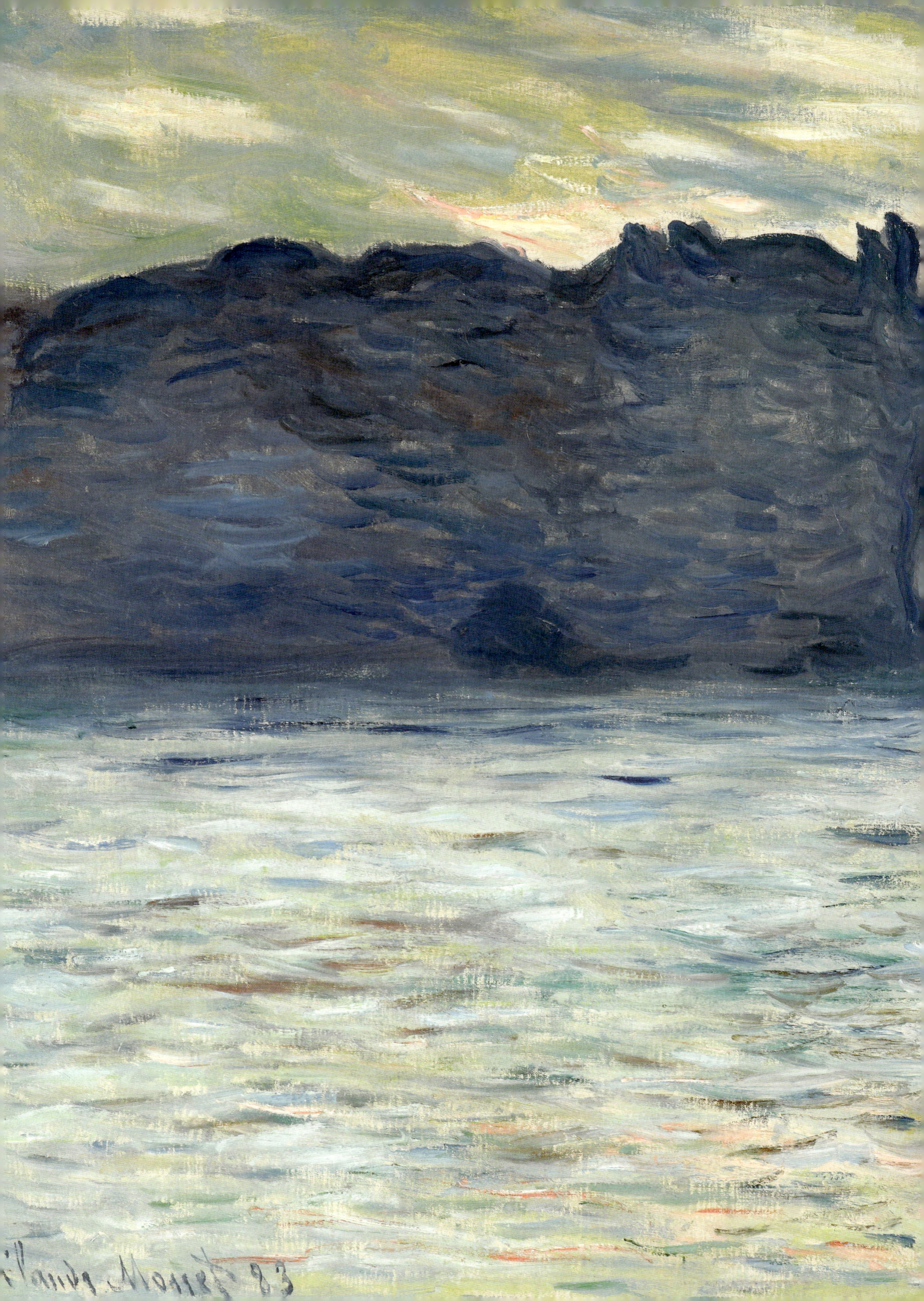

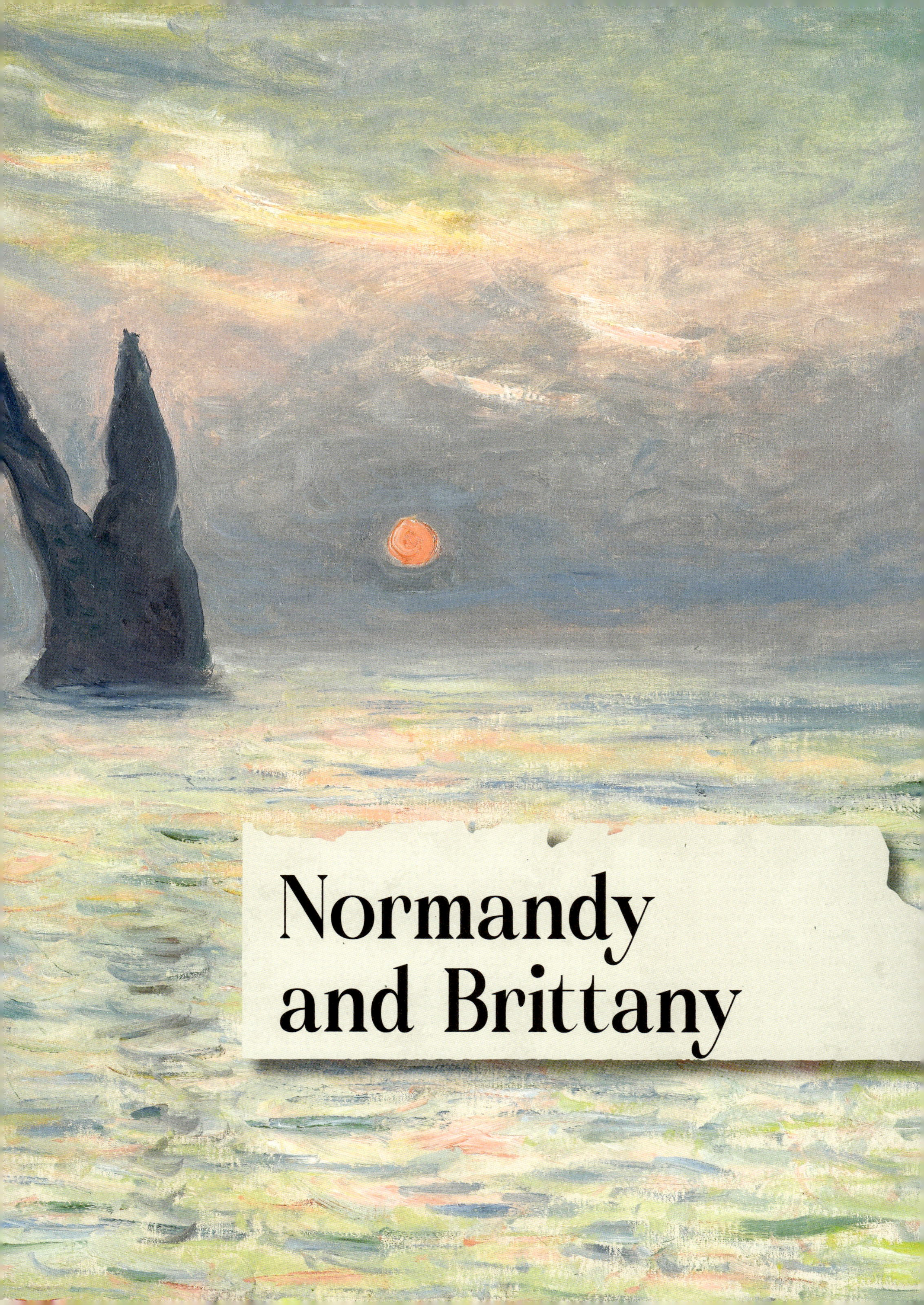

Normandy and Brittany

18. Giverny

Giverny is near the medieval village of Vernon, not far from where the Epte joins the Seine. The unadorned house that Monet discovered in 1883, and then rented from Monsieur Singeot, stood far from the road in the middle of a vast swampy area, connected to the towns by a small railway. It was surrounded by an uncultivated Eden of about one hectare, which the boxwood hedges (the garden's only ornament) lent no particular charm. Monet had the vision to see in that awkward little duckling the elegant, snow-white swan of tomorrow. Purchasing the house and grounds in 1890, the artist set to work transforming it. He began by cutting down the firs and cypresses, which have given the spot a melancholy air. But he left the trunks, using them as supports for climbing rosebushes. These wild, twisting roses soon intertwined, creating a vault streaked with multicoloured petals above the paths. When the trunks died, they were replaced with metal trellises, but these were not strong enough to support the luxurious frenzy of fevered flowers. At the beginning, one would have said that the music of a quartet flowed from that garden. Now that the abundance of irises was joined by peonies, phlox, delphiniums, asters, gladiolas, dahlias and chrysanthemum, planted in place of the more typical flowerbeds, it would have been described as orchestral. Maurice Barrès described the flowering sanctuaries he had seen in Italy as *syllabes chantantes, terrasses parfumées*, more imaginary than real.[32] And indeed, at Giverny, Symbolism found its Alhambra, its Tivoli, its Versailles: Monet's imaginative water

pp. 112–113
Claude Monet, *The Cliff, Étretat, Sunset*, 1883. Raleigh, North Carolina Museum of Art

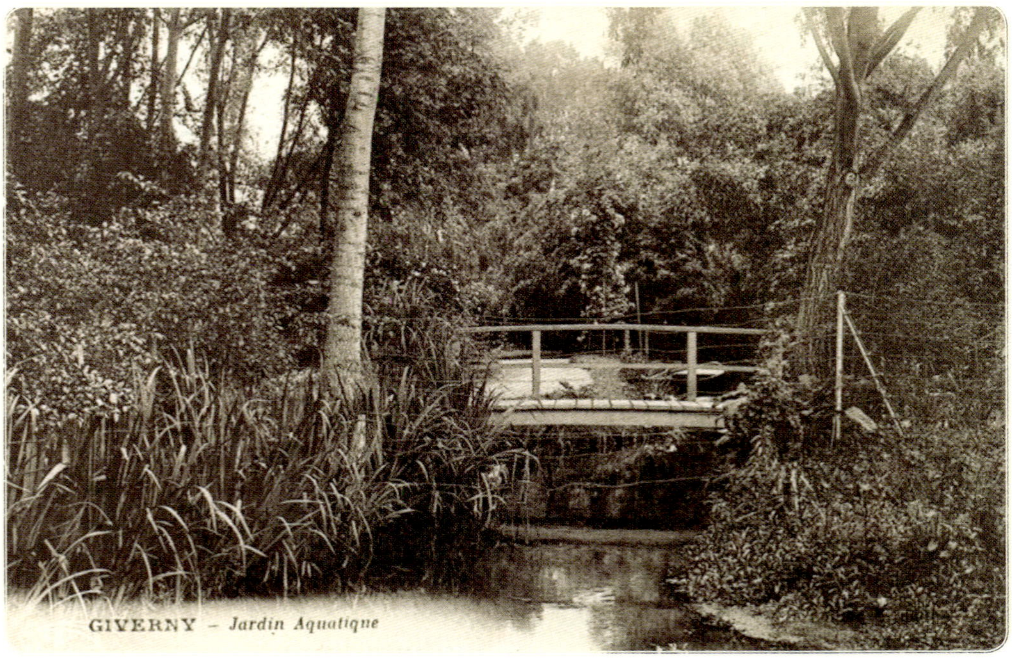

The water garden at Giverny

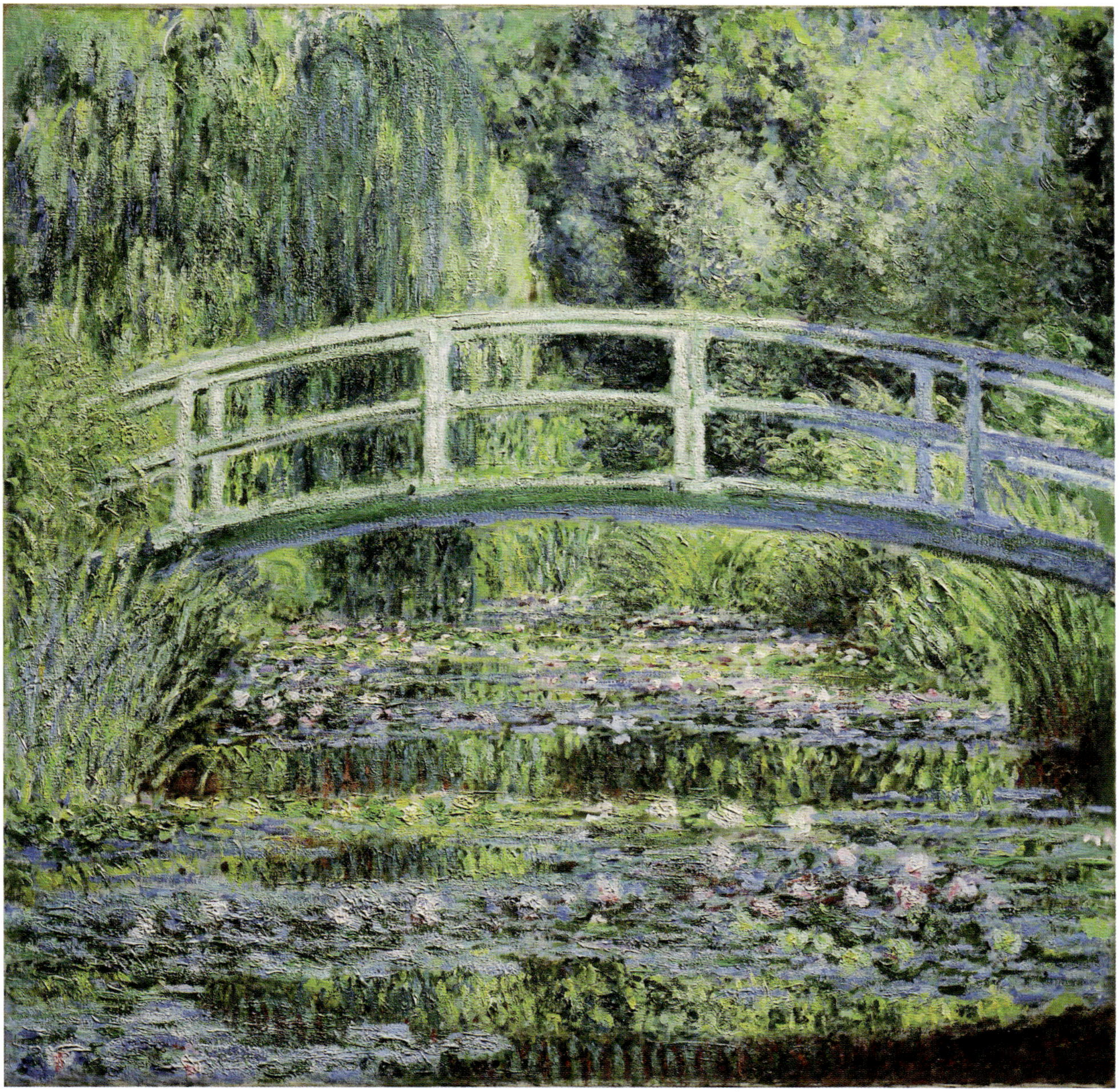

Claude Monet, *Water Lilies and Japanese Bridge*, 1899. Princeton, Princeton University Art Museum

architecture and living pillars were like a backdrop for the scene of Ophelia's suicide, as imagined by John Everett Millais, or the flower duet in Léo Delibes's *Lakmé*, while the vases of Émile Gallé and Hector Guimard's lianas later emerged from its views, imprisoned in glass.

This miracle was made possible by the diversion of the Ru, a branch of the Epte. Part of the land was drained, part of it reshaped by the brook. The garden's greatest glory was the artificial lake. The artist himself described it as:

> a pond that I created about fifteen years ago, about 200 metres in circumference, fed by a branch of the Epte River. It is edged by irises and various aquatic plants framed by trees, in particular poplars and willows, many of which of the weeping variety. This is where I painted the water lilies with a Japanese-style bridge.[33]

Monet's iris garden at Giverny

Claude Monet, *Water Lilies*, 1906. Chicago, Art Institute of Chicago

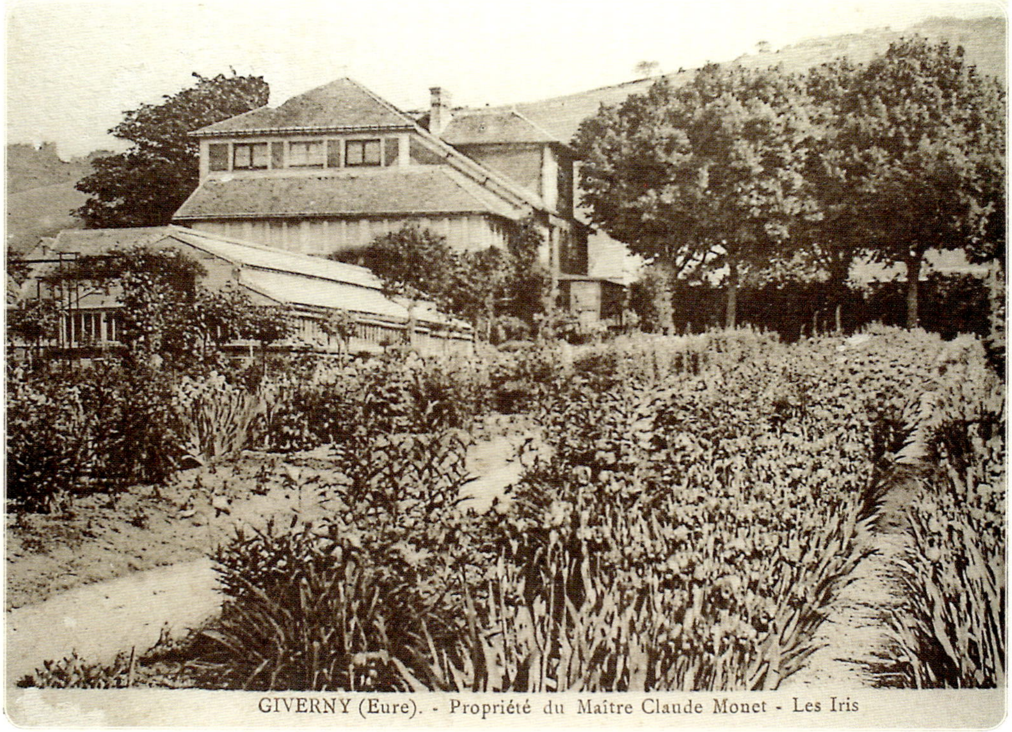

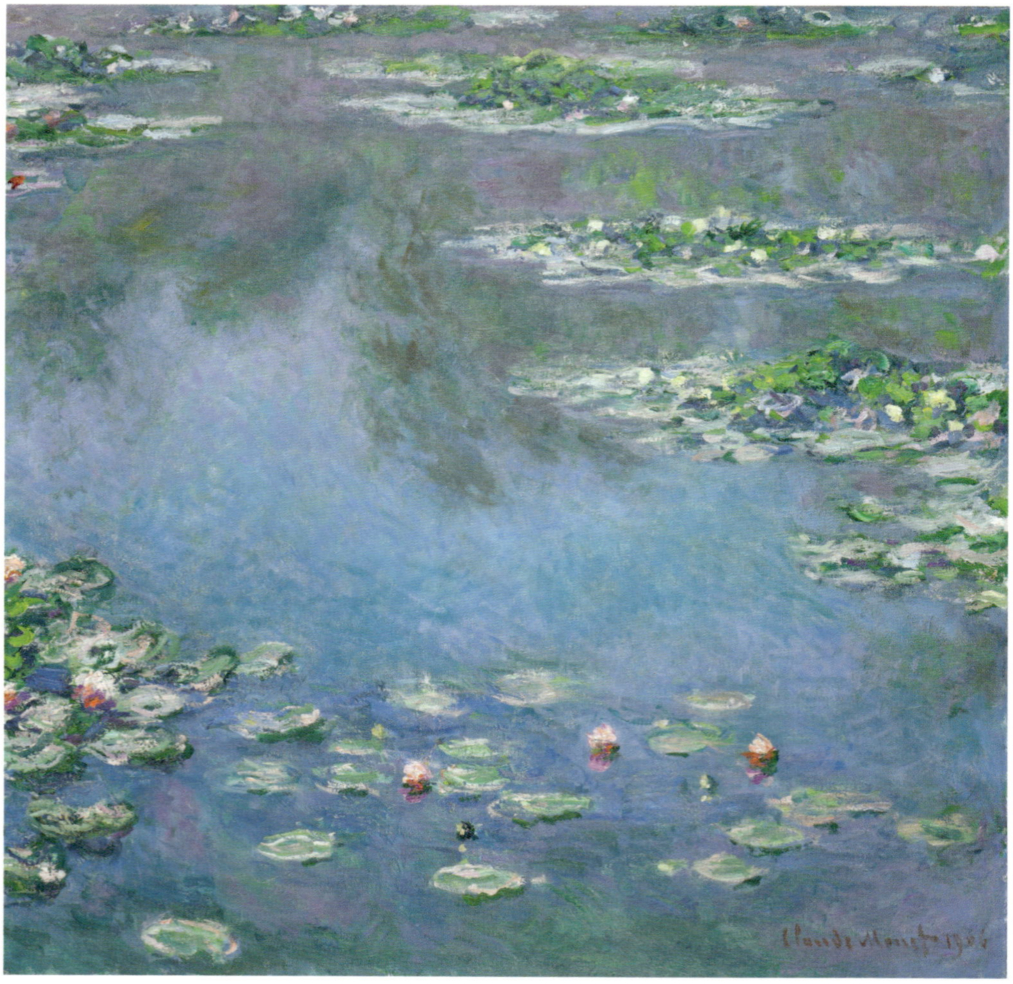

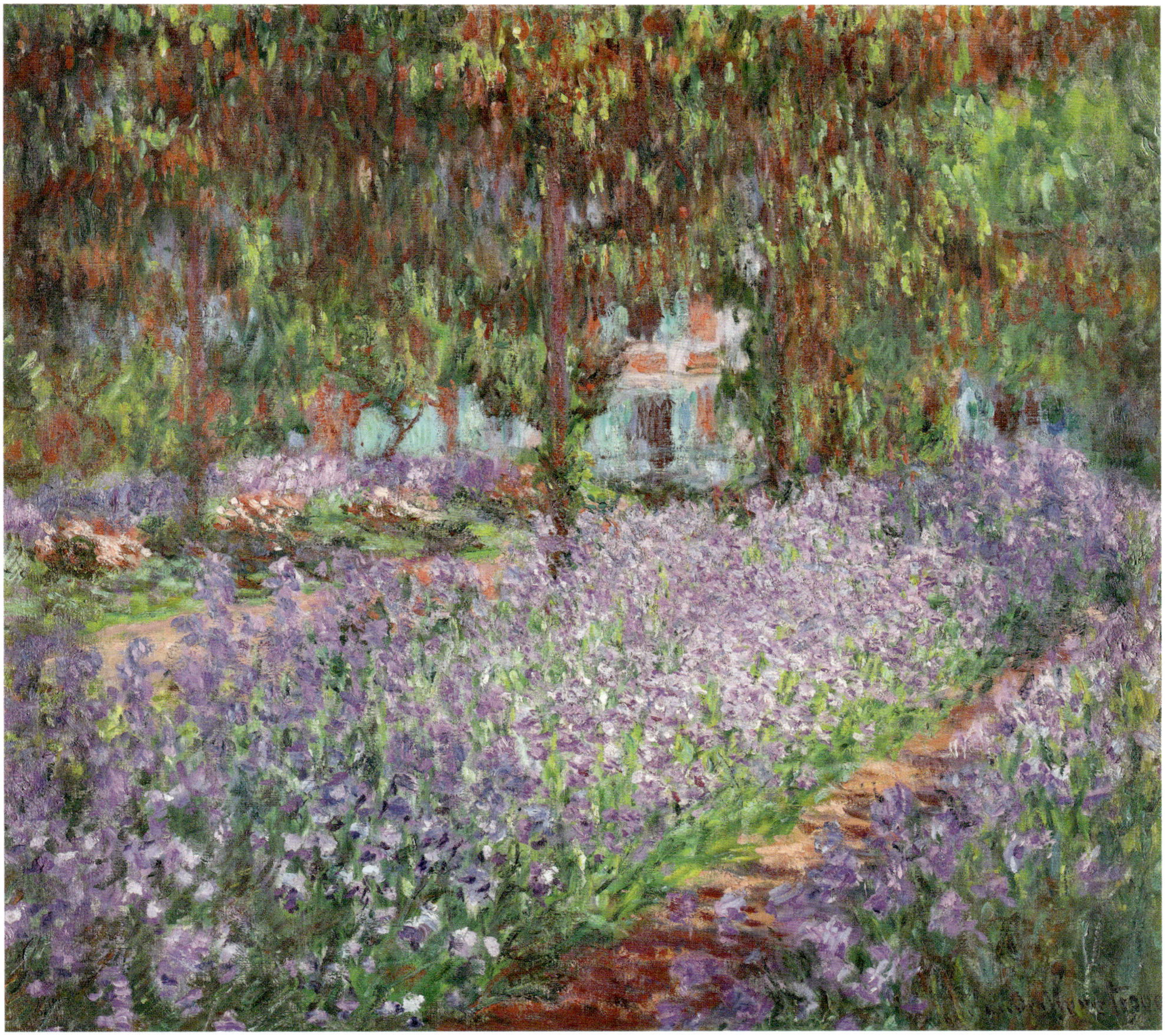

Claude Monet, *The Artist's Garden at Giverny*, 1900. Paris, Musée d'Orsay

As Monet's vision weakened, his tired eyes were still filled with colour during his walks around the grounds. In 1918 he confessed:

> I no longer perceived colours with the same intensity; I no longer painted light with the same accuracy. Reds appeared muddy too, pinks insipid and the intermediate and lower tones escaped me. As for forms, they always appeared clear and I rendered them with the same decision.[34]

Proust considered Giverny a work of art, a 'true transposition of art rather more than a model for pictures, a picture already executed within nature itself which becomes illuminated from beneath by the gaze of a great painter', the first sketch of his latest masterpiece, the series of *Water Lilies*.

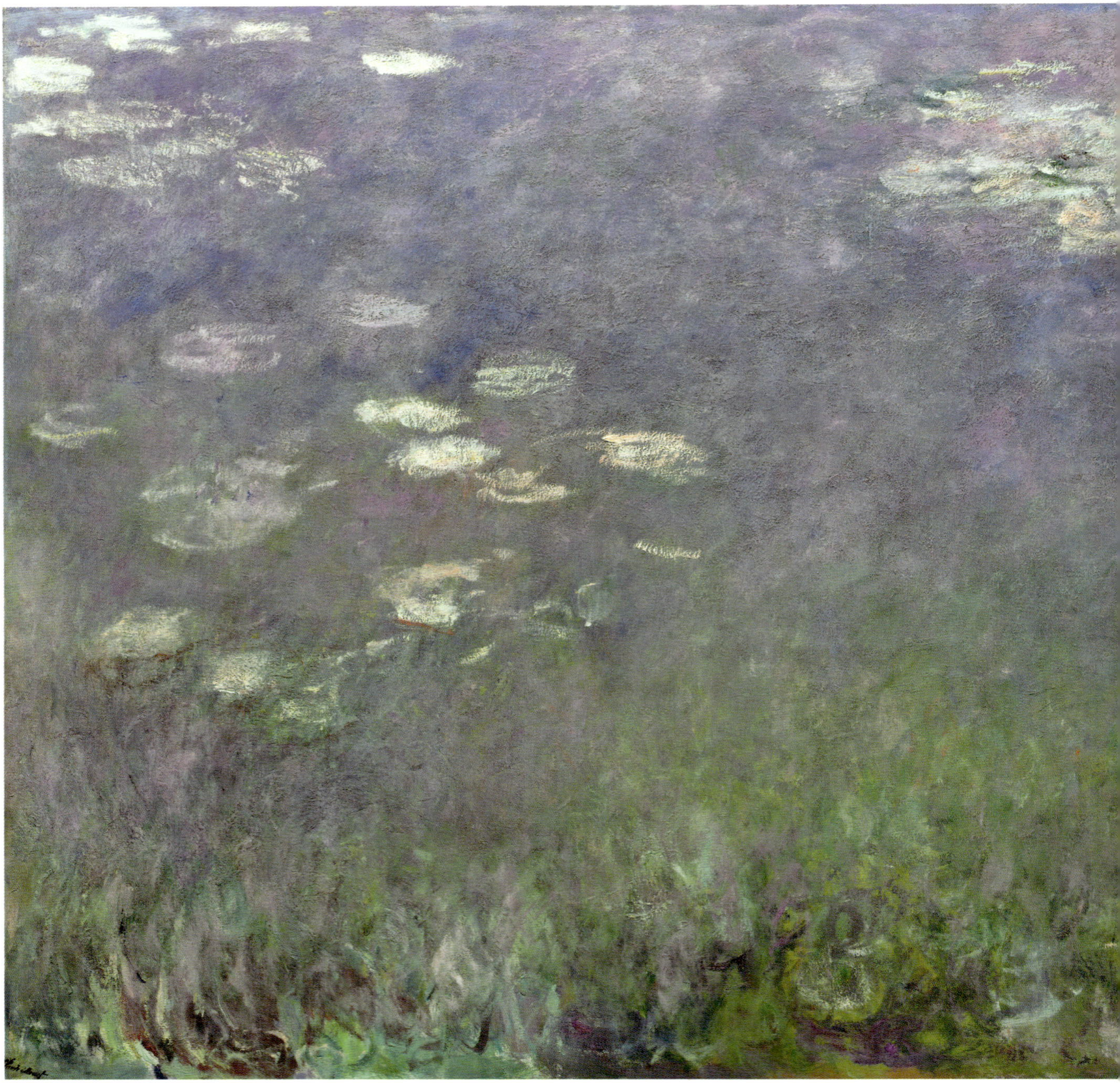

Claude Monet, *Water Lilies*, 1915–1926. Cleveland, Cleveland Museum of Art

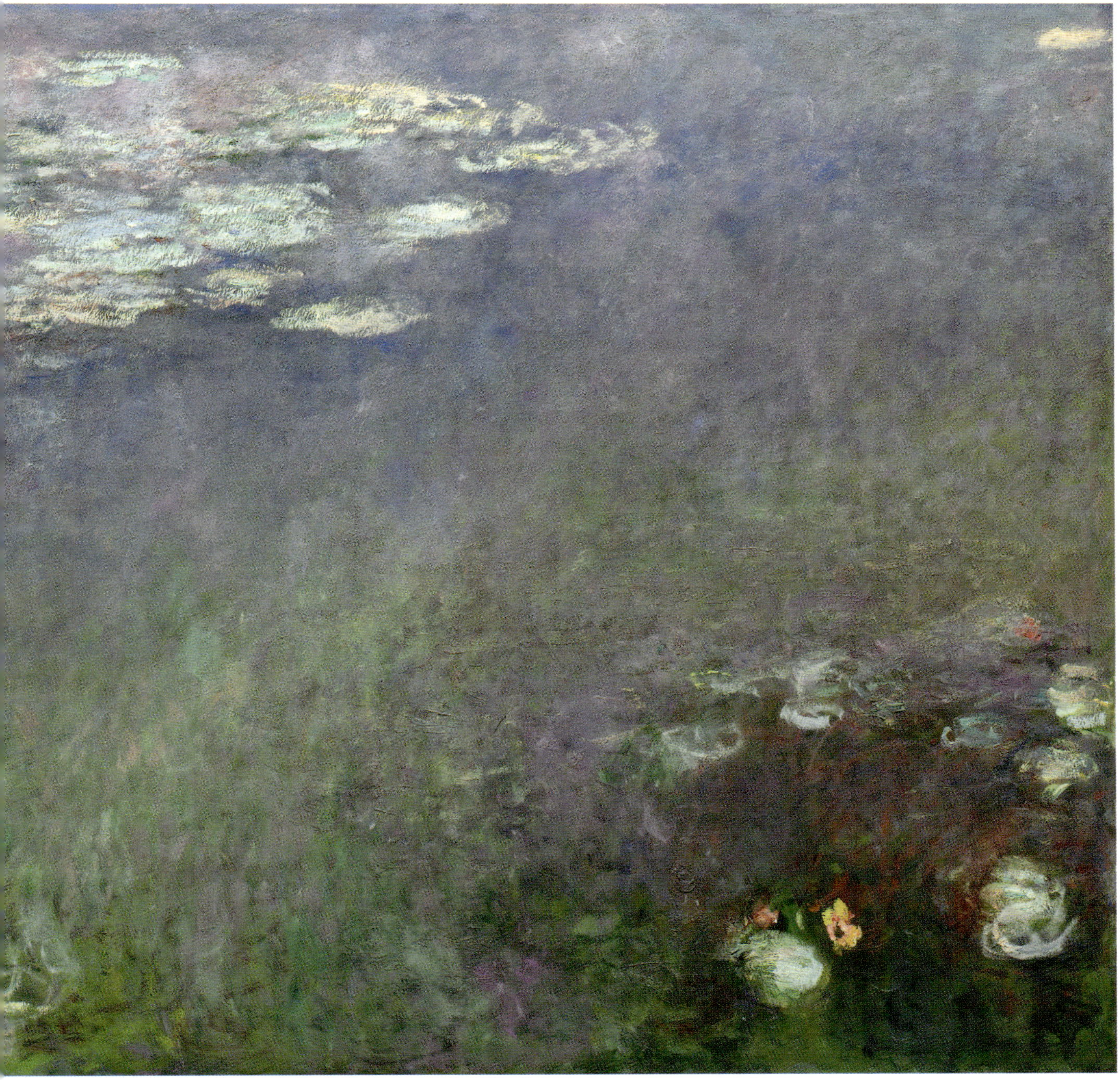

19. The Estuary of the Seine: Le Havre, Honfleur

Fashions can change a place overnight; the one for beach holidays, imported from England, had quickly spread throughout the romantic, patriarchal Normandy of Barbey d'Aurevilly. And yet, Beuzeval, a modest village separate from the seaside resort of Houlgate, still had its mills along the Drochon Torrent, when one of them was rented by the Morisot family for the summer of 1864. The areas nearby were perennially and placidly steeped in memories of the history of France: Dives-sur-Mer, from which William the Conqueror set out for Hastings, and Caen, with its noble medieval abbeys. Not to forget Cabourg, immortalised in *Recherche* and beloved by the aristocracy of Faubourg Saint-Germain. These tiny villages, like all the ones between Cabourg and Honfleur, such as Deauville and Trouville, more or less met the same fate: transformed from humble fishing villages into stylish, modern resorts. When Empress Eugénie stayed in Dieppe, the modern fashion for beach holidays received its official stamp of approval.

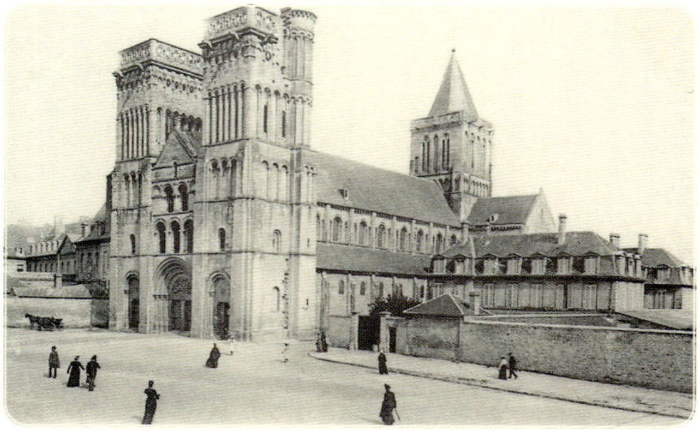

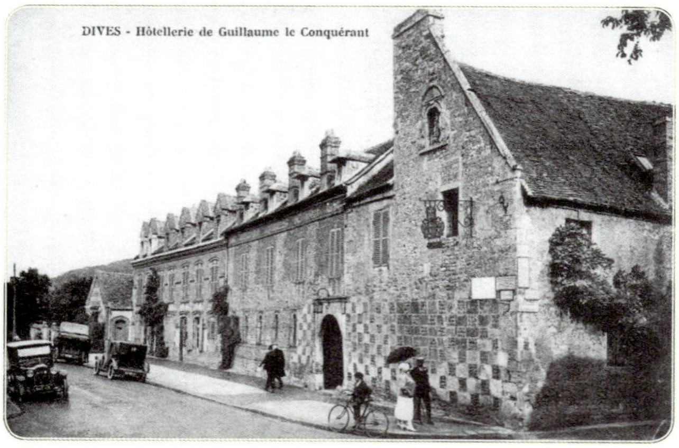

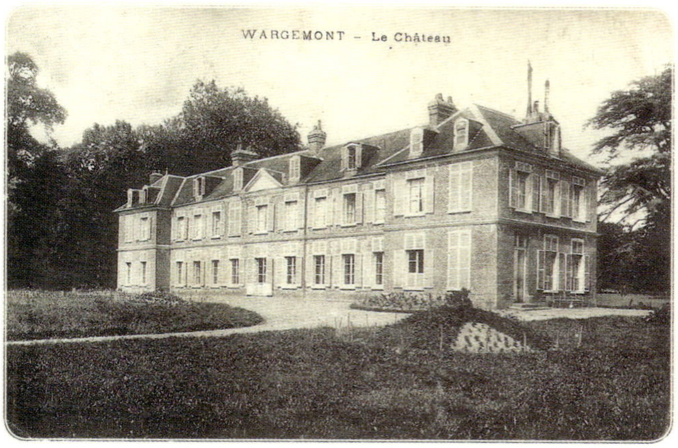

The Normandy coast offered the Impressionists' brush a calmer, more refined way of life than the one in merry, carefree Bougival. And indeed, a conversation-piece-like quiet seems to spread from the gentlemen painted by Monet sitting on the *Terrace at Sainte-Adresse* or the ones lazing about on the promenade in his *Hôtel des Roches Noires à Trouville.* Berthe Morisot was inspired by the nearby village of Petites Dalles for a gentle, country idyll, *Reading*, which portrays her sister sitting in a field and reading a book. Whereas Renoir, so fond of Montmartre's humble little houses, stayed in Wargemont as the guest of the banker Paul Bérard, painting his family and the rose garden that surrounded the castle.

The most fascinating of these towns, however, was Étretat, with its white cliffs, immortalised

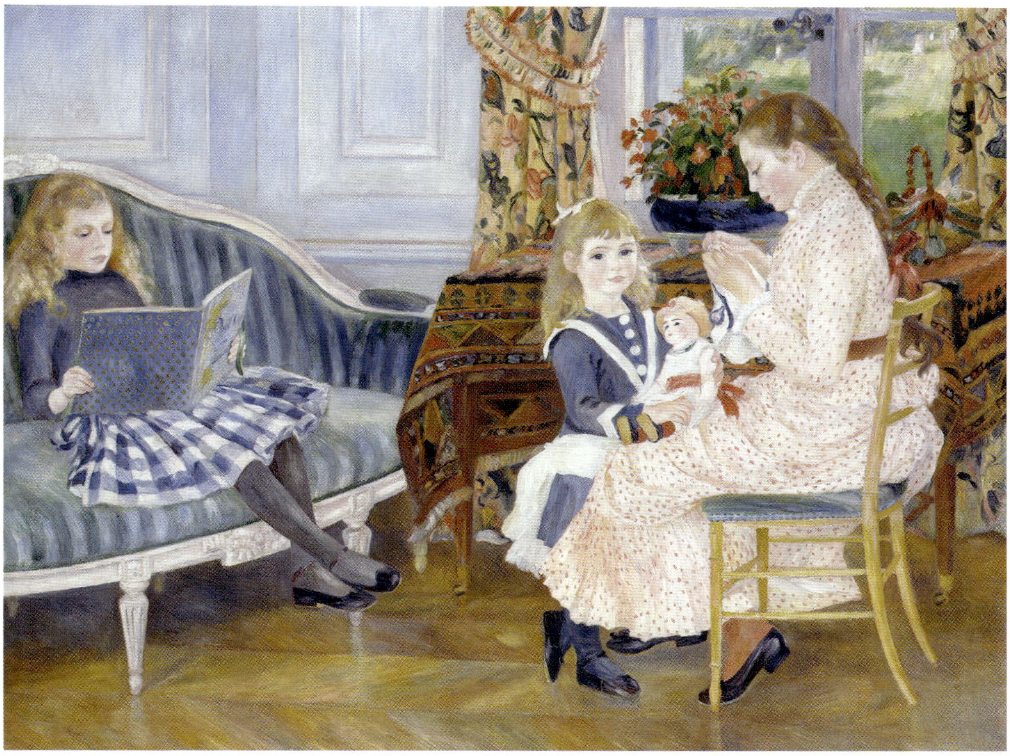

p. 120
Caen, Abbaye aux Dames

Dives-sur-Mer, the inn of William the Conqueror

Wargemont Castle

Pierre-Auguste Renoir, *Children's Afternoon at Wargemont*, 1884. Berlin, Alte Nationalgalerie

Berthe Morisot, *Reading*, 1873. Cleveland, Cleveland Museum of Art

by Courbet and Monet (pp. 112–113). The little town, beloved by poets and writers, had also welcomed, like a northern Capri, many of the exiles from across the English Channel who had incurred the disapproval of strict Victorian morality.

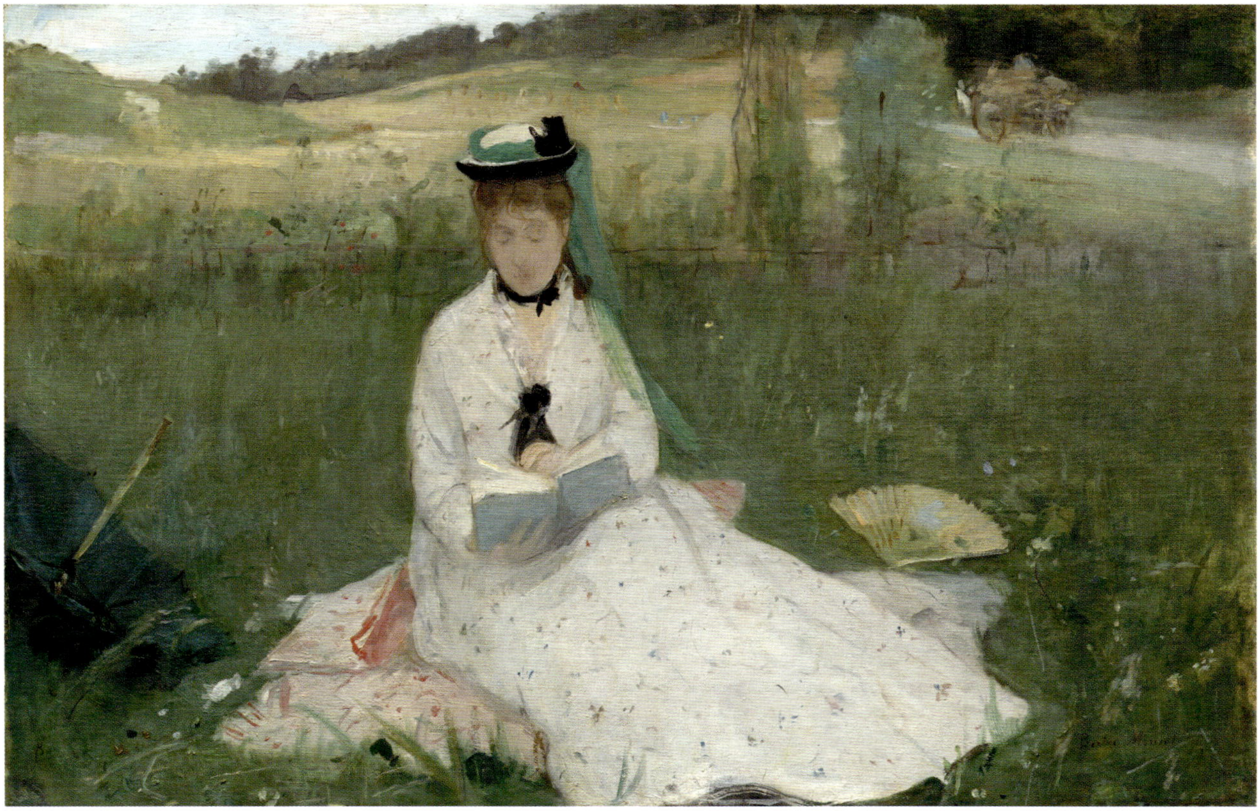

Claude Monet, *Terrace at Sainte-Adresse*, 1867. New York, The Metropolitan Museum of Art Boats at Étretat

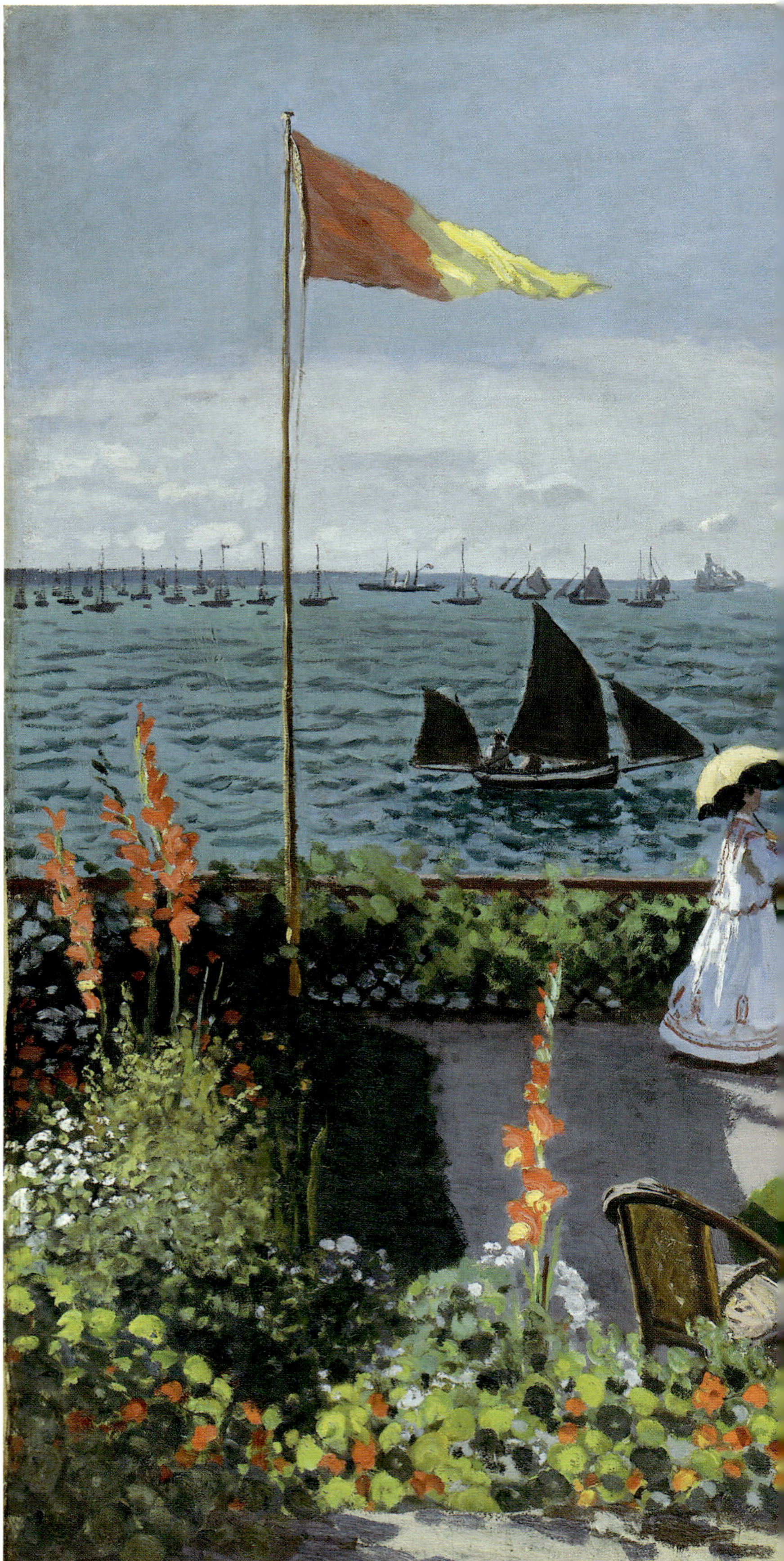

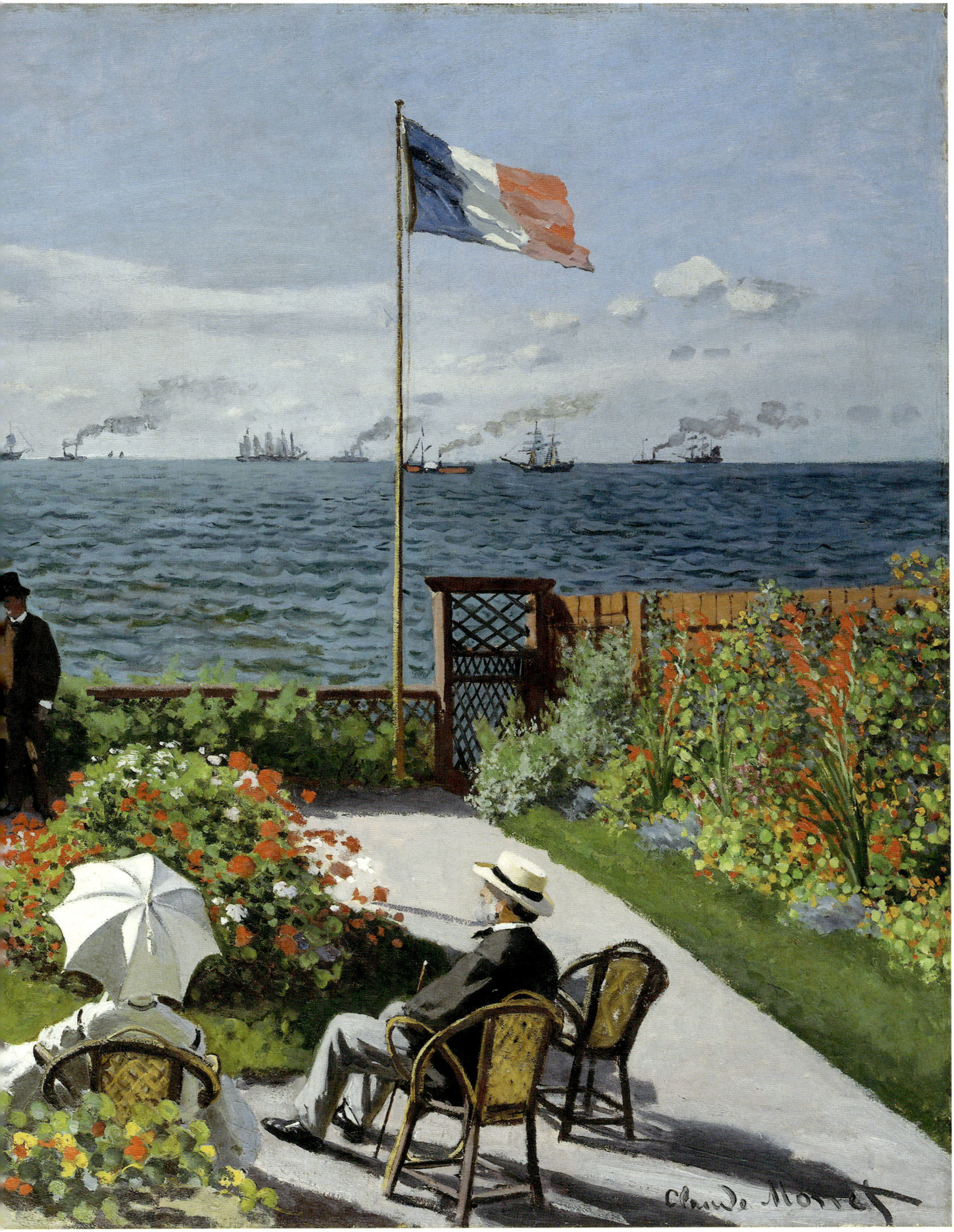

This was where Swinburne spent his days in the company of his friend George Powell and a well-dressed monkey. Once famous, the cottage, which was called Chaumière de Dolmancé in homage to one of the libertines in the Marquis de Sade's *Philosophy in the Bedroom*, with its desks full of bones and fantastical paintings, must have provided a perfect backdrop for the 'depraved Englishman' type that was, on the model of George Selwyn in Edmond de Goncourt's *Faustin*, popular in European literature at the time. But Monet kept his distance from this pernicious atmosphere and in 1885, having moved his family to rue du Havre, devoted himself to painting. Maupassant described him whilst working in the summer on the famous painting *Belle-Île, Rain Effect*:

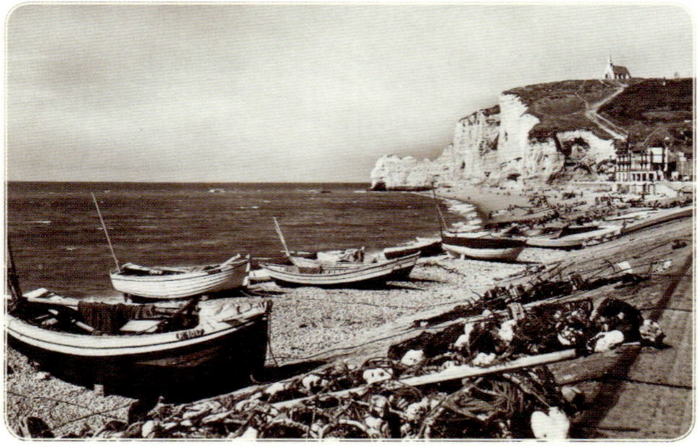

Boats in Étretat

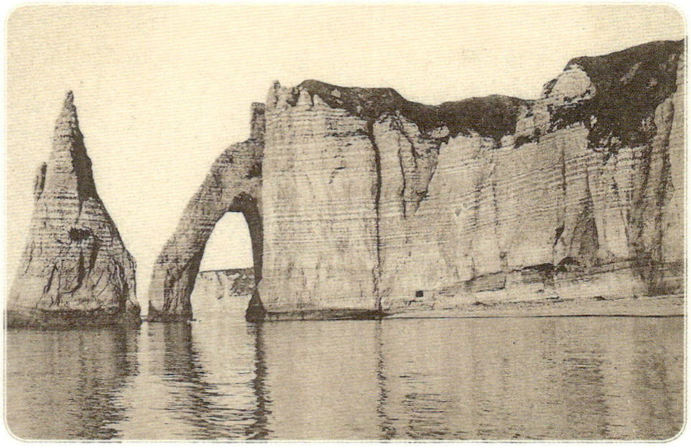

Étretat, the Porte d'Aval and L'Aiguille at high tide

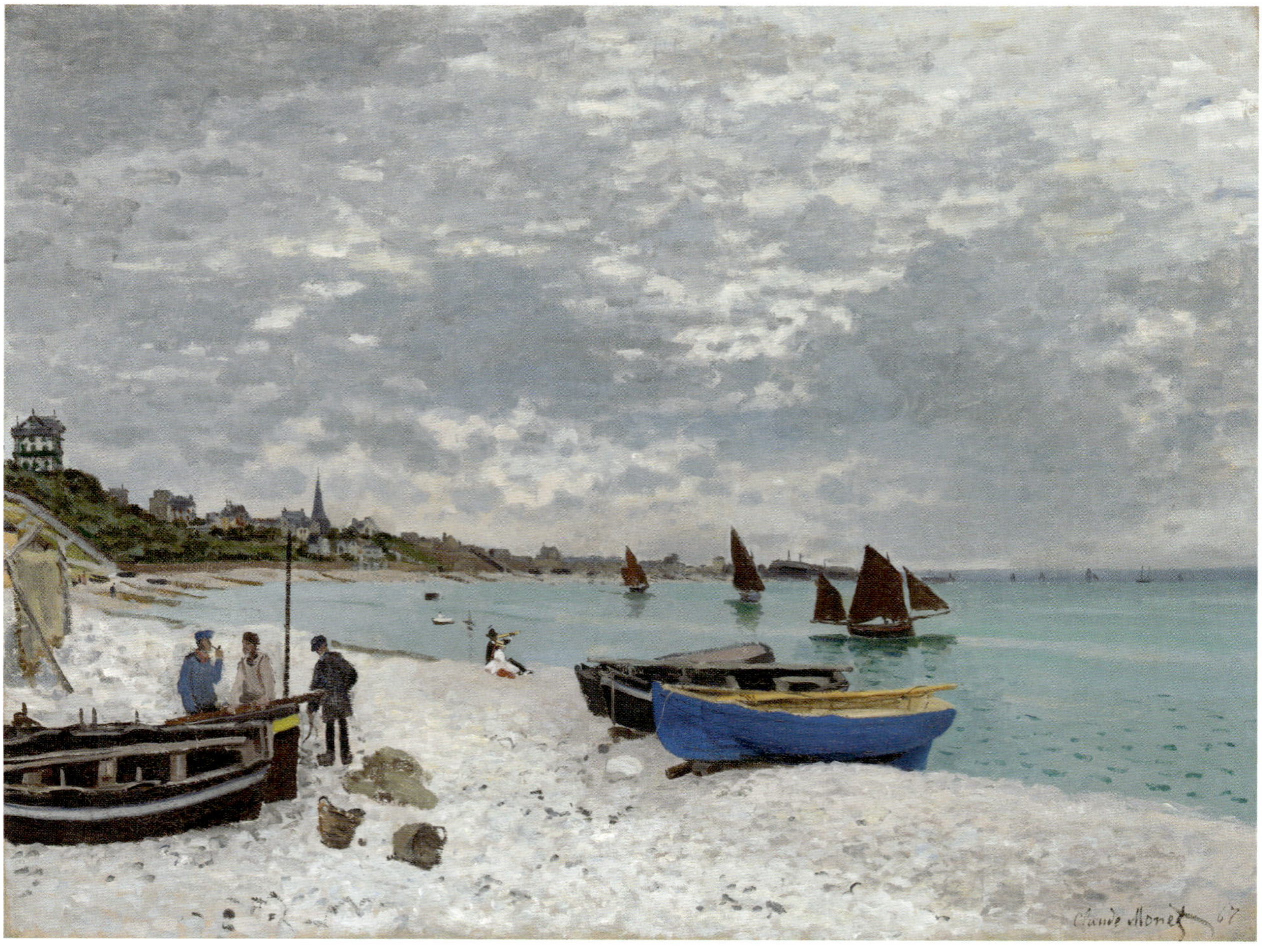

Claude Monet, *The Beach at Sainte-Adresse*, 1867. Chicago, Art Institute of Chicago

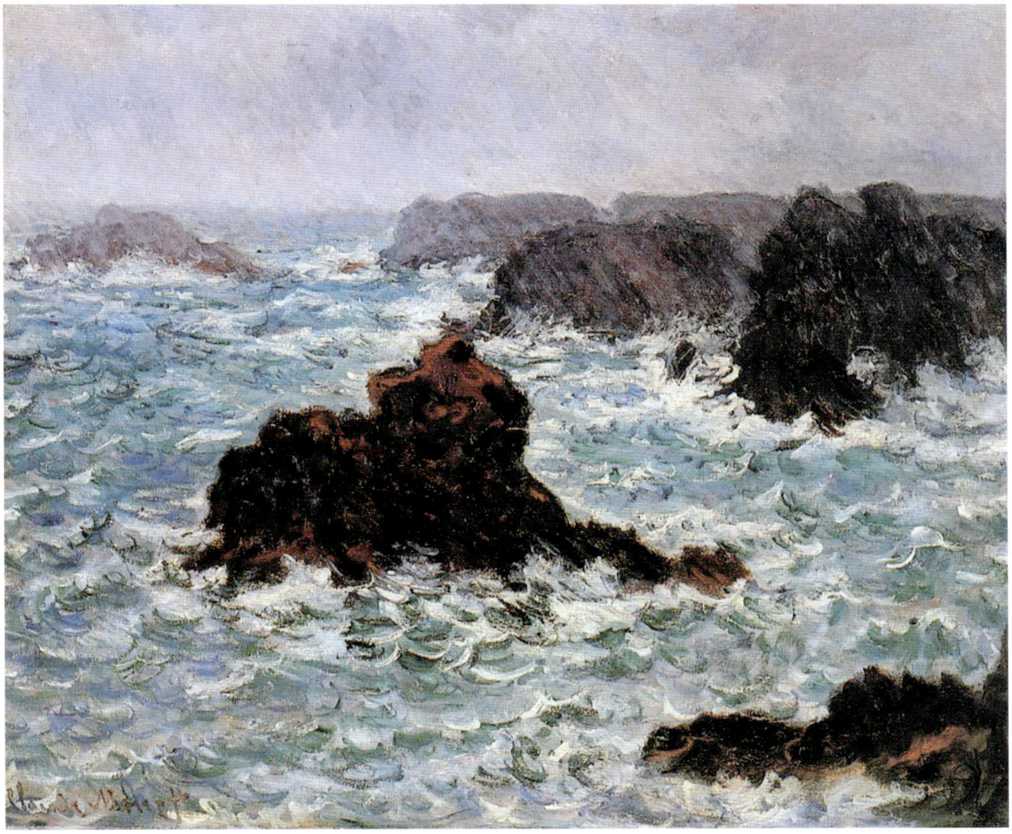

Claude Monet, *Belle-Île, Rain Effect,* 1886. Tokyo, Artizon Museum

> I have seen him thus seize a glittering shower of light on the white cliff and fix it in a flood of yellow tones which, strangely, rendered the surprising and fugitive effect of that unseizable and dazzling brilliance. On another occasion he took a downpour beating on the sea in his hands and dashed it on the canvas—and indeed it was the rain that he had thus painted, nothing but the rain veiling the waves, the rocks and the sky, hardly distinct under this deluge.[35]

For that matter, until 1875 he had gone at least twice a year to Normandy, where he had also found refuge from his creditors in 1866. Le Havre, where Monet spent his childhood, was an opulent mercantile port that had gradually expanded beyond its original nucleus, founded by Louis XII in 1509 on the marshy, unstable land that formed the estuary of the Seine. In the middle of the nineteenth century, all the raw material and industrial products, as well as the wine and spirits for which France is still renowned, travelled from there. Walking through it, its affluence was clear, from the smart blocks of flats and houses that lined the boulevards. Sainte-Adresse, where the Monet family owned property, was just as elegant but a bit more select. One got there by tram and, if one wanted, one could go from there to the lighthouse of La Hève that dominated the coast or to Trouville, which was renowned for its beach.

The maritime and commercial glory of Honfleur, on the other river front, was instead long behind it. The ruins of its old fortifications, attesting to an illustrious past along with the governor's palace, gave it an indefinable and lifeless appearance rather than a majestic one. Those who went there to paint, like Courbet, Millet, Corot, Diaz and Daubigny, were primarily interested in its shores and environs, which were so teeming with artists (who found convenient accommodation at mére Toutain's inn)

pp. 126–127
Claude Monet, *Port of Le Havre,* 1874. Philadelphia, Philadelphia Museum of Art

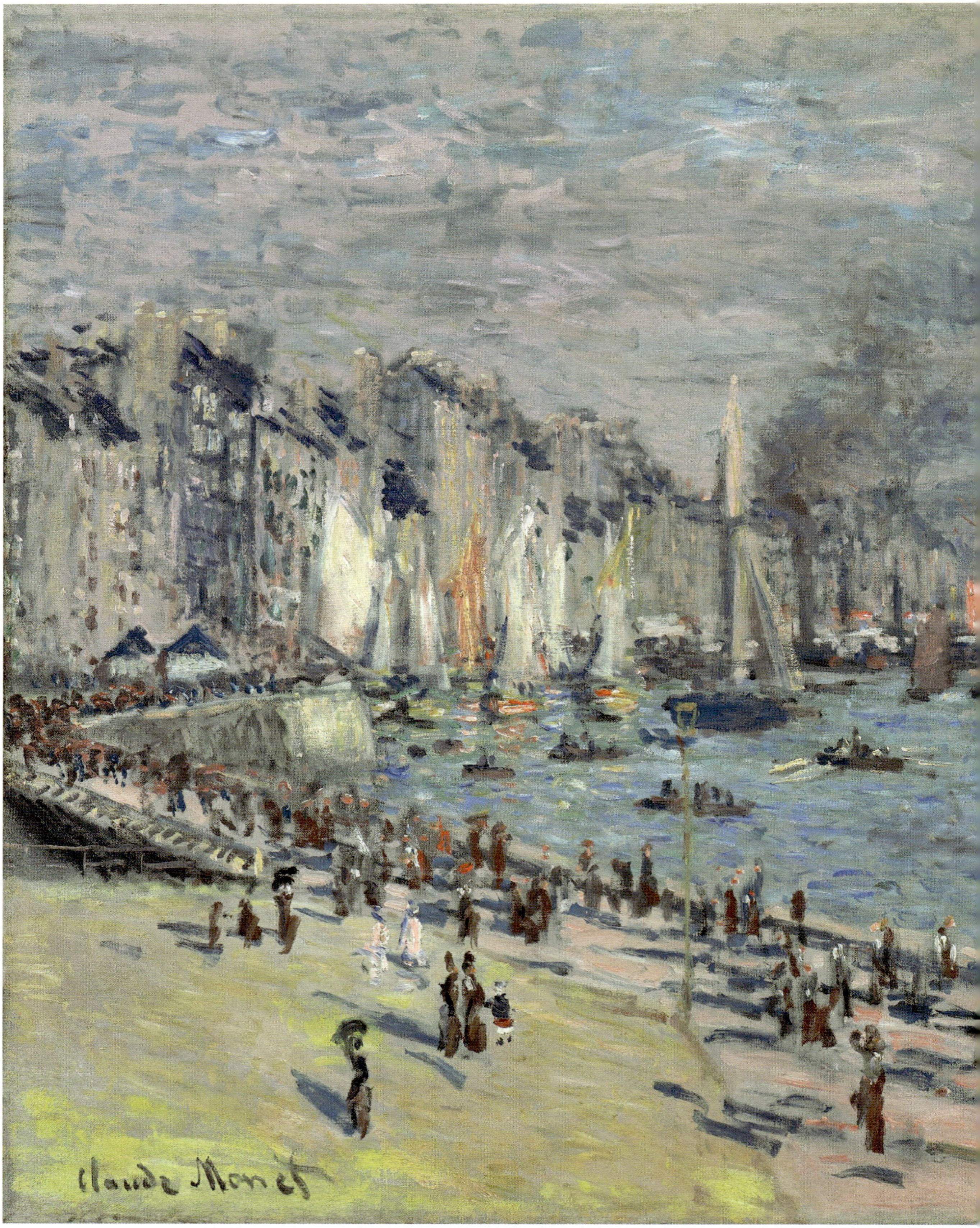
Claude Monet

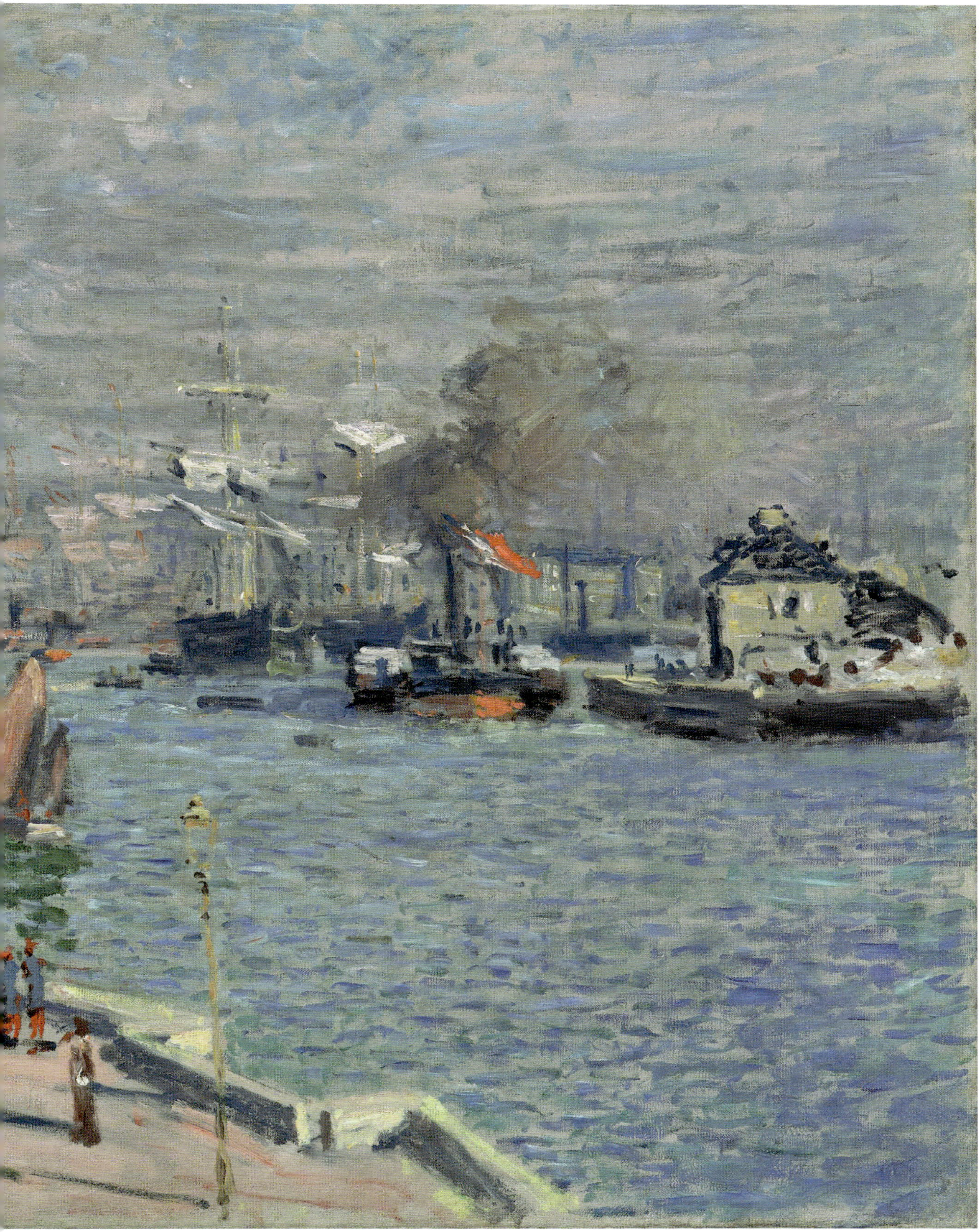

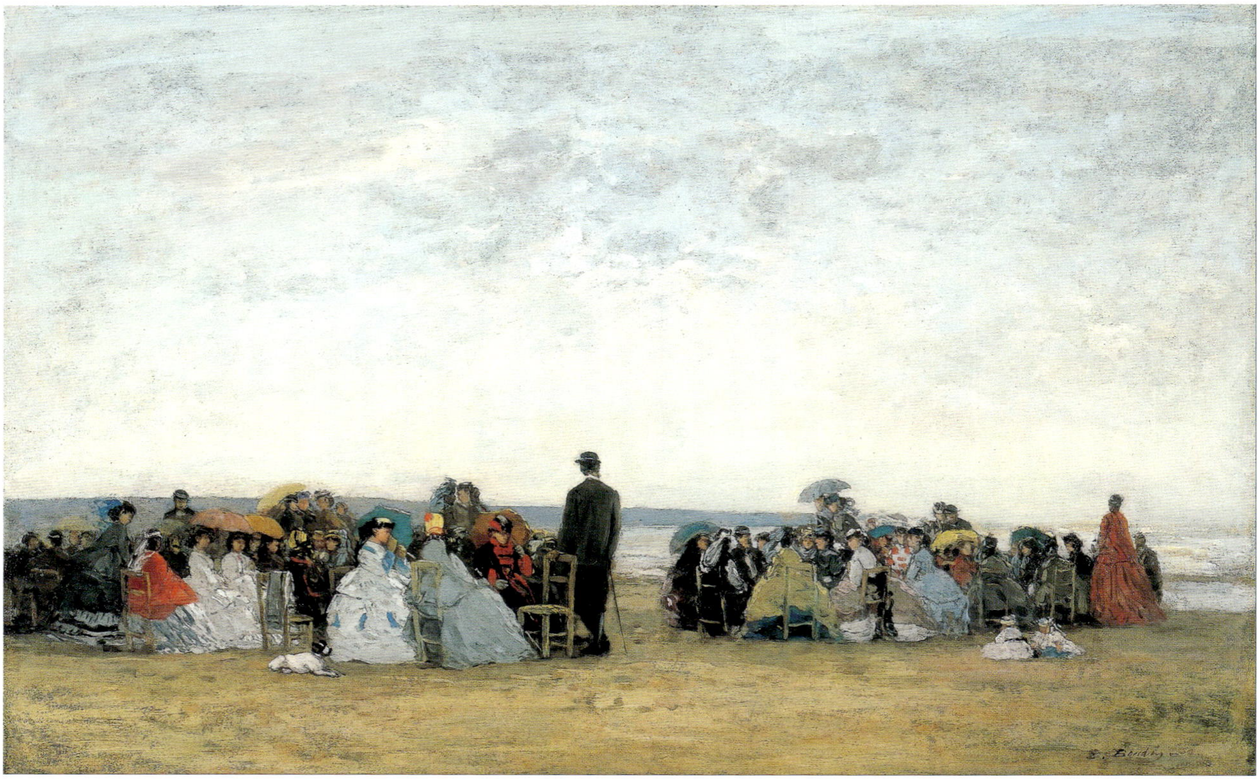

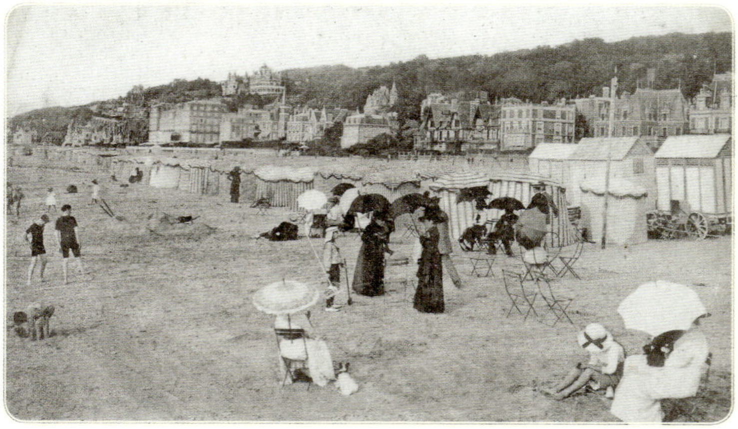

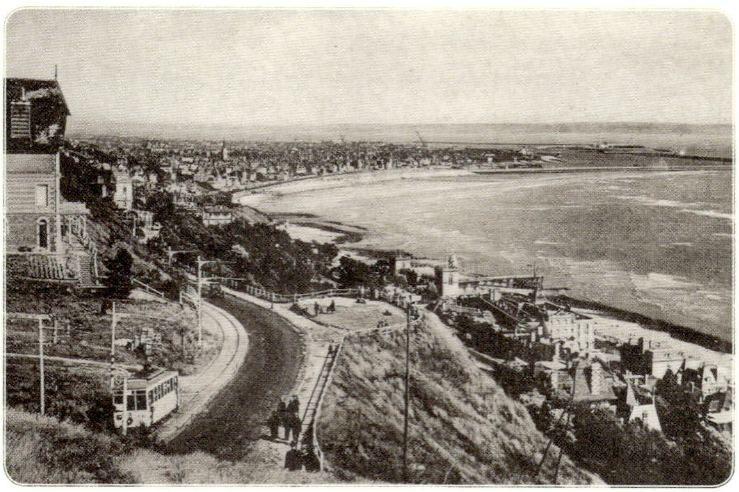

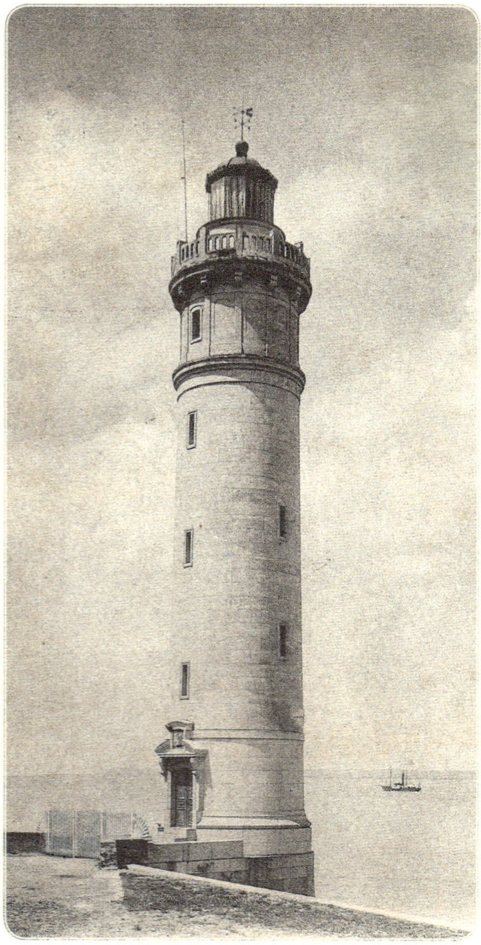

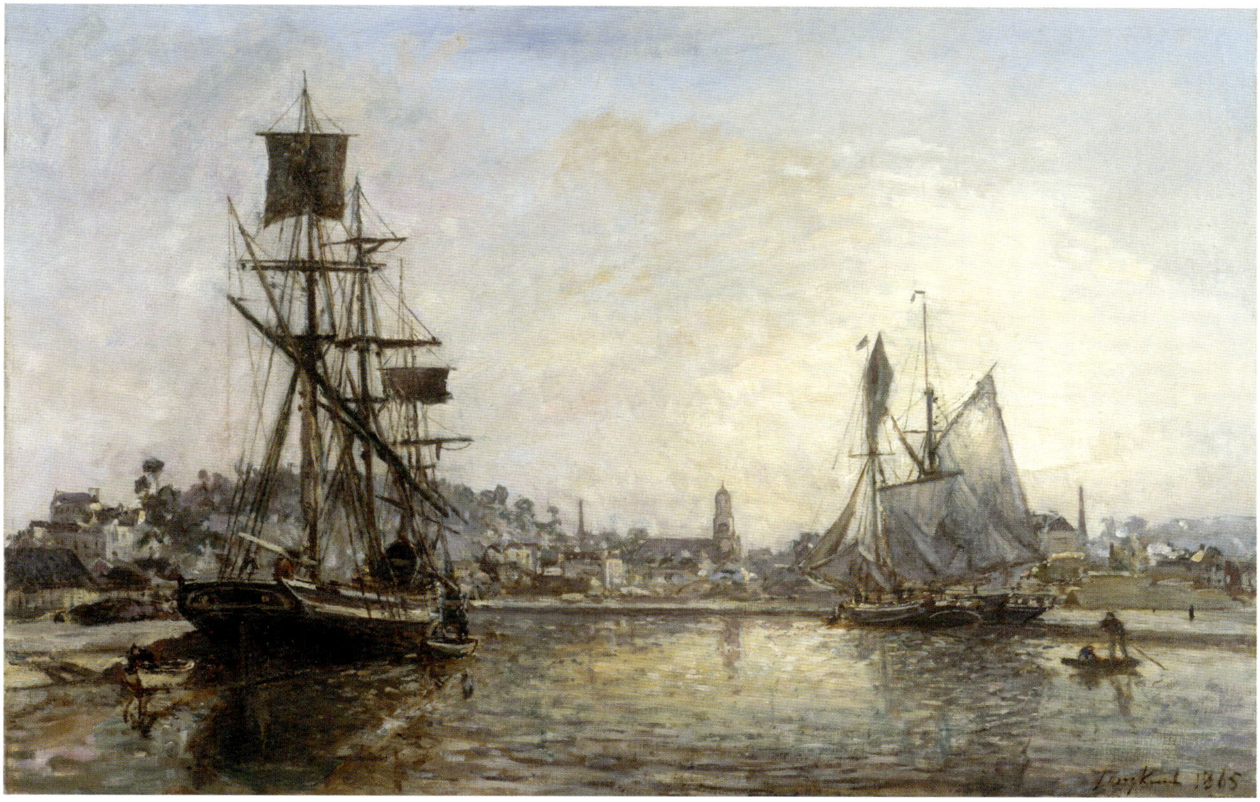

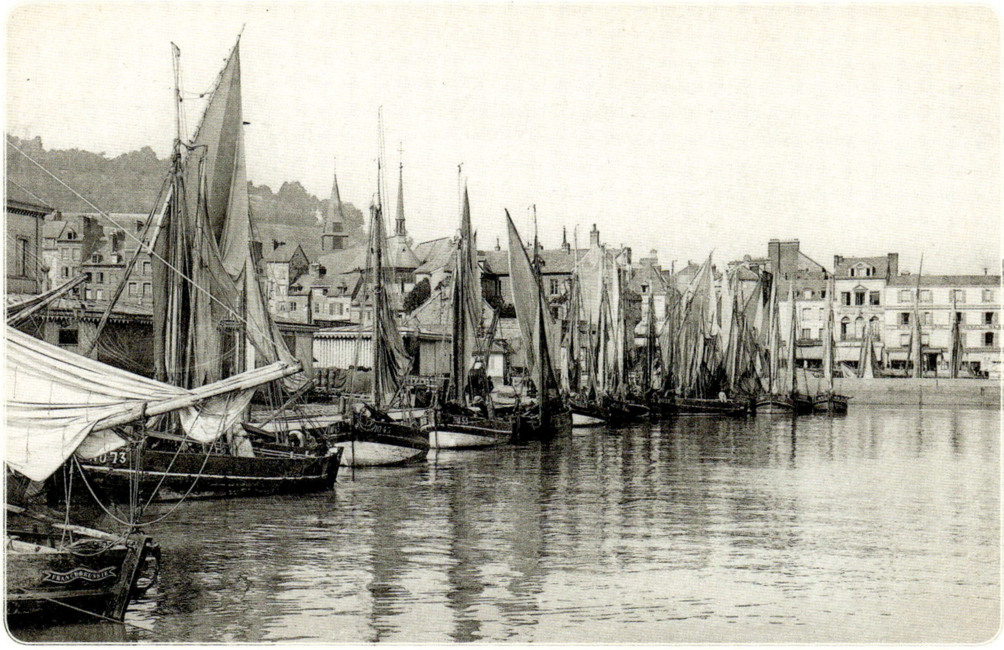

p. 128
Eugène Boudin, *The Beach Near Trouville*, *c.* 1865. Tokyo, Artizon Museum

Trouville and the Trouville beach

Panoramic view of the beach at Sainte-Adresse with the tram on the left, *c.* 1905

The lighthouse of Honfleur

Johan Barthold Jongkind, *Honfleur,* 1865. New York, The Metropolitan Museum of Art

Boats in the port of Honfleur

that it was nicknamed the 'Barbizon of Normandy'. Monet had moved to Honfleur in the spring of 1864, where he was joined by Bazille. In the autumn, he was still there, painting the mole with Boudin and Jongkind. The paintings from these months have similar titles—Jongkind's *Honfleur*, Monet's *The Lighthouse of Honfleur*—and can be considered the first seeds of the movement.

20. Pont-Aven and Le Pouldu

At the end of the nineteenth century, Brittany was still backwards and archaic. In many of its villages, filled with old houses with slate roofs, the farmers still dressed in the way of their ancestors and preserved a form of

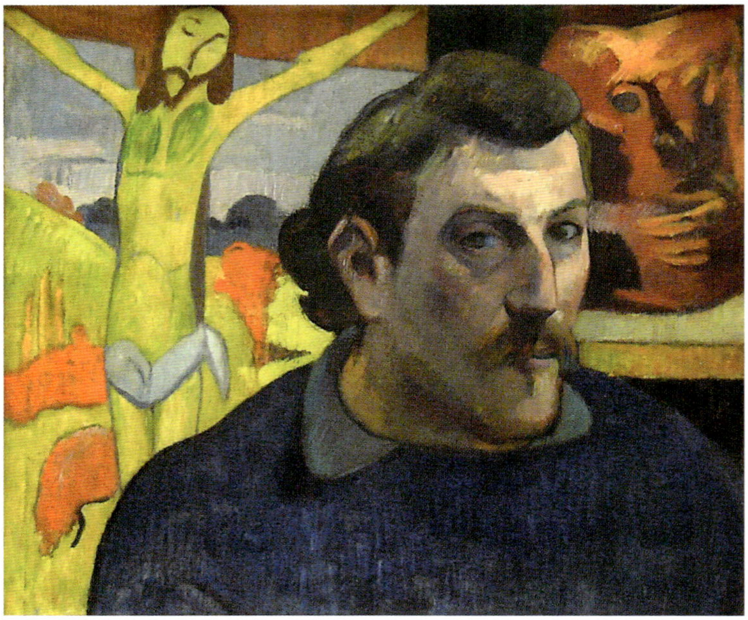

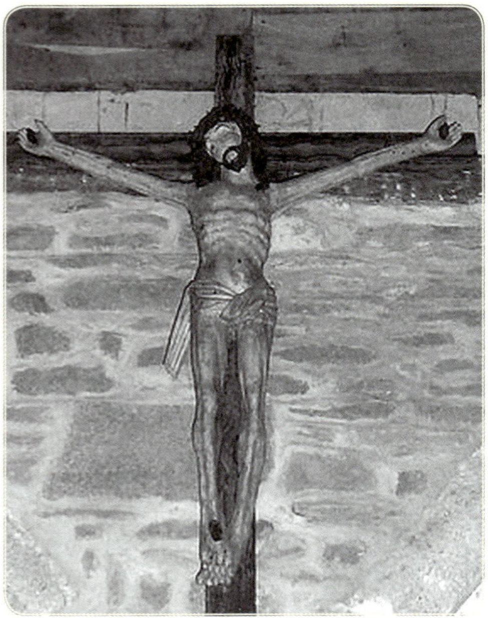

Paul Gauguin, *Self-Portrait with Yellow Christ*, 1890–1891. Paris, Musée d'Orsay

Christ in polychrome wood, Pont-Aven, chapel of Trémalo

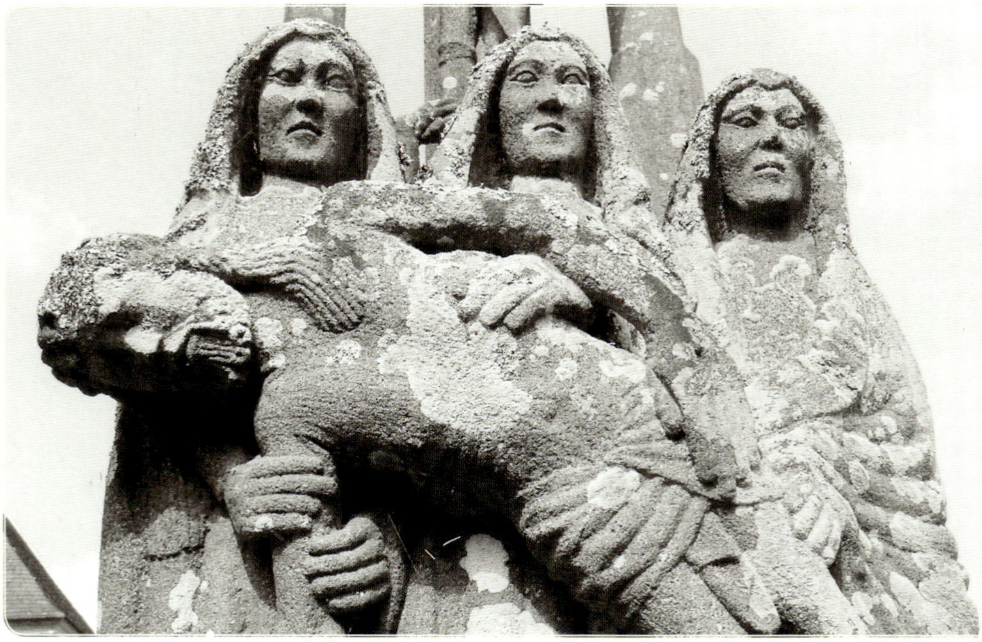

Pietà from the Calvary of Brasparts

mystical, primitive Catholicism. It was a fervent, naive religion that was expressed in small sacred symbols crudely sculpted in wood and rock and used the native Breton

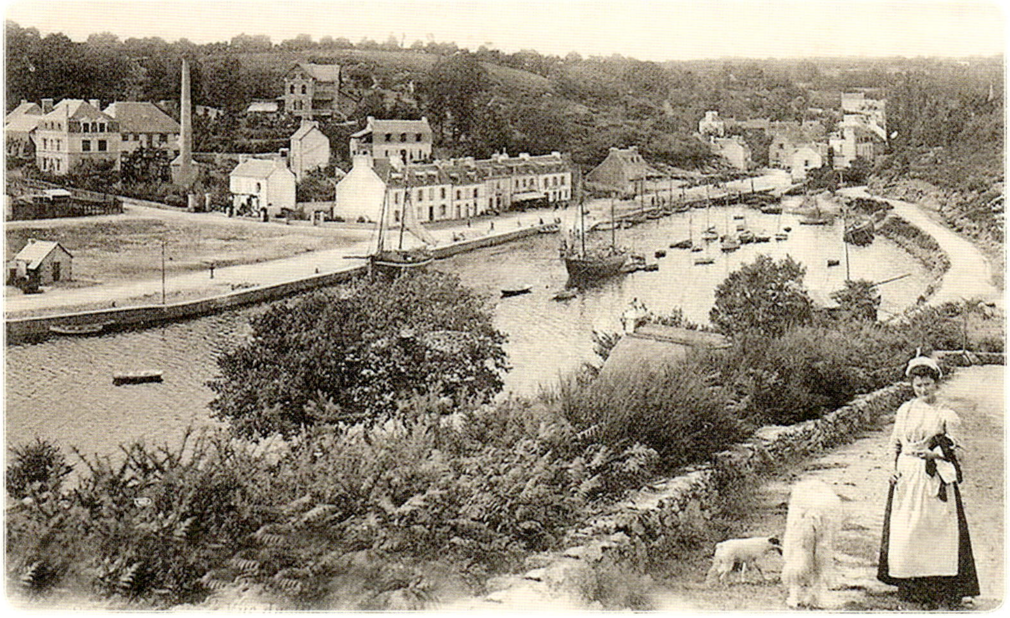

The small harbour of Pont-Aven

Paul Gauguin, *Landscape in Brittany. The David Mill*, 1894. Paris, Musée d'Orsay

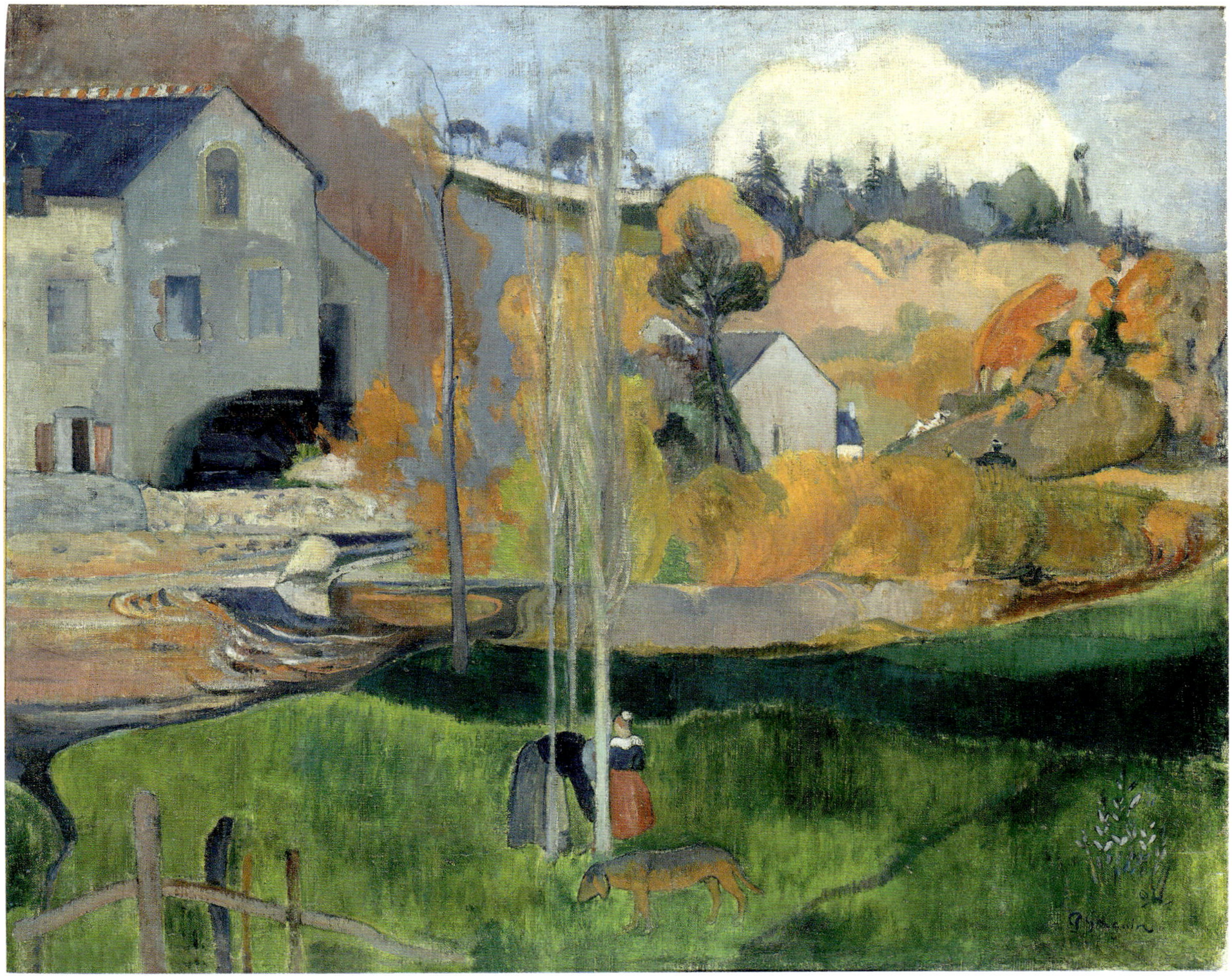

Women in traditional Breton costume in Pont-Aven

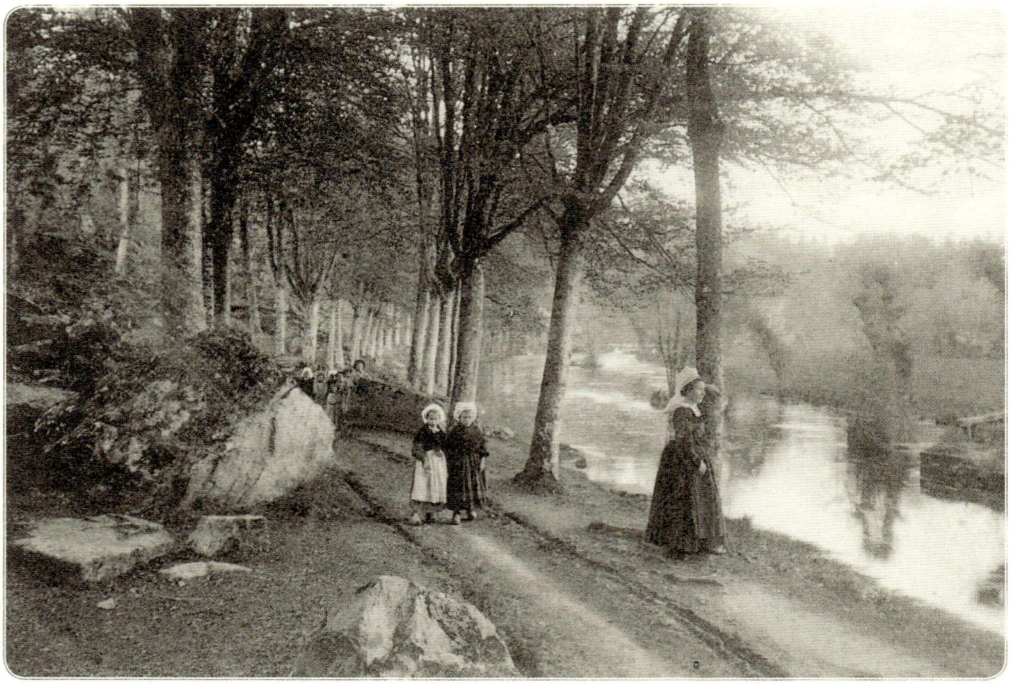

The Laïta River near Le Pouldu

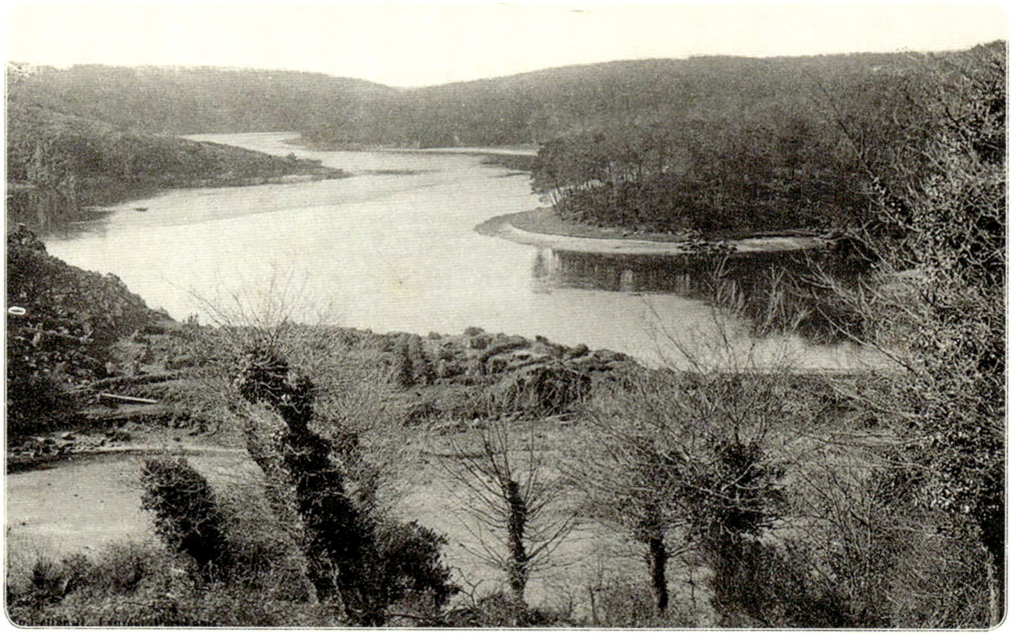

language. When Gauguin visited the region for the first time in 1886, he was immediately inspired: the primitivism that he had looked for in Martinique and later found in Tahiti, he now asked of Brittany. The Pre-Raphaelites went back to the art from before Raphael and John Ruskin to the Gothic. Gauguin went much further, rediscovering the expressions of a naive, popular form of art, like the polychrome crucifix in the chapel of Trémalo or the stone *Pietà* from the Calvary in Brasparts, the former inspiring his *Yellow Christ*; the latter, his *Green Christ*. 'I love Brittany', he wrote to his friend Schuffenecker, 'I find the wild and the primitive here. When my clogs resonate on this granite ground, I hear the muffled, powerful thud that I'm looking for in painting.'[36]

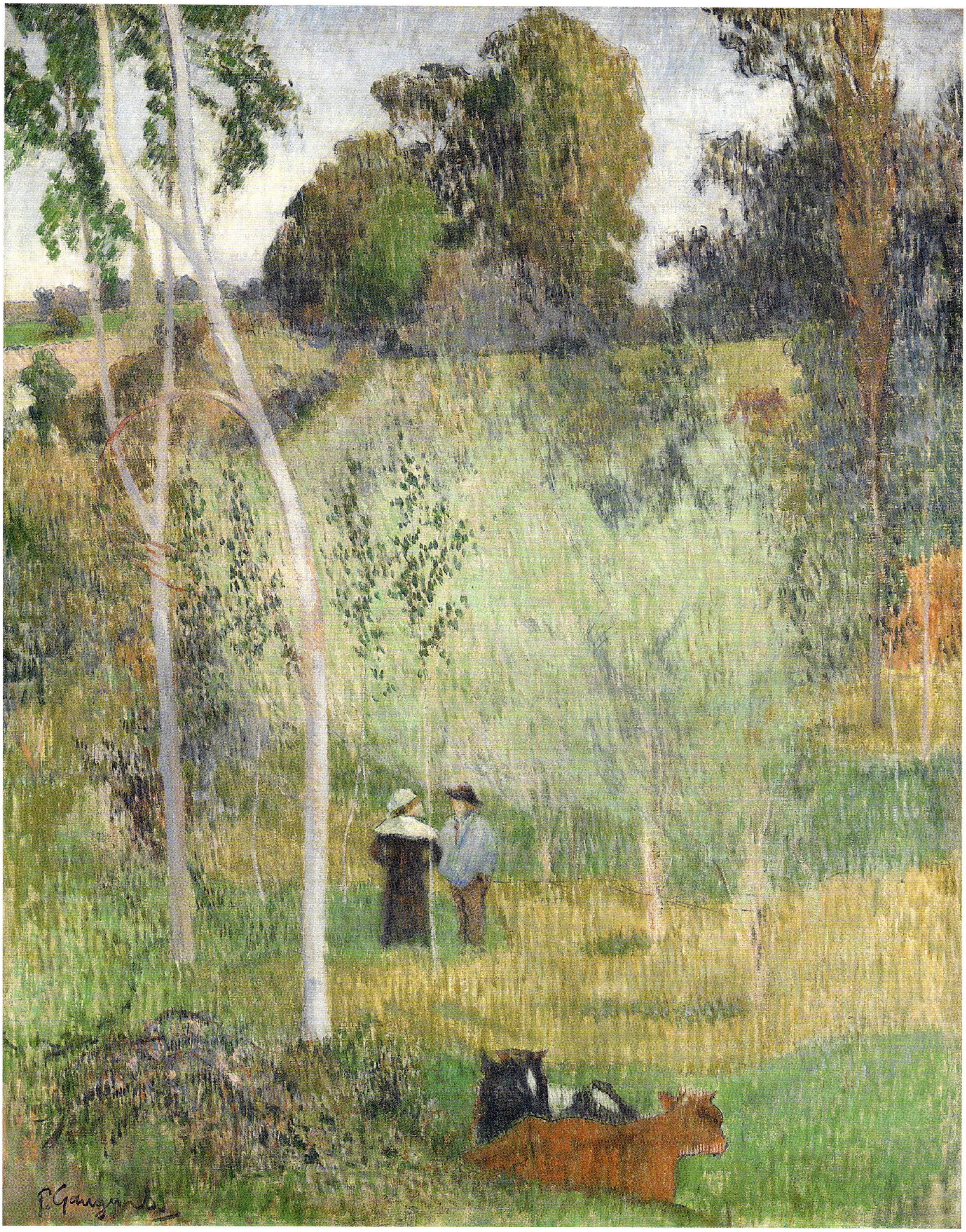

Paul Gauguin, *Shepherds in a Field*, 1888. Private Collection

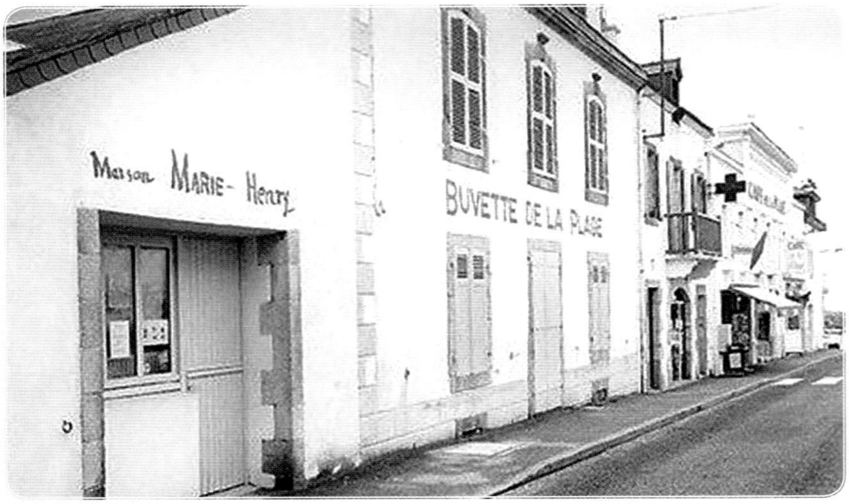

The inn of Marie Henry at Le Pouldu

He moved to Pont-Aven, a village on the banks of the river by the same name, dotted with mills and, climbing up the steep, woody incline, farms, thickets and little churches. Arriving at the rise that dominated the village, you could see the mouth of the river and its sandy gulf. Gauguin painted numerous views of it, sometimes inspired by the landscape, other times by the farmers' clothing. When he was tired, he would go back to the guesthouse run by Marie-Jeanne Gloanec, where he was staying and where Émile Bernard, Charles Laval, Meijer de Haan and other artists would gather. They talked about abstraction and synthesis (during one walk, Gauguin told the younger Paul Sérusier to make the trees yellow if he saw them as yellow, the shadows ultramarine blue and the leaves vermilion, without worrying too much about mimetic fidelity), however, while these meetings in some ways recalled those of the Impressionists at Café Guerbois, the Batignolles School had had a less esoteric nature than the one of Pont-Aven. The former's manifestos had been called *Luncheon on the Grass and Impression, Sunrise*, not the *Talisman*, as Paul Sérusier's first painting in this style was titled.

The gatherings at Marie-Jeanne Gloanec's guest house were revived a few years later in Le Pouldu, on the mouth of the Laïta River, fifteen miles from Pont-Aven, in the hotel run by Madame Marie Henry. André Gide went there as well and, years later, on 29 July 1889, described it in the following passage.

> The village consisted of just four houses, two of which were inns. The more modest seemed the more pleasant, so I went inside, being very thirsty. A servant showed me into a room with roughcast, whitewashed walls, and left me there sitting in front of a glass of cider. The sparse furnishings and complete absence of wall-hangings made it that much easier for me to notice a fairly large number of canvases and stretchers stacked up against the wall. As soon as I was alone, I rushed over to these canvases and turned them around, contemplating each one with increasing pleasure. They seemed to show nothing more than childish daubs, but the colours were so unusually bright and gay that I had no other thought than to stay.[37]

A new religion originated amidst those desolate dunes in the middle of a community that some period sources described as semi-wild, devoted almost exclusively to gathering algae and pieces of wood stranded by the tide. The younger artists saw Gauguin as the prophet of a new creed: did he not restore sight to those who could no longer see, resuscitating a dead art? Maurice Denis described him as

> the undisputed master, the one surrounded by paradox. We admired his talent, eloquence, gesture, physical strength, cruelty, inexhaustible imagination, romantic manner and

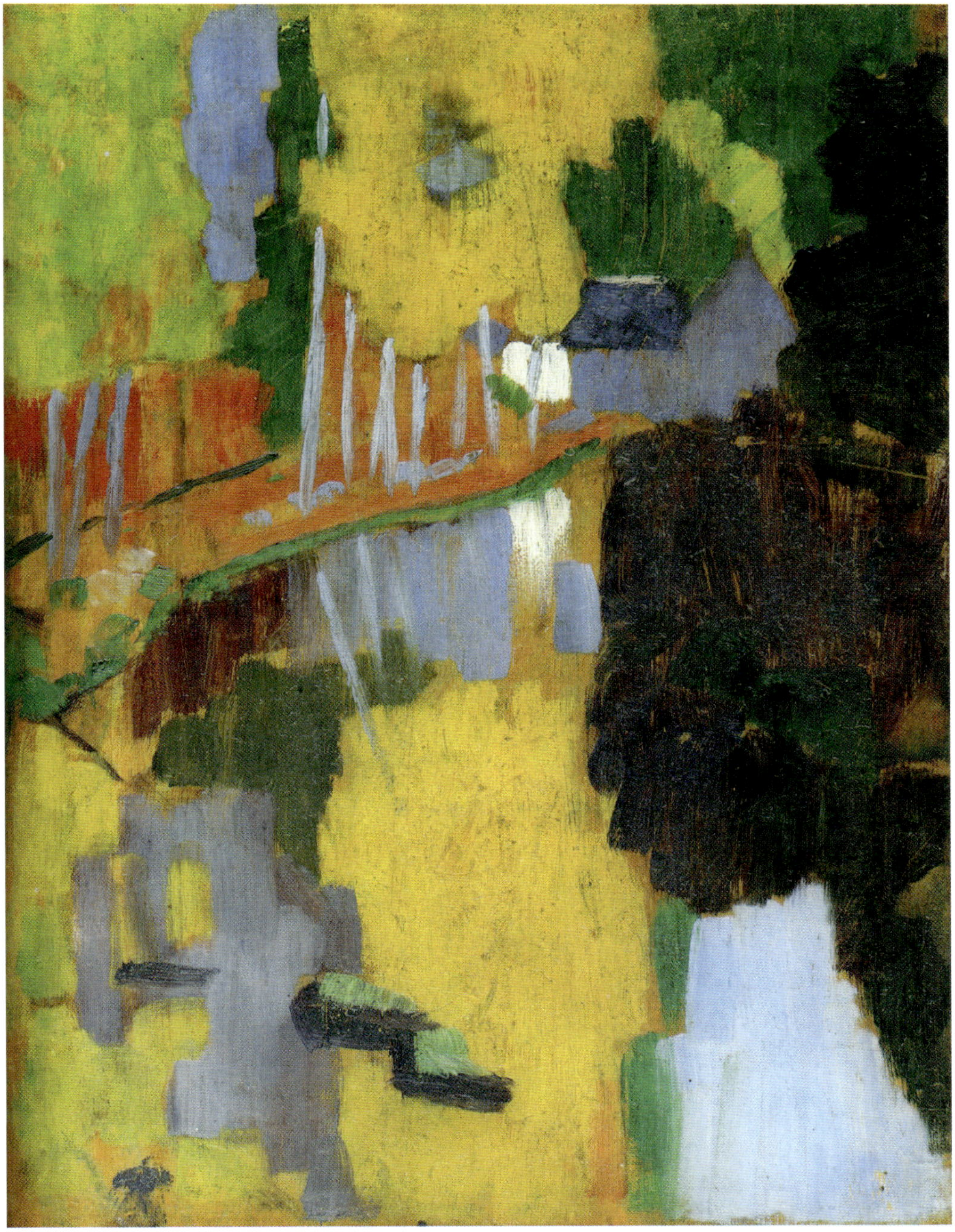

Paul Sérusier, *The Talisman (Bois d'Amour)*, 1888. Paris, Musée d'Orsay

ability to resist alcohol. The mystery of his ascent was that he furnished us with one or two very simple, necessarily true ideas, at a moment when we were totally without instruction.[38]

But the master did not stay long. His dream was to go to Tahiti, and he set sail in 1891.

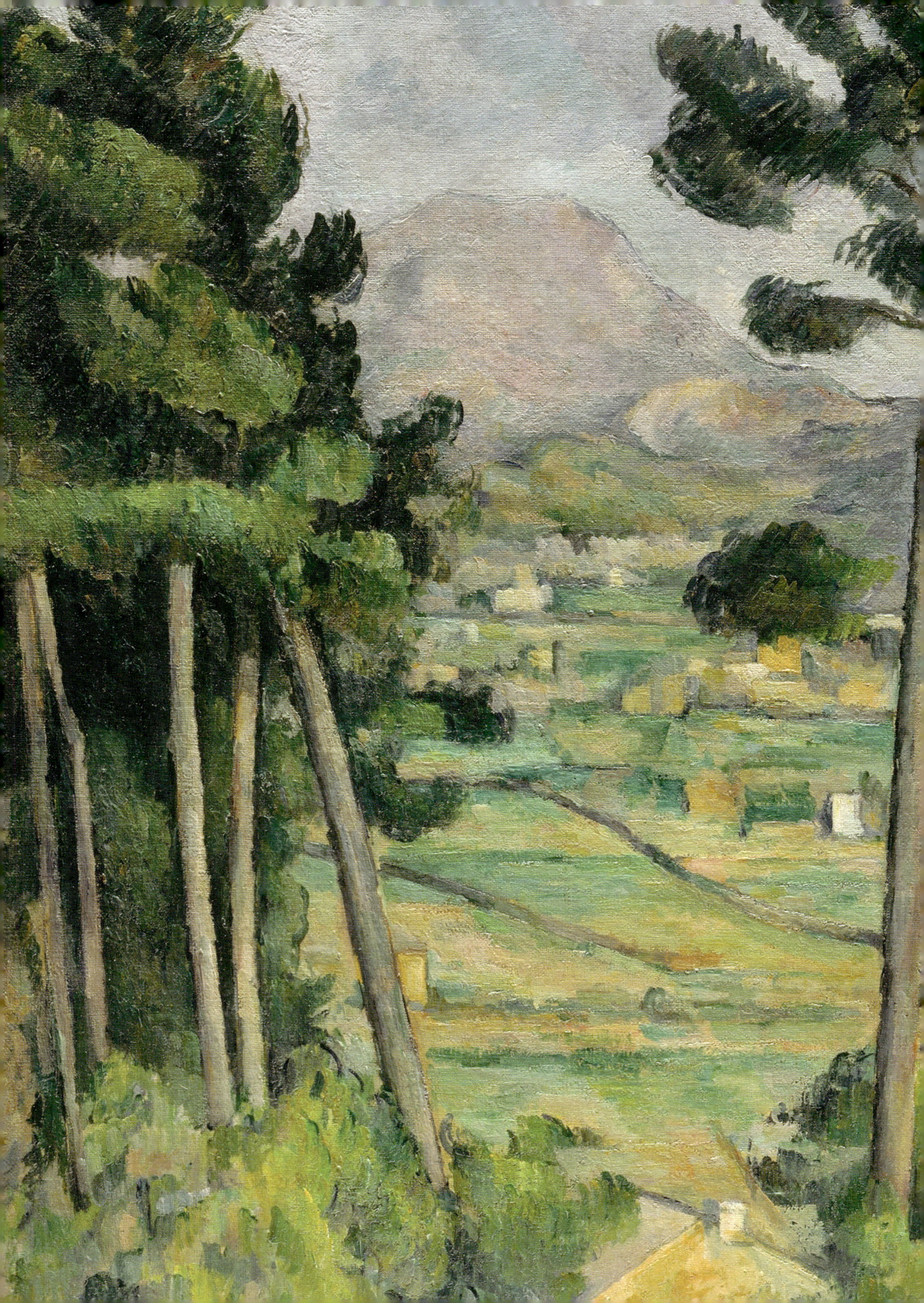

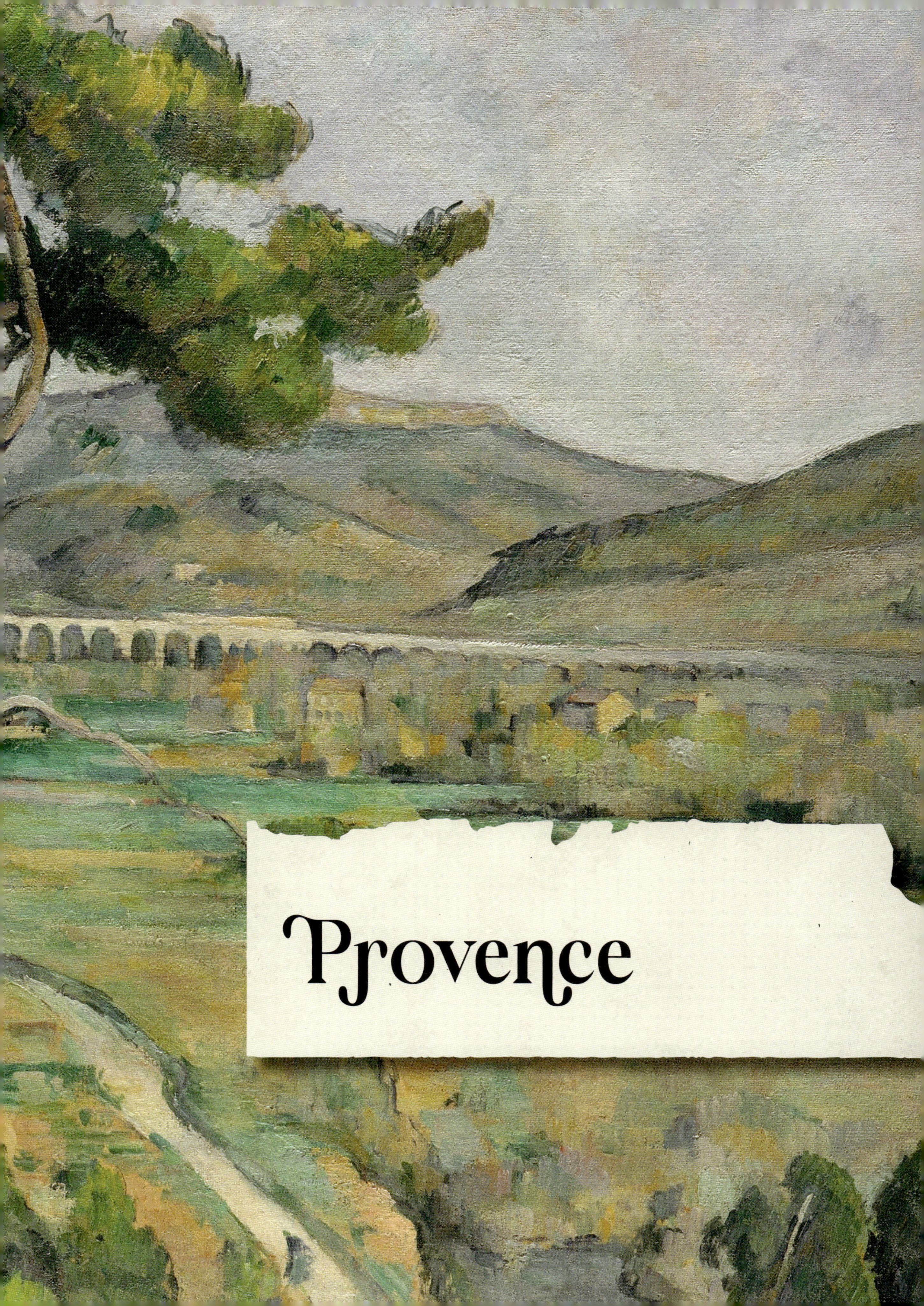

Provence

21. Aix-en-Provence

Aix-en-Provence, where Cézanne was born in 1839 and where he attended the Collège Bourbon with Zola, was isolated at the time. Anyone who visited it at the end of the previous century or at the beginning of the nineteenth century would not have found many differences: the same streets, lined with the same elegant, vertical eighteenth-century buildings, leading to the same trees, golden in autumn or bright with the intense heat of summer, against a sky that was more or less always the same blue. A simple melody of houses, courtyards and squares, like a pavane, joined by the murmur of the fountains like a liquid arpeggio for guitar. Leaving cours Mirabeau and its cafés, you could immediately start exploring the environs. The weather was always pleasant, the region gentle and lazy, rich in vineyards, almond trees and olive groves. Mont Sainte-Victoire, which dominated the panorama with its bare, grey-blue mass, was the harshest note in a landscape of otherwise gently rolling hills.

Although he left Aix for Paris when he was twenty-two, Cézanne always went back and indeed, starting in 1881 his time in the capital grew shorter and shorter. He was there briefly in the spring of 1882 and again in 1883. Among the Impressionists,

pp. 136–137
Paul Cézanne, *Mont Sainte-Victoire and the Viaduct of the Arc River Valley*, 1882–1885. New York, The Metropolitan Museum of Art

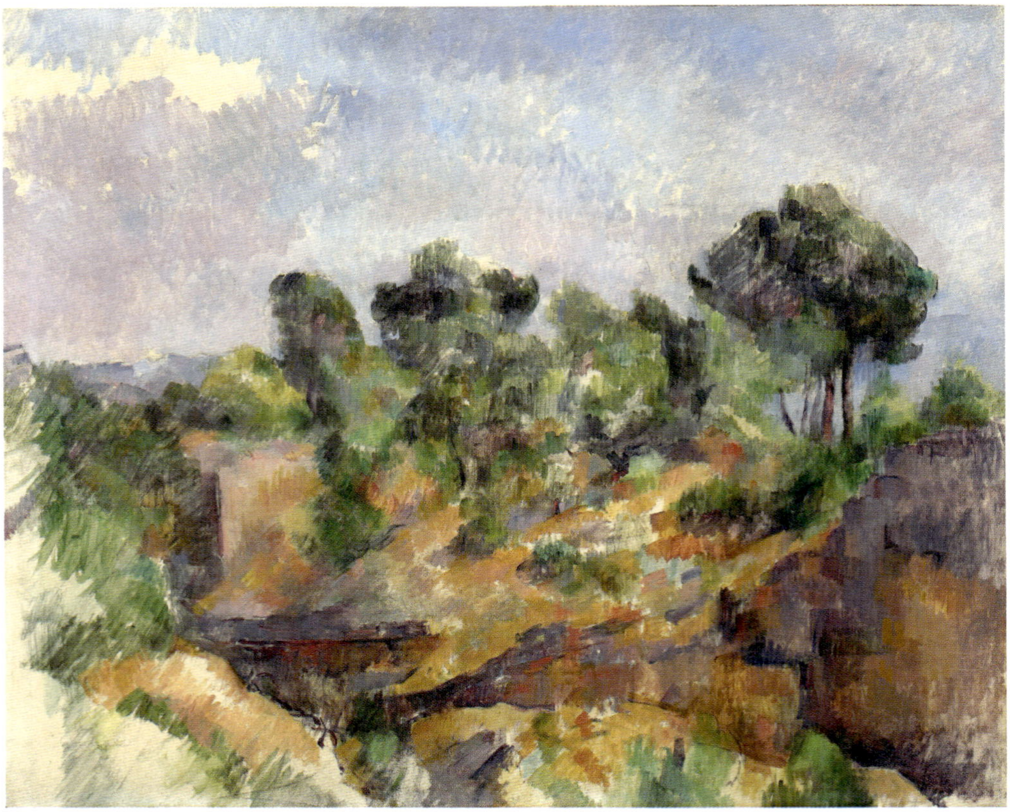

Paul Cézanne, *Bibémus*, 1894–1895. New York, Solomon R. Guggenheim Museum

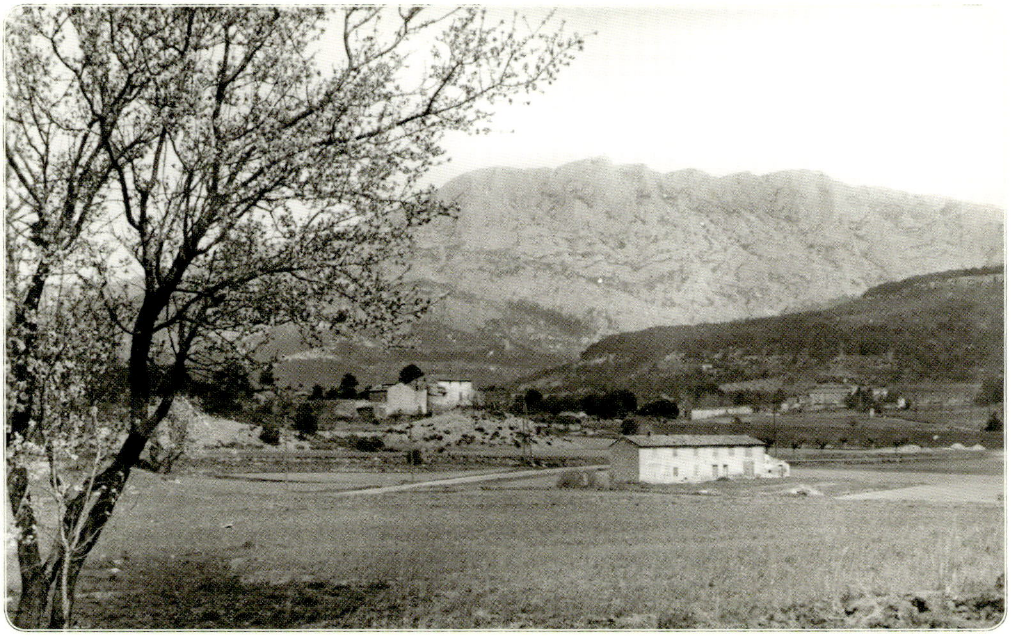

Mont Sainte-Victoire near Aix-en-Provence

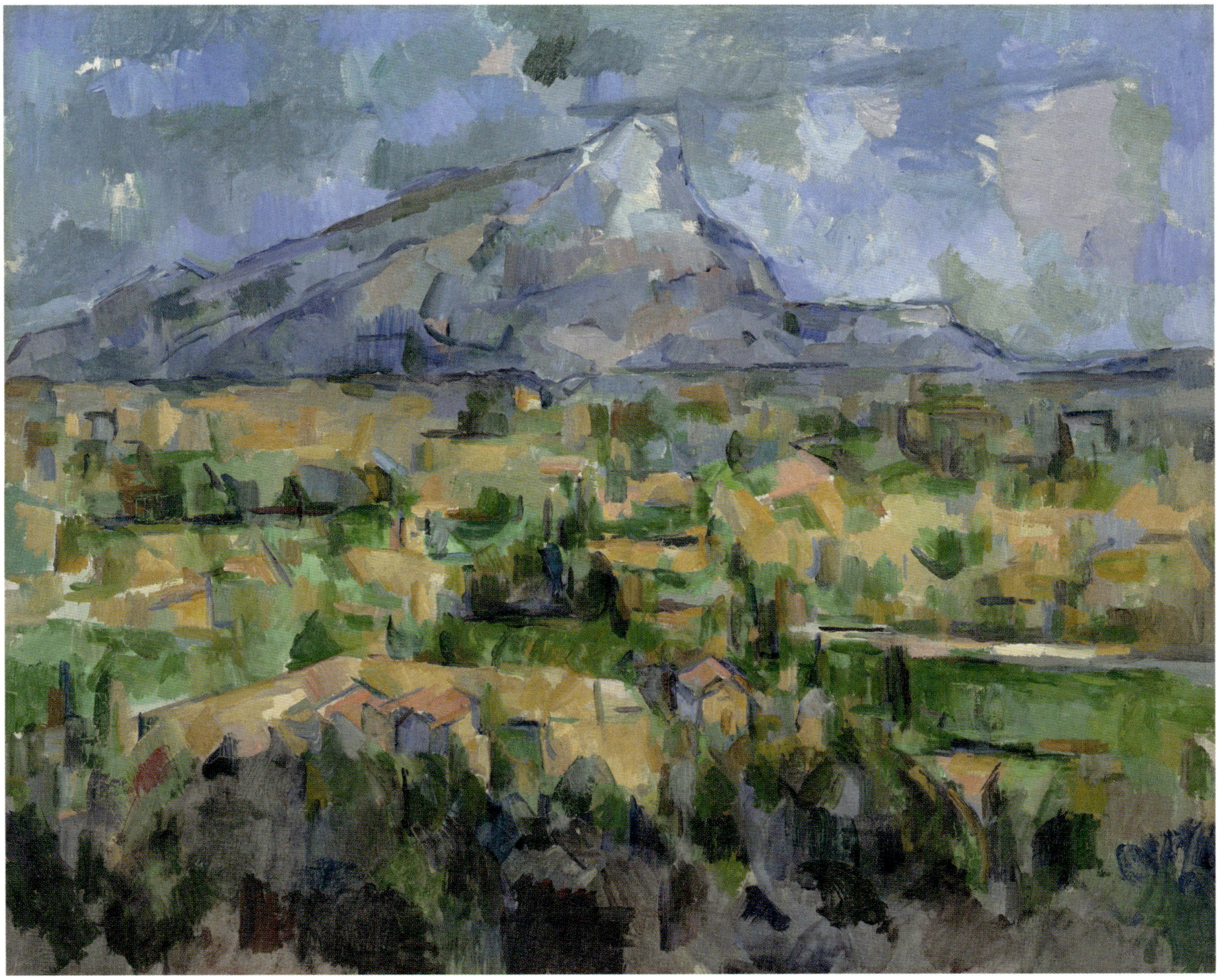

Paul Cézanne, *Mont Sainte-Victoire*, 1902–1904. Philadelphia, Philadelphia Museum of Art

he was the one who least felt the need for the city. He was immune to the pleasures of the intellectual skirmish typical of the gatherings at Café Guerbois and Café de la Nouvelle Athènes, since his touchy, shy nature meant that he had no taste for engaging in it, and nor was he interested in scenes of modern life. According to Baudelaire, beauty is made up of two elements: the eternal and the contingent. Cézanne, in his search for beauty, was stirred by only one of these. His friends had portrayed objects in specific atmospheric conditions. Monet's sheaves changed according to the hour of the day, while Sainte-Victoire was depicted by Cézanne in terms of its trigonometric stability and spatial substance. It was as if a question that had been long turned round and round by the skilful sophistry of a sceptic was now in the hands of an austere monk. And there is something anchoritic—including in the appearance adopted by the artist: bald, bearded and thin, like St Anthony in medieval paintings—in his years of seclusion in Provence: first in Estaque, near Marseilles, and Gardanne, then his father's estate, the Jas de Bouffan, near Aix. For him, nature was no longer a plaything of light. Unlike the Impressionists, in whose paintings colour almost dissolved form, Cézanne used colour contrasts to clarify the space and planes. Like other painters, he perceived an almost astringent quality in the southern light that let outlines emerge. As he wrote about the view of the bay of Estaque: 'It is like a playing card. Red roofs over the blue sea [...] The sun is so terrific here that it seems to me as if the objects were silhouetted not only in black and white, but in blue, red, brown, and violet.'[39]

In 1885, his brother-in-law bought an estate in Bellevue, near Aix, and Cézanne began to spend a lot of time there. He also loved the quarries at Bibémus, for their wild, tortuous appearance, and Château noir, on the road to Le Tholonet, which he would have liked to buy; not being able to, he contented himself with painting it.

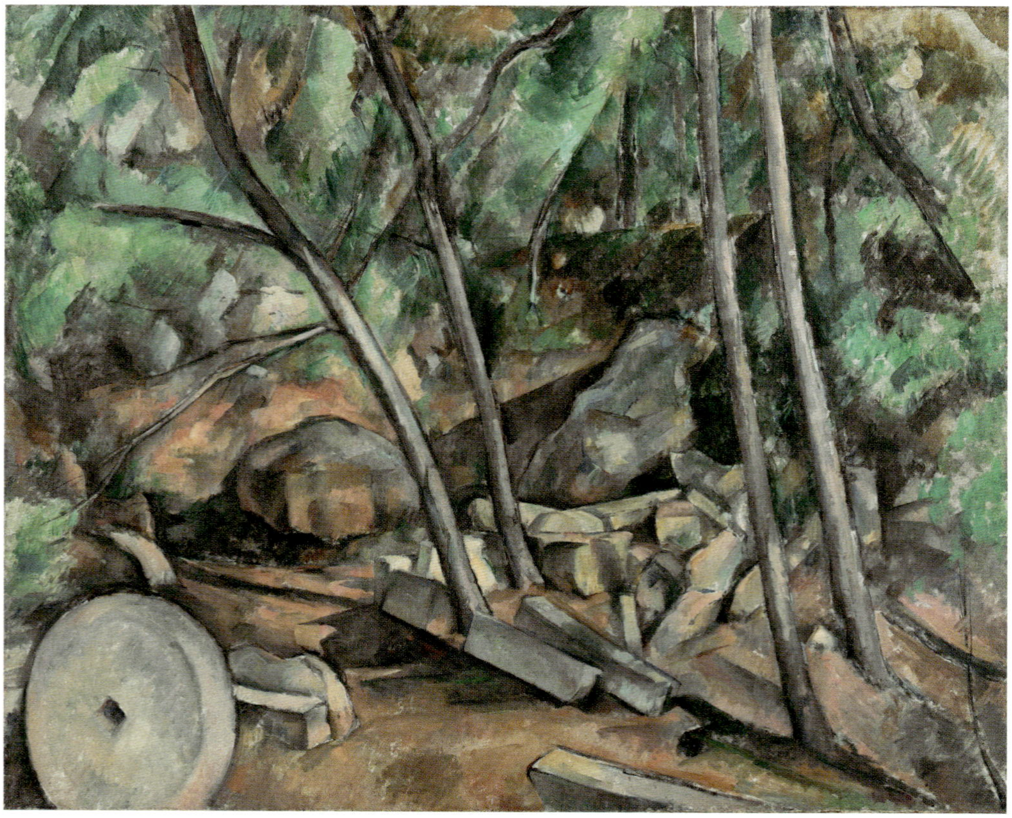

Paul Cézanne, *Millstone in the Park of the Château Noir*, 1892–1894. Philadelphia, Philadelphia Museum of Art

p. 141
Le Tholonet, lo Château noir

Paul Cézanne, *Château Noir*, 1900–1904. Washington, National Gallery of Art

Generally, he found in the surrounding countryside a landscape continually circumscribed and interrupted by trees, hills and rises, and so more interesting, in terms of the solid and structural aspects he was drawn to, than the vast seafronts of the north or the lazy, fleeting river bends, immersing the eye as if in something soft and undefined.

Increasingly solitary, he was, however, often visited by admirers, like Maurice Denis and Émile Bernard. He would take them to the hills around Aix, where he was working, and endlessly repeat: 'Everything, especially in art, is theory developed and applied in contact with nature'.[40]

He died on 22 October 1906, in the house at 23 rue Boulegon where he spent his final years.

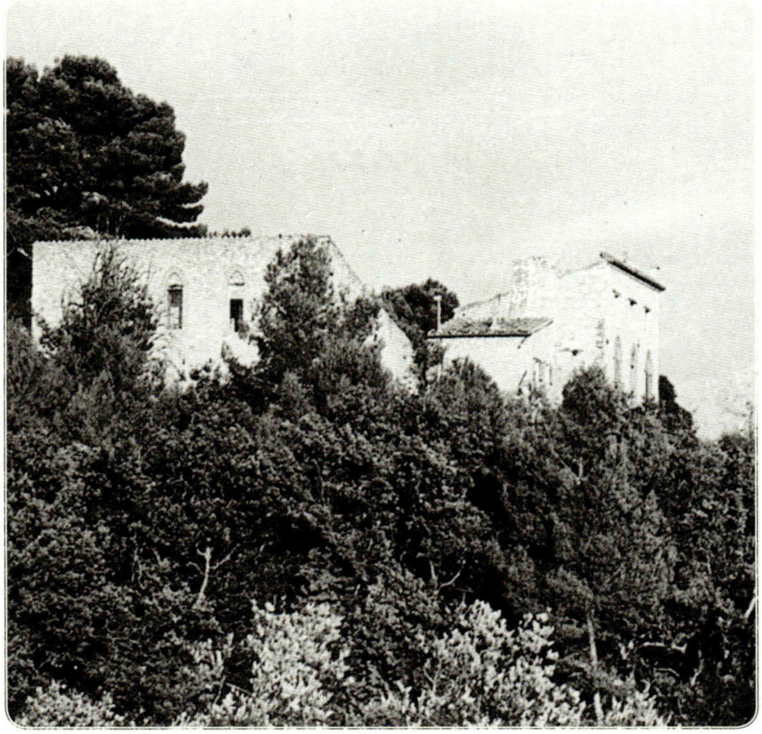

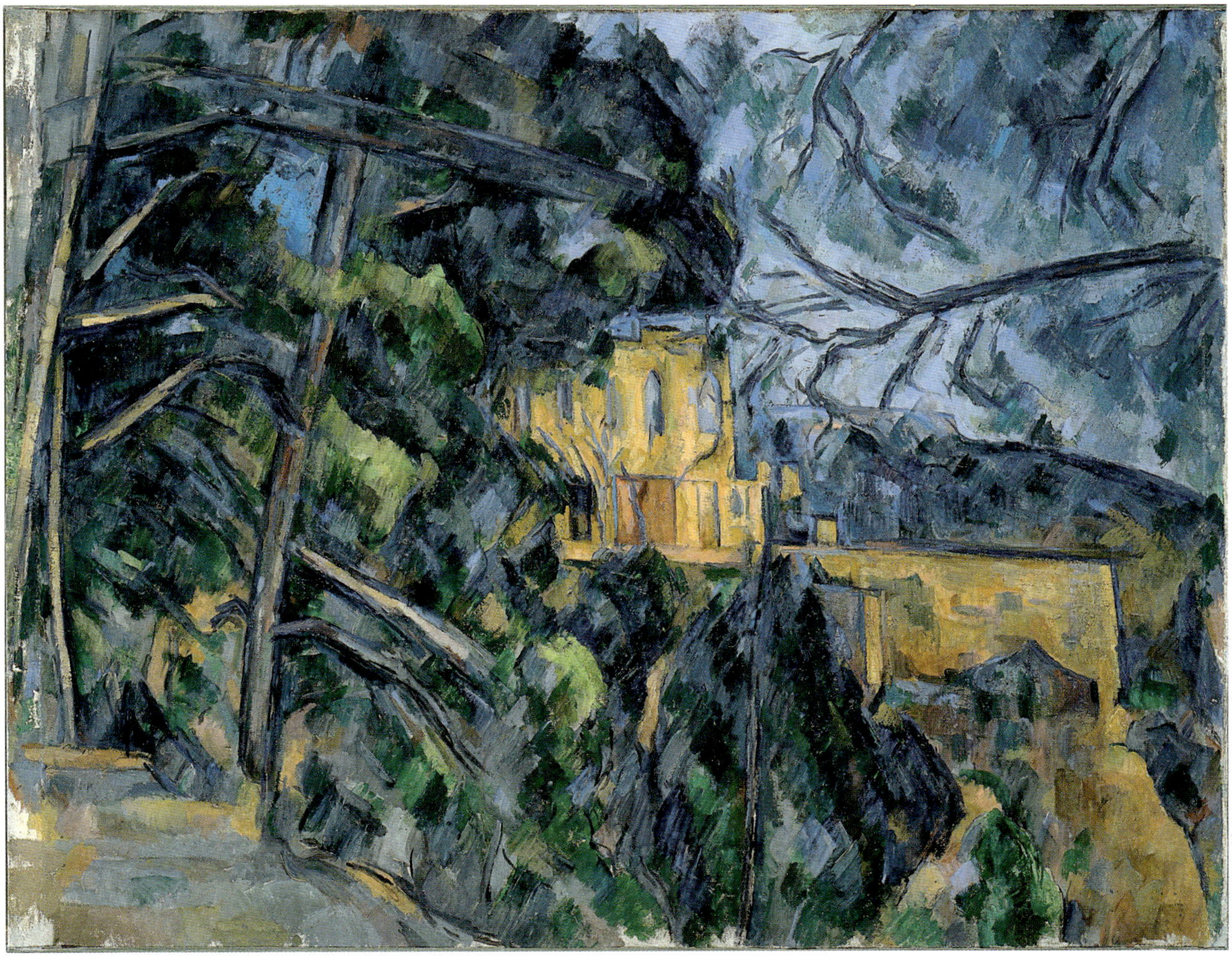

22. Arles

Arles, The Alyscamps

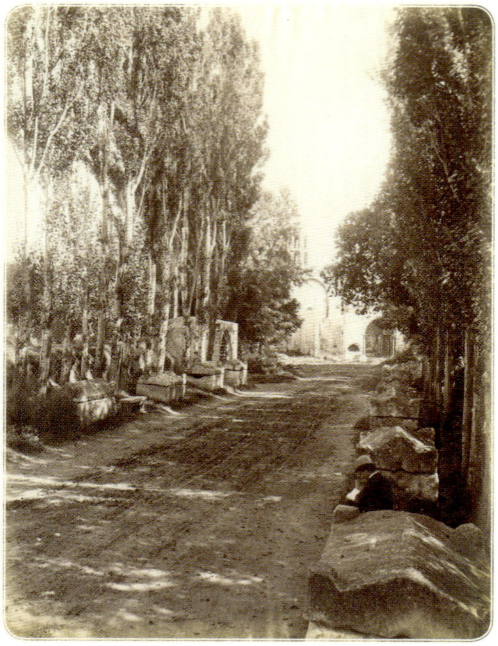

Vincent van Gogh, *Les Alyscamps*, 1888. Private Collection

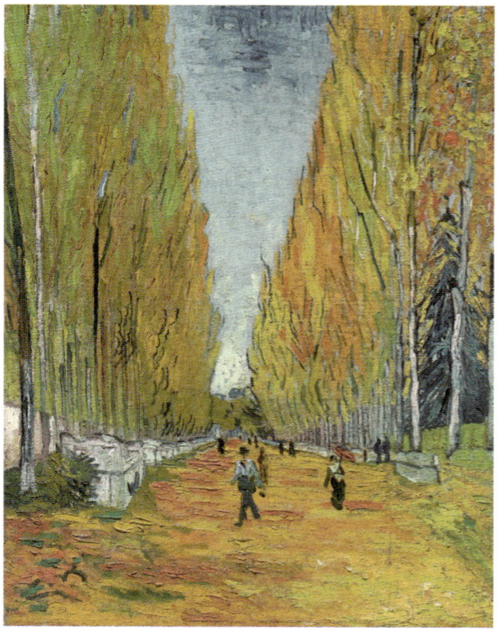

With the sole exception of Cézanne, who left rather soon in favour of Provence, the Impressionists preferred the quiet light of the north to the crisp one of the south, the latter sharply sculpting masses and crudely isolating volumes. The play of the sun on freshly melted sleet, the sparkle of grass covered with dew, the pale pink of dawn, the burnished gold of sunset bathing the solitary earth of the forests, the iridescence of water rippled by the hulls of small boats: this whole unstable, fluctuating world, found in paintings by Sisley, Renoir and Monet, was, however, like the vision of Mallarmé's faun, impossible to keep hold of and soon gave way to the needs of a sharper, more severe style. Synthesists and Symbolists needed the landscape to offer up vigorous lines and reinforced contours. The simple, clear-cut eurhythmics of Poussin, the harmony of a classical pediment, succeeded the liquidity of Lorrain. Signac looked for this transparency of form in Saint Tropez, Gauguin in the environs of Arles, but no one was as struck by the region as Van Gogh.

When the Dutch artist arrived in Arles for the first time in February 1888, it was the middle of winter, and a thick blanket of snow suffocated the countryside. Nature offered little enchantment, but then came the thaw, the almond trees bloomed and the gentle, still countryside took on the vague look of a Japanese print, as we read in one of Van Gogh's letters to Gauguin: 'I still have in my memory the feelings that the journey from Paris to Arles gave me this past winter. How I watched out to see "if it was like Japan yet"! Childish, isn't it?'[41] Besides the Far Eastern air, Van Gogh found other familiar aspects in Arles. He had been trained on the work of Jean-François Millet and Eugène Delacroix and now he was seeing the warm hues of *Women of Algiers* envelop the noble, simple peasants portrayed in *The Angelus*. 'I am convinced that nature down here is just what one needs to give one color',[42] he wrote to his brother Theo, and then went on to talk about the colours of the houses, the hues of the trees and the verdant hills, with a feeling of panic plenitude in which he saw analogies with Richard Wagner's operas:

nature here is extraordinarily beautiful. Everything and everywhere. The dome of the sky is a wonderful blue, the sun has a pale

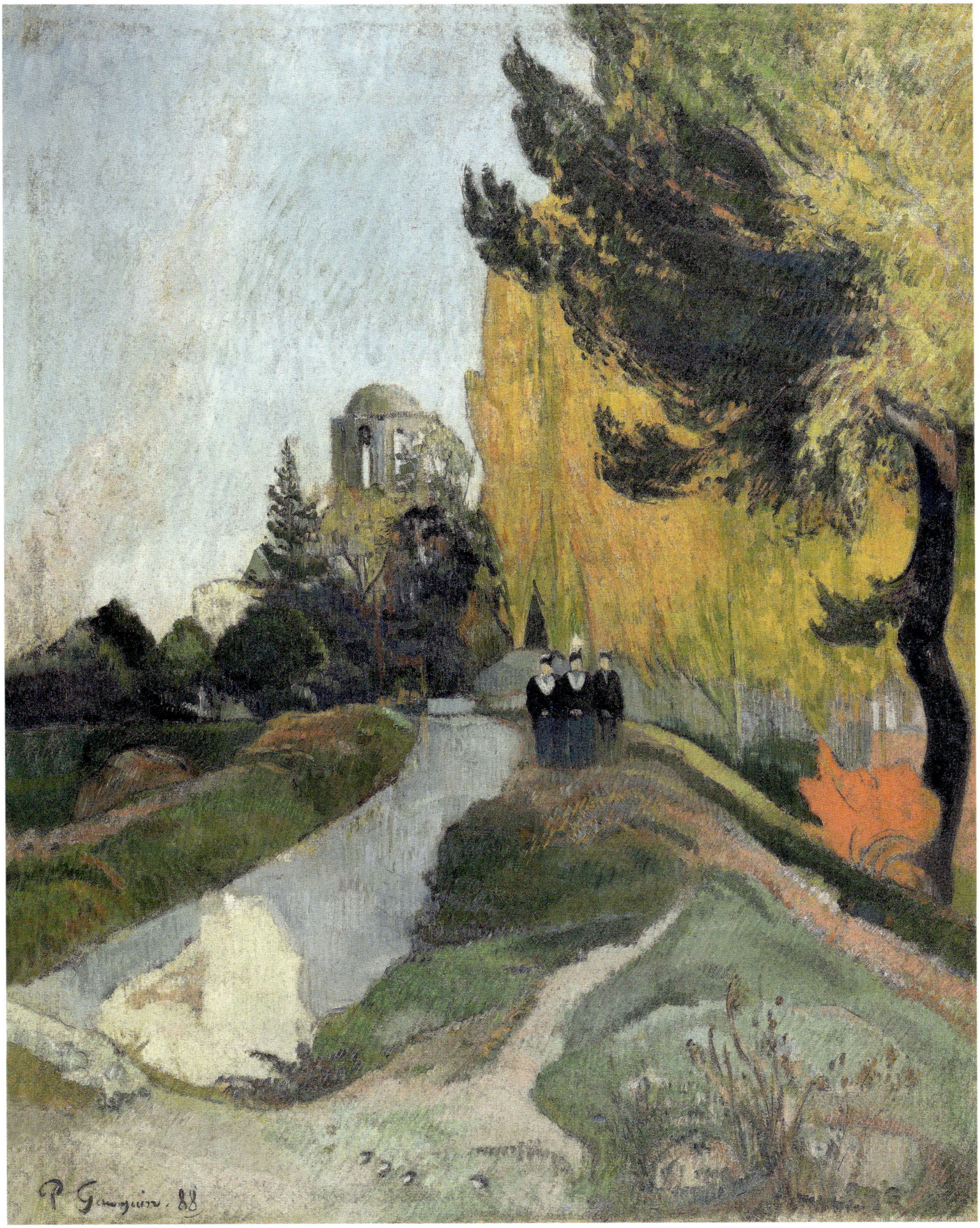

sulphur radiance, and it's soft and charming, like the combination of celestial blues and yellows in paintings by Vermeer of Delft. I can't paint as beautifully as that, but it absorbs me so much that I let myself go without thinking about any rule.[43]

Paul Gauguin, *Les Alyscamps*, 1888. Paris, Musée d'Orsay

Meanwhile, he walked along the banks of the Rhône and the necropolis of Alyscamps, he visited the ruins of Montmajour and the Crau Plain, and he was moved before the fishermen's houses in Saintes-Maries-de-la-Mer: all subjects that should have also excited Paul Gauguin, Émile Bernard, Charles Laval and the other artists with whom he hoped to found a community in the south. He was deluding himself. The same light that had inspired Van Gogh held less of an ambiguous fascination for Signac, who wrote in his diary:

> In this town, the light reflected everywhere absorbs all the local colours and exalts the shadows. The paintings that Van Gogh made in Arles are wondrous for their force and intensity, but they do not at all render the luminosity of the South. With the pretext that they are in the South, people expect to see red, blue, green, yellow [...] And yet, on the contrary, it is the North—for example Holland—that is 'colourful' (local colours), while the South is 'luminous'.[44]

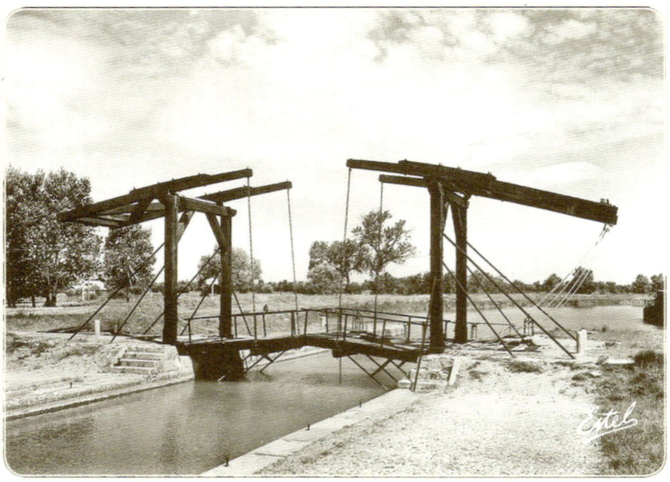

Arles, Langlois Bridge

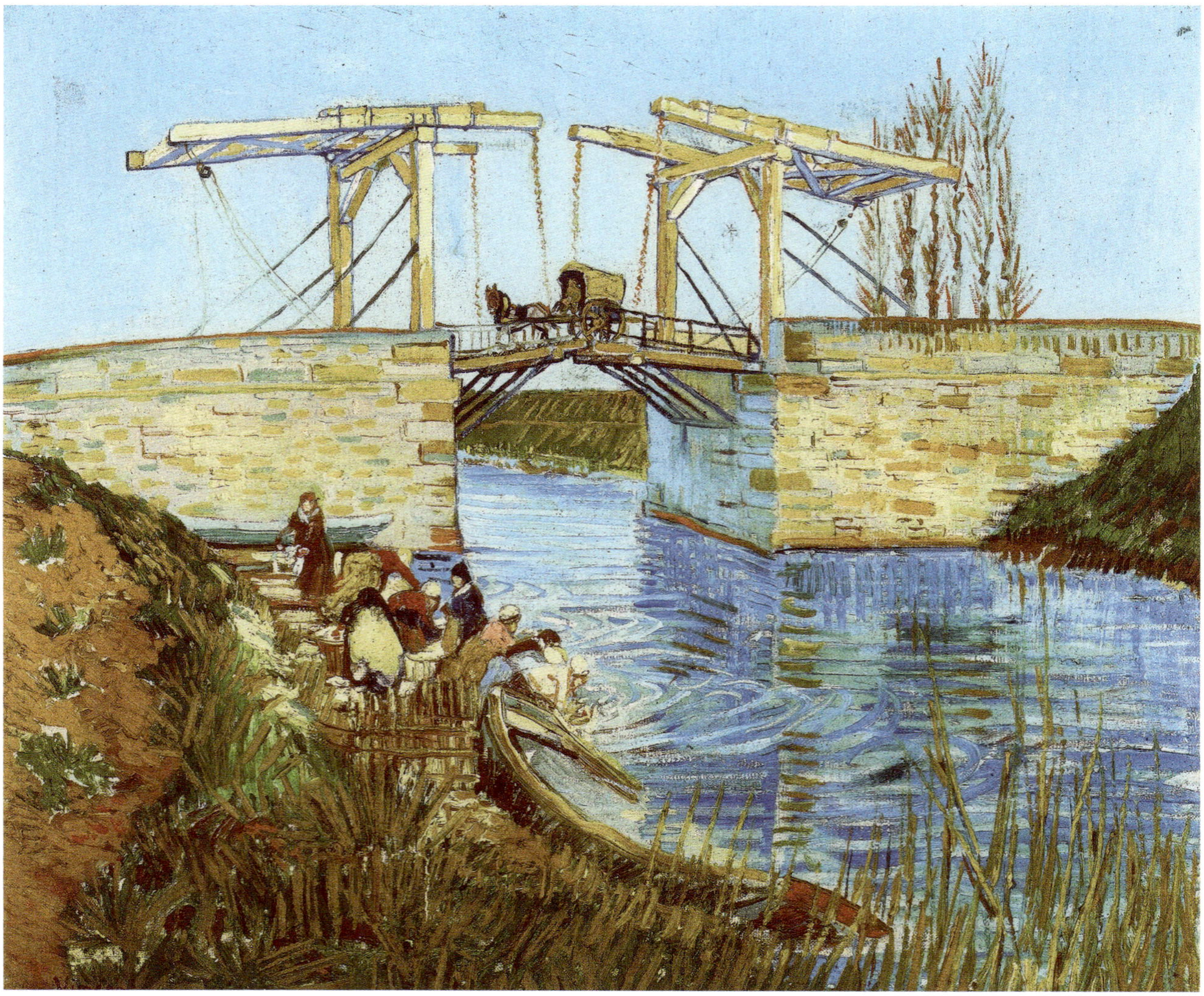

Vincent van Gogh, *Langlois Bridge at Arles*, 1888. Otterlo, Kröller-Müller Museum

During this period, Van Gogh painted *The Brothel*, *Les Alyscamps*, *Garden at Arles* and *Langlois Bridge at Arles*, in which the influence of Japanese prints is explicit; Gauguin painted *Washerwomen of Arles*, *Les Alyscamps* and *Landscape near Arles*. They often went to paint in the same places, like the Alyscamps or Café de Nuit, and made portraits of the same people, like Madame Roulin. Van Gogh remained, however, troubled.

The end of their friendship is well known. According to what Gauguin wrote years later in his memoires (*Avant et Après*, 1903), Van Gogh, upset by the idea of his friend's impending departure, went to him brandishing a razor, but one look from Gauguin was enough to bring him momentarily to his senses. In reality, he had not at all calmed down and, shutting himself in his house, cut off his ear after a few moments of paranoid hallucinations.

Gauguin left the next day. It was 25 December 1888. Van Gogh, after spending long periods in hospital, died in 1890.

Vincent van Gogh, *Garden at Arles*, 1888. The Hague, Gemeentemuseum Den Haag

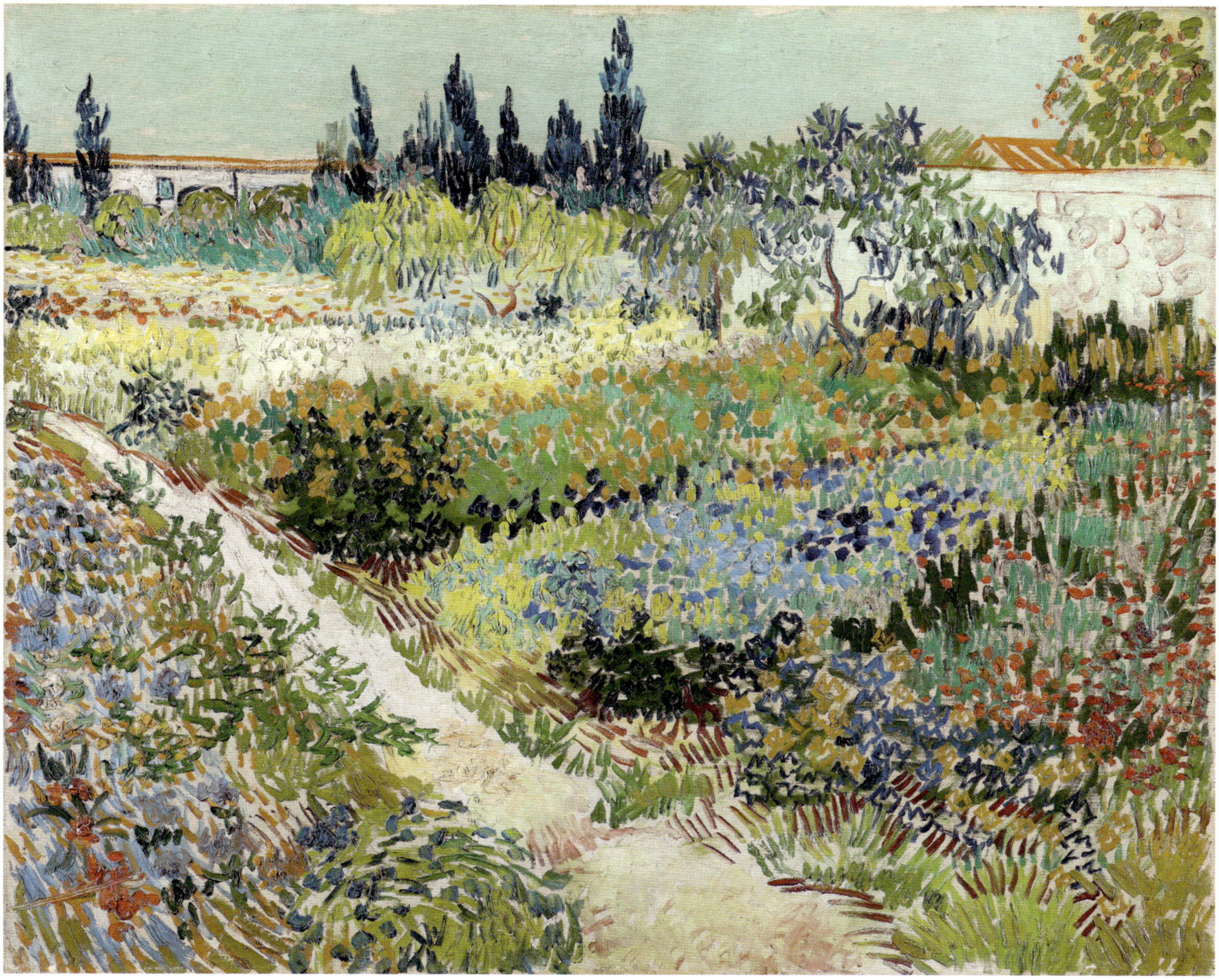

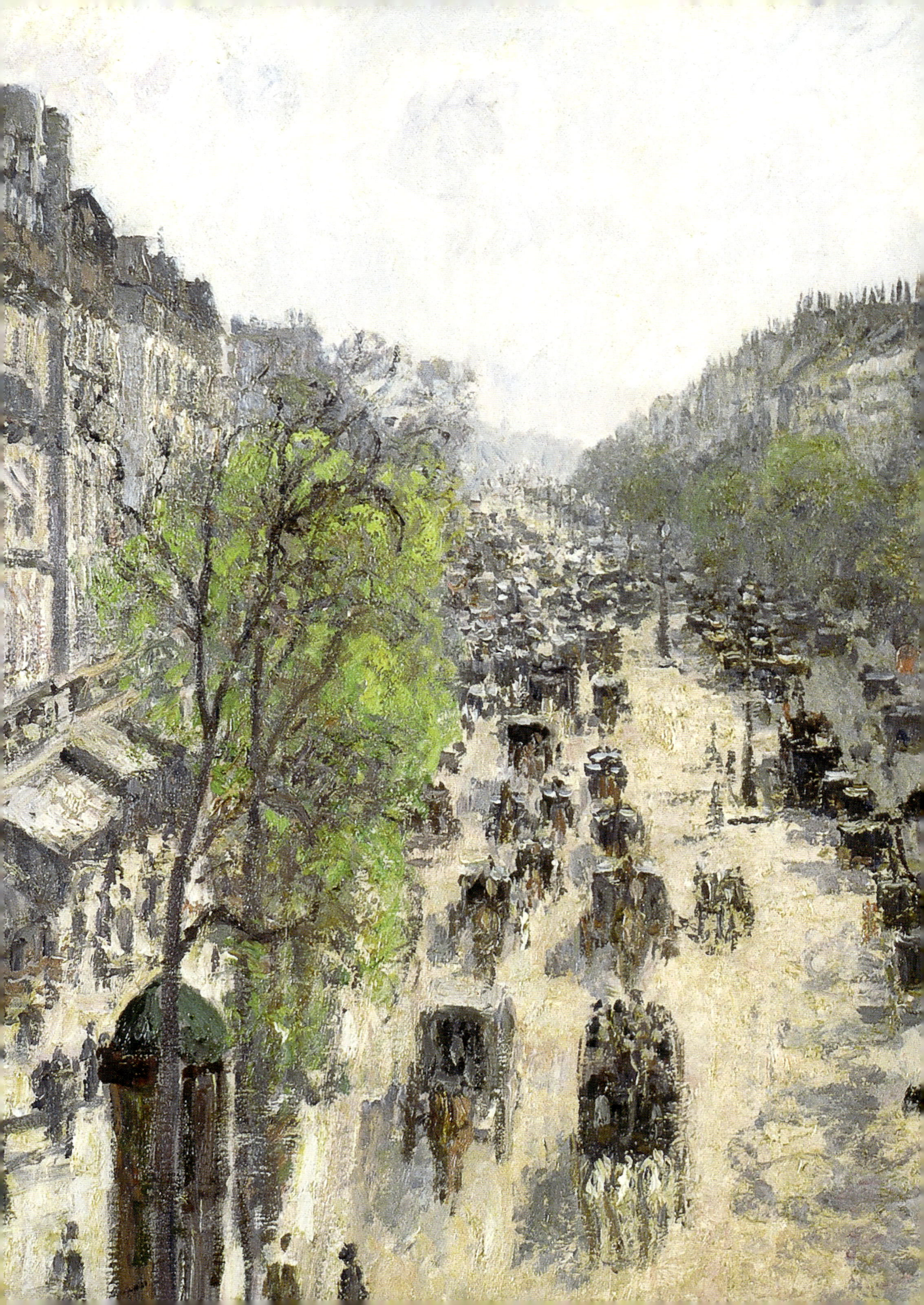

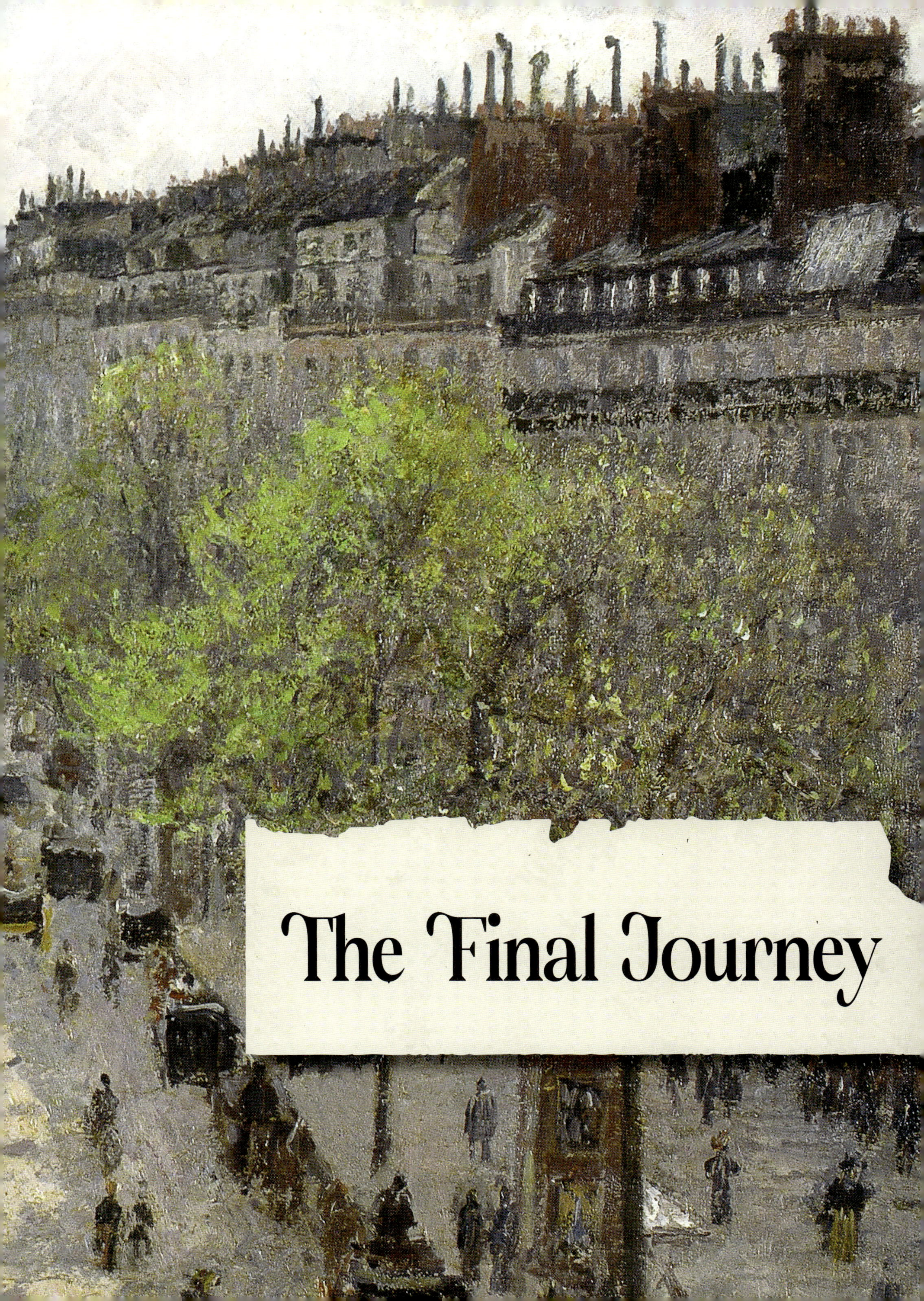

The Final Journey

23. Montmartre Cemetery

avenue Rachel

A little above place de Clichy, near rue Lepic, where many artists had their studios, is the cemetery of Montmartre. Less charming than the one of Montparnasse, with its noble geometric paths flanked by tall lindens that, when in bloom along with the other plants and trees made the place look like a peaceful Edenic refuge, the cemetery in avenue Rachel, in its labyrinthine vastness, did not even aspire to be—like that of Père-Lachaise—a chthonic copy of the city of the living. Insufficiently wealthy, its tombs a bit jumbled together, it preserves something of the quarter's old character. It is alone—everything around it having changed—in still holding up the slightly worn banner of the *bohème*. It is the final resting place of Henri Murger, author of *Scènes de vie de bohème*, Marie Duplessis, the 'Lady of the Camellias' who inspired Verdi's *La traviata*, and Zola, the Impressionists' first champion. Here lie also the mortal remains of the Goncourt brothers, who, it is true, were not admirers of Renoir's associates, but shared their subjects, their passion for Japan and, sometimes, even something of their style. It is often the case that people who are similar are made to not understand each other. Also buried here are Gustave Moreau, Matisse's teacher, Jacques Offenbach, composer of the most famous cancan, and the renowned Nijinsky, star of Djagilev's Ballets Russes, whose funerary statue portrays him as Stravinsky's *Petrushka*. Continuing through the cemetery, we come to the tombs of Ferdinand Beert and Louise Weber, the star of the Moulin Rouge: the former took the moniker Fernando, directing the circus; the other the name Goulue, and directed nothing if not the lust of men during the final, beloved quarter of the

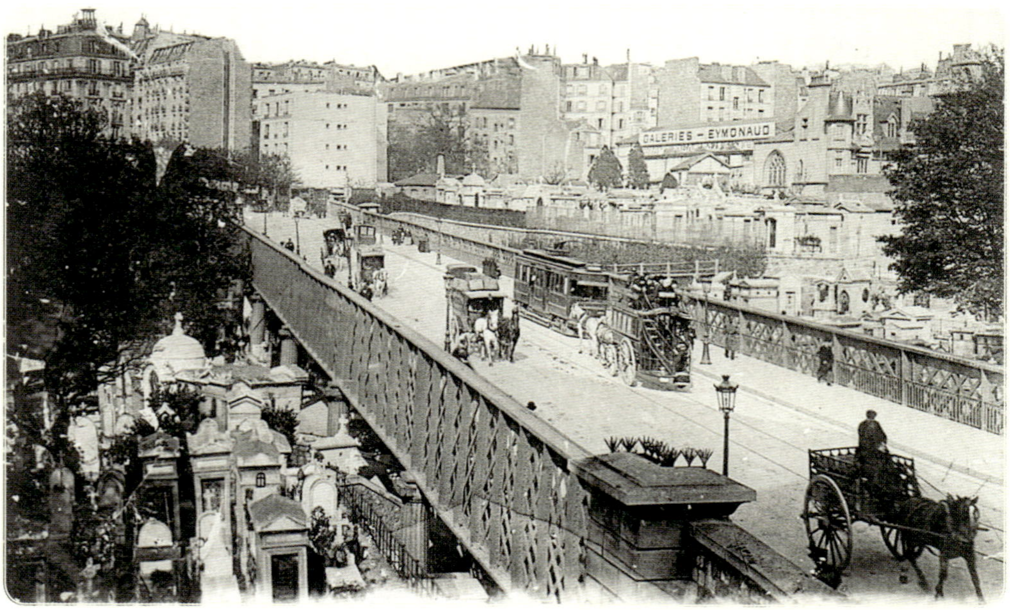

pp. 146–147
Camille Pissarro, *Boulevard Montmartre, Spring Morning*, 1897. Private Collection

The Caulaincourt Bridge above the Montmartre cemetery

century. Among these shades, we of course also find Degas, whose austere chapel is between two that are a bit loftier. When I visited a few years ago, the door was broken and its melancholy sadness almost evoked the old age of the artist, who died bitter and half-blind.

If, like in a medieval *Totentanz*, the dead were to abandon their tombs in the night, they would be astonished to find themselves all together, in that unique little corner of Montmartre spared all the upheaval that, in the name of salubrity and modernisation, has washed away its poetically sordid and mendicant soul: artists, models, acrobats, poets, musicians and painters, like it was long ago, when the dancers kept

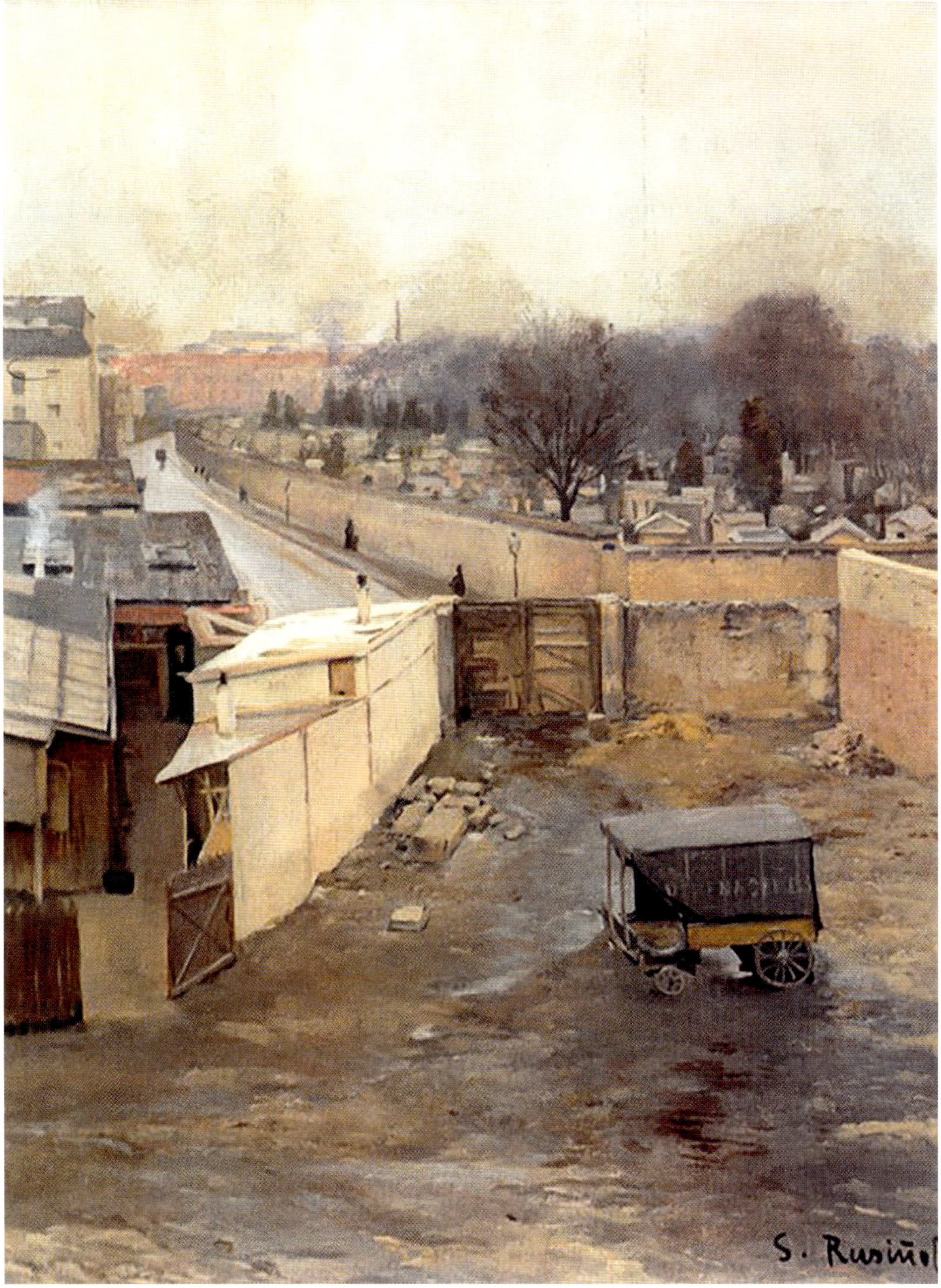

Santiago Rusiñol, *View of the Montmartre Cemetery*, 1891. Sitges, Cau Ferrat Museum

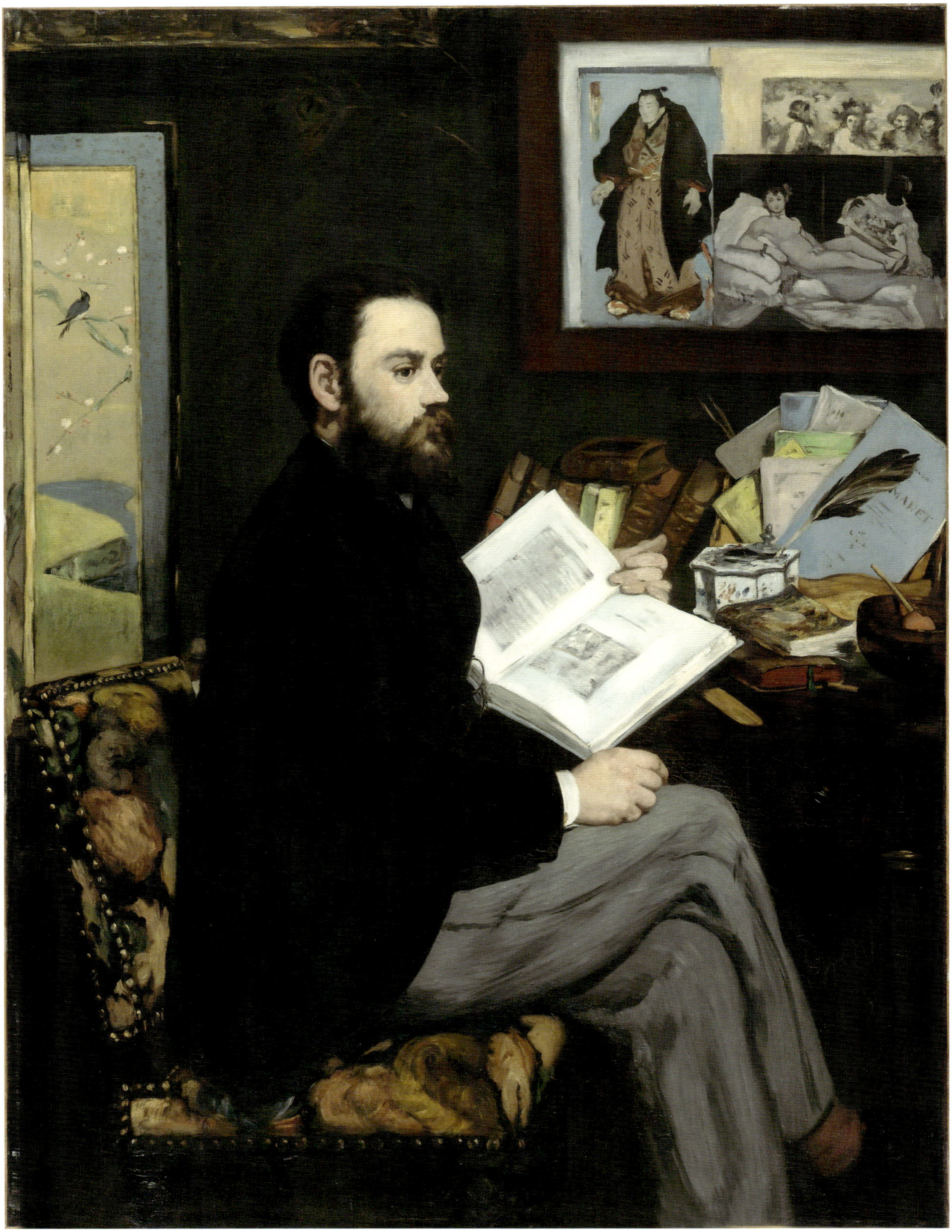

p. 150
Édouard Manet, *Portrait of Émile Zola*, 1868. Paris, Musée d'Orsay

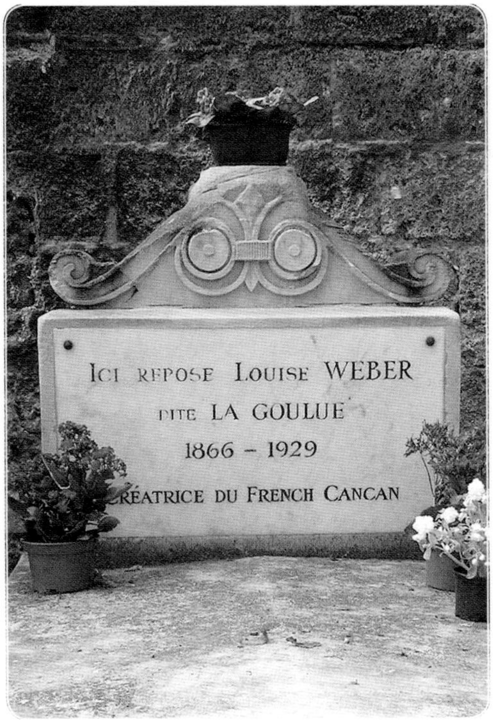

Tomb of Louise Weber, called 'La Goulue'

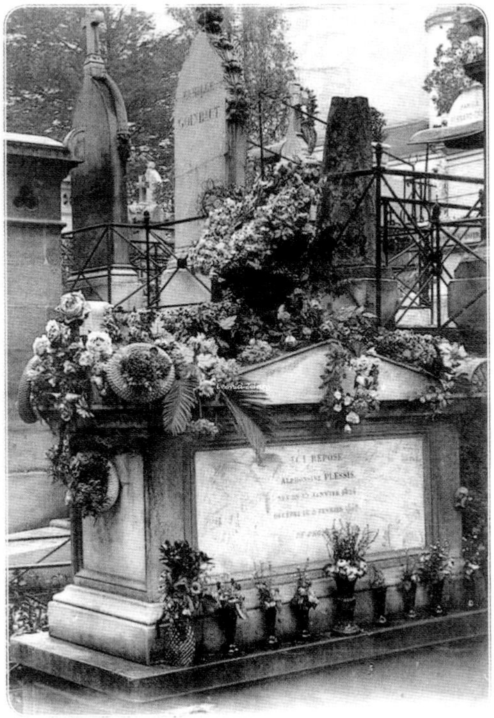

Tomb of Alphonsine Plessis, the 'Lady of the Camellias'

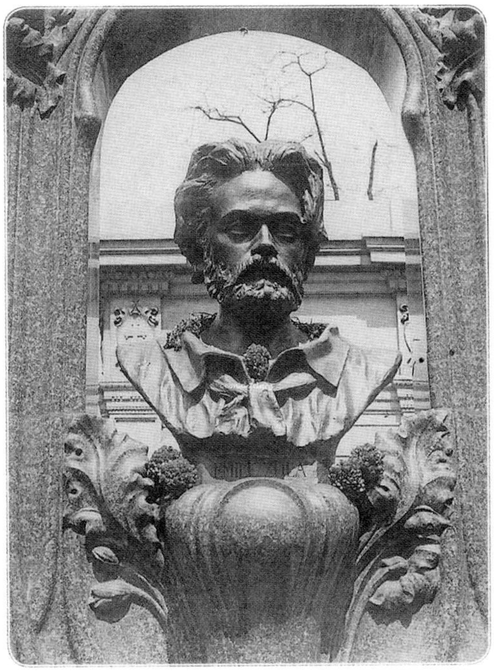

Tomb of Émile Zola

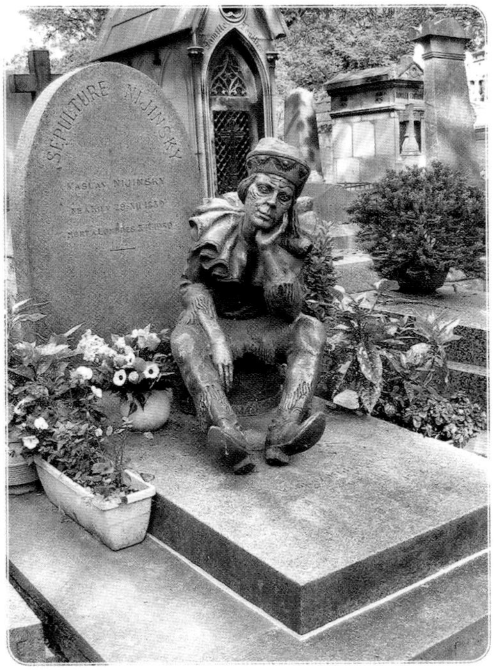

Tomb of Vaslav Nijinsky

going until the point of exhaustion, like the girl in Andersen's fairy tale, and the painters portrayed them, slightly elated by absinthe. But with the rooster's crow, the illustrious dead would return to their graves, aware that the obstinate dome of Sacré-Cœur had triumphed over the demonic grace of those places, which had hosted some of the greatest geniuses of the nineteenth century.

pp. 152–153
Vincent van Gogh, *View of Paris from Montmartre*, 1886. Basel, Kunstmuseum Basel

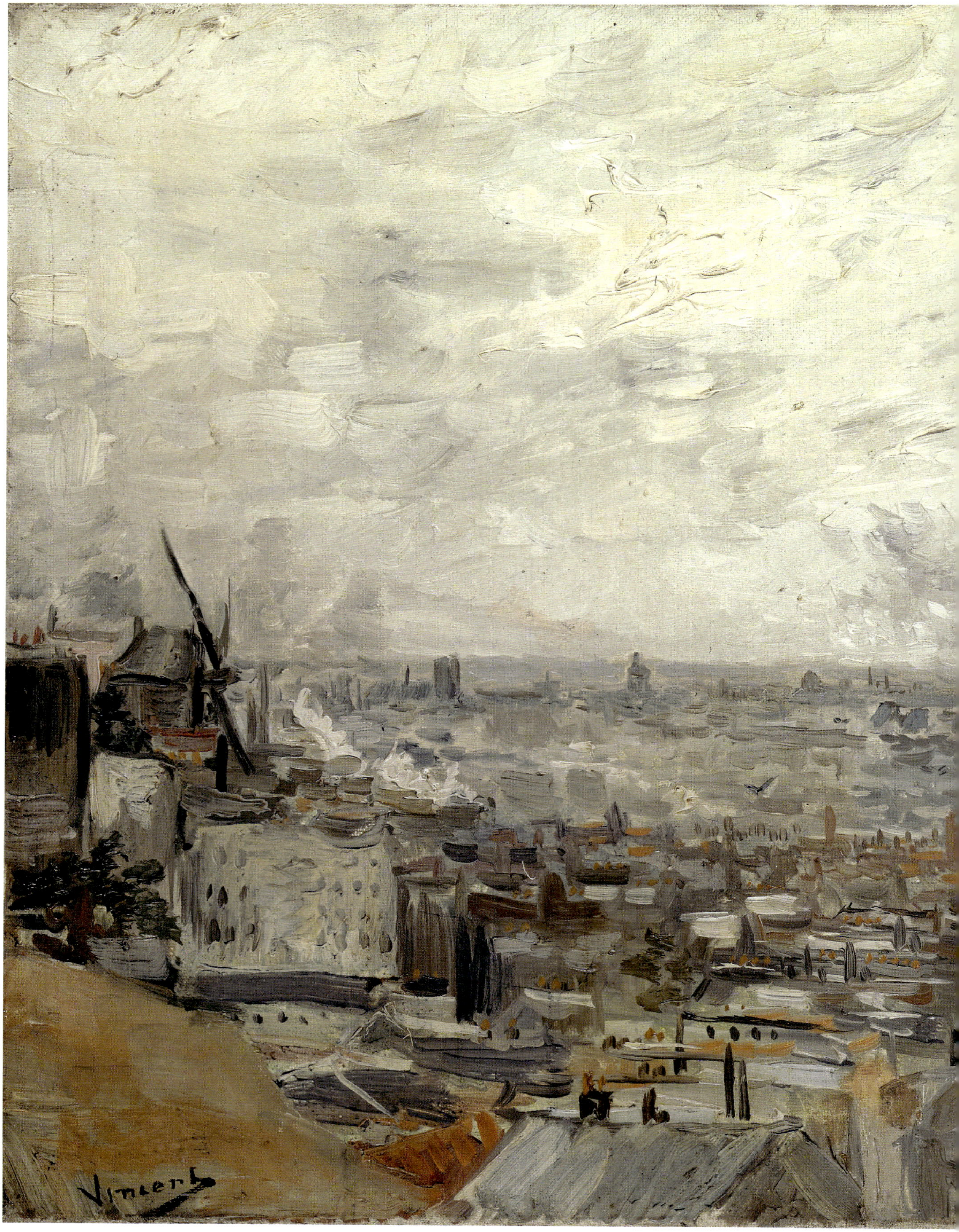

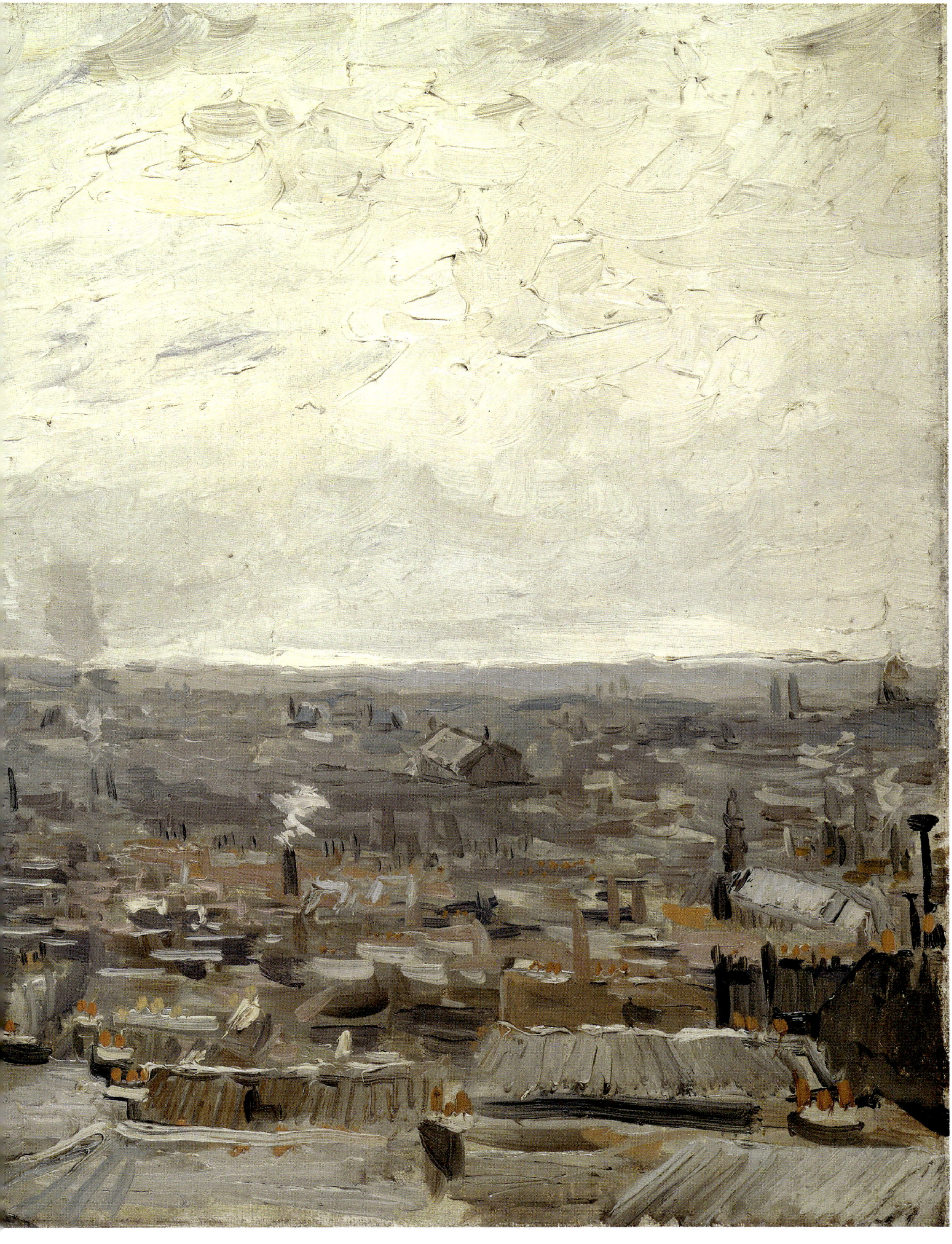

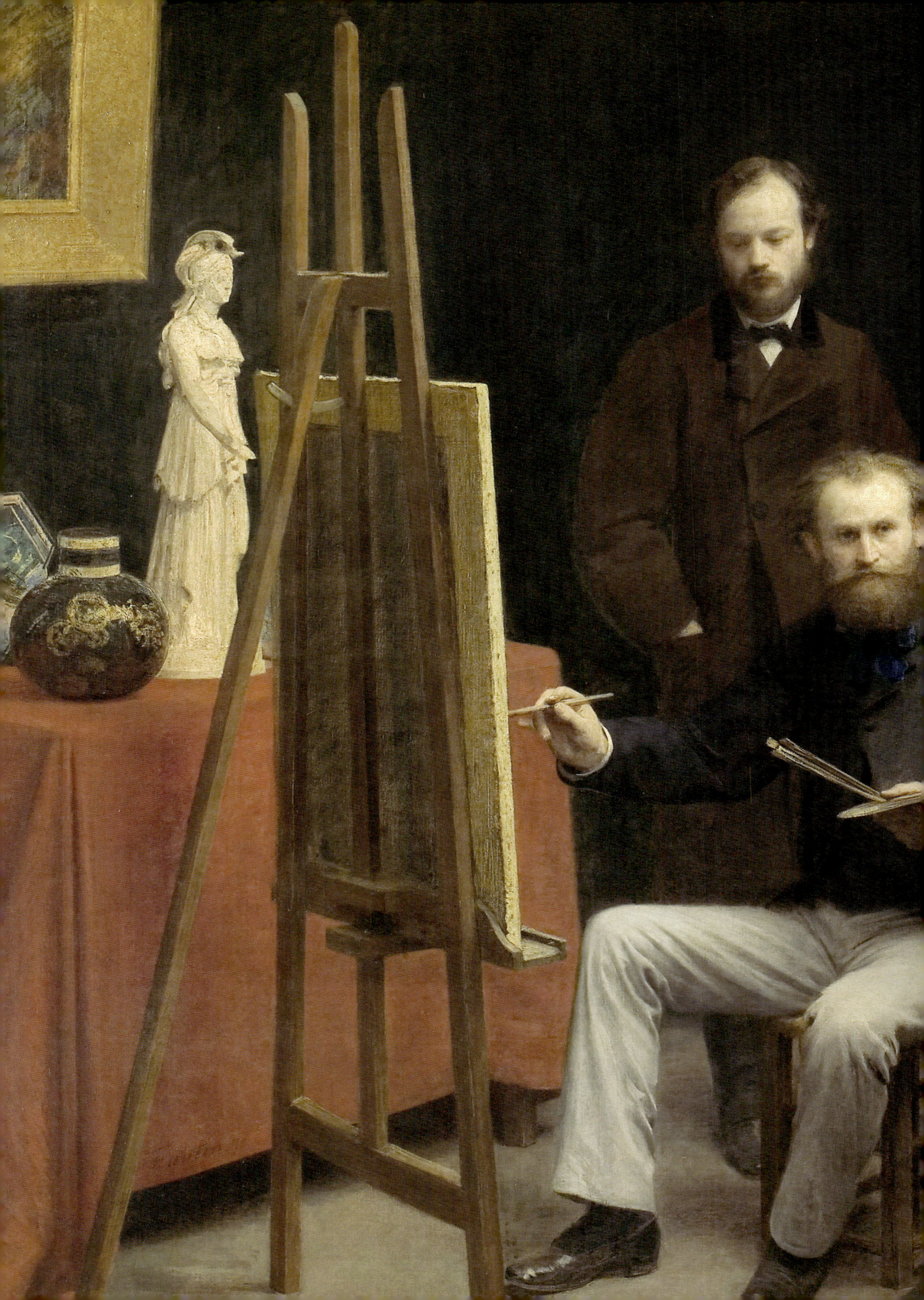

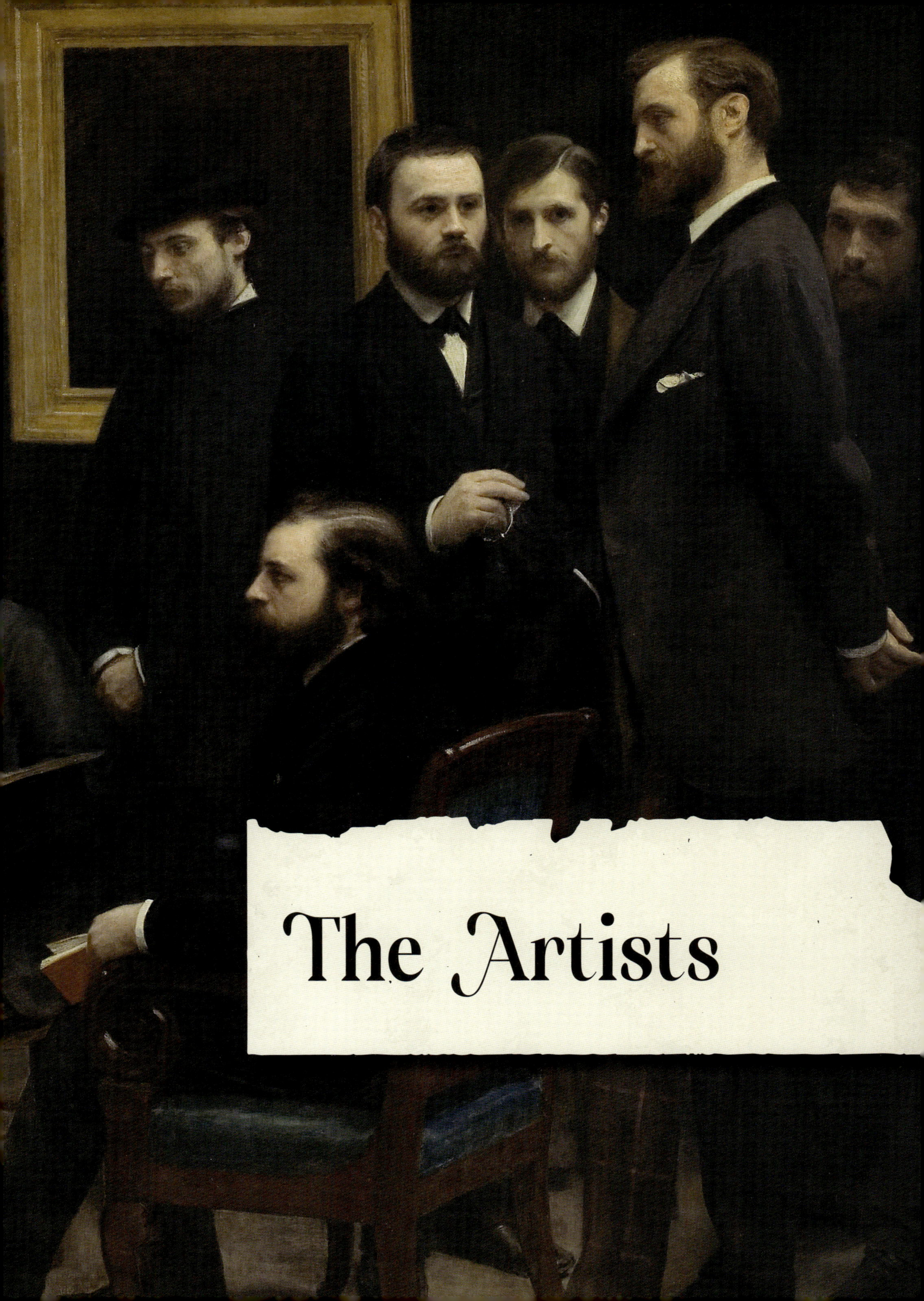

The Artists

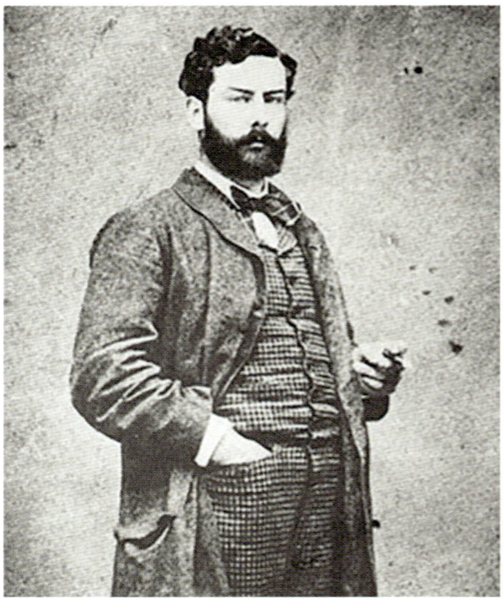

Alfred Sisley
Paris 1839–Moret-sur-Loing 1899

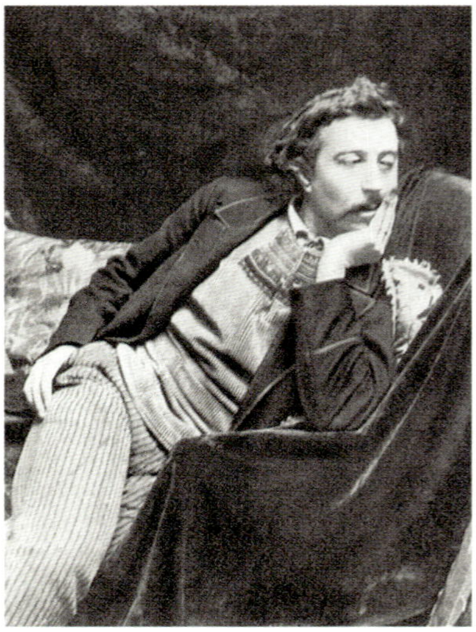

Paul Gauguin
Paris 1848–Hiva Oa (French Polynesia) 1903

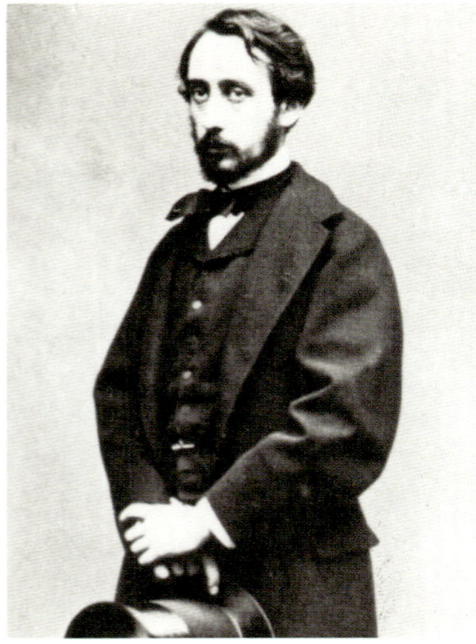

Edgar Degas
Paris 1834–1917

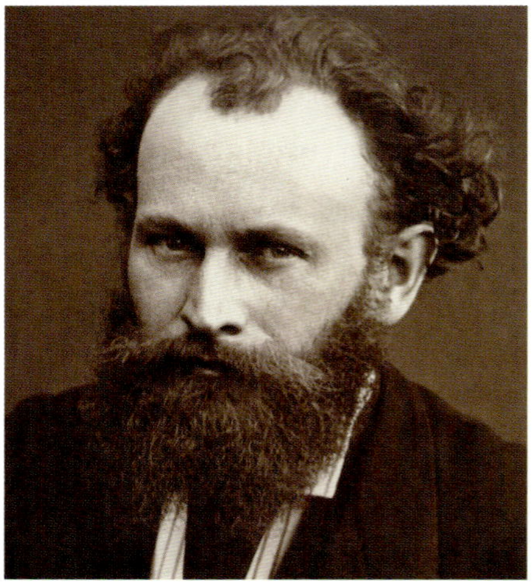

Édouard Manet
Paris 1832–1883

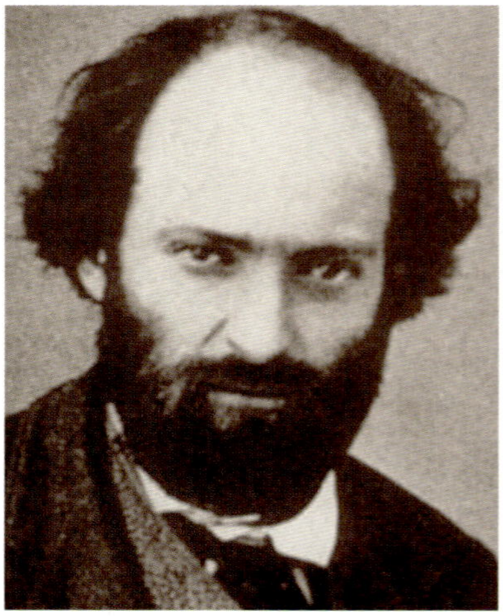

Paul Cézanne
Aix-en-Provence 1839–1906

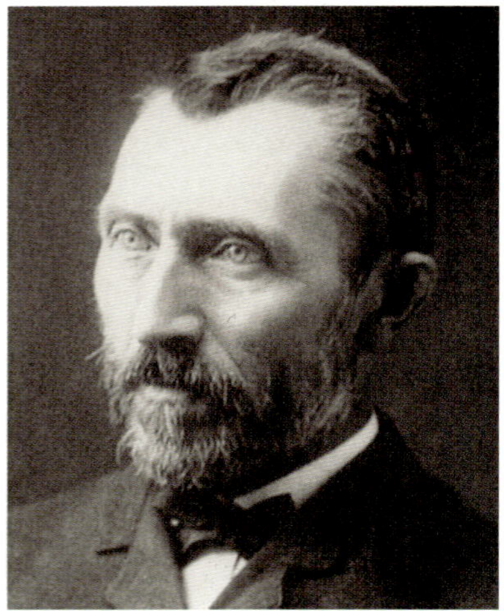

Vincent van Gogh
Zundert 1853–Auvers-sur-Oise 1890

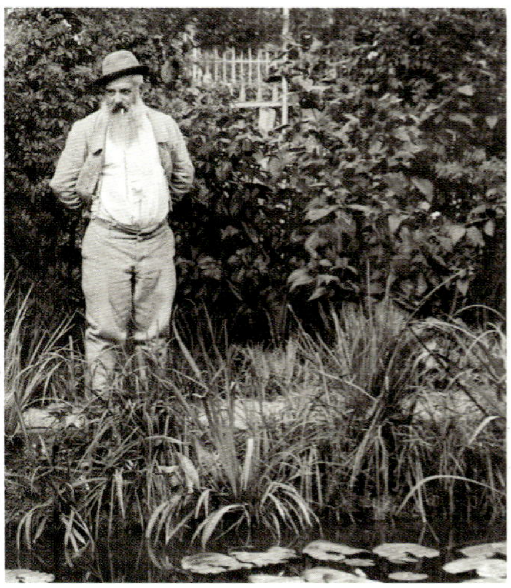

Claude Monet
Paris 1840–Giverny 1926

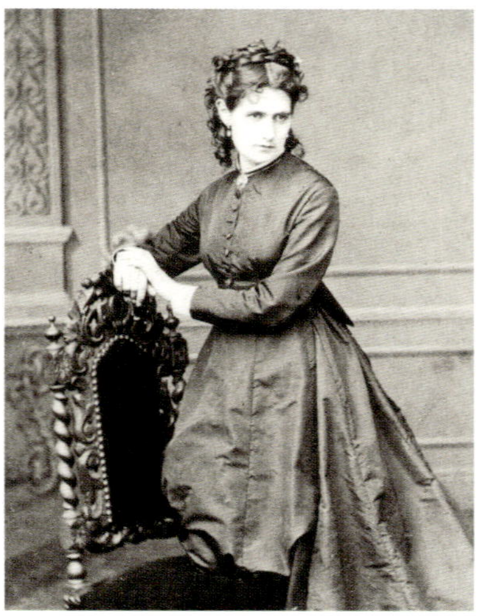

Berthe Morisot
Bourges 1841–Paris 1895

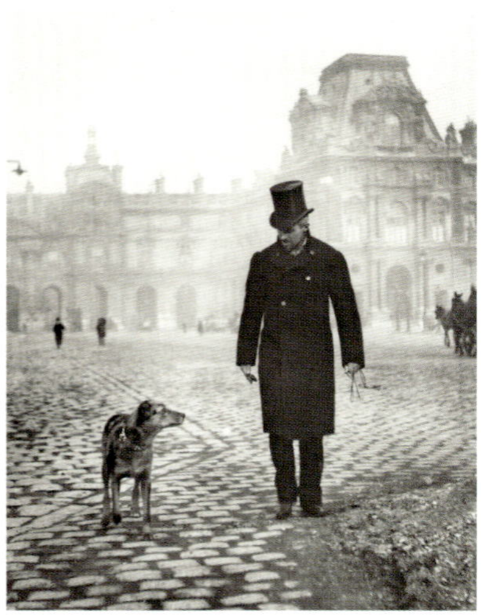

Gustave Caillebotte
Paris 1848–Gennevilliers 1894

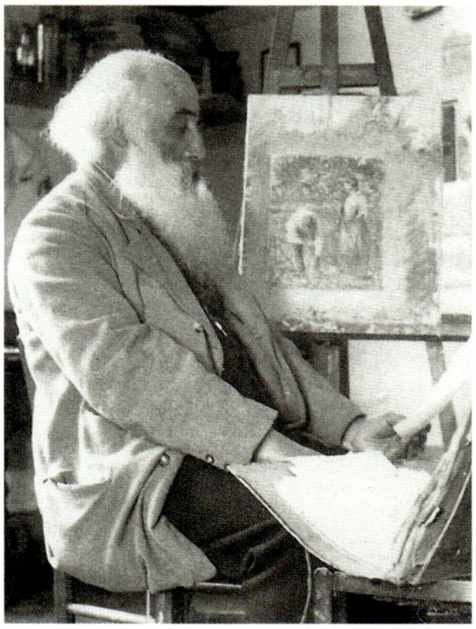

Camille Pissarro
Charlotte Amalie (Virgin Islands) 1830–Paris 1903

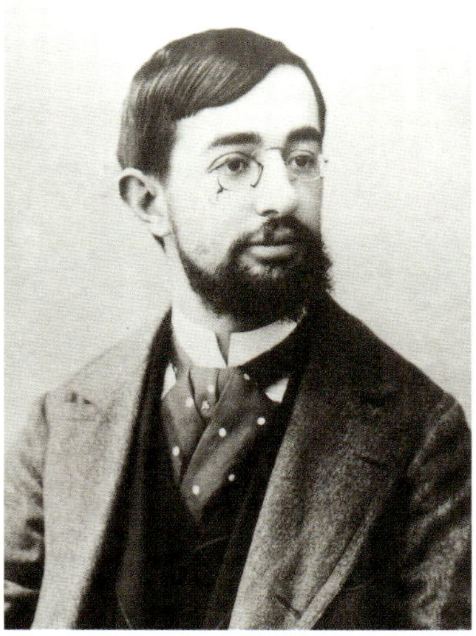

Henri de Toulouse-Lautrec
Albi 1864–Saint-André-du-Bois 1901

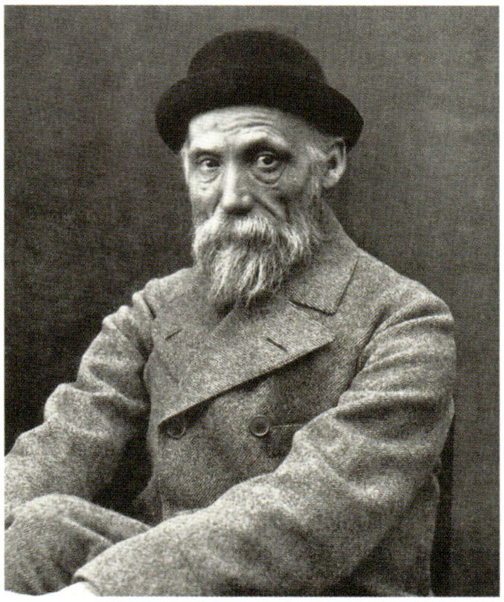

Pierre-Auguste Renoir
Limoges 1841–Cagnes-sur-Mer 1919

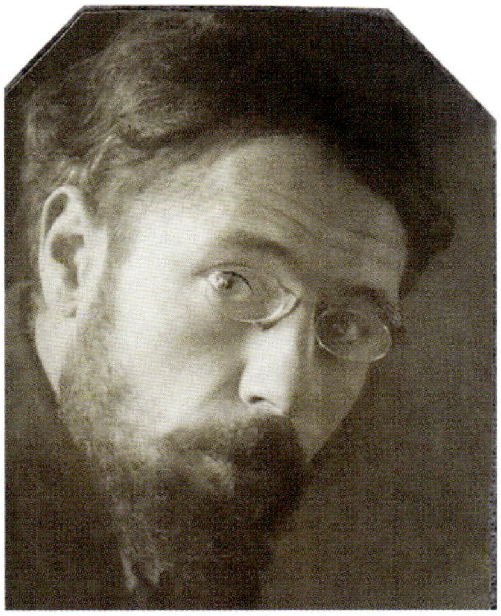

Pierre Bonnard
Fontenay-aux-Roses 1867–Le Cannet 1947

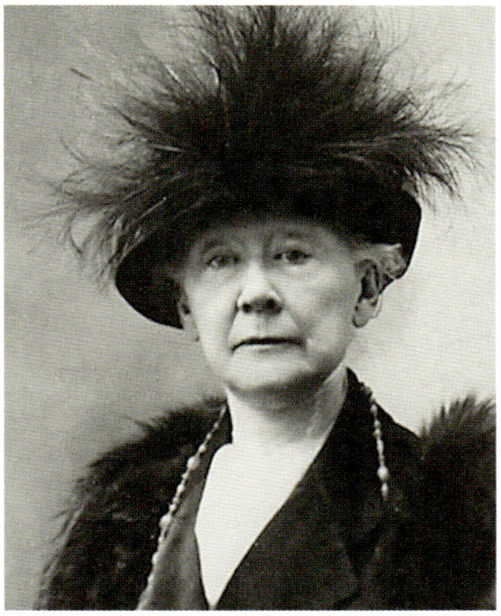

Mary Stevenson Cassatt
Pittsburgh 1844–Le Mesnil-Théribus 1926

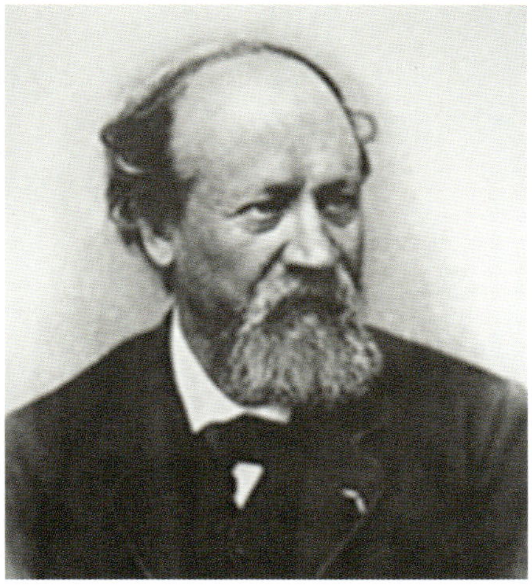

Eugène-Louis Boudin
Honfleur 1824–Deauville 1898

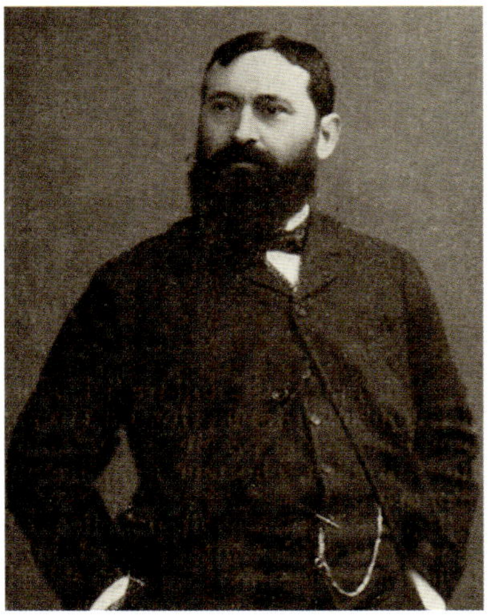

Giuseppe De Nittis
Barletta 1846–Saint-Germain-en-Laye 1884

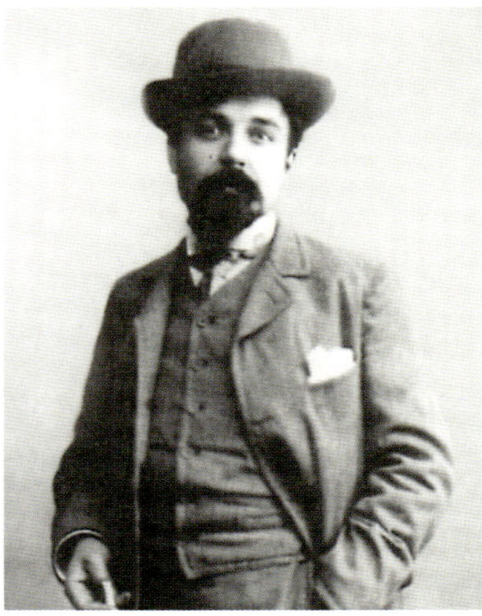

Maurice Denis
Granville 1870–Saint-Germain-en-Laye 1943

pp. 154–155
Henri Fantin-Latour, *Studio in Batignolles*, 1870. Paris, Musée d'Orsay

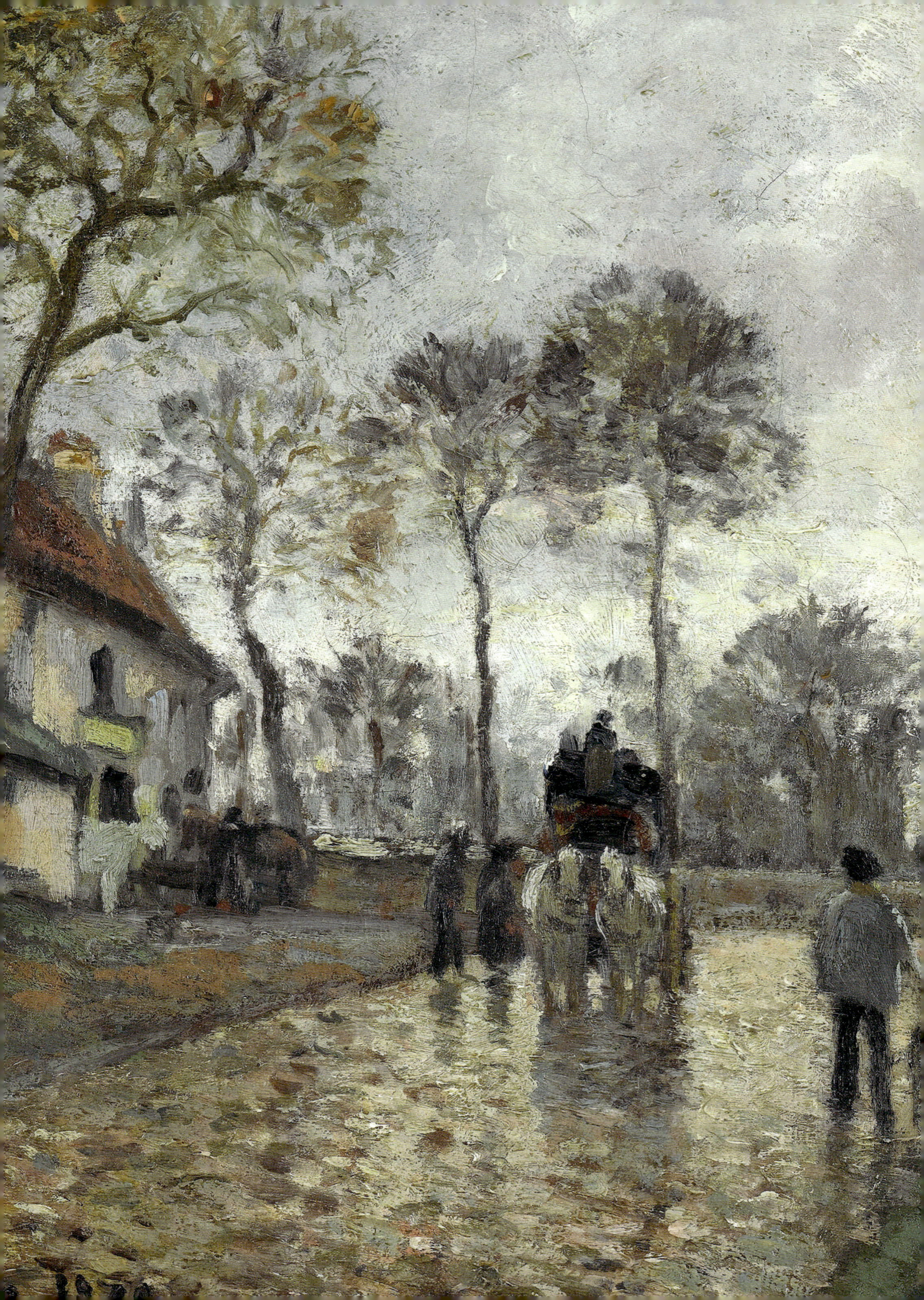

Notes

1. R. and M. Wittkower, *Born Under Saturn: The Character and Conduct of Artists*, New York 1963.
2. C. Waern, *Some Notes on French Impressionism, The Atlantic Monthly* 69, 414 (1892), pp. 535–541.
3. É. Bernard, 'Julien Tanguy dit le "Père Tanguy"', *Mercure de France* 76, 276 (1908), pp. 600–616: 604.
4. *Le Figaro*, 3 April 1876.
5. J. Renoir, *Renoir*, Paris 1962; *Born Under Saturn: The Character and Conduct of Artists*, New York 1963, p. 154.
6. Henri, count of Chambord (1820–1883), grandson of Charles X, was the legitimist pretender to the French throne.
7. A. Vollard, *Recollections of a Picture Dealer*, Boston 1936, p. 70.
8. Ibid., p. 81.
9. Émile Zola, *L'œuvre*, Paris 1886, p. 169.
10. Ibid., p. 159.
11. J. Rewald, *The History of Impressionism*, New York 1973, p. 313.
12. E. Duranty, 'La double vie de Louis Seguin', *Gazette des Beaux-Arts* 88 (1976), pp. 235–239. In the story, it is called 'Café Barbois'.
13. Claude Monet, in F. Thiébault-Sisson, 'Claude Monet. Les années d'épreuves', *Le Temps* 40, 14.414 (26 November 1900), p. 3.
14. A. Silvestre, *Au pays des souvenirs: mes maîtres et mes maîtresses*, Paris 1887, pp. 161–162.
15. É. Zola, *Le ventre de Paris*, Paris 1888 (1873), p. 18. Zola is describing the painter Claude Lantier, but in his notes for the volume, the third in the Rougon-Macquart series, he calls him Cézanne.
16. C. Baudelaire, *Curiosités esthétiques*, Paris 1868, p. 432.
17. G. Moore, *The Confessions of a Young Man*, edited and annotated by the author, London 1904 (1886), p. 86.
18. J. de Neuville, *Les joyeuses dames de Paris*, Paris 1867, p. 129.
19. J. Lorrain, *Fards et poisons*, Paris 1903, pp. 204–205.
20. G. Moore, *Memoirs of My Dead Life*, New York 1923, p. 50.
21. A stage name composed of the phonetic transcription of *chahut*, a type of acrobatic dance, and *chaos*.
22. E. de Goncourt, *Les Frères Zemganno*, Paris 1879, p. 51.
23. D. Bona, *Berthe Morisot. Le secret de la femme en noir*, Paris 2000, p. 264.
24. É. Zola, *Nana*, Paris 1881, pp. 407–408.
25. G. Moore, *Memoirs of My Dead Life*, New York 1923, p. 28.
26. É. Zola, *La bête humaine*, Paris 1890, p. 34.
27. G. de Maupassant, 'La femme de Paul', in *La maison Tellier*, Paris 1891, p. 278.
28. 'C'était un grand château du temps de Louis treize. Le couchant rougissait ce palais oublié': V. Hugo, *Passé*, XVI, in *Les voix intérieures*, 1837.
29. G. Flaubert, *L'éducation sentimentale*, Paris 1910 (1869), p. 463.
30. J. Renoir, *Renoir*, Paris 1962, p. 127.
31. J.-K. Huysmans, *À rebours*, Paris 1922 (1884), p. 30.
32. M. Barrès, *Quelques cadences*, Paris 1904, p. 29.
33. Cited in *Donations Claude Roger-Marx* (Parigi, Musée du Louvre, Cabinet des dessins, Pavillon de Flore, 27 novembre 1980–19 avril 1981), Paris 1980, p. 9.
34. Cited in P. Lanthony, *Les yeux des peintres*, Lausanne 1999, p. 30.
35. G. de Maupassant, *Chroniques*, new expanded edition, Paris 2019, p. 914.
36. Letter from Gauguin to Émile Schuffenecker, Pont-Aven, February 1888, in *Correspondance de Paul Gauguin 1873-1888*, ed. V. Merlhès, Paris 1984, p. 141.
37. A. Gide, *Si le grain ne meurt*, Paris 1926, p. 88.
38. M. Denis, *Théorie. Du symbolisme et de Gauguin vers un nouvel ordre classique. 1890-1910*, Paris 1920, p. 168.
39. Letter from Cézanne to Pissarro, Estaque, 2 July 1876, cited in J. de Beucken, *Un portrait de Cézanne*, Paris 1955.
40. Letter from Cézanne to Charles Camoin, Aix, 22 February 1891, cited in D. Giraudy, *Camoin: sa vie, son œuvre*, Marseilles 1972.
41. Letter from Van Gogh to Gauguin, Arles, 17 October 1888, vangoghletters.org.
42. J. Rewald, *Post-Impressionism: From Van Gogh to Gauguin*, New York 1956, p. 215.
43. Letter from Van Gogh to his brother Theo, Arles, 18 September 1888, vangoghletters.org.
44. 'Extraits du journal inédit de Paul Signac', ed. J. Rewald. vol. I: 1894–1895, in *Gazette des Beaux-Arts* 36 (1949), p. 106.

Camille Pissarro, *Stagecoach in Louveciennes*, 1870 (detail). Paris, Musée d'Orsay

About the Author

Giorgio Villani holds a doctorate in comparative literature and studies the history of taste and relations between literature and sculpture. He has published articles on these subjects in *Paragone*, *Rivista di Letterature Moderne e Comparate e Storia delle arti* and *Antologia Vieusseux*. He has written numerous books, including *Il Convitato di pietra. Apoteosi e tramonto della linea curva nel Settecento* (Olschki 2016), *Un atlante della cultura europea. Vittorio Pica, il metodo e le fonti* (Olschki 2018, Premio Casentino), *Dentro una conchiglia. Note d'arte sul liberty e sul déco* (Bordeaux 2022), *Tra ieri e oggi. Temi dell'immaginario* (Palumbo 2022). He is a contributor to *Alias* (the cultural supplement of *Il Manifesto*), *FMR* and *Il Giornale dell'Arte.*

Photo Credits

The publisher is at the disposal of rights holders for any unidentified iconographic sources or to correct errors in attribution.

Basel, Kunstmuseum Basel: pp. 15, 152–153
Berlin, Staatliche Museen, Alte Nationalgalerie (bpk, Bildagentur fuer Kunst, Kultur und Geschichte, Berlin): p. 121
Buffalo, Albright-Knox Art Gallery: p. 104
Cambridge, Mass., Harvard Art Museums / Fogg Art Museum: p. 43
Chicago, Art Institute of Chicago: pp. 53, 60, 62, 90, 111, 124
Cleveland Museum of Art: pp. 118–119, 121
Copenhagen, Ny Carlberg Glyptotek: p. 98
Florence, Alinari Archive: p. 22; Florence, Scala / bpk, Bildagentur fuer Kunst, Kultur und Geschichte, Berlin: pp. 52, 89; Florence, Scala / New York, The Metropolitan Museum of Art / Art Resource: pp. 93, 122–123; Florence, Scala / The Solomon R. Guggenheim Foundation/Art Resource: p. 138; Florence, Scala / Paris, RMN-Grand Palais / Musée du Louvre: pp. 47, 102; Florence, Scala / Paris, RMN-Grand Palais / Musée d'Orsay: pp. 4, 10–11, 27–28, 34–37, 39–41, 51, 66–67, 69, 74, 76–77, 84–85, 87, 99, 100, 101, 117, 131, 143, 150, 158
Houston, Museum of Fine Arts: p. 58
Kansas City, The Nelson-Atkins Museum of Art: p. 38
London, The Courtauld Gallery: pp. 56, 70
London, Bridgeman / Detroit, Detroit Institute of Arts: p. 106; London, Bridgeman, The Courtauld Gallery: p. 23
London, The National Gallery: pp. 61, 81
London, Victoria and Albert Museum: p. 65
Munich, Neue Pinakothek (bpk, Bildagentur fuer Kunst, Kultur und Geschichte, Berlin): cover
New York, The Metropolitan Museum of Art: pp. 2, 26–27, 46, 88, 129, 136–137
Norwich, Norwich Castle Museum: p. 91
Otterlo, Kröller-Müller Museum: p. 144
Paris, Bibliothèque nationale de France: p. 59
Paris, Musée Marmottan-Monet: p. 33
Paris, Musée d'Orsay: pp. 7, 91, 130, 135, 154–155
Paris, Musée Rodin, ph. Jean de Calan: p. 13
Paris, Petit Palais, Musée des Beaux-Arts de la Ville de Paris: pp. 21, 107
Paris, Photo Archives Durand-Ruel © Durand-Ruel & Cie.: p. 17
Philadelphia, Philadelphia Museum of Art: pp. 44, 126–127, 139–140
Princeton, Princeton University Art Museum: p. 115
Raleigh, North Carolina Museum of Art: pp. 112–113
Sitges, Cau Ferrat Museum: p. 149
Stockholm, Nationalmuseum: pp. 96–97, 105, 109
The Hague, Gemeentemuseum Den Haag: p. 145
Tokyo, Artizon Museum: pp. 125, 128
Toledo, OH, Toledo Museum of Art: p. 100
Washington, D.C., National Gallery of Art: pp. 31, 34, 64, 71, 80, 88, 141
Washington, D.C., Phillips Collection: pp. 94–95

FSC www.fsc.org
MISTO
Carta da fonti gestite in maniera responsabile
FSC® C017635

Printed on the presses of Petruzzi Stampa, Città di Castello, Perugia, in the month of May 2024
Ex Officina Libraria Jellinek et Gallerani

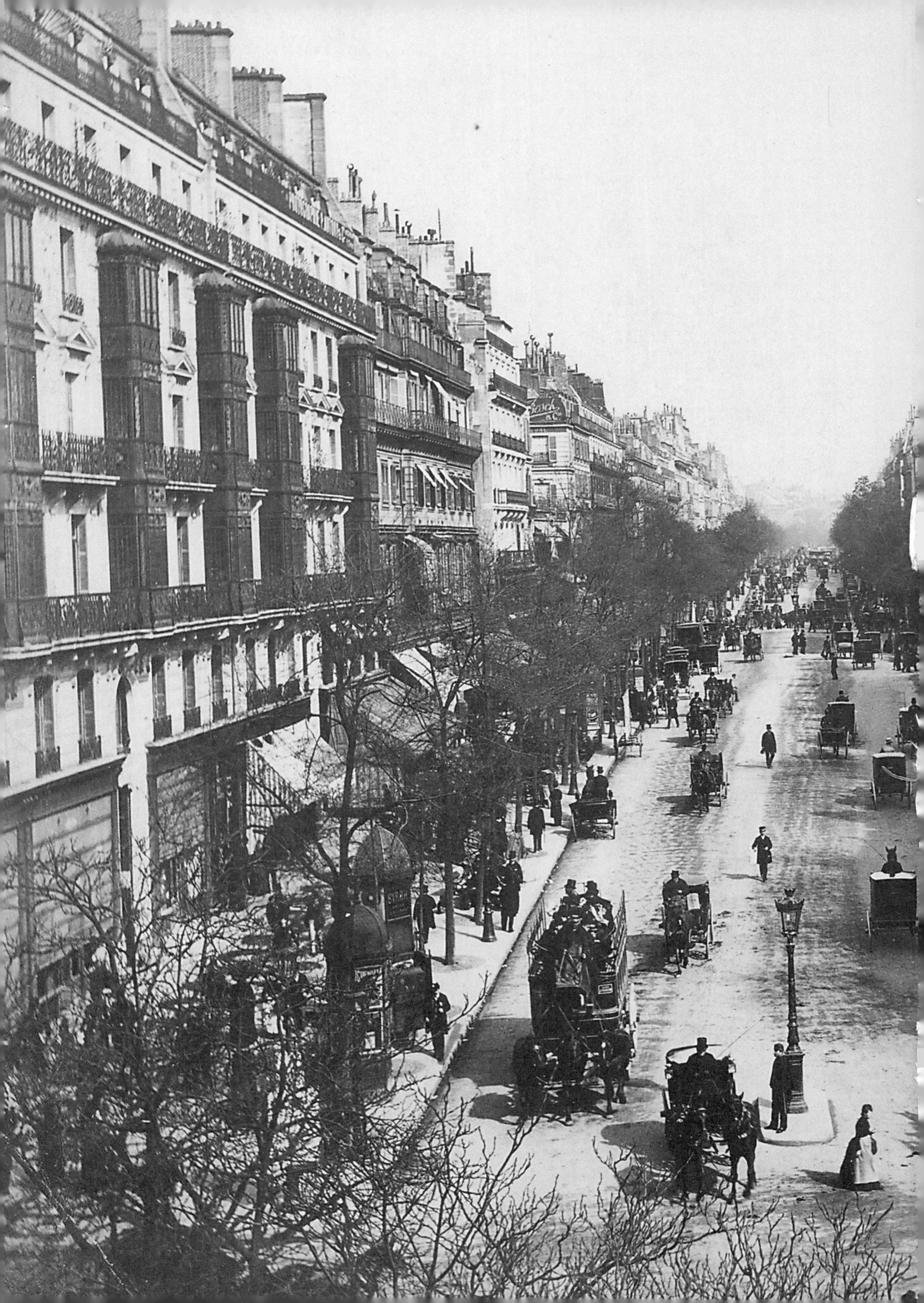